W9-AEV-138

SEEING THROUGH
THE MEDIA

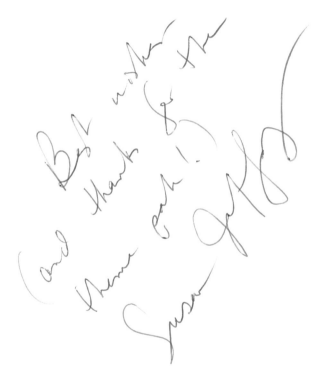

SEEING THROUGH THE MEDIA

The Persian Gulf War

Edited by Susan Jeffords and Lauren Rabinovitz

Rutgers University Press

New Brunswick, New Jersey

Library of Congress Cataloging-in-Publication Data

Seeing through the media : the Persian Gulf War / edited by Susan
    Jeffords and Lauren Rabinovitz.
        p.   cm. — (Communications, media, and culture)
    Includes bibliographical references and index.
    ISBN 0-8135-2041-X (cloth) — ISBN 0-8135-2042-8 (pbk.)
    1. Persian Gulf War, 1991—Press coverage—United States.
I. Jeffords, Susan, 1953–   . II. Rabinovitz, Lauren, 1950–.
III. Series.
DS79.739.S44   1994
070.4′499567044′28—dc20   93-25725
                                                               CIP

British Cataloging-in-Publication information available

"Time and the Television War" by Victor J. Caldarola was originally published in *Public Culture*, the Bulletin of the Society for Transnational Cultural Studies, vol. 4, no. 2 (Spring 1992). Reprinted by permission.

"The Media's War" by Ella Shohat was originally published in *Social Text*, no. 28 (1991). Reprinted by permission.

"The Gendered Gulf" by Cynthia Enloe was originally published in *Collateral Damage: The New World Order at Home and Abroad*, ed. Cynthia Peters (Boston: South End Press, 1992). Reprinted by permission.

*In memory of William Rabinovitz and Steve Valentik,
who taught us as children how to see through things
and who help us remember as adults why it matters*

Contents

Acknowledgments

First and foremost, we wish to thank Richard Abel, without whom this book truly could not have happened. He invited both of us to participate in a symposium in the fall of 1991 entitled "The Gulf War in Media Discourse" at Drake University, where we first met one another and decided that together we would undertake this book. Dick provided not only the opportunity but also the structure and leadership for our first mutual consideration of the significance of the Persian Gulf War and the media. To him and to the faculty and students of the Cultural Studies Program at Drake University who shared their ideas and questions with us, we owe a lot for helping us to define the contours and basic questions of this book. We also wish to thank Norman Solomon, who was the third speaker at that event, for helping us to think more deeply about the perspectives we brought to our scholarship on the war and the media.

We are grateful to all the book's contributors for their hard work, their diligence in meeting deadlines, and their commitment to the idea of the book. In fact, all of the scholars who were doing work on the Persian Gulf War helped us to think about what role scholarly critique could play in political activism.

At the University of Iowa, the collective MediaWatch played important roles in encouraging scholars to speak out publicly during the Persian Gulf War and in gathering media materials that were the basis for some of the papers and observations in this book. In addition, the Department of Communication Studies and the American Studies Program at the University of Iowa provided support wherever needed. The Center for Advanced Studies, University of Iowa, and Jay Semel and Lorna Olson provided both the environment and material support so that many of the ideas herein could bear fruit.

Bruce Gronbeck offered helpful advice and suggestions. Chuck

Kleinhans generously aided in photograph preparations. Tom Engelhardt took an especially serious interest in the book's development that contributed much at several key points. Sara Cody and Margaret Gers provided research assistance, and Dev Stahlkopf helped us immensely at the times when we needed it most.

Our editor Leslie Mitchner was an active partner at every phase of this book's preparation, and her support and ideas contributed a significant amount to anything we have accomplished here. George Custen was a valuable reader who helped us to hone ideas.

Greg Easley and Greg Powell lived with this project from start to finish, providing advice, insights, and a lot more without which this book could never have been completed. To them, we are always grateful.

SEEING THROUGH
THE MEDIA

Lauren Rabinovitz and Susan Jeffords

Introduction

Seeing Through the Media: The Persian Gulf War is a study of how the
media operated during the 1990–1991 Persian Gulf War. But more
than simply summarizing the kinds of media productions that took
place during the war, this book offers a critical assessment of the role
the media played in forging the social consensus needed for support of
the war and the national identity that defined the shape that consensus
would take. In so doing, we provide not only a way of analyzing how
that war was narrativized and produced but also a means for understanding more broadly how the U.S. media respond to and manufacture crisis events. As these essays show, one of the key points of analysis
for interpreting the media's role in the formation of national identity is
visibility, both as the literal "seeing" the media offers in terms of images, descriptions, and narratives, and as the encoded distinctions between what can be "seen" and not seen in and through the media. In
diverse ways, these essays analyze how history, television production,
the home front, and patriotism were written and rewritten, imaged
and reimaged to construct the past, to control information, to form social consensus, and to frame national identity—four functions assumed by the media during the Persian Gulf War.

The formal aspects of how the media do their work as an industry
are many and varied, and there are numerous textbooks that provide
ample lessons on this subject. In general, however, the media practice
their craft by making stories, that is, narratives that follow certain implicit rules of storytelling for how individuals respond to a series of
events, take action, and follow through to some outcome or effect. Such
rules of storytelling help structure much of what the media produce,
whether the results are categorized as news or entertainment. There
are other forms in the media controlled less by storytelling techniques
than by other rhetorical strategies, and these usually appear as either
announcements or conversations. What is important here, however, is

the role that different rhetorical devices play in shaping what passes for information. They produce, circulate, and organize meaning through three levels that include, but are also bigger than, the individual texts: economic-industrial production, linkages across different texts, and the cultural practices of everyday life.

At the first level, the media produce meanings through the conditions of industrial and economic production. In the United States, this means that because the media are privately rather than publicly owned, they always function to try to produce revenue for their owners. The effect of this economic imperative in the United States is that the media are always selling themselves and competing with one another to differentiate their "products." So, for example, during the Persian Gulf War, "getting the story" became an important thread that not only served to differentiate among media outlets for which had the most successful journalists, but was itself the major subject of information in the crucial hours when the United States began bombing Baghdad. The ongoing hours of Cable News Network (CNN) telephone reports by Bernard Shaw, Peter Arnett, and John Holliman from their room in Baghdad's Al-Rashid Hotel, when all communications between Baghdad and the outside world were apparently cut off, became a much ballyhooed moment of drama in the Persian Gulf War. Although it offered little news about the progress or nature of the war itself, it was a drama of journalists getting the story. The well-known economic effect of this drama is that it boosted Ted Turner's Cable News Network. CNN jumped 27.1 percent in the ratings, which allowed it to set higher fees for advertisers. Its advertising rates went from an average price of $3,500 per thirty-second spot to more than $20,000 per spot.[1]

At the second level, the media also make meanings through their contextualization in what might be called "secondary texts," or those supporting intertextual frameworks that may guide audience expectations and predispositions toward certain meanings while excluding others. For example, the medium of television depends additionally upon advertisements and schedules printed in newspapers to guide, frame, and interpret audience's attentions. Indeed, entire magazines —themselves another mass medium—like *TV Guide* exist to "explain" and to interpret television to audiences. During the Persian Gulf War, *TV Guide* sprinkled news stories about the media coverage of the war throughout its issues and prominently framed the war in relationship to television's coverage of it. Fan magazines steeped in star discourse have served a similar purpose for the movie industry or for the television industry's production of soap operas. Movies, magazines, books, radio, and television may all recirculate a similar or shared story, each

"Secondary texts" like billboards, banners, buttons, and T-shirts were used prominently during the Persian Gulf War.

version accumulating meanings dependent upon the viewers' knowledge of other versions.

A textual network that shapes meanings in the media may extend beyond the media themselves. Most concretely, an event like the Olympics may be promoted and broadcast on television and radio as well as advertised and reported in daily newspapers and magazines, but its identifiable features and ultimate significance also depend upon its manufacture as an event through a variety of public displays. Billboards, banners, buttons, and T-shirts are all commodities that reproduce and disseminate the semiotic language of the media in everyday objects. Merchandising tie-ins, like scratch-card games to predict athletic winners at nationwide fast-food restaurants or Olympic athletes' likenesses on cereal boxes, only make the connections more explicit between the ideological work of commerce and the media. In this light, billboards supporting the Persian Gulf War, buttons both for and against the war, T-shirts, bumper stickers, and even yellow-ribboned wreaths available in stores throughout the United States became important elements in the process by which the media made the war meaningful.

At the third level, the media also make their meanings within a broader cultural contextualization in which audiences make active use of their frameworks of personal experience, social environment, and political systems of belief. Certainly people watch television, read newspapers, or listen to the radio with intermittent attention and often while engaging in other activities. Such a mode for reception influences the way the media are understood just as much as do people's discussions with one another about their understandings. New technologies even allow people to extend their roles in shaping "media texts." Whether one zaps across television channels with a remote control so that various incongruous bits constitute the object, "time shifts" by employing videocassette recorder technology, or makes an interactive game out of sampling media materials with new computer technologies, the result is that audiences experiencing media in new ways do so through interpretive frameworks that extend beyond the specifics of the media message.

It is also important to remember that there are hierarchical forms of knowledge produced and circulated that are the products of unequal power relations. During the Persian Gulf War, for example, commercial television networks, whose "products" saturated the U.S. population's television sets, dominated the public sphere with their high-technology and economic investments in both the production and distributin of news. But they were not the only significant media voices, and th y were not the only ones interpreting and managing war information. An intelligent, articulate alternative press remained active throughout the duration of the war. From Paper Tiger TV's series about the war aired in public access cable outlets to *Extra!*'s exposure of network news' biased reporting to the editorials, exposés, and critiques that dominated the leftist literary press (e.g., the *Nation*, the *Village Voice*, *Mother Jones*, *Z Magazine*), alternate media fought the propagandistic strength of mainstream media with their own accounts that constructed the war differently. But they did so without equal access to the public sphere or equivalent power in shaping public opinion.

Standing in sharper relief to the ongoing flow of information produced day in and day out, twenty-four hours a day, and across the social spaces in which we live out our lives is the media's segmentation of life into "events." The media's construction of certain kinds of happenings into something culturally eventful provides a periodic focus and organization for daily U.S. life. Through its construction of events, the media serve an important social function by working to organize and orchestrate the relationship of the individual to the community. The Persian Gulf War is one such media event.

There are, however, many kinds of media events. The most common or frequent examples are sporting events like the Olympics, the World Series, or the Super Bowl. Following a regular cyclical calendar, these events punctuate the flow of the seasons just as much as do holidays. The second type of media events are official state events like a royal wedding in England, John F. Kennedy's funeral, or President Bill Clinton's inauguration. This type of event happens less frequently than the regularized sports media events. But official state events do correspond to a more loosely organized schedule according to political cycles (every four years) or to life cycles of the heads of state (birth, wedding, death). A third type of media event is the political or juridical event; these generally do not occur according to any regular, preplanned schedule. Instances of this type are Clarence Thomas's Supreme Court confirmation hearings and Anita Hill's testimony, the Watergate hearings, the Oliver North hearings, and the William Kennedy Smith rape trial. A fourth type of media event is the cultural event of celebration. Examples of this type are the annual Macy's Thanksgiving Day parade, the 1976 July 4 Bicentennial celebration, the Miss American pageant, or the Academy Awards ceremonies. Although these follow a schedule according to a social calendar, the time of occurrence could be set either seasonally or arbitrarily. What becomes interesting as well here is how it is possible for one type of event to become or to meld with another, producing a different set of meanings about the happening itself. The best-known example of this is probably Bill Clinton's presidential inauguration, which may be better seen as both an official state event and a cultural event of celebration. In fact, what made this event so significant was the ways in which the government and the media orchestrated it so as to turn an official state occasion into a party for the entire nation, effectively making a new presidential administration's meaning contingent upon a media ritual of national celebration.

Media events always receive extensive coverage by U.S. media, saturating everyday routines with such a high degree of detail, attentiveness, and seriousness that the events themselves become defined as exceptional and separated from the ordinariness of everyday life. They occur simultaneously with the moment in which they are viewed. In other words, they are broadcast "live," and although they may be spatially separated from the audience, they are temporally co-present. They have identifiable beginnings and ends, knowable or approachable before the occurrence of the event itself. The fixed duration allows the event to be further distinguished from everyday life as a specially marked segment. In summary, media events may be formally characterized in these ways: (1) they are "live" or simultaneously performed and viewed; (2) they have fixed beginnings and ends that mark their status as a definable segment of life; (3) they have a high amount of detail and focus that separates them from everyday or ordinary types of public information.

Media events are special occasions for enacting values, beliefs, and norms through a play of symbols and behavior. Media events have become increasingly conventionalized as ritual experiences disconnected from viewers' spatial presence at the enactment. Such conventionalization has encouraged cultural adoption of the media event as a ritual of spatial collectivity *because of* simultaneous temporal presence. In other words, the social community in the football stadium where the Super Bowl is played (although it may be an important element of the media event's performance) becomes less important as a cultural community than the communities defined by those who gather around television sets to watch the game either as groups of TV viewers in the same places or as a group of TV viewers simultaneously watching television in different places. The new electronic community, as Walter Ong described in 1982, upholds a participatory mystique, fosters a communal sense, concentrates on the present moment, and uses formulas to accomplish such ends.[2]

These four types of media events, however, are not the only kind of special segmentation that occurs in the mass media. When bad or even catastrophic things happen, they may be organized by the media as media crises. The October 19, 1989, San Francisco earthquake, the explosion of the space shuttle *Challenger*, the rescue of Baby Jessica from a Texas well shaft, the Los Angeles riots of 1992, the student riots in Tiananmen Square in 1989 in Beijing, China, and the Persian Gulf War are all media crises. A media crisis sometimes exhibits many of the properties and proportions of a media event except that its duration is not known beforehand because the end point is indeterminate. This means that, unlike in a ritualized media event, its narrative can never by fully prescribed because no one really knows how or when something might make the cause-and-effect logic of a narrative implausible. In order, then, to avoid any possibility of having to deny or reverse explanations once they are made, a media crisis generally employs a structure of explanation that forestalls origins of causality or displaces them onto generalizations that are so large that they do not explain anything.

An example here will help to illustrate the point. When the FBI began a tank and tear gas assault on David Koresh and his Branch Davidian religious cult followers in Waco, Texas, in April 1993 after a widely publicized fifty-one-day standoff, television did not immediately turn this into a media crisis. Only when the Branch Davidians' compound caught fire and became a raging inferno did all the television networks interrupt their regular programming to cover this occurrence as a crisis event. As Meaghan Morris has observed, "TV *generates* the real to the extent that any interruption in its processes of doing so is experienced as more catastrophic in the lounge room than a 'real' catastrophe elsewhere."[3] This is where the crisis begins even though the FBI's repeated efforts that morning to flush out the religious cult, which were filmed by television cameras with telescopic lenses a mile and a half away, might be regarded as equally catastrophic.

When the compound went up in flames, network television began uninterrupted coverage (except for interspersed commercial advertisements) of the burning building, on-the-spot journalists describing what they saw and thought, and reporters at television studios commenting on and orchestrating the various elements of coverage. Only at this point, and even though they did not actually know the fates of the people in the building, did the media focus on the occurrence, because, among other things, it was now clear that there was a culminating end to the chain of actions, one of human tragedy. During television coverage, they repeatedly cut to the footage shot earlier that morning of an army tank with a boom puncturing the walls and windows of the compound and lobbing in tear gas canisters. This signature sequence (both at the moment and in the following days) became through its repeated retrospective inclusion and the reporters' voice-over commentaries the causal event and origin of the blazing inferno as well as of people's deaths *even though* the reporters said separately that Koresh and his followers probably had set the fire themselves. This exemplifies how the media guide a set of actions toward one explanation over another and how a crisis takes shape even when the end of the crisis is indeterminate.

Crises may have different origins that in turn produce different types and degrees of uncertainty or threat to the very social community whom the media serves. The rescue of Baby Jessica was an individual's crisis, which invoked collective worry or anxiety only to the degree that others could identify or sympathize with the actors in the crisis. The outcome, while a life-and-death situation to the child and her rescuers, was irrelevant for the continuity of the rest of the country except insofar as Jessica became a figure for a metaphoric national community of concerned citizens. The periodic reports of her rescue and the continuous coverage of its climax were only a narrative extension at the national level of local media's announcements that intercede and scroll across television programs when a child is missing. Both function at different levels to construct a crisis around a missing, kidnapped, or hurt child, and they alert the viewer to one's inclusion in a media community defined by its concern for such children.

Sometimes, as in the 1989 San Francisco earthquake, the crisis may have as its origin a "natural" catastrophe, that is, forces beyond the control of the nation, groups, or individuals. The "natural" media crisis has fatalistic origins. It is interesting that a television network chose to cover this disaster, since the media generally do not construct crises from weather-induced catastrophes. Hurricane Andrew in 1992 caused more devastation over a longer period of time and wider geographic region than did the San Francisco earthquake, but it did not provide an occasion for the kind of attention, detail, or immediacy offered in San Francisco. Some of this might be attributed to the difficulties that journalists encounter when trying to visit disaster sites firsthand or to get information relayed to them when communications systems have been destroyed. Many commentators have even cynically noted that the San Francisco earthquake received so much attention because TV crews were already there to broadcast a World Series baseball game when the earthquake struck, and faced with hours of paid airtime to fill, the network chose to cover the canceled ball game with the disaster. San Francisco provides an instance of a media event (the World Series) that turned into a media crisis. Yet it was important in the television coverage that the crisis became focused through its attentiveness to a dramatic narrative—the attempts to rescue people buried in their cars when the lower deck of the Oakland Bay Freeway collapsed.

The crisis most dangerous for the social structure, however, is one produced by a disruptive show of force that threatens the existing power relations and hierarchy of the social order. War and riots are two such examples, and whereas one may typically treat the former as a threat coming from outside the dominion of the nation, the latter is from within it. The Los Angeles riots and the Tiananmen Square riots provide two interesting counterexamples of riots, since the former was broadcast to the United Stated about a threat from within the United States and the latter was broadcast to U.S. audiences about an internal threat in another country. Both potentially implicate destruction of the existing community, and they may produce fear and uncertainty or elation and hope depending on one's relation to the politics of the possible change.

When a media crisis is a war, the media's coverage of events as they unfold may also be one of the key resources, if not often the only resource, for citizens to learn about their country's military engagements. In particular, nonmilitary citizens have little access to military actions that are taking place at a distance. Reports from journalists who are on the scene provide information as well as interpretation of military events. At the same time, given the proliferation of media outlets in technologized societies, the media not only can provide information about military engagements, but they can shape and influence those events themselves.

There are three primary avenues of citizen access to information about military activities in contemporary U.S. society. The first venue for public information is the government, as it announces declarations of war, military commitments, troop movements, casualties, and battles. Government sources, however, want to control the flow, type, and amount of detailed information about military activities in order, ostensibly, to keep such details from reaching enemy troops. The U.S. government, for example, did not announce the invasion of Grenada in 1983 until after the assault had already taken place. In addition, since a particular political administration's public approval can often be tempered by its military successes or failures, government representatives often find it tempting to offer the best possible interpretations of military events. For example, we now know that the percentages of bombs that hit their assigned targets in the Persian Gulf War in 1991 were greatly exaggerated during the early government reports about the war (the famous "precision" laser-guided bombs were determined to have missed their targets 40 percent of the time).

Most pointedly, the government is unlikely to provide information that could prove useful to those sections of the population who may oppose a particular military commitment and who might endanger support for the war by publicly wielding such "negative" information in the formation of oppositional public opinion. During the Vietnam War, opponents of a U.S. presence in Vietnam often relied on government information that they gained surreptitiously or covertly rather than on information freely supplied by the government. One of the most famous examples is Daniel Ellsberg's publication of what came to be known as the Pentagon Papers, obtained surreptitiously by a former government employee. Over a period of time, former soldiers, Vietnamese citizens, independent researchers, and even a few former government employees came forward with information that contradicted the reports made available by the U.S. government.

A second source of public information and of the material for the formation of public opinion is the military itself, both in its official capacity as a government department—through the Pentagon, the chairman of the Joint Chiefs of Staff, or individual military commanders—and in its more informal channels—through soldiers and their families. An example of official reporting is General Norman Schwarzkopf's now famous January 23, 1991, television briefing in which he provided information about U.S. military progress in the Persian Gulf War. Examples of the latter include letters home, some of which themselves become memorialized, as in the letters from U.S. soldiers in the Vietnam War that have been published in books, placed in glass compartments as part of the New York Vietnam Veterans Memorial, and read on television during the Persian Gulf War.[4] Other types of informal sources include speeches made by soldiers in front of civic groups or classrooms as well as gossip around military bases. Of course, the duration of a military engagement determines the relative importance of formal and informal revelations, since more official military responses dominate in the short run because they have immediate access to widespread media outlets. Only as war wears on for a longer period of time or after a war is completed do personal communications and individual expressions find access to public communications and publications networks.

But, like the government, the military has its own investments in not revealing anything that could negatively affect its own public image, activities, and status. During peacetime, this is pronounced enough, as in the 1992 scandals surrounding the Tailhook convention in which U.S. Navy pilots sexually harassed civilian and military women, and the military made internal efforts to hush up damaging information about the pilots' behavior. But, during wartime, when protection of the military's image may be seen not simply as a nicety but as a necessity for winning a war, such cover-ups of information may be more frequent and widespread. Some of the most notorious examples come again from the Vietnam War: the My Lai massacre, which was revealed only after a helicopter door gunner who witnessed the event came forward; the rape and murder of a Vietnamese woman by a squad of soldiers who kidnapped her to provide "personal R & R," revealed only when a military chaplain pressed the issue (an incident that is the source for the 1969 book and 1988 film *Casualties of War*); or in the numerous cases of torture, rape, and brutality unreported by the military but that eventually came to light as former GIs testified to crimes they had witnessed during what came to be known as the Winter Soldier Investigation.

The third avenue for citizen access to information about military activities is that constructed by eyewitness observers and journalists unconnected to either the government or the military. In this vein, the journalist functions as a professional observer or interpreter or both. Although eyewitness accounts of war are as old as war itself, journalistic observation and management of war information in the United States began with the ability to disseminate such reports quickly and widely in mass-circulation newspapers during the Civil War. Such accounts may be linguistic or visual, made up of the written word, the pictorial, the photographic, sound, or a combination of these elements.

The mass media, however, do not function separately from the government or the military in their coverage of wars. In fact, they often reproduce or interpret the government's and military's war reports as well as generate their own first- and secondhand accounts. Conversely, the military and the government may censor media reports and repress or reshape what is said. During the Persian Gulf War, the government prevented journalists from traveling alone in the war zone and denied journalists access to certain areas, thereby ensuring a different kind of censorship by restricting visibility of military events transpiring and their consequences. In addition, all mass media reports of the war had to be approved by a military public relations officer before they could be printed or broadcast.[5]

It is important to remember that the media function as more than a watchdog over military and government information access in a kind of checks and balances system, although such a role is important. The media can also shape the ways in which war itself is waged. The most infamous case of this in U.S. history is, of course, publisher William Randolph Hearst's use of his *New York Examiner* in the propagation of the Spanish-American War in 1898. Hearst not only penned extravagant, inflated editorials challenging the U.S. government to prove that it was not weak in the face of Spanish actions in Cuba, but he sent a reporter to stage a media event that would encourage public support of the war. Hearst's "rescue" of Evangelina de Cisneros brought the woman to New York City, where he promoted the publication of her memoirs and a speaking tour in which she told what is now recognized as a fabricated tale of rape, kidnapping, and torture at the hands of the Spanish government in Cuba.

While cases of military censorship may seem easily pinpointed and flamboyant examples like Hearst outmoded in a modern, technologized society, the media shape public opinion as well as government and military activities in a variety of subtle ways. If the media prove to be the dominant or, often, the only means available for public access and discussion about military activities, then it is all the more crucial that public stagings, readings, and interpretations themselves be scrutinized for their power in shaping public opinion and policy. For example, CBS news anchor Walter Cronkite's 1967 statement that the Vietnam War was "unwinnable" is now regarded by historians as a political shift taken by a trusted figure that encouraged people to turn away from the government's position on the war.

By extension, the media's role in the Persian Gulf War is important to study precisely because it provides some of the most explicit and troubling examples of how the mainstream media constructed public support in ways that made it easier, if not altogether possible, for the Bush administration to proceed with the war. Such examples are numerous: from *The New Republic* cover photo of Saddam Hussein that airbrushed his mustache to look more like Adolf Hitler's; to CNN's Wolf Blitzer's ecstatic coverage of the opening hours of the bombing of Iraq in which he never questioned Pentagon assessments that the Iraqi Republican Guard had been "decimated"; to the failure of the majority of U.S. media to question U.S. military assertions that the oil slick devastating the coast of Saudi Arabia was the result of the Iraqi sabotage of oil pipelines (rather than, for example, the result of the U.S. bombing of four Iraqi tankers). Media participation in and promotion of the Persian Gulf War helped to create an atmosphere that discouraged questioning the Bush administration's claims about Iraq, Saddam Hussein, or the value of the war itself.

One key example of this media failure is worth examining in greater detail. In October 1990, testimony before the U.S. House of Representatives Human Rights Caucus told of Iraqi atrocities, particularly how Iraqi soldiers had removed babies from incubators in a Kuwait hospital and taken the incubators back to Iraq, leaving the infants to die on the hospital floor. The story was disseminated by the mainstream media and circulated quickly around the country. It became a justification cited by many people (including seven U.S. senators) for going to war against Iraq. The story was eventually revealed

Iraqi baby-atrocity testimony given by "Nayirah," daughter of Kuwaiti ambassador to the United States.

as a well-orchestrated propaganda campaign engineered by the public relations firm of Hill and Knowlton (a firm that was headed by former vice president Bush's chief of staff, Craig Fuller). Hill and Knowlton made numerous videos (called "video news releases") about Iraqi destruction of Kuwait and distributed these tapes to television news programs, many of which simply replayed them as "news." Although journalists eventually revealed that the incubator incident was propaganda, their articles did not appear until long the war was over.[6] As Douglas Kellner concludes, "The baby atrocity story was, therefore, a classic propaganda campaign to manufacture consent to the Bush administration policies. . . . The media which repeated these lies without skepticism or inquiry also revealed itself to be a naive instrument of U.S. propaganda."[7] The amount of public attention drawn to this story and its influence in leading many people to believe that the United States was justified in going to war to stop such atrocities indicate how important such media reports are to the production of modern warfare.

Although the Persian Gulf War was officially over and ended in April 1991, subsequent events (including the revelation of the falsity of the "baby atrocity" story) continue to revisit the Persian Gulf War, to reframe its meanings, and to extend its life. In both December 1992 and January 1993, the United States threatened again to air bomb Iraq, and President Bush's administration presented that possibility as part of a continuation of the Persian Gulf War. The investigation of Iraqi nuclear facilities continues in 1993 to be a source of contention between Iraq and the U.N. And in 1993, President Clinton ordered the bombing of Iraq in retaliation for an alleged assassination attempt on George Bush during his visit to Iraq. One of the things we hope this book will enable us to understand is the way in which Iraq and the Middle Eastern context have been rediscussed and represented in subsequent events that are related to the Persian Gulf War and will probably continue for some time given the economic and political forms of the Middle East in U.S. foreign policy and global relations.

In this volume, we have gathered essays that examine the media in their diverse forms: newspaper journalism, television situation comedies, advertising, videocassette documentaries, television talk shows, war photography, television news, tabloid journalism, and mass-market spin-offs such as bumper stickers, buttons, and, most popular during the Persian Gulf War, yellow ribbons. But rather than group the essays by individual medium, we have arranged them in terms of what we feel to be the primary functions the media served during the war: reconstructing history, controlling the dissemination of information, creating social consensus, and solidifying national identity. It is, finally, these functions, rather than any particular subject matter or apparatus, that describe the role the media played in promoting, reporting, and producing the Persian Gulf War. We hope to provide a beginning point for analyzing how the media worked during the Persian Gulf War and how we might best begin to see through it.

Such an arrangement also serves to make these essays more readable to a broader audience as well as more useful as a classroom tool. In addition to grouping the essays by their emphasis on U.S. media in a global or national framework, we have arranged them from the more general to the more specific kinds of analyses, so that the initial essays in each section pave the way for the more focused analyses in subsequent essays. Interestingly enough, the first essay in each section was written during the war. Finally, an appendix offers a general chronology of the war that should assist in placing the events discussed in these essays in a historical context.

What the essays in this book have in common is that they examine the coverage of the war as a result of readable social formations and discourses, not only on war itself but also on such things as femininity and masculinity, racial difference, technology, and history. They are concerned with how these discourses were presented and shaped by the commercial industrial practices of the media and what strategies the media developed. For most of the authors, these strategies in the Persian Gulf War required a redefinition of the concepts of the basic frames through which we interpret the world. As Todd Gitlin's study of media coverage of the New Left during the Vietnam War showed, the way that the media selects, interprets, constructs, and emphasizes symbols for patterns of recognition and emphasis is singularly important for how we understand world events.[8] So, although Mimi White and Victor J. Caldarola may emphasize the redefinition of time accomplished through the media's presentation of war and Lauren Rabinovitz and Robyn Wiegman may stress realignments of gender, what is important is the degree to which the media's role in this war offered important reframings of how we view the world.

The authors emphasize many of the most significant facets of media production during the Persian Gulf War. Ella Shohat provides an overview of the media's role in the war through her indictment of the mainstream media for its support of the war, and H. Bruce Franklin offers a general look at this role through his historical perspective on the purpose of photographs and images in the production of warfare. The essays on Cable News Network (CNN) by Mimi White and TV network news documentaries by Michelle Kendrick acknowledge the important role that broadcast journalism played in coverage of the war.

But the number of essays that address television's role in the war indicates the broader impact this medium had in formulating public opinion and constructing national identity. As these essays show, along with ones by Victor J. Caldarola, Tom Engelhardt, Dana L. Cloud, Robyn Wiegman, Lauren Rabinovitz, Daniel C. Hallin, Therese Saliba, and Margot Norris, the influence of television in national war making goes far beyond the production of journalism and news programs. It includes situation comedies, talk shows, soap operas, video packaging, and advertisements. To understand the role that medium plays in contemporary society, even in the crisis of war, which seems to be so straightforwardly politics rather than culture (and therefore newsworthy rather than entertainment), it is necessary to look beyond the news to appreciate the numerous, complex, and subtle ways in which public information is shaped, packaged, and disseminated to assist in the formation of a shared national "experience," even if that experience is communally defined simply as watching the same television programs.

Essays that focus on other media institutions indicate the same philosophy of looking beyond mainstream newspapers for an assessment of media operations. Holly Cowan Shulman puts the U.S. media into a broader international context in her examination of the role of

Western radio broadcasts in the Arab world. Venise T. Berry and Kim E. Karloff examine the representations of the Persian Gulf War through popular black magazines, and Leonard Rifas investigates how tabloids attempted to repress social dissent in their focus on celebrity support for the war. Both Cynthia Enloe and Therese Saliba argue for the ways in which images of women were used to reinforce presuppositions about warfare as well as the anti-Arab racism that enabled this particular war.

For several reasons, we chose to focus on CNN, tabloids, sitcoms, popular magazines, and news coverage by commercial television networks rather than look at the significant voices from the alternative media that appeared throughout the war. First and foremost, we wanted to emphasize how the dominant media assisted in the production of the war, whether through their outright support of the Bush administration and its policies, their unquestioning acceptance of Pentagon and military statements, their often "gee-whiz" replications of Pentagon images from the war, or a more sophisticated blending of sentimental persuasion and blackmail by combining entertainment forms with hard-edged news. Second, because we are interested in how the media function in the formation of national identity, we insisted on focusing our examination on those media forms that are defined as popular venues in order to analyze the construction of national self-images and beliefs as well as the widespread demonization of the "enemy." Third, we were interested, quite simply, in those media that reached and affected the largest numbers of people in this country as the best way to understand the role of media in war making.

With this emphasis, we do not wish to diminish the importance of the alternative media during the war. Paper Tiger TV, *Extra!*, *In These Times*, *Middle East Report*, The *Nation*, *Z Magazine*, *Mother Jones*, and *Village Voice* as well as independently published essay-pamphlets by Noam Chomsky, Edward Said, and others all offered precise and devastating critiques of the Bush administration and the war it fought. But these media were not as influential for the majority of U.S. citizens as were images of precision bombing, Patriot missiles, tearful families, injured U.S. pilots, flaming oil wells, and oil-streaked waterfowl. As a study by Justin Lewis, Sut Jhally, and Michael Morgan concludes, the one aspect of the war that the majority of U.S. citizens knew most about was not U.S. ambassador April Glaspie's questionable statements to Saddam Hussein about whether the United States would respond to "inner-Arab" affairs, not the history of U.S. support for Iraq during the Iran-Iraq War, not the environmental damage caused by U.S. bombing of Iraq, and not the numbers of Iraqi dead caused by the war.[9] It was the Patriot missile, that image of U.S. technology and "defense" capability touted during the war as the savior of Israel. People knew this because it was the image most popularized and spectacularized through television. In such a context, for all the sophistication of alternative critiques of the war, jingoistic support for the Bush administration's war won out. Any attempt to understand the basis for this support depends less upon assessments of the range of public discourses than upon their popularity.

For similar reasons, we have limited our scope to discussions of U.S. media. While it is absolutely essential to consider the wide range of media presentations of the war—including those Western media that offered wider, less censored materials than the U.S. media as well as non-Western media, particularly those of Arab countries, that offered radically alternative interpretations of U.S. and allied actions —such a task was beyond the scope of a single volume. We felt it important to focus on the United States for two primary reasons: it would allow us to present a more comprehensive picture of a single media crisis in its wide array of forms, and it would assist in analyzing the role of the media in the formation of national identity, particularly as that identity is shaped during the crisis of wartime.

Notes

1. "War Continues to Boost CNN's Ratings," *Broadcasting*, Feb. 4, 1991, 32.
2. Walter J. Ong, *Orality and Literacy: The Technologizing of the Word* (New York: Methuen, 1982), 136.
3. Meaghan Morris, "Banality in Cultural Studies," in *Logics of Television: Essays in Cultural Criticism*, ed. Patricia Mellencamp (Bloomington: Indiana University Press, 1990), 18.
4. For books of U.S. soldiers' letters home, see Bernard Edelman, ed., *Dear America: Letters Home from Vietnam* (New York: Norton, 1985). On ABC's *Prime-Time Live*, celebrity actors read soldiers' letters home from the Civil War up through the Vietnam War at the end of a program dedicated to Persian Gulf War coverage.
5. Jacqueline E. Sharkey, *Under Fire: U.S. Military Restrictions on the Media from Grenada to the Persian Gulf* (Washington, D.C.: Center for Public Integrity, 1991).
6. John MacArthur's op-ed piece in the *New York Times*, which revealed that the congressional witness was, in fact, the daughter of the Kuwaiti ambassador to the United States, did not appear until Jan. 6, 1992. An ABC *20/20* story on the incident aired Jan. 17, 1992.
7. Douglas Kellner, *The Persian Gulf TV War* (Boulder: Westview Press, 1992), 117.
8. Todd Gitlin, *The Whole World Is Watching: Mass Media in the Making and Unmaking of the New Left* (Berkeley and Los Angeles: University of California Press, 1980).
9. Justin Lewis, Sut Jhally, and Michael Morgan, *The Gulf War: A Study of the Media, Public Opinion, and Public Knowledge* (Amherst, Mass.: Center for the Study of Communication, 1991).

SEEING THROUGH HISTORY

The War for the Past

During the Persian Gulf War, history was not just the framework in which war occurred or the backdrop for justifying new action but became thematized as part of the meaning of the war itself. Popular emphasis on the Vietnam War provided a means for reframing a discourse of national history and U.S. military actions by attempting to overturn the "bad vibes" of the Vietnam War. When the Persian Gulf War began, the most recent images of U.S. involvement in a full-scale foreign war were those of tortured U.S. prisoners of war in *The Deer Hunter* (1979), the futility of the death and destruction in Vietnam as portrayed in Oliver Stone's *Platoon* (1986), and the larger-than-life superhero Rambo acting as a single-man army amidst an inept, bureaucratically frozen U.S. military (*First Blood*, 1982; *Rambo: First Blood, Part Two*, 1985). These were not images that could favorably consolidate national opinion for a new war on foreign soil, nor could they encourage military participation and home front patriotism. In order for the United States to wage a new war, the public memory of the old war would have to be overturned or erased.

The Pentagon explicitly chose this strategy, saying that censorship policies about photographing war casualties and press pool restrictions were responses to the effects of a certain kind of war publicity that attended the Vietnam War. President Bush himself promised repeatedly that this would not be "another Vietnam." Policy decisions about this war were made in light of the effects of public opinion in the other war. While such direct attempts at social control are well known, less has been said about their relationship to the technology of contemporary war journalism and the degree to which the media also enthusiastically embraced the figure of the Vietnam War as a ghost for constructing the Persian Gulf War.

The essays in this section explain why the media would want to do this and what they had to gain. At stake was another battle—one for dominance in shaping public opinion—a battle waged by both the government and the media with the expensive apparatus of modern television rather than with guns. Michelle Kendrick pursues this route by showing how the major television news networks, particularly through their packaged videocassettes, acted as efficient salespeople for President Bush's refrain for a war defined against an unsatisfactory war in the past. She shows how the presentation of the Persian Gulf War packaged as a sophisticated narrative of redemption accomplished two things: it wrote the Persian Gulf War as a story whose inclusive terms dictated that the outcome could only be one of success, and it rewrote the Vietnam War

as an imperfect war of the past that has in the present been sur-
mounted. For Kendrick, the implications are important because
they are indicative of broader ideological moves to redefine U.S.
identity and strength in a post–Cold War world where U.S. economic affluence and domination face erosion both because of the
political shifts in Europe and because of Japanese economic ascendancy. The media are complicit with the government in reframing
the past into a self-congratulatory feel-good narrative for the sake
of spurring U.S. power in an economically declining situation.

Daniel C. Hallin thickens the concept of war rhetoric as played
out during the Vietnam War by giving it both temporal dynamism and
formalistic depth. Just as Kendrick argues for a critique of war
when one war is functionally defined in relation to another, so does
Hallin also show how the Vietnam War was taken out of its geopolitical contexts to make it instead "a part of a timeless American
tradition of war." In this regard, he cites instances in which the Vietnam War was constructed in the media in relationship to World War II
or to American Indian wars of the eighteenth and nineteenth centuries. Both authors argue persuasively for how the discourse of a
particular war—the Persian Gulf War as well as the Vietnam War—is
fully embedded in a discourse of the traditions of U.S. wars as set
out in U.S. popular culture. For them, a critique of the current construction of war is possible only when one interrogates the history
of war vocabulary through which current images are made.

Since these wars have been hailed as the two great television
or "living-room" wars of modern society, these authors consider
further the technologically determined dynamics of the discourses
of the Vietnam and Persian Gulf wars. But, as George Gerbner has
pointed out, images of the Vietnam War usually took days or at least
hours to reach U.S. audiences. The Vietnam War may have been the
first "living-room war," but it was a war that still displaced information temporally. In other words, the Persian Gulf War is the first war
in which war information was broadcast as temporally co-present
with its audience. The instantaneousness of news encouraged
certain kinds of images—those images that could be generated
relatively easily and spontaneously from the positions that U.S. journalists were allowed to occupy. Unlike the Vietnam War, where following soldiers fighting on the ground required a great deal of time
and labor for the initial results of brief segments, Persian Gulf War
reporters had relatively little access to the soldiers and little time to

sort out the relative importance of an abundance of impressions, information, and images. Instead, they relied upon self-contained images of intense movement and visual drama, the images that argued for the "triumphant technology" itself of war: Patriot missiles being launched, jet fighters taking off, video feedback of smart bombs, and traces of bomb fire in the night sky.

H. Bruce Franklin, too, considers the relationship between technology and the images produced of war. More than Kendrick or Hallin, he argues that the images produced of war are a result of the technologies that image war. To support his position, he sketches a history of this relationship from the Civil War to the present. In the Civil War, the government made little attempt to control the images of war, even when men like Mathew Brady manipulated the new medium of photography to create hundreds of images of war dead. Franklin argues that the new technology of photography, with its dependence on long exposure times and the photographer's need to stay close to his horse-drawn laboratory wagon, could only produce certain kinds of images, scenes far removed from battle in which the stillness of the depicted human subjects overwhelmed many of the intellectuals who viewed these images as poignant essays about tragic death.

Franklin's essay reminds us how important it is to be aware of the historical development of the media. The production of photographs of the Civil War slightly prefigures the rise of the mass media in the United States. As a result of the exploitation of new communications technologies during the second industrial revolution in the late nineteenth century, new printing methods, chemicals, and machinery made possible the production of newspapers on a grand and economical scale. The rise of the penny press in the late nineteenth century was only the first of the mass media to address a literate population increasingly concentrated in industrialized, urban areas and caught up in daily life bifurcated by work and leisure, public and private spaces. This is the world that Mark Twain satirizes in *A Connecticut Yankee in King Arthur's Court* (1889), a general critique of industrial capitalism and a specific critique of technologized warfare to which Franklin refers.

By the time the United States entered the Spanish-American War in 1898, both the media and government played new and different roles in relationship to each other in the imaging of war. During the Spanish-American War, newspapers not only developed a new role in producing the direction of war (as the example of William Randolph Hearst shows), they were also an important source of regular information on the progress of that war, providing information in less time than it took for soldiers' letters to reach home and reproducing it in a more extensive geographic reach than public officials could achieve in their coverage of the important news of the war. Such spatial and temporal foreshortening was made possible by the telegraph.

The Spanish-American War was also the first war covered by the movies. Barely a few years old, movies depicted this war not so much to convey detailed photographic information about the events of the war itself as to stir public opinion about the war. Since motion picture footage was sold by the foot to exhibitors who cut and arranged the footage according to their programmatic interests and needs, the Spanish-American War became constructed in the movies through obviously re-created battle scenes, images of waving flags, and toy-boat battles as well as through limited footage shot on location. Song slides and piano backup for patriotic songs about the country and the war were combined with different types of relevant film images that were important for their references to known events rather than for their accurate depiction of events. The effort was not so much one to convey public information as to produce an emotionalized patriotism.

By World War I, as Franklin implicitly argues, movies had become a full partner in imaging war in order to inform the people what the war looked like. But, as Franklin says, the military's and government's increased control in restricting access to combat spaces severely limited cinema's ability to achieve this end. Instead, documentary films claimed their veracity as war information while neglecting to mention the constructedness of their information. In opposition to the documentary's rhetoric of realism, genre fiction films perpetuated the Spanish-American War tradition of producing emotionalized patriotism as enacted through the rhetoric of storytelling.

Franklin uses the juxtaposition of these opposite forms of filmmaking in World War I to travel the distance from how the importance of producing realistic war images and emotionalized icons of war has given way in this century to increasingly depersonalized icons of what has come to be called techno-war. He argues that as the government exerts increasing control over the production of war images and since technology for war itself is increasingly a technology of seeing apparatus, the visual representation of war has reached an apogee in the Persian Gulf War, in which we have the distilled images of a perfectly technologized war machine yet without the critique leveled by a Mark Twain or the human element of suffering as captured by a novelist like Stephen Crane.

These essays emphasize what is at stake in erasing or remaking public memory. They show how history is not just the accumulation of facts about the past but an active process of constructing the present.

H. Bruce Franklin

From Realism to Virtual Reality: Images of America's Wars

The Industrial Revolution was about one century old when modern technological warfare burst upon the world in the U.S. Civil War. During this century human progress had already been manifested in the continually increasing deadliness and range of weapons, not to mention other potential military benefits of industrial capitalism. But it was the Civil War that actually demonstrated industrialism's ability to produce carnage and devastation on an unprecedented scale, thus foreshadowing a future more and more dominated by what we have come to call techno-war. Immense armies were now transported by railroad, coordinated by telegraph, and equipped with an ever-evolving arsenal of mass-produced weapons designed by scientists and engineers. The new machines of war—such as the repeating rifle, the primitive machine gun, the submarine, and the steam-powered, iron-clad warship—were forged by other machines. Industrial organization was essential not only in the factories where the war machines were manufactured but also on the battlefields and waters where these machines destroyed each other and slaughtered people.

Prior to the Civil War, visual images of America's wars were, almost without exception, expressions of romanticism and nationalism. Paintings, lithographs, woodcuts, and statues displayed a glorious saga of thrilling American heroism from the Revolution through the Mexican War.[1] Drawing on their imagination, artists pictured action-filled scenes of heroic events, such as Emanuel Leutze's 1851 painting *Washington Crossing the Delaware.*[2]

Literature, however, was the only art form capable of projecting the action of warfare as temporal flow and movement. Using words as a medium, writers had few limitations on how they chose to paint this action, and their visions of course had long covered a wide spectrum. One of the Civil War's most distinctively modern images was expressed by Herman Melville in his poem "A Utilitarian View of the Monitor's Fight." Melville sees the triumph of "plain mechanic power" placing war "Where War belongs— / Among the trades and artisans," depriving it of "passion": "all went on by crank, / Pivot, and screw, / And calculations of caloric." Since "warriors / Are now but operatives," he hopes that "War's made / Less grand than Peace."[3]

The most profoundly deglamorizing images of the Civil War, however, were produced not by literature but directly by technology itself. The industrial processes and scientific knowledge that created technowar had also brought forth a new means of perceiving its devastation. Industrial chemicals, manufactured metal plates, lenses, mirrors, bellows, and actuating mechanisms—all were essential to the new art and craft of photography. Thus the Civil War was the first truly modern war not only in how it was fought but also in how it was imaged. The romantic images of warfare projected by earlier visual arts were now radically threatened by images of warfare introduced by photography.

Scores of commercial photographers, seeking authenticity and profits, followed the Union armies into battle. Although evidently more than a million photographs of the Civil War were taken, hardly any show actual combat or other exciting action typical of the earlier paintings.[4] The photographers' need to stay close to their cumbersome horse-drawn laboratory wagons usually kept them from the thick of battle, and the collodion wet-plate process, which demanded long exposures, forced them to focus on scenes of stillness rather than action. Among all human subjects, those who stayed most perfectly still for the camera were the dead. Hence Civil War photography, dominated by images of death, inaugurated a grim, profoundly antiromantic realism.

Perhaps the most widely reproduced photo from the war, Timothy O'Sullivan's "Harvest of Death, Gettysburg," is filled with the corpses of rebel soldiers, rotting after lying two days in the rain. Stripped of their shoes and with their pockets turned inside out, the bodies are strewn around the central figure, his mouth gaping gruesomely.

The first of such new images of war were displayed for sale to the public by Mathew Brady at his Broadway gallery in October 1862 in a show entitled "The Dead of Antietam." The *New York Times* responded in an awed editorial:

The living that throng Broadway care little perhaps for the Dead at Antietam, but we fancy they would jostle less carelessly down the

"A Harvest of Death, Gettysburg."

great thoroughfare . . . were a few dripping bodies, fresh from the field, laid along the pavement. . . .

Mr. Brady has done something to bring home to us the terrible reality and earnestness of war. If he has not brought bodies and laid them in our dooryards and along the streets, he has done something very like it. At the door of his gallery hangs a little placard, "The Dead of Antietam." Crowds of people are constantly going up the stairs; follow them, and you find them bending over photographic views of that fearful battle-field, taken immediately after the action. . . . You will see hushed, reverend [*sic*] groups standing around these weird copies of carnage, bending down to look in the pale faces of the dead, chained by the strange spell that dwells in dead men's eyes.[5]

Oliver Wendell Holmes went further in explicating the meaning of the exhibition, which gives "some conception of what a repulsive, brutal, sickening, hideous thing it is, this dashing together of two frantic mobs to which we give the name of armies":

Let him who wishes to know what war is look at this series of illustrations. These wrecks of manhood thrown together in careless heaps or ranged in ghastly rows for burial were alive but yesterday. . . . It was so nearly like visiting the battlefield to look over these views, that all the emotions excited by the actual sight of the stained and sordid scene, strewed with rags and wrecks, came back to us.[6]

Three decades after end of the Civil War, the surging forces of militarism and imperialism were reimaging the conflict as a glorious episode in U.S. history. The disgust, shame, guilt, and deep national divisions that had followed the Civil War, such as followed the Vietnam War, were being buried under an avalanche of jingoist culture, the equivalent of contemporary Ramboism, even down to the cult of muscularism promulgated by Teddy Roosevelt.

It was in this historical context that Stephen Crane used realism, now flourishing as a literary mode, to assault just such treacherous views of war. As Amy Kaplan has shown, *The Red Badge of Courage* (1895), generally viewed as the great classic novel of the Civil War, can be read much more meaningfully as Crane's response to the romantic militarism that was attempting to erase from the nation's memory the horrifying lessons taught by the war's realities.[7] Not subject to the technological limitations of the slow black-and-white photographs that had brought home glimpses of the war's sordid repulsiveness, Crane was able to image the animal frenzy that masqueraded as heroic combat and even to add color and tiny moving details to his pictures of the dead: "The corpse was dressed in a uniform that once had been blue but was now faded to a melancholy shade of green. The eyes, staring at the youth, had changed to the dull hue to be seen on the side of a dead fish. The mouth was opened. Its red had changed to an appalling yellow. Over the grey skin of the face ran little ants. One was trundling some sort of a bundle along the upper lip."[8]

Other literary reactions to the new militarism looked even further backward to project images of a future dominated by war. Melville's *Billy Budd*, completed in 1891, envisions this triumph of war in the aftermath of the American Revolution on the aptly named British warship H.M.S. *Bellipotent*, where the best of humanity is hanged to death by the logic of war, the common people are turned into automatons "dispersed to the places allotted them when not at the guns," and the final image is of a sterile, lifeless, inorganic mass of "smooth white marble."[9]

In *A Connecticut Yankee in King Arthur's Court*, published in 1889, Mark Twain recapitulates the development of industrial capitalism and extrapolates its future in a vision of apocalyptic techno-war. Hank Morgan and his young disciples of techno-war have run "secret wires" to dynamite deposits under all their "vast factories, mills, workshops, magazines, etc." and connected them to a single command button so that nothing can stop them "when we want to blow up our civilization."[10] When Hank does initiate this instantaneous push-button war, "in that explosion all our noble civilization-factories went up in the air and disappeared from the earth." (476) Beyond an electrified fence, the techno-warriors have prepared a forty-foot-wide belt of land mines. The first wave of thousands of knights triggers a twentieth-century style explosion: "As to destruction of life, it was amazing. Moreover, it was beyond estimate. Of course we could not *count* the dead, because they did not exist as individuals, but merely as homogeneous protoplasm, with alloys of iron and buttons" (478). After Hank and his boys trap the rest of the feudal army inside their electric fence, Hank electrocutes the first batch, a flood is released on the survivors, and the boys man machine guns that "vomit death" into their ranks: "Within ten short minutes after we had opened fire, armed resistance was totally annihilated. . . . Twenty-five thousand men lay dead around us" (486). The number of dead exactly matches the total casualties in America's costliest day of war, the Battle of Antietam, thus recalling Brady's exhibition, "The Dead of Antietam." Twain's vision is even more horrific because the victors themselves are conquered by "the poisonous air bred by those dead thousands." All that remains of this first experiment in industrialized warfare is a desolate landscape pockmarked by craters and covered with unburied, rotting corpses.

Twain's vision of the future implicit in industrial capitalism began to materialize in the First World War, when armies slaughtered each other on an unprecedented scale, sections of Europe were turned into a wasteland, and weapons of mass destruction first seemed capable of actually destroying civilization. Meanwhile, the scientific, engineering, and organizational progress that had produced the modern machine gun, long-range artillery, poison gas, and fleets of submarines and warplanes had also created a new image-making technology that broke through the limits of still photography. Just as the Civil War was the first to be extensively photographed, World War I was the first to be extensively imaged in motion pictures.[11]

World War I generated millions of still photographs, many showing scenes at least as ghastly as the corpse-strewn battlefields of the Civil War, and now there was also authentic documentary film of live action. But for various reasons the most influential photographic images from World War I, though realistic in appearance, displayed not reality but fantasy.

Filmmakers who wished to record actual combat were severely restricted by the various governments and military authorities. At the same time, powerful forces were making a historic discovery: the tremendous potential of movies for propaganda and for profits. This was the dawn of twentieth-century image making.

In the United States the most important photographic images were movies designed to inflame the nation, first to enter the war and then to support it. Probably the most influential was *The Battle Cry of*

Peace, a 1915 smash hit movie that played a crucial role in rousing the public to war against Germany by showing realistic scenes of the invasion and devastation of the Unites States by a rapacious Germanic army. Once in the war, the public got to view an endless series of feature movies, such as *To Hell with the Kaiser, The Kaiser, the Beast of Berlin,* and *The Claws of the Hun,* each outdoing the other in their pictures of German bestiality. Erich von Stroheim's career began with his portrayal of the archetypal sadistic German officer in films like *The Unbeliever* and *Heart of Humanity,* where in his lust to rape innocent young women he murders anyone who gets in the way, even the crying baby of one intended victim. This genre is surveyed by Larry Wayne Ward, who describes the 1918 Warner Brothers hit *My Four Years in Germany,* which opens with a title card that tells the audience they are seeing "Fact Not Fiction":

> After the brutal conquest of Belgium, German troops are shown slaughtering innocent refugees and tormenting prisoners of war. Near the end of the film one of the German officials boasts that "America Won't Fight," a title which dissolves into newsreel footage of President Wilson and marching American soldiers. Soon American troops are seen fighting their way across the European battlefields. As he bayonets another German soldier, a young American doughboy turns to his companions and says, "I promised Dad I'd get six."[12]

Before the end of World War I, the motion picture had proved to be a more effective vehicle for romanticizing and popularizing war than the antebellum school of heroic painting that had been partly debunked by Civil War photography. Indeed, the audiences that thronged to *My Four Years in Germany* frequently burned effigies of the kaiser outside the theaters and in some cases turned into angry mobs that had to be dispersed by police.[13]

To restore the glamour of preindustrial war, however, it would not be sufficient to glorify just the men fighting on the ground or even the aviators supposedly dueling like medieval knights high above the battlefield. What was necessary to reverse Melville's "utilitarian" view of industrial warfare was to romanticize the machines of war themselves.

The airplane was potentially an ideal vehicle for this romance. But photographic technology would have to go a bit further to bring home the thrills generated by destruction from the sky because it would have to be seen from the sky, not from the ground, where its reality was anything but glamorous. The central figure in America's romance with warplanes, as I have discussed at length in *War Stars: The*

Superweapon and the American Imagination (1988), was Billy Mitchell, who also showed America and the world how to integrate media imagery with techno-war.

In 1921, Mitchell staged a historic event, using bombers to sink captured German warships and turning the action into a media bonanza. His goal was to hit the American public with immediate, nationwide images of the airplane's triumph over the warship. The audacity of this enterprise in 1921 was remarkable. There were no satellites to relay images, and no television; in fact, the first experimental radio broadcast station had begun operation only in November 1920.

Back in 1919, Mitchell had given the young photographer George Goddard his own laboratory, where, with assistance from Eastman Kodak, Goddard developed high-resolution aerial photography. As soon as Mitchell won the opportunity to bomb ships, he put Goddard in command of a key unit: a team of aerial photographers provided with eighteen airplanes and a dirigible. Mitchell's instructions to Goddard were unambiguous: "I want newsreels of those sinking ships in every theater in the country, just as soon as we can get 'em there." This demanded more than mere picture taking. With his flair for public relations, Mitchell explained to Goddard: "Most of all I need you to handle the newsreel and movie people. They're temperamental, and we've got to get all we can out of them."[14] Goddard solved unprecedented logistical problems, flying the film first to Langley Field and thence to Bolling Field for pickup by the newsreel people who would take it to New York for development and national distribution. The sinking of each ship, artfully filmed by relays of Goddard's planes, was screened the very next day in big-city theaters across the country.

This spectacular media coup implanted potent images of the warplane in the public mind. Mitchell himself became an overnight national hero as millions watched the death of great warships on newsreel screens. He was a prophet. The battleship was doomed. The airplane would rule the world. And America was now much closer to the media creation of the Persian Gulf War than to Melville's "Utilitarian View of the Monitor's Fight," which might appear as antiquated as the ironclad warship itself. The "utilitarian view" of techno-war as lacking "passion" was wrong, for what could be more thrilling and erotic than aerial war machines? The evidence is strewn throughout modern America: the warplane models assembled by millions of boys and young men during World War II, the thousands of warplane magazines and books filled with glossy photographs that some find as stimulating as those in "men's" magazines, and Hollywood's own warplane romances, such as *Top Gun* (1986)—one of the most popular movies of the

1980s—or *Strategic Air Command* (1955), in which Jimmy Stewart's response to his first sight of a B-47 nuclear bomber is, "She's the most beautiful thing I've ever seen in my life."

One of the warplane's great advantages as a vehicle of romance is its distance from its victims. From the aircraft's perspective, even the most grotesque slaughter it inflicts is sufficiently removed so that it can be imaged aesthetically. The aesthetics of aerial bombing in World War II were prefigured in 1937 by Mussolini's son Vittorio, whose ecstasy about his own experience bombing undefended Ethiopian villages was expressed in his image of his victims "bursting out like a rose after I had landed a bomb in the middle of them."[15] These aesthetics were consummated at the end of World War II by the mushroom clouds that rose over Hiroshima and Nagasaki.

Bracketed by these images, the aerial bombing of World War II has been most insightfully explored in *Catch-22* (1961) by Joseph Heller, a bombardier with sixty combat missions. The novel envisions the triumph of fascism through the very means used to defeat it militarily. The turning point of the novel is the annihilation of an undefended antifascist Italian mountain village, which allows fascist forces, embodied by U.S. Air Corps officers, to gain total control.[16] The military purpose of the American bombing of the village is to produce publicity photos of tight bomb patterns.

General Peckem privately confides that although bombing this "'tiny undefended village, reducing the whole community to rubble,'" is "'entirely unnecessary,'" it will allow him to extend his power over the bombing squadrons. For he has convinced them that he will measure their success by "a neat aerial photograph" of their "*bomb pattern*—'a term I dreamed up,'" he confides, that "'means nothing.'" The pretext for destroying the village is to create a roadblock to delay German reinforcements, but Colonel Korn admits, "'We don't care about the roadblock.' . . . Colonel Cathcart wants to come out of this mission with a good clean aerial photograph he won't be ashamed to send through channels. Don't forget that General Peckem will be here for the full briefing, and you know how he feels about bomb patterns.'"[17]

Of course pictures of bomb patterns were not the most influential American form of photographic image making in World War II. The still photos published in *Life* alone could be the subject of several dissertations, and World War II feature movies about strategic bombing have been discussed at length by myself and many others. One might have wondered in 1945 how the camera could possibly play a more important role in war.

The answer came in Vietnam, the first war to be televised into tens of millions of American homes.[18] The glimpses of the war's reality were so horrendous and so influential that these images have been scapegoated as one of the main causes of the U.S. defeat. As appalling as these public images were, however, few had meanings as loathsome as the pictures that serve as the central metaphor of Stephen Wright's novel *Mediations in Green* (1983).

The hero of the novel, like the author, works as a photo analyst in an intelligence unit whose mission is to aid the torture and assassination campaign known as Operation Phoenix, the genocidal bombing, and the ecocidal defoliation originally designated Operation Hades. The official name for his job is "image interpreter."[19] He scrutinizes reconnaissance films to find evidence of life so that it can be eliminated. Not just humans are targets to be erased by the bombing; trees themselves become the enemy. Anyone in the unit who has qualms about this genocide and ecocide is defined—in a revealing term—as a "smudge" and thus also becomes a target for elimination. The perfect image thus should have nothing left of the human or the natural. From the air, the unit's own base looks like "a concentration camp or a movie lot" (199). The climax of the novel comes when the base is devastated by an enemy attack intercut with scenes from *Night of the Living Dead*, that ghoulish 1968 vision of America that is being screened as entertainment for the American torturers, bombers, and image interpreters.

Perhaps the most influential and enduring single image from the Vietnam War—and certainly the most contested—is one that exploded into the consciousness of millions of Americans in February 1968 as they actually watched, in the comfort of their own homes, the chief of the Saigon national police execute a manacled NLF (National Liberation Front) prisoner. In a perfectly framed sequence, the notorious General Nguyen Ngoc Loan unholsters a snub-nosed revolver and places its muzzle to the prisoner's right temple. The prisoner's head jolts, a sudden spurt of blood gushes straight out of his right temple, and he collapses in death. The next morning, newspaper readers were confronted with AP (Associated Press) photographer Eddie Adams's potent stills of the execution. The grim ironies of the scene were accentuated by the cultural significance of the weapon itself, a revolver, a somewhat archaic handgun symbolic of the American West.

Precisely one decade later this image, with its roles now reversed, was transformed into the dominant metaphor of a Hollywood production crucial to reimaging the history of the Vietnam War: *The Deer Hunter*. This lavishly financed movie, which the New York Film Critics' Circle designated the best English-language film of 1978 and which

General Nguyen Ngoc Loan, head of South Vietnam's police and intelligence, executing a prisoner in 1968.

received four Academy Awards, including Best Picture of 1978, succeeded not only in radically reimaging the war but in transforming POWs into central symbols of U.S. manhood for the 1980s and 1990s.

The reimaging was blatant, though most critics at the time seemed oblivious to it. The basic technique was to take images of the war that had become deeply embedded in America's consciousness and transform them into their opposite. For example, in the first scene in Vietnam, a uniformed soldier throws a grenade into an underground village shelter harboring women and children, and then with his automatic rifle he mows down a woman and her baby. Although the scene resembles the familiar TV sequence of GIs in Vietnamese villages as well as *Life*'s photographs of the My Lai massacre, he turns out not to be an American soldier but a North Vietnamese soldier. He is then killed by a lone guerrilla, who is not a Viet Cong but our Special Forces hero, played by Robert DeNiro. When two men plummet from a helicopter, the images replicate a familiar telephotographic sequence showing an NLF prisoner being pushed from a helicopter to make other prisoners talk;[20] but the falling men in the movie are U.S. POWs attempting to escape from their murderous North Vietnamese captors.

The structuring metaphor of the film is the Russian roulette game that the sadistic Asian Communists force their prisoners to play. The crucial torture scene consists of sequence after sequence of images replicating and replacing the infamous historical sequence in which General Nguyen Ngoc Loan placed a revolver to the right temple of an NLF prisoner and killed him with a single shot. Prisoner after prisoner is hauled out of the tiger cages (which also serve as a substitute image for the tiger cages of the Saigon government) and then forced, by the demonic North Vietnamese officer in charge, who always stands to the prisoner's right and our left, to place a revolver to his own right temple. Then the image is framed to eliminate the connection between the prisoner's body and the arm holding the revolver, thus bringing the image closer to the famous execution image. One sequence even replicates the blood spurting out of the victim's right temple.

The Deer Hunter's manipulation of this particular image to reverse the roles of victim and victimizer was used over and over again by other vehicles of the militarization of U.S. culture in the 1980s. Take, for example, *P.O.W.: The Escape*, an overtly militaristic 1986

In The Deer Hunter *(1978), General Loan's revolver metamorphoses into a North Vietnamese revolver, and his NLF prisoner is replaced by South Vietnamese and U.S. prisoners forced to play Russian roulette.*

P.O.W.: The Escape *(1986) transforms General Loan's execution into a North Vietnamese prison commander murdering a U.S. prisoner.*

POW rescue movie inspired by *Rambo* and starring David Carradine as superhero. The bestiality of the Asian Communists is here embodied by a North Vietnamese prison camp commander who executes a U.S. prisoner with a revolver shot to the right temple in a tableau modeled even more precisely than *The Deer Hunter*'s on that sequence of General Loan executing the NLF prisoner. Then, just in case viewers missed it, this scene is replayed later as the movie's only flashback.

Toward the end of the 1980s, however, the militarism of U.S. culture went even further in manipulating this image, shifting the role of archenemy from the Vietnamese Communists to the photographers themselves. For example, the cover story of the November 1988 issue of the popular comic book *The 'Nam* portrays photojournalists, both still photographers and TV camera people, as the real villains because they put the original image on the "front page of every newspaper in the states!" The cover literally reverses the original image by showing the execution scene from a position behind the participants. This offers a frontal view of the photographer, whose deadly camera conceals his face and occupies the exact center of the picture. The prisoner appears merely as an arm, shoulder, and sliver of a body on the left. The only face shown belongs to the chief of the security police: it displays the righteous—even heroic—indignation that has led him to carry out this justifiable revenge against the treacherous actions of the "Viet

Cover story of the November 1988 issue of The 'Nam *glorifies General Loan and makes the photographer into the villain.*

The 'Nam *images the photographer as the shooter and the camera as the most destructive weapon.*

G.I.s spell out The 'Nam's *message about photographs and TV.*

Cong" pictured in the story. The climactic image is a full page in which the execution scene appears as a reflection in the gigantic lens of the camera above the leering mouth of the photographer, from which comes a bubble with his greedy words, "Keep shooting! Just keep shooting!" "Shooting" a picture here has become synonymous with murder and treason. In the next panel, two GIs register their shock, not at the execution, but at a TV cameraman shooting the dead body:

"Front page of every newspaper in the states!"

"Geez . . ."

One could not imagine a more complete reversal of the acclaim accorded to those Civil War photographers for bringing the reality of war and death home to the American people.

The logic of this comic-book militarism is inescapable: photographers must be allowed to image for the public only what the military deems suitable. It is the logic that has been put into practice by each of the United States' wars since the Vietnam War. Nonmilitary photographers and indeed all journalists were simply banished from the war zone during the 1983 invasion of Grenada. Partly because of this, the major media accepted a pool system for the 1989 invasion of Panama and meekly went along with the military's keeping even these selected journalists confined to a U.S. base throughout most of the conflict. A European reporter who attempted to report directly from the scene was actually shot to death when the military unit sent to arrest him became involved in friendly fire with another group of U.S. soldiers.

The almost complete absence of photographic images was quite convenient for the Grenada and Panama invasions, which were carried out so swiftly and with such minimal military risk that they required no congressional or public endorsement. And for the first several days after U.S. troops were dispatched to confront Iraq in August 1990, Secretary of Defense Dick Cheney refused to allow journalists to accompany them.[21] The Pentagon seemed to be operating under the belief that photographic and televised images had helped bring about the U.S. defeat in Vietnam. But for the Gulf War, with its long build-up, potential for significant casualties, and intended international and domestic political purposes, *some* effective images would be essential.

To control these images, the U.S. government set up pools of selected reporters and photographers, confined them to certain locations, required them to have military escorts when gathering news, set up stringent guidelines limiting what could be reported or photographed, and subjected all written copy, photographs, and videotape to strict censorship.[22] Most of those admitted to the pools represented the very newspapers and TV networks that were simultaneously mounting a major campaign to build support for the war. Journalists were forced to depend on military briefings, where they were often fed deliberately falsified information. Immediately after the ground offensive began, all press briefings and pool reports were indefinitely suspended. In a most revealing negation of the achievement of Civil War photography, with its shocking disclosure of the reality of death, the Pentagon banned the press entirely from Dover Air Force Base during the arrival of the bodies of those killed in the war. Responding to an American Civil Liberties Union (ACLU) legal argument that it was attempting to shield the public from disturbing images, the Pentagon replied that it was merely protecting the privacy of grieving relatives.[23]

Although the media were largely denied access to the battlefields, the Gulf War nevertheless gained the reputation of the first real-time television war, and the images projected into American homes helped to incite the most passionate war fever since World War II. These screened images ranged from the most traditional to the most innovative modes of picturing America's wars.

Even the antiquated icon of the heroic commanding general, mis-

Techno-war triumphs in TV sequence of a smart bomb destorying an Iraqi building.

sing for about forty years, was given new life. Although hardly as striking a figure as the commander in Leutze's *Washington Crossing the Delaware* or the posed picture of General Douglas MacArthur returning to the Philippines during World War II, a public idol took shape in the corpulent form of General Norman Schwarzkopf in his fatigues, boots, and jaunty cap.

But perhaps the most potent images combined techniques pioneered by Billy Mitchell, General Peckem's quest for aerial photos of perfect bomb patterns, the medium of television, and the technological capabilities of the weapons themselves. After all, since one of the main goals was to create the impression of a "clean" techno-war, almost devoid of human suffering and death, conducted with surgical precision by wondrous mechanisms, why not project the war from the point of view of the weapons? And so the most thrilling images were transmitted directly by the laser-guidance systems of missiles and by those brilliant creations, "smart" bombs. Fascinated and excited, tens of millions of Americans stared at their screens, sharing the experience of these missiles and bombs unerringly guided to a target by the wonders of U.S. technology, a target identified by a narrator as an important military installation. The generation raised in video arcades and on Nintendo could hardly be more satisfied. The target got closer and closer, larger and larger. And then everything ended with the explosion. There were no bloated human bodies, as in the photographs of the battlefields of Antietam and Gettysburg. There was none of the agony of the burned and wounded that had been glimpsed on television relays from Vietnam. There was just nothing at all. In this magnificent triumph of techno-war, America's images of its wars had reached perfection.

Notes

1. William A. Frassanito, *Antietam: The Photographic Legacy of America's Bloodiest Day* (New York: Charles Scribner's Sons, 1978), 27–28.
2. Alan Trachtenberg, *Reading American Photographs: Images as History, Mathew Brady to Walker Evans* (New York: Hill and Wang, 1989), 74.
3. *Collected Poems of Herman Melville*, ed. Howard P. Vincent (Chicago: Hendricks House, 1947), 39–40.
4. William C. Davis, "Finding the Hidden Images of the Civil War," *Civil War Times Illustrated* 21, no. 2 (1982): 9.
5. "Brady's Photographs: Pictures of the Dead at Antietam," *New York Times*, Oct. 20, 1862.
6. Dr. Oliver Wendell Holmes, "Doings of the Sunbeam," *Atlantic Monthly* (12 July 1863): 11–12.
7. Amy Kaplan, "The Spectacle of War in Crane's Revision of History," in *New Essays on the Red Badge of Courage*, ed. Lee Clark Mitchell (Cambridge: Cambridge University Press, 1986), 77–108.

8. Stephen Crane, *The Red Badge of Courage: An Episode of the American Civil War*, ed. Henry Binder (New York: Avon Books, 1983), 37.

9. See H. Bruce Franklin, "From Empire to Empire: *Billy Budd, Sailor*," in *Herman Melville: Reassessments*, ed. A. Robert Lee (London: Vision Press; Totowa, N.J.: Barnes & Noble, 1984), 199–216.

10. Mark Twain, *A Connecticut Yankee in King Arthur's Court*, ed. Bernard L. Stein (Berkeley and Los Angeles: University of California Press, 1979), 466.

11. During the Spanish-American War, the Edison Company recorded some motion pictures of the embarking troops but was unable to obtain any battle footage. Later the company re-created battle scenes in a mountain reservation near Edison's headquarters in Essex County, New Jersey. See "Historian Remembers the Main, Spain-America Conflict," (Newark) *Star-Ledger*, Feb. 11, 1992.

12. Larry Wayne Ward, *The Motion Picture Goes to War: The U.S. Government Film Effort during World War I* (Ann Arbor, Mich.: UMI Research Press, 1985), 55–56. This volume is an excellent source of information on U.S. government and commercial filmmaking and World War I.

13. Ibid., 56.

14. Quoted in Burke Davis, *The Billy Mitchell Affair* (New York: Random House, 1967), 16.

15. *Voli sulle ambe* (Florence, 1937), a book Vittorio Mussolini wrote to convince Italian boys they should all try war, "the most beautiful and complete of all sports"; as quoted in Denis Mack Smith, *Mussolini's Roman Empire* (New York: Viking, 1976), 75.

16. For extended analyses of the significance of this event, see Clinton Burhans, Jr., "Spindrift and the Sea: Structural Patterns and Unifying Elements in *Catch-22*," *Twentieth Century Literature* 19 (1973): 239–250, and H. Bruce Franklin, *War Stars: The Superweapon and the American Imagination* (New York: Oxford University Press, 1988), 123–127.

17. Joseph Heller, *Catch-22* (New York: Dell Publishing, 1962), 334–337.

18. When the Korean War began in mid-1950, there were fewer than ten million TV sets in the United States. Americans' principal visual images of the war came from newsreels shown before feature films in movie theaters and from still photos in magazines.

19. Stephen Wright, *Meditations in Green* (New York: Bantam, 1984), 39.

20. "How Helicopter Dumped a Viet Captive to Death," *Chicago Sun-Times*, Nov. 29, 1969; "Death of a Prisoner," *San Francisco Chronicle*, Nov. 29, 1969.

21. Everette E. Dennis et al., *The Media at War: The Press and the Persian Gulf Conflict, A Report of the Gannett Foundation* (New York: Gannett Foundation Media Center, 1991), 14.

22. Ibid., 17–18.

23. Ibid., 20–22.

Daniel C. Hallin

Images of the Vietnam and the Persian Gulf Wars in U.S. Television

Since the Vietnam War, it has commonly been assumed that television has a pacifist bias: it shows the true horror of war in a way that whatever the political context of a particular conflict, leads the mass public quickly to tire of the violence. In fact, the technology of television has no more inherent bias than the typewriter or the still camera. It can present war as horrible or glorious or simply as commonplace; and the image it prefers is determined, like other social representations, by politics, economics, and culture far more than by technology.

In the case of the Vietnam War, television's image of war followed closely the prevailing balance of political opinion. In the early years, when antiwar sentiments were still marginal, television presented war as generally glorious and rational. Later, as the balance of opinion shifted, television's image of war became progressively less positive. The short and successful war in the Persian Gulf predictably brought back to the screen the positive image of war that prevailed in the mid-1960s. This essay summarizes the image of war presented by U.S. television in three periods: the early days of the "living-room war" in Vietnam, from July 1965 roughly through the Tet offensive in 1968;[1] the later days of Vietnam, roughly after the Tet offensive; and the Persian Gulf War of 1991. The discussion of Vietnam coverage is a condensation of an argument I made in greater detail in The "Uncensored War": The Media and Vietnam.[2] The methodology of the study is explained in much greater detail there. The discussion of Persian Gulf War coverage is a preliminary report on a study in progress.[3]

War as Masculine Courage and Mastery:
Vietnam, 1965–1968

For a reader of a major U.S. newspaper, the ideological context for Vietnam in 1965 was the political struggle of the Cold War. Television did report the politician's arguments about the need to stand firm against "Communist aggression" and to prevent the falling dominoes of Southeast Asia from threatening the security of the Free World. But for television, the primary political context for Vietnam lay in a different, less conscious level of ideology. Television presented war not so much as a political instrument but as an arena of human action, of individual and national self-expression. This understanding of war, as it was manifested in most of television's Vietnam War reporting in the early days of the Vietnam War, can be summarized in the following set of unspoken propositions.

War Is a National Endeavor. Television correspondents commonly spoke of the war in the first-person plural, as an action of the nation as a whole: "our forces, our bombers."

War Is an American Tradition. Sometimes television reports would explicitly evoke the memory of World War II, placing Vietnam in a continuous tradition descending from it. NBC's Dean Brelis, for instance, closed one report (aired on the Fourth of July, 1966), by signing off from "the First Infantry Division, the Big Red 1 of North Africa, Omaha Beach, Normandy, Germany, and the now the Cambodian border." The effect was to take Vietnam out of historical context, making it instead a part of a timeless U.S. tradition of war, understood in terms of its most powerful and positive symbols. At times, this tradition would be pushed even further back, as correspondents used the language of the frontier. Americans in Vietnam, for instance, referred to Vietcong-controlled territory as "Indian country," a phrase that reporters sometimes adopted.

War Is Manly. A society's political ideology is closely tied to its conceptions of sexual identity. The understanding of war that dominated U.S. thinking in the 1950s and 1960s went along with certain ideas about what it is "to be a man." Two elements are especially important: toughness and professionalism. War was seen as manly, first of all, because it was thought to give a man, and a nation, the opportunity to prove they could "take it," that they could face danger and pain without flinching. "They are marines," said NBC's Garrick Utley, narrating a report about an early amphibious landing in Vietnam. "They are good, and they know it. But every battle, every landing, is a new test of what a man and a unit can do."[4] And Dean Brelis, in the Fourth of July, 1966, report that he signed off by invoking the memory of Omaha Beach, reported, "But they were bloody, and that's what they wanted. They had chased the hills and the mountains looking for the enemy and after many frustrations they had found him, and the price is blood and tears." Network policies intended to avoid offense to the audience, and particularly to relatives of the dead or wounded, limited the use of particularly graphic footage of U.S. casualties.[5] This report was one of the few really bloody ones to be aired; yet it illustrates why it should not be assumed that the capacity of television to represent the suffering of war makes it an inherently pacifist technology. Suffering and death are part of the mystique of war. By seeking them out, Brelis's infantrymen proved they had, as a football coach would say, "motivation" and "desire"; and these were an important part of the American ideal of masculinity of the Cold War era.

War also gave men a chance to prove mastery and control, to show that they were not only tough but were "pros"—men who could "do the job." On occasion, the connection with sexual imagery would be expressed directly. On December 12, 1967, for instance, NBC ran a report on a new helicopter, the Cobra. Reports on new technologies were common and usually stressed the skill of the men who controlled them. "Mr. Davis," the correspondent asked, "what do you like best about piloting the Cobra?" The pilot replied, "It's kind of like a hard woman: it's something you can't like very well, but you can love it."

Winning Is What Counts. This theme is closely related to the conception of masculinity discussed above. It is interesting to contrast that conception with another image of masculinity that competes with it in U.S. culture. If we turn from the 1950s and 1960s back to the 1930s, and from John Wayne to Jimmy Stewart, we see a very different kind of masculine ideal. The hero of Frank Capra's *Mr. Smith Goes to Washington* (1939), for instance, is an awkward and sensitive country boy who stands in contrast to tough and professional Washington and in the end wins both the "girl" and the respect of the younger generation because he, unlike Washington's "pros," sticks to his convictions. He is masculine because he is independent and firm in his moral beliefs. The male hero of Vietnam coverage is masculine for very nearly the opposite reason: he renounces individuality and dedicates himself single-mindedly to the pursuit of ends he does not question—winning, doing the job.

A great deal of the language of television reporting of Vietnam put the war on this sort of footing. While some television reports would put it "above" moral or political judgment by reference to the Cold War, what was far more common was language that essentially put the war *below* such judgment by treating it as a sporting event or a day's work. Bruce Morton of CBS, for instance, closed one report, based on

Defense Department bombing footage, with this narration: "This next run was a pilot's dream, the bomb landing squarely on a railroad bridge. The Communists will have to detour now, and the flow of supplies will be slowed. Barges make a handy target for pilots with some spare rockets as they head for home, perhaps planning a ward-room party after hitting that bridge."[6] Notice the similarity of this report to the typical beer commercial that shows workers coming home after a long day to enjoy the rewards of a job well done.

Here are some other characteristics of the language of Vietnam reporting that have the same effect of "purging" the war of political and moral implications:

> Use of words that portray war as a technical process, for example, "clear" an area, "work them over," "take out" a target, "mop up."
> Action words that give violence a trivialized, cartoonlike character: "American marines with heavy air and artillery support *smashed* a Viet-cong unit near Saigon";[7] "Above the DMZ . . . U.S. naval power is *pounding* communist targets."[8]
> The language of sport: "[O]ur airplanes should have even better shooting in the days ahead";[9] "[T]he total score now stands at 695 enemy bodies counted and several hundred more captured."[10]

War Is Rational. Eventually, one of the things that may have soured the American public on the war in Vietnam was the fact that it was a war of attrition, without fronts or fixed objectives, and therefore appeared irrational: it was never clear whether any given battle or operation should be considered a victory or defeat, or how it contributed to the achievement of more general strategic objectives. But this was not how the war appeared on television in the early years. Here the role of the anchor was particularly important. Film reports from Vietnam were typically preceded by a battlefield summary by the anchor that served to give the day's events the appearance of structure Americans had come to expect from their wars, complete with "fronts" and "big victories" and a sense of driving, goal-directed energy. On August 25, 1965, for instance, Walter Cronkite reported:

> American air force jets gave Communist Vietnamese their heaviest clobbering of the war today, hurling almost half a million pounds of explosives at targets in the North. . . . In [one] raid, the first at purely economic targets, they dropped one-and-a-half-ton bombs, the biggest yet used in this war. In the south, Vietcong mortars fired into the big U.S. air base at Bien Hoa, 15 miles from Saigon, and light American casualties were reported. And the International Red Cross in Geneva today got an urgent appeal from the Vietcong for medical and

and surgical supplies, an indication that our bombing raids and infantry sweeps are taking a heavy toll of all kinds of Red equipment.

These summaries were based on the daily press briefing in Saigon (known to reporters as the "Five o'Clock Follies"), and the claims of victory presented there were taken most of the time at face value, with the result that, of all those battles or operations in the pre-Tet period for which journalists offered an assessment of success or failure, 62 percent were presented as victories for the United States and South Vietnamese, 28 percent as successes for the other side, and only 2 percent as inconclusive. The United States and its allies were also generally reported as holding the military initiative; this was the case in 58 percent of television reports on military engagements. The "enemy" was described as holding the initiative in 30 percent. (By some estimates the reality was the other way around: the Office of Systems Analysis in the Defense Department estimated in 1967 that "the VC/NVA started the shooting in over 90% of the company-sized fire fights."[11] This impression of U.S. initiative was reinforced by a heavy emphasis on the potency of U.S. firepower and the technology that delivered it. It must have been very hard in this early period for the average television viewer to imagine the possibility that U.S. arms might not ultimately be successful in Vietnam.

The New Image of War: Vietnam, 1968–1973

By 1968 or 1969—the change was gradual, so it cannot be dated precisely—the United States was deeply divided about the war. The division existed at all levels: among political elites in both parties and throughout the government, in the mass public, and among the soldiers in the field, who were the principal characters in television's drama of war. Television was not in the vanguard of this change: the positive image of war of the early years persisted until the wider political change was fairly well advanced. But eventually a very different television image began to develop.

It would not be accurate to say that even in the later years television positioned itself in opposition to the war. It was still unusual for TV journalists to take an openly critical stance. Most of the time, the war was reported from inside U.S. policy: a story had a "happy ending," in other words, when U.S. policy succeeded, a "sad ending" when it did not. The Americans, and to a lesser extent the South Vietnamese, were still the "good guys," though they were now more fallible, less macho than the good guys of pre-Tet mythology. A 1970 report on the pacification program illustrates this well. "The idea," the correspondent explained, "is to take an area that was formerly controlled by the Communists, an area where the natives were driven out, and give it back to them, help them to relocate and make sure they're safe."[12] How were the "natives" driven out of their homes? Presumably, since it was a Communist-controlled area, by U.S. military action—but the correspondent said nothing about this. Journalists still deeply believed that American motives were good, and there remained a strong tendency to emphasize the positive in reporting U.S. actions. Some elements of the old hero image of U.S. troops—the image of the pilot as a hero of technology, for instance—also persisted, as did television's image of the "bad guys" on the other side.

But the change was nevertheless dramatic. Let us go through, one by one, the characteristics of television's pre-Tet image of war.

War Is a National Endeavor. Before Tet, Vietnam was "our" war. After Tet, as the war became an object of political debate, it became simply "the" war: first-person plural was used only by correspondents in the field, who still identified closely with the troops they accompanied into battle.

War Is an American Tradition. After Tet, it became extremely rare for news reports to mention World War II. Vietnam was now cut off from that legitimizing connection with tradition (and, perhaps, the tradition itself was at the same time protected from Vietnam).

War Is Manly. The change here can be seen in the handling of casualties. Never after Tet does one hear a comment like "They were bloody, but that was what they wanted." There was increasing focus on the costs of war to U.S. troops, and less inclination either to bury them in statistics or to treat them as proof of the masculinity of war. Every Thursday the Public Affairs Office in Saigon released the weekly casualty figures, or "body count." And for years the networks put them up, every Thursday, usually next to little U.S., South Vietnamese, and NLF or North Vietnamese flags. In the later years of the war, however, they began apologizing in various ways for the coldness of the numbers. At times they would use still photographs of wounded soldiers instead of the flags. And at times they would introduce them with a comment, like this one by David Brinkley on June 26, 1969: "Today in Saigon they announced the casualty figures for the week and, though they came out in the form of numbers, each one of them was a man, most of them quite young, each with the hopes he will never realize, each with family and friends who will never see him again. Anyway, here are the numbers."

In reporting from the field, too, there was an effort to humanize the costs of the war. One thing that made the pre-Tet "living-room war" seem so pale in comparison to other accounts was the fact that the people killed almost never had names—or families, friends, childhoods, and so on, which go along with having names. In part, this was because television took care not to identify specific U.S. casualties to ensure that relatives not yet officially notified would not learn the fate of their loved ones from the evening news. But later, as the political consciousness changed, reporters began to think of ways around this problem. One report closed with film of a number of soldiers looking down at the bodies of three friends killed that day, remembering them.[13] The bodies were never shown and the people were not named, but the story was much more powerful than many more graphic ones. It is important to add here that it was the costs of the war to Americans that were stressed more heavily in the later years, more than its costs to the Vietnamese.

Winning Is What Counts. When Lyndon Johnson was preparing his March 31, 1968, address on the war, aides persuaded him to change the opening from "I want to talk to you of the war in Vietnam" to "I want to talk to you of *peace* in Vietnam." And from that point forward, the message Americans heard was—to quote a 1968 cable sent by NBC News to its correspondents in the field—"We are on our way out of Vietnam."[14] Richard Nixon entered office promising that he would end the war, and though he also promised "peace with honor," he never publicly talked about military victory. For all the polarization that followed Tet, a new national consensus of sorts had been formed: everyone agreed the country wanted out of Vietnam. One interesting statistic bears this out. When statements reported on television in the post-Tet period—most of them from administration officials or members of Congress—were coded according to the criteria used in evaluating Vietnam policy, about 42 percent of the classifiable statements were argued on the basis of whether administration policy would help end the war. An additional 23 percent referred to related themes, including the costs of the war to the United States and the need to protect U.S. troops and get back prisoners of war. Fewer than 6 percent referred to the familiar themes of the pre-Tet period, halting Communist aggression, preserving democracy, and so on.

This had a profound effect on the morale of U.S. troops. The fighting continued while troops were being withdrawn and indecisive peace talks were proceeding in Paris, and increasingly U.S. troops began to question and to resist risking their lives in a cause to which the country was no longer fully committed. The most extreme manifestation of this was the increase in "fraggings"—assaults by soldiers on officers considered too willing to risk their men's lives—from 126 incidents in 1969 to 333 in 1971 despite a declining number of troops.[15]

The soldiers were the primary characters in television's drama of war, and as their morale declined, the tone of television coverage changed. Early reports were full of soldiers expressing their "motiva-tion" to fight and to win. Later there were often reports like one that appeared on ABC in 1972, about an officer persuading reluctant troops to go on a mission by convincing them it was not an offensive opera-tion. The correspondent closed it by saying, "One thing does seem for sure: the average American soldier no longer wants any part of this war, even in a defensive posture."[16]

War Is Rational. Finally, the image of the efficient U.S. war ma-chine moving inexorably toward victory was supplanted to a large extent by an image of war as eternal recurrence, progressing nowhere. The percentage of engagements described in television reports as vic-tories declined from 62 percent before Tet to 44 percent after, and those described as inconclusive or "stalemated" rose from 2 percent to 24 percent. The typical story on ground combat in the post-Tet period would be a matter-of-fact report on the day's activities, without any direct statement one way or the other about their larger significance, but with a closing line something like, "The Special Forces and the en-emy fought this battle to a standstill. And there was nothing left but to tend to the wounded, and fight again another day."[17]

In other reports, the theme of endless repetition was expressed more directly:

> These tanks and armored personnel carriers are assaulting an area called the "Country Store" [because so much enemy equipment had been captured there over the years]. It illustrates one of the frustra-tions of fighting here. The troops have held so many assaults here they've long ago lost count of the number. . . .
>
> There are dozens of areas in Vietnam like this one. We enter, ei-ther fight the enemy or find they've just left, we leave, and the Com-munists return. The soldiers on these vehicles will serve their full twelve-month tour of duty here and then return home. Most will be-lieve they've accomplished something. But in all probability it will still be business as usual at the Country Store.[18]

War as Patriotic Celebration and Technological Triumph: The 1991 Persian Gulf War

After the Persian Gulf War virtually every major U.S. newspaper or television news broadcast had a story observing that the victory in the Persian Gulf had "exorcised the ghosts of Vietnam." And it is true that the Persian Gulf War turned back the clock culturally in many ways in the United States. Certainly television's image of war during the Gulf conflict looked very much like the image that prevailed in the early years of the Vietnam War. Here it will be useful to go once again through the major elements of that image.

War Is a National Endeavor. The Persian Gulf War, like the Vietnam War in its early days, was again "our war" for American journalists.

War Is an American Tradition. References to World War II returned in Persian Gulf War coverage. Gulf War coverage, moreover, stressed patriotic themes far more heavily than Vietnam coverage did even in the early days. There was a heavy volume of stories about support for the war at home, usually reported with a reverential tone television reserves for consensual events it regards as above politics. On President's Day, for example, NBC closed its evening news broadcast with a story on public support for the war, reported from Mount Rushmore.[19] "The polls continue to show overwhelming public support for President Bush's plans and policies in the war," began anchor Tom Brokaw. "NBC's Jim Cummins tonight is at an American shrine." The correspondent began, against shots of the monument and a U.S. flag being raised, "What could be more American than Mount Rushmore on President's Day? Perhaps the mood of the people who drove up here, through a foot of snow." The rest of the report was taken up with interviews with two tourists who expressed support for the war. It closed with the camera slowly zooming in on the monument, and a woman saying, "It's the freedom of the American people and of the world. And that's worth fighting for. Our forefathers did it for us." After this closing story appeared the logo NBC used throughout its war coverage: a fighter-bomber superimposed over the U.S. flag, and the words "America at War."

Flag-waving at home was not a significant part of Vietnam War coverage. The difference probably reflects greater self-consciousness about patriotism in post–Vietnam War America, and the strength of the common view that the United States lost in Vietnam because it didn't have the "will" to win. It may also reflect changes in television news. The U.S. television industry is far more competitive than it was in the early days of the Vietnam War, and the news divisions are under much greater pressure to produce high audience ratings. This often results in considerable pressure to give audiences what they are assumed to want, to play to strong popular sentiments.[20] It may also be that the economics of advertising had a role in television's intense patriotism during the Persian Gulf War. Despite considerably increased ratings during the war, advertisers were reluctant to buy time, fearing that war broadcasts were not a good environment for advertising. And CBS executives were reported to have offered to "insert the commercials after segments that were specially produced with up-beat images or messages about the war, like patriotic views from the home front."[21]

War Is Manly. The women's movement rose to prominence between the Vietnam and the Persian Gulf wars, producing considerable changes in culture and weakening the gender privilege associated with war; U.S. forces in the Persian Gulf included many women. Very few Americans, moreover, were killed in the Persian Gulf or even faced combat with an enemy that could return their fire. So it is perhaps not surprising that the machismo, the toughness, of television's earlier image of war was less pronounced in the Persian Gulf conflict. The male heroes of the Persian Gulf appeared as far less removed from domesticity than those of the Vietnam War, more like weekend warriors than men of the frontier. General Schwarzkopf, for example, appeared on the cover of *People* magazine with his wife and the title "Honey, I'm Home." It is also interesting that there was far more coverage during the Persian Gulf War than during the Vietnam War of the families of soldiers at war (perhaps reflecting, again, not only changes in culture, and the fact that mothers were now at war, but also television's greater sensitivity to the interests of the mass audience).

But powerful parts of the old image of war as a masculine adventure nevertheless were revived in Persian Gulf War reporting, particularly those associated with technical mastery and professionalism. This we can see as we look at the remaining themes, the focus on winning and the rationality of war—which again are closely connected to each other.

Winning Is What Counts. In the Persian Gulf War, winning was once again what counted. This can be seen most dramatically in the technical language that dominated the reporting. This language had three primary sources. First, there were the soldiers, who in modern warfare must be masters of technology—and in the process come to think and speak in technical terms. A battleship gunner, for instance, told one CBS correspondent, "The 16-inch is of course a great counter-the-other-guy's-firepower type of weapon. . . . We prefer shooting at their artillery, their structures. Don't waste the 16-inch on *people*—you can do that with other things!"[22] It will come as no surprise that the correspondent did not make an issue of the moral attitude this statement seems to represent. No journalist wanted to appear as disrespectful to the ordinary U.S. soldier, who more than any other aspect of the war belongs to the realm of the sacred.

Second, there were the experts, whose language sounded something like this: "We can use our aircraft as long as we think we can keep finding valuable targets and killing them before we commit the land forces. We're going to wait . . . as we let air power take what is an inevitable toll and we can undermine and almost destroy the cohesiveness of Iraq's forces."[23] The language of the military strategist is an abstract technical language largely devoid of any sense of violence: targets are "killed" but people aren't.[24] These experts appeared in Persian Gulf coverage in two guises: allied military briefers, and military analysts

—usually former military or Defense Department personnel—hired by the networks as commentators.

Experts were far more important to Persian Gulf War than Vietnam War coverage. This was true primarily because of the limitations journalists faced covering the Gulf War. The military controlled their movements far more tightly than it had in Vietnam, giving them less access to soldiers in the field and making them more dependent on official briefers and experts who could comment on the official briefings. Even if the military had not controlled the journalists so tightly, the shortness of the war would have meant that the journalists would have had little time to develop sources of their own in the field. To this it should be added that modern U.S. TV news places far greater emphasis than the TV news of an earlier era on analysis of day-to-day events; experts are also used far more often, for instance, in election coverage, and there too, they tend to speak in technical rather than political or other terms.[25] The experts, by the way, generally spoke about U.S. forces in the first person, including those hired by the networks who in theory were appearing as journalists and not as government spokespersons. They, after all, were in fact military insiders.

Finally, the journalists themselves largely adopted the technical language of the experts. Thus NBC's anchor, Tom Brokaw, opened one broadcast by saying, "Good evening, it was the most concentrated attack yet by allied forces. From the air, sea and with artillery they pounded Iraqi troops and armor concentrations in southern Kuwait for three hours. It was the real thing, and yet it was also a useful test of the complexities of mounting an all-out attack with so many forces from many different nations."[26]

As these examples suggest, there was relatively little emphasis on casualties in Persian Gulf coverage. In general, the Persian Gulf War appeared as an extremely "clean" war: it looked on television as the ABC expert described it, "targets" were killed, people were not. There are technical factors that are important to understanding this. The Persian Gulf War was a one-sided war mainly fought by air power and artillery, in which journalists had little access to the battlefield, little access to the places where people were dying. The closest parallel is to coverage of the air war in Vietnam, which U.S. journalists covered mainly in two ways: by interviewing pilots and by showing bomb sight films released by the Defense Department. We should remember, though, that in the case of Vietnam, when political attitudes changed, ways were found to report things that had not been reported. The dearth of reporting on casualties in the Persian Gulf War, it is safe to assume, reflects both the fact that journalists were not normally there to witness them *and* the return of the definition of war as a job to be done without sentiment and without moral or political qualms.

War Is Rational. The Persian Gulf War was unquestionably successful, at least if one defines it, as U.S. television did, essentially as a contest between two "teams" and not as a policy intended to shape the political future. The kind of rationality at issue here is the internal, technical rationality of a game—if you make the right moves, you will win—not rationality in any deeper sense. "Our side" clearly won. This is crucial to understanding the return of a strongly positive image of war; if the Gulf War had dragged on, images from the later period of Vietnam, recirculated in much of American popular culture, would have been readily available to be applied. But the Patriot missiles and smart bombs hit their targets, at least as far as we could see on our TV screens, the military plans the experts showed on their electronic chalkboards worked, and the troops came home in triumph. There is no question that the Persian Gulf War appeared on television as rational in a way that the Vietnam War in the end did not.

Only one more point needs to be emphasized here, and that is the centrality of technology to television's image of the Persian Gulf War. If the main characters of the first living-room war were the soldiers, the main characters—and heroes—of the second were the experts and the weapons themselves. Again, it should be remembered that the journalists had relatively little access to the soldiers and that the latter did little fighting on the ground. Overwhelmingly the dominant images of Persian Gulf coverage were the images of triumphant technology: the Patriot streaking up to hit a Scud in the night sky; the cruise missiles arching gracefully toward their targets; the jet fighters landing at sunrise or sunset (a favorite TV visual) with soldiers watching and giving the thumbs-up sign; and most characteristically, the smart-bomb video. All of these are perfect visual images for television—fire and moving machines are among the images most favored by video editors—as well as having deep cultural appeal.

It is hard to say, of course, what will be the long-term impact of the Persian Gulf War, as people experienced it through television. Its shortness and its low cost for the United States may well limit the depth of its impact; it is more comparable to the Falklands War for Britain than to World War II or the Vietnam War. But one can easily imagine a sort of synthesis of the "lessons" of the Vietnam War and the Persian Gulf War: a view that war is still a good thing, a "positive experience" for the nation, as long as patriotic spirit is displayed and as long as machines and not people do the fighting.

Notes

1. The phrase comes from Michael Arlen, *Living-Room War* (New York: Penguin, 1982).

2. Daniel C. Hallin, *The "Uncensored War": The Media and Vietnam* (New York: Oxford University Press, 1986; Berkeley and Los Angeles: University of California Press, 1989). Statistics are from a content analysis of 779 randomly selected television broadcasts, from all three networks, for the period from Aug. 1965 through Jan. 1973.
3. Daniel C. Hallin and Todd Gitlin, "The Gulf War as Popular Culture and as Television Drama," *Political Communication*, in press.
4. NBC, Sept. 9, 1965.
5. The military also threatened to restrict television's access if pictures of U.S. casualties considered too bloody were shown. See Francis Faulkner, "Bao Chi: The American News Media in Vietnam, 1960–1975" (Ph.D. diss., University of Massachusetts, 1981), 236; and William M. Hammond, *Public Affairs: The Military and the Media, 1962–1968* (Washington, D.C.: Center of Military History, United States Army, 1988), 237–238.
6. CBS, May 2, 1967.
7. NBC, July 5, 1966.
8. CBS, Apr. 28, 1967.
9. NBC, Sept. 10, 1965.
10. NBC, Feb. 2, 1966.
11. Guenter Lewy, *America in Vietnam* (New York: Oxford University Press, 1978), 82–83.
12. NBC, Aug. 4, 1970.
13. CBS, Nov. 26, 1970.
14. Edward Jay Epstein, *News from Nowhere: Television and the News* (New York: Random House, 1973), 17–18.
15. Lewy, *America in Vietnam*, 146–147.
16. ABC, May 28, 1972.
17. CBS, Oct. 1, 1968.
18. CBS, June 18, 1969.
19. NBC, Feb. 18, 1991.
20. I have developed this theme, along with its connection with patriotism, in "We Keep America on Top of the World," in *Watching Television: A Pantheon Guide to Popular Culture*, ed. Todd Gitlin (New York: Pantheon, 1986).
21. Bill Carter, "Few Sponsors for TV War News," *New York Times*, Feb. 7, 1991, C17.
22. CBS, Feb. 9, 1991.
23. ABC, Feb. 6, 1991. The analyst is Tony Cordesman, a former Defense Department analyst and aide to a conservative congressman.
24. For a fascinating discussion of the connection between gender ideology and the culture of military strategists, see Carol Cohn, "Sex and Death in the Rational World of Defense Intellectuals," *Signs: A Journal of Women in Culture and Society* 12, no. 4 (1987): 685–718.
25. Daniel Hallin, "Sound Bite News: Television Coverage of Elections, 1968–1988," *Journal of Communication* 42, no. 2 (1992): 5–24.
26. NBC, Feb. 12, 1991.

Michelle Kendrick

Kicking the Vietnam Syndrome: CNN's and CBS's Video Narratives of the Persian Gulf War

Prior to the outbreak of the Persian Gulf War, during the time of national debate over U.S. involvement, government and military leaders sought to assuage a country uneasy at the thought of U.S. soldiers once again fighting overseas. They reiterated one particular theme—the comparison of the current crisis to the Vietnam War—a theme that became constitutive of many later narratives of the Persian Gulf War. The tenor of the comparison was consistently reassuring: this crisis was not a replay of that "unhappy conflict in Asia"; this war was not going to be another Vietnam. In a December news conference, President George Bush assured the country, "If there must be war, I promise there will not be any murky endings."[1] On January 16, 1991, he carefully restated his promise in a televised speech: "I've told the American people before that this will not be another Vietnam, and I repeat this here tonight. Our troops will have the best possible support in the entire world, and they will not be asked to fight with one hand tied behind their back." General Normal Schwarzkopf, in an initial address to troops stationed in the Middle East, made the same promise: "This is not going to be another Vietnam. We're going to wrap this thing up and get you all home as soon as possible." Congressional representatives like Stephen J. Solarz (D-N.Y.), too, took up the chorus of denial and difference:

> I find myself supporting a policy in the Persian Gulf that might well lead to a war that many believe could become another Vietnam. . . .

And yet I cannot accept, or be dissuaded by, the analogy with Vietnam. . . . In Vietnam no vital American interests were at stake. . . .
The war in Vietnam dragged on for years and ended in an American
defeat. A war in the Gulf . . . is likely to end with a decisive American
victory in months, if not weeks.[2]

Solarz, like Bush and Schwarzkopf, guaranteed the U.S. public that
there would be material and ideological differences between the wars.
In essence, they promised that this war would conform to a narrative
already written against the legacy of the Vietnam War. Furthermore,
Solarz's political affiliation as a Democrat, as one who has been generally critical of U.S. foreign policy, suggests that the promise of "never
again" subsumed traditional political differences (those of Democrats
versus Republicans) within its overarching ideology.[3]

What I investigate in this essay are the ways in which this public
promise translated into products of popular culture and the ways in
which the rhetoric of "never again" functioned as a constitutive force
in the construction of Persian Gulf War narratives. Specifically, I trace
this process in two videocassette documentaries, CNN's *Desert Storm:
The Victory* (1991) and CBS's *Desert Triumph* (1991).[4] My focus is two-
fold: to examine the ways in which these videos use broadcast footage
to construct a seemingly coherent narrative of the U.S. triumph in the
Persian Gulf War, and to show how these videos enforce particular
readings of these images to make good on the "never again" promise.[5]
These commercial videos, which were publicly sold both during and
after the war, continually foreground the political promise of difference, translating an overarching ideological message into their representations and aesthetics. As a result, the Vietnam War comes to
function in these videos as a secondary, embedded narrative that defines the Persian Gulf War against itself—continually accentuating the
distinctions between the two conflicts. Despite the Bush administration's continual references to World War II as the allegory of choice,[6] it
is the Vietnam War that haunts these videos—its chaotic, nonlinear,
postmodern elements are evoked, in both verbal and visual representation, to make the Persian Gulf War by contrast seem a coherent
narrative. Such representations define the war against that which it is
not, paradoxically repudiating while continually maintaining a necessary connection with the Vietnam War. At the same time, however, that
the Persian Gulf War narrative is constructed "against" the Vietnam
War, the Vietnam War itself is inscribed in a coherent narrative that
controls and (re)defines its "chaos," which is shown to include moral
ambiguity, weaknesses, indecision, challenges to American military
power, national fragmentation, and bodily fragmentation. The "never
again" promise, therefore, is implemented through a binary construc-

tion that simultaneously defines the Persian Gulf War in a narrative of redemption and reconstitution and redefines the Vietnam War in a carefully constructed and controlled narrative of chaos, weakness, fragmentation, and multiplicity.

Furthermore, the process of narrative construction that takes place in these video products of popular culture reflects a larger process of political containment and ideological (re)definition that attempts to (re)construct a national identity for the United States. Following World War II, the United States enjoyed unrivaled affluence and political and military might. Since that time, however, there has been a gradual erosion of U.S. economic power, most recently in challenges from Japan. The end of the Cold War, moreover, has had the consequence of devaluing our military might abroad, while domestic harmony and the identity of the United States as a democracy have been challenged by multiculturalism, feminism, and gay and lesbian rights. The plethora of promises of "never again" is indicative of broader ideological moves to (re)define the United States' identity in terms that can recoup national strength and coherence, terms unified through discourses that privilege corporate values. As I discuss later, examining how these videos work to define, contain, and narrate the Vietnam and Persian Gulf wars can help to elucidate broader ideological processes that attempt to repudiate chaos and multiplicity and to create a narrative of redemption predicated on corporate aesthetics of organizational unity, efficiency, and order.

In order to understand the process of narrative (re)construction that these videos employ, one first needs to understand how they establish a relationship between two "narrative levels" that elucidates their mechanisms of coherence. Literary theorist Gerard Genette differentiates between the primary narrative (which he calls the diegetic level) and narratives that are embedded within it (metadiegetic-level narratives). In Genette's terms, "metanarrative is a narrative within the narrative, the metadiegesis is the universe of this second narrative, as the diegesis . . . designates the universe of the first narrative."[7]

In the CBS and CNN videos, the diegetic level is the narrative of the events of the Persian Gulf War: the political machinations, the tactical decisions, the end results. Operating on the metadiegetic level are embedded fragments of the nonnarrative of the Vietnam War. That is, situations, conditions, and opinions concerning the Vietnam War are the always present undercurrent, the "second level," and they interact with the diegetic narrative, in both explicit and implicit ways, in thematic relationships of contrast. Thus, the second-level narrative of the Vietnam War interacts with the Persian Gulf War narrative to reinforce the unity and coherence of the first-level narrative. Disruptions are represented primarily on the second level (though, in the constructive process, these disruptions are contained, ordered, and controlled for the purpose of their necessary interaction with and contrast to the Persian Gulf War). The Vietnam War is represented as chaotic, confusing, disruptive, and multiplicitous, whereas the Persian Gulf War is represented as orderly, linear, and unified.[8]

In many ways, of course, the Persian Gulf War is extraordinarily disorderly, harboring within its structure many loose ends that resist compaction into a clean narrative form. Its causes are complex and rooted in years of imperialist rule, border tensions, and the past two decades of U.S. involvement in the Persian Gulf. The closure promised in these videos ignores such aspects of the crisis as the Kurdish civil war and subsequent actions, the question of possible war crimes, the nondisclosure of the number of Iraqi dead, the American/allied deaths by friendly fire (in a war touted for its accuracy), Saddam Hussein's continuing rule, the difficulty of enforcing the United Nations regulations concerning nuclear and biological weapons, the turbulent Arab/Israeli disputes, continued U.S. dependence on imported oil and recent revelations of technological failures and media cover-ups. These particular avenues of potential disorder, however, are either ignored completely in the Persian Gulf War videos or are included but downplayed and dismissed by the admission into the videos of the emphatic "never again" rhetoric.

Both the CBS and CNN videos' dramatic emphasis on narrative coherence represents the Persian Gulf war as orderly.[9] Narrative coherence is anticipated even before the videos properly begin. The titles, *Desert Storm: The Victory* and *Desert Triumph*, explicitly highlight an allied interpretation of the cessation of hostilities.[10] Brief summaries on the videos' packages promise viewers "the complete story of the Persian Gulf War" and proclaim, "THIS IS THE COMPLETE STORY OF THE AMERICAN TRIUMPH IN THE GULF." The explanatory text of the CBS video reinforces the narrative completeness: "These historic tapes offer the complete visual chronicle of the War in the Persian Gulf." A promise of a complete narrative, of closure and containment, occurs no fewer than three times in CBS's packaging. CNN's packaging also emphasizes narrative, promising its viewers a "historic" and "compelling tale." Aristotelian aesthetics are conflated with history; historical fact conforms to the formal demands of traditional narrative.

CBS's video emphasizes closure by beginning the narrative with the "end" of the war. Positioning the war retrospectively, news anchor Dan Rather's opening lines are, "By February 28, 1991, it was over. Men and machines had fought and died here in the drifting sand, and now the winds had begun to erase their footprints, leaving the rest for time

Used throughout CNN's video, this screen reports important dates from the Persian Gulf War. Note the time line at the bottom of the screen. (Desert Storm: The Victory, Turner Home Entertainment, CNN, 1991)

itself to consume." Rather's voice accompanies images of desert stretches empty except for the hulks of destroyed machinery. Such a beginning posits the entire video as a flashback on a finished story, a conventional gambit for foregrounding closure and binding the story within a tight narrative frame. Furthermore, a display of empty desert and abandoned machines gives viewers the (false) impression of U.S. absence in the Persian Gulf.[11]

Formal elements in CNN's video contribute to an overarching organization of order and control. This narrative is tidily divided into "chapters": The Air War, The Ultimatum, and The Hundred Hour Ground War. Within each chapter, important dates appear on the screen above a time line, which is marked with incremental lines that are a precise distance apart. Moving steadily across the screen (right to left), accompanied by upbeat, percussive music, this time line creates the impression of the progress of each chapter of the war as aesthetically controlled and measured, marked and verifiable.

Another strategy that regulates and contains the primary narrative is the video's continual evocation of nature metaphors that naturalize U.S. aggression and depoliticize our involvement in the Persian Gulf. The foremost of these metaphors, of course, is the operation name, "Desert Storm." Deployed liberally throughout the videos, this metaphor elides the complexity, turmoil, and political character of a human war through the fixed causes, inevitable progression, and visible boundaries of a storm. This metaphor functions on many levels to confer upon the allied forces certain qualities associated with catastrophic natural phenomena—incredible power, the ability to destroy outside the bounds of morality, and the ability to inspire awe.

As it was for the war as a whole, this metaphor is part of the constitutive framework for the videos' narrative, enclosing the war within the limits of its logic and imagery. With a clear beginning, a turbulent but comprehensible progression, and a distinct end, the storm as metaphor contains and orders the events of the Persian Gulf War. For example, CNN's video, *Desert Storm: The Victory*, describes prewar tensions and the breakdown of diplomatic maneuvers as "storm clouds" that "had been forming over the gulf for months [and] were finally about to break." These political tensions are also described later as "small but mounting signs of the storm to come." Applied in this fashion, the storm metaphor contributes to the sense of the war as inevitable, a natural result of the regional tensions and Saddam Hussein's "madness." The political debate, moreover, is conflated with the aesthetics of a mounting storm front, and the outbreak of the war is explicitly demarcated within a temporal frame as localized and identifiable as two clashing storm fronts.

The progression of the war is also metaphorically equated to the raging of the storm. CNN mixes the imagery of nature's force and human folly, announcing, "Sunday morning, rain lashes the desert. Black clouds from burning oil wells rise to meet thunder. The time had come for a desert storm." Nature and humanity fuse within this description so that the natural components of a storm, such as rain and thunder, are the metaphoric markers of the war's commencement. Specific actions occurring during the progression of the war are also assimilated into the metaphor. CNN reporter Bernard Shaw, for example, describes bombing as "a powerful new rain . . . from the sky." His words naturalize and even aestheticize political agency (and with it the ethical ramifications of the intense bombing raids) while they naturalize and render immaterial the bombs' destructive effects—they fall like "rain" on the Iraqis.

Ultimately, in harmony with the rest of its metaphoric frame, CNN's video declares, "The war was over. The storm had passed." Evoked in this manner, the storm metaphor works to simplify the cessation of hostilities with the image of the "passing" of the storm. The metaphor cleanly closes off the narrative, precisely marking the far boundary of the temporal frame and resisting further complications or possible disruptions that may result from the outcome of the war.

Such repetitive and excessive insistence on containment and closure has its roots in the metadiegetic influence of the Vietnam War. An often noted characteristic of the Vietnam War is that it resists inscription in traditional narrative—resists, in fact, any linear troping.[12] One reason for this seems to lie in the ambiguity that surrounds its time frame. Susan Jeffords, in her book *The Remasculinization of America*, writes:

> The "end" of the Vietnam War itself is difficult to identify. Is it the fall of the Saigon government in 1975? the withdrawal of American troops from battle in 1973? the Tet Offensive in 1968, when, according to many historians, the war was perceived by the American public to be lost? And is its beginning with the large-scale introduction of American Troops in 1965? with the commitment of American financing and advisors in 1962? the assumption by the United States government of the debts and institutions of the French in Vietnam in 1945? or the Declaration by Ho Chi Minh of an Independent Vietnam in 1945?[13]

Without clear beginning and insistent closure, the Vietnam War has often been characterized as a "quagmire," and the lack of discernible boundaries has been a significant factor in the labeling of the Vietnam War as "postmodern." Kate Beaird Meyers concludes, "Vietnam histories have one thing in common: they are all, to some extent, fragmentary," in part because "the length of the war is still debated."[14] Thomas Myers is more to the point: "Within its unresolved story elements and abundant symbolic possibilities, the [Vietnam] war as lived history had a distinctly postmodernist composition."[15]

Refusing aestheticization within traditional narrative patterns, foregrounding its open and unresolved features, literally haunting the present with a political, domestic backlash (often labeled the "Vietnam syndrome"), the Vietnam War functions as a constitutive force in the creation of Persian Gulf War narratives. These new narratives are written to restore order, where "order" means renewed U.S. power, control, and identity.[16] Many people initially feared that the Persian Gulf War would become a second postmodern war, a similar site for chaos, fragmentation, and disorder. War protesters took to the streets chanting "Hey, Hey Uncle Sam, we remember Vietnam" and dressed in plastic to symbolize the Vietnam War's infamous body bags. Before the outbreak of hostilities, media commentaries theorized that war in the

Persian Gulf might become a "prolonged war of attrition, similar to Vietnam"[17] and might mean "blood, gore, pain, retribution, and hate for years to come."[18] In order to resist this rhetoric, the political promises and the subsequent narrative of the Persian Gulf War, therefore, had to emphasize containment and closure. After all, Bush's gamble, when he promised no "murky endings," was to have events work as a narrative of order and control that, in effect was *already written* against the Vietnam War.

CBS's and CNN's videos demonstrate this process of assembling a narrative for the Persian Gulf War on and against the "fragments" of the Vietnam War. After CNN's video introduces Norman Schwarzkopf, he addresses the troops: "This is not going to be another Vietnam. We're going to wrap this thing up and get you all home as soon as possible." Schwarzkopf's implicit message, of course, is that the Vietnam War (and the leaders in charge of that war) resisted closure, and his promise is that this war is consciously being constructed to avoid that pitfall.

Schwarzkopf's on-screen promise is one of CNN's first explicit references to the Vietnam War. Directly succeeding this, a voice-over narrator reinforces the difference between the wars—"Haunted by Vietnam, the general and his staff devise a never-again strategy"— while Vietnam War clips are shown. Beginning with slow-motion footage of helicopters hovering above a clearing and soldiers leaping out to run to the jungle, the shot dissolves to black-and-white footage of wounded soldiers, grimacing and screaming as they are jarred by the men carrying them. The sequence ends with a freeze frame of a young white soldier, his mouth open in a silent scream, straining against the hands that are attempting to hold him on the stretcher.

The nightmarish quality of the grainy black-and-white footage, further enhanced in slow motion, sharply contrasts with the bright, sunlit expanses of the Persian Gulf War footage. The choice of black-and-white footage is one aesthetic manifestation of the proposed ideological differences between the wars. In fact, this particular scene, accompanied by somber music, portrays the Vietnam War (from the viewpoint of the soldiers at least) as an utterly mysterious event, which was the site for physical pain and existential anguish. The viewer can then juxtapose these images with the clarity of the Persian Gulf War, as it is exemplified both rhetorically, in the video reiterations of the allies' clear, morally unambiguous purpose for fighting, and aesthetically, in the splendor and beauty of the sunlit desert shots.

Moreover, the visual representation of wounded U.S. soldiers in the Vietnam War specifically relates the "never again" strategy to the bodily coherence of "our" troops in the Persian Gulf. Before the out-

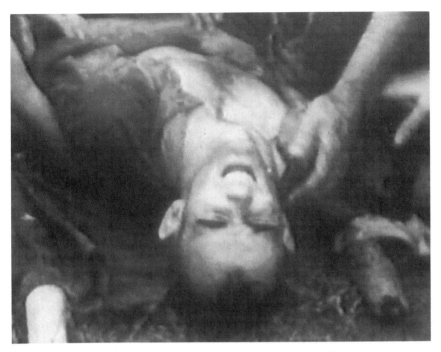

Black-and-white archival footage of a wounded soldier from the Vietnam War. (Desert Storm: The Victory, Turner Home Entertainment, CNN, 1991)

break of the Persian Gulf War, one widely publicized fear was that this war would result, like the Vietnam War, in thousands of dead or wounded U.S. "boys." Within the videos' representation, however, wounds, dying, death, and the destruction and fragmentation of human bodies are emphatically relegated to the "other" war. While there is CNN footage from the Basra road, it shows only dead Middle Eastern men (none of our "boys"), and these figures are generally unrecognizable as bodies; they are charred lumps, whose human features have been all but eradicated.[19] In neither video is there battlefield blood, bodily fragmentation of soldiers, or even any concrete physical evidence of their pain and suffering[20]—except in the archival footage of the Vietnam War. In those instances when it is impossible to avoid talking about the allied dead, they are metonymically represented by a crushed helmet, an empty boot, or a piece of wrecked machinery. War equipment thus eclipses human bodies, shifting attention from the physical beings affected by the war onto the technology. Thus one particularly potent potential disruption within this narrative—the dead or maimed allied body—is defused by the visual and vocal reassurances that the "never again" strategy, the strategy that "won" the war, ensured the bodily coherence of our troops. Furthermore, this emphasis on bodily coherence foregrounds the political promise of a new United States identity that is founded on unity and coherence (against the fragmentation and disorder of the Vietnam War). Order and containment are promised even on the tangible level of the human body.[21]

Following the wounded-soldier footage, the next few minutes of CNN's video are a point-by-point comparison of the Persian Gulf War to the Vietnam War, as if the phantom of "Nam," once roused, must be exorcised through a ritual of comparison and denial. Four explicit comparisons are made: the first clarifies differences in military command; the second, in presidential leadership; the third, in battle plans; and the fourth, in technology. The first two comparisons deal with the focus and unity of command in the Persian Gulf War. While a narrator's voice-over declares, "In Vietnam each division of the military conducted its own air campaign," Vietnam War footage is shown, consisting of hazy, unsteady film clips, shots from the ground, showing two jets carpet bombing a section of jungle, creating huge fireball explosions and flying debris. The video cuts to a banking jet against a cloudless blue sky, and the voice-over assures viewers, "This time all air activity is coordinated under one command." Images of devastation —explosions, fire, flying debris—belong to the Vietnam War, whereas the Persian Gulf War offers aesthetically pleasing images of technological sophistication.[22] Similarly, the chaos and destruction of the Vietnam War are linked directly to the multiplicity of command. The Persian Gulf War, on the other hand, because it is efficiently unified "under one command," is antiseptic and beautiful.

The video delineates the responsibility for this particular difference (and perhaps all the differences between the two wars) in the next comparison between Lyndon Johnson and George Bush. Here, the voice-over informs viewers, "In Vietnam President Johnson was involved in choosing enemy targets to strike. . . . This time that does not happen." Brief clips show each president in a similar public relations situation—surrounded by a crowd, smiling and shaking hands. Amidst *reporters*, Johnson is the focus of dozens of flashing cameras. Since the degree of Johnson's involvement has often been characterized by Vietnam historians and analysts as a form of self-aggrandizement and inefficient managing that endangered U.S. soldiers and was ultimately a factor in the U.S. defeat, this shot subtly criticizes his position.[23] Bush, on the other hand, is shown among the *troops*—young men and women in camouflage who mill excitedly about him. There are no press cameras evident, and the camera's position is distant, contrasting the low-angle close-up of Johnson. Each framing, therefore, also suggests the stance of the crisis managers in each of the wars. Johnson's selfish usurpation of media glory and his abuse of managerial power are represented by his position at the center of the flashing cameras. This image underscores Johnson's (selfish) managerial style that resulted in a division between the war's decision makers and those who would pay the price for their decisions. In contrast, the Persian Gulf War's commander in chief mingles with the troops and thus is represented as an efficient manager who depoliticizes control and effectively delegates command and unifies the war effort.

The two subsequent comparisons also position the Vietnam War as fragmented and chaotic. A voice-over announcing that "in 'Nam there was confusion over the battle plan" accompanies footage of a Vietnam War battle, replete with images of chaos: soldiers run and fall, crowd into foxholes, shoot, shout, and throw grenades. The dark, grainy footage adds to the air of mystery and to the impenetrability of the surrounding jungle. Within this image, the enemy cannot be seen; thus the jungle metaphorically becomes the amorphous, invisible other.

The next sequence, however, stylistically and rhetorically poses a contrast. The shots begin with footage of one of the technological wonders of this war, the Stealth bomber, while a voice-over narrator explains: "This time there is clarity and simplicity. Pound the enemy from the air, mop up on the ground." The subsequent shot is the now famous view through the "eye" of a smart bomb and the consequent collapse of a building as it is struck directly. Moving from the subjective Vietnam War soldier's "eye" view to the objective "eye" of the smart bomb emphasizes the antiseptic nature of the Persian Gulf War, with its clean, well-designed, perfectly functioning technology. It is a sharp contrast to the chaos both created by and captured in the subjective human soldier of the Vietnam War. Finally, a line of Abrams tanks moves through the desert and mops up on the ground, displaying a sharply geometrical and cleanly efficient U.S. technological superiority.

The technological differences between the Vietnam and Persian Gulf wars are especially significant and pointedly marked. The singular representation of Vietnam War technology is a solitary tank, apparently stuck, in a muddy sinkhole, surrounded by the tangle of jungle vegetation. The narrator explains, "In Vietnam weaponry and terrain did not match. This time the arsenal is nearly perfect," as a shot cuts to an Apache helicopter rising from the far side of a sand dune. The contrast occludes the widely publicized concern that the desert sand might quickly destroy valuable weaponry systems and instead glorifies and aestheticizes the "nearly perfect" technological arsenal of the Persian Gulf War.

An aesthetically pleasing shot of technological sophistication, this photo is typical of CNN footage of the Persian Gulf War. (Desert Storm: The Victory, Turner Home Entertainment, CNN, 1991)

The point-by-point comparison defines and contains each of the war narratives against the other. Throughout the comparison, the Vietnam War is disorderly, subjective, and multiplicitous, whereas the Persian Gulf War is unified, ordered, and efficient. Perhaps most striking is the emphasis on the technological products of the military industrial complex, which are always and everywhere aestheticized and fetishized; the Persian Gulf War becomes their showcase. In CNN's video, Patriot missiles are referred to as "the first heroes" of the war, so effective that the media and the viewing public canonized them; long, elaborate sections of both CNN's and CBS's videos describe weapons systems in loving detail, supplying viewers with such statistics as tonnage, range, and the like. The footage from the Vietnam War, by contrast, does not focus on technology but on the effects of weaponry systems—death, destruction, and the subjective experiences of fear, panic, and confusion.

CBS's video also explicitly juxtaposes the two wars, including a long monologue by a leading military authority, retired U.S. Marine Corps general George Crist, who, seated before an enlarged map of the Middle East, begins his rather detailed comparison by ironically denying that there *can be any comparison:* "When we first started in early August, the plane trips, and all the way up to the war, when the war itself really started, all the pundits wanted to compare this thing to the Vietnam War. How we fought, how we're organized, and *yet there was no comparison at all*" (emphasis mine). Although Crist emphasizes, at first, what he sees as the absolute opposition between the wars, he continues with a detailed analysis that explicitly contrasts the fighting forces. The U.S. soldiers of the Vietnam War, according to Crist, were uncommitted riffraff who "couldn't wait to get out the door." They were "an army of draftees, an army taken off the streets of ghettos," whereas "the army that went to [the Persian Gulf War] came out of the ashes of Vietnam and the lessons from Vietnam." Crist continues,

> About an all-volunteer force, the officers were graduates of school after school after school, where they not only practiced the arts of war but studied the arts of war. We had grown a professional armed force that had been trained intensely, receiving these new high-tech weapons and learning how to use them and how to use them well. . . . It was not a citizen's army. It was a true professional's army. The fact that this was an army of careerists, not draftees [, means that] when they get loose on the battlefield they prevail over an army whose officers ran and were conscripted.

Crist's distinction between the two wars is quite literally black-and-white. He implies that the Vietnam War was fought primarily by people of color who lacked commitment, education, and dedication. On the other hand, he portrays the new army, rising phoenixlike from the "ashes of Vietnam," as one composed of "practiced" warriors who studied the "arts of war." Crist's characterization of the "all-volunteer" army stresses education, training, the soldiers' willingness to subordinate themselves to their country's good, and the absolute nature of their commitment. Through his suggestion that the Vietnam War was lost, in part, because of its soldiers' "ghetto" origins, Crist implies, moreover, that the opposite is true of the Persian Gulf conflict, positing either a predominately Anglo army or, at the very least, a kind of racial and class unity not operative during the Vietnam War.

In this rhetoric, the "professional" nature of the current army is glorified not for its strength, aggression, or courage but rather for its education, training, and mastery of "high" technology. The unity of the Persian Gulf War troops, Crist suggests, is grounded in the soldiers' dedication to their careers. The troops are thus represented as dedicated "employees" who win the war because they are well trained and well managed. The shots following Crist's speech emphasize, once again, the differences. First ground, then tangles of bushes, then sky— all clearly shot by someone wildly running—spatialize disorientation amidst sniper fire and hoarse shouts in the jungle. The final shot of the sequence dissolves to a huge fireball rising above a distant patch of jungle. Again, the jungle is a dramatic trope for the enigmatic war in Vietnam. The images of disorientation, manifest fear, and massive destruction contrast with the subsequent single shot of the Persian Gulf War: a soldier seated before a wall of technological apparatus—video monitors, keyboards, switches, and colored lights. The camera cuts to one of the video screens that displays the simulated image of a helicopter rising to the center of crosshairs. The antiseptic primacy of technology is signified in the wall of monitors, representing U.S. technological superiority and suggesting both absolute control over and a crucial distance from the powers of destruction. The soldier before the video display terminal is the new "professional" warrior who uses a keyboard rather than a rifle.

Later in the video, General Crist again compares the Vietnam War to the Persian Gulf War, when he celebrates the unity that prevailed among the allied forces of the Persian Gulf War. "It was a textbook war," he said, which had some "very big firsts. . . . One was the melding together of the services, all the air under one commander, all the ground forces under one commander. . . . In no war had [the United States] ever been able to overcome interservice rivalry right down on the battlefield. . . . Nowhere had U.S. and allied forces been able to come together and operate in such a way that they did here." The unity that Crist praises comes from the formation of a hierarchy "under one commander." The "interservice rivalry" of previous wars (read Vietnam), Crist claims, has been overcome by an efficient and well-structured organization. Again, the contrast between the two wars is made implicitly, and potential disruptions are not handled by the video documentary, particularly the prewar apprehensions that the U.S. combat force would be composed of disproportionate numbers of minorities, as was the case in the Vietnam War.

The CBS video includes one final comparison between the wars. The harmony and racial unity (resulting from efficient organization) that prevailed among the troops during the Persian Gulf War was matched, the video goes on to explain, by unity on the home front. In a multitude of visual and vocal reassurances, each video collection stresses the solidarity of U.S. citizens behind the war effort. Antiwar demonstrators, political dissenters, and those with opinions contrary to the official line of the United States government are given little coverage. What coverage there is again invokes the specter of the Vietnam War that renders the Persian Gulf War protesters innocuous. For example, CBS shows footage of a war protest, focusing its shots mainly on long-haired, shabbily dressed youth and ignoring the issues brought up by the waving placards ("No blood for oil," "There is no boot camp for war widows"). Dan Rather explains solemnly, "Although peace demonstrators took to the streets both before and during the war, their protests never shook the nation like they had during the Vietnam conflict." Thus the disruption and dissent that occurred during the Persian Gulf crisis is again occluded by the incorporation into the narrative of a greater disruptive force—the Vietnam War protests. Persian Gulf War protesters are stripped of their validity, import, and effectiveness with one sentence.

The drive for narrative coherence within these videos pits the audiovisual images of the Persian Gulf War against those of the postmodern Vietnam War. In so doing, these videos reflect a larger process of (re)constructing and refining a narrative of national identity for the United States. In their article on the consensus-building, media-sponsored spectacles that took place on the home front during the Persian Gulf War, Jochen and Linda Schulte-Sasse examine "the importance of aestheticized experiences of collective unity and superiority for the cultural reproduction of U.S. society and of war as a means of simulating a unified body politic."[24] They argue that events, such as the rally in San Diego in which several thousand people created an American flag with their bodies, construct an "aesthetic experience [that] compensat[es] for a dysfunctional reality."[25] Similarly, the "aestheticized experiences of collective unity and superiority" in CNN's and CBS's videos construct a narrative of national identity, utilizing a rhetoric of unity and order.

This need to reinscribe a national identity is, in part, an anxiety-ridden response to the country's "dysfunctional reality" in a global marketplace in which the United States is steadily losing economic ground. The revisions of the history of the Vietnam War occur, in part, in order to subsume U.S. anxieties within a coercive corporate ideology that attempts to totalize an order aesthetically that it cannot achieve politically. Therefore, the videos concentrate on the rhetoric and representation of culturally recognized corporate values—order, organization, expediency, containment and control of losses, efficiency, delegation, maximization of profits, professionalism, and the showcasing of technologically superior products.[26] If the Vietnam syndrome functions metonymically for a global erosion of U.S. prestige and power, then the new narrative of the Persian Gulf War signifies a shift to a new corporate culture in which U.S. national identity is renewed in primarily capitalist terms.[27]

Although these videos' revisions indicate broader ideological moves, it is important to understand their specific ramifications for the way the U.S. public conceives of both wars. Consigning the Vietnam War to the "underside" of this narrative—placing the Vietnam

War in the position of a mistake now rectified—could close off critical investigation of that conflict, as President Bush declared, in one of his first speeches after the war, "We have finally kicked the Vietnam syndrome." Rather than examining critically the ways in which wars have become corporate ventures carried on by more brutal means, these narratives foreground and celebrate this fact. By representing military technology in glorified terms and images, these videos of the Persian Gulf War are redeeming warfare as a U.S. economic product and cultural commodity.

Notes

1. From "Excerpts from President's News Conference on Crisis in Gulf," *New York Times*, Dec. 1, 1990.
2. Stephen J. Solarz, "The Stakes in the Gulf," *The New Republic*, Jan. 7, 1991: reprinted in *The Gulf War Reader*, ed. Micah L. Sifry and Christopher Cerf (New York: Random House, 1991), 269. Solarz is a Democratic member of the U.S. House of Representatives from New York and a senior Democrat on the Foreign Affairs Committee.
3. So firm was Solarz's belief in the fundamental differences between the wars that Solarz later was a principal sponsor of the "Authorization for Use of Military Force against Iraq Resolution."
4. *Desert Storm: The Victory*, prod. Turner Home Entertainment, CNN, 1991. *Desert Triumph*, CBS News, prod. Joel Heller, 1991. CNN sold a video during the war entitled "Desert Storm: The War Begins," and after *Desert Triumph* it released a six-videocassette collection entitled *War in the Gulf: The Complete Story*. All together these video collections sold more than 500,000 copies. Both of these videos were sold at checkouts in local supermarkets. CNN also has a six-videocassette set coming out to commemorate the anniversary of the war. CBS's video set was available at video stores.
5. Since I completed this essay, several studies have appeared that analyze the ways in which the concerns of narrative, or more broadly of the discourses of theory, shape and are shaped by the visual images of the Persian Gulf War broadcast in America and Europe. See particularly Christopher Norris, *Uncritical Theory: Postmodernism, Intellectuals, and the Gulf War* (Amherst: University of Massachusetts Press, 1992).
6. One particularly memorable instance of the use of this allegory occurred on Oct. 15, 1991, at a campaign stop in Dallas, when Bush informed the crowd, "We are dealing with Hitler revisited." Literary critic John Carlos Rowe points out that one of the ways in which Vietnam is "contained" is through the Bush administration's use of this analogy. Rowe writes, "That analogy has had the rhetorical effect of underscoring the negative example of the Vietnam War. 'Contained' between World War II and the Persian Gulf victory, Vietnam could be treated as an 'anomaly.'" See John Carlos Rowe, "The 'Vietnam Effect' in the Persian Gulf War," *Cultural Critique* 19 (Fall 1991): 124.
7. Gerard Genette, *Narrative Discourse: An Essay in Method* (Ithaca, N.Y.: Cornell University Press, 1988), 233.
8. Genette explains that the relationship between the two levels of narrative varies from text to text; metadiegetic narratives can have an explanatory function, working to explain the history behind the primary narrative, or they can maintain a "purely thematic relationship, therefore implying no spatio-

temporal continuity between metadiegesis and diegesis," evoking instead "a relationship of contrast . . . or of analogy" (*Narrative Discourse*, 233).

9. Perhaps the most striking feature of the videos—and some would argue of the Persian Gulf War as it was manifested in a myriad of representations, such as news reports, television documentaries, docudramas, and informational publications—is the emphasis on order, control, and containment within their primary narratives. The Persian Gulf War, as portrayed in these videos, is narrative with a vengeance, complete with villains, heroes, deadlines, linear progression toward an ending that is implicit in the beginning, and an emphatic sense of closure. In the truest Aristotelian fashion, these videos script primary narratives of a war that had a clear beginning (the day after the Jan. 15 deadline), middle (the switch from the airwar to the ground), and end (a cease-fire after one-hundred hours of ground war).

10. *Desert Storm: The Victory*, prod. (CNN) Turner Home Entertainment, 1991, 101 minutes; *Desert Triumph*, CBS News, prod. Joel Heller, 1991, 217 minutes.

11. Moreover, both Rather's opening line, "By Feb. 28, 1991, it was over," and the CNN section entitled "The Hundred Hour Ground War" deliberately obfuscate the fact that the biggest battle took place well after the cease-fire. The "engagement," as it was called on news reports and in the papers, took place on Mar. 2, 1991, when allied troops destroyed 247 Iraqi tanks and armored fighting vehicles and set ablaze more than 500 military transport vehicles. The number of Iraqis killed remains undisclosed, but *Seattle Times* report of Mar. 8, 1991, quoted an allied commander as saying, "We really waxed them."

12. For example, Thomas Myers, *Walking Point: American Narratives of Vietnam* (New York: Oxford University Press, 1988), 23; and Kate Beaird Meyers, "Fragments and Mosaics: Vietnam War 'Histories' and Postmodern Epistemology," *Genre* 21 (Winter 1988): 547.

13. Susan Jeffords, *The Remasculinization of America: Gender and the Vietnam War* (Bloomington: Indiana University Press, 1989), 6–7.

14. Meyers, "Fragments and Mosaics," 547.

15. Myers, *Walking Point*, 23.

16. One way in which the lack of closure evidences itself in the Persian Gulf War videos is through the metaphors of haunting that are often associated with the Vietnam War. Dan Rather tells viewers that the "specter of that unhappy conflict in Asia would hang over much of [the Persian Gulf War]," and CNN's video speaks of a military "haunted" by the Vietnam War.

17. James Ridgeway and Dave Lindorff, "Feeling the Draft," *Village Voice*, Dec. 25, 1990.

18. *Z Magazine*, Feb. 1991, 24.

19. See Margot Norris's essay in this volume.

20. The only blood shown, besides in connection with the Vietnam War, is blood on the faces of Israeli women who are the victims of Saddam's bombing of Israel.

21. For a brilliant analysis of U.S. censorship of body counts and thus the creation of "the fiction and the ideology of the "technological utopianism" that has become the central defense narrative in George Bush's "new world order," see Margot Norris's essay "Military Censorship and the Body Count in the Persian Gulf War," *Cultural Critique* 19 (Fall 1991): 223–245.

22. It is significant that the image of technological sophistication used in this juxtaposition is a warplane, for it has been argued that the warplane and its "effects" are the easiest to dissociate. H. Bruce Franklin, in his book *War Stars: The Superweapon and the American Imagination* (New York: Oxford University Press, 1988), took note of this when writing about the Vietnam War: "The American people were appalled once they learned that U.S. ground troops were massacring and burning whole villages such as My Lai. Why was this more

reprehensible than massacring and burning countless villages from the air? Because one of the distinguishing features of the airplane as an instrument of genocide is the dissociation it offers from its own effects. The interior of the plane does not even seem to be in the same universe as the victims on the ground" (119).

23. For further discussion of Johnson's role during the Vietnam war, see Stanley Karnow, *Vietnam: A History* (New York: Viking Press, 1983), or David W. Levy, *The Debate over Vietnam* (Baltimore: John Hopkins University Press, 1991).

24. Jochen and Linda Schulte-Sasse, "War, Otherness, and Illusionary Identifications with the State," *Cultural Critique* 19 (Fall 1991): 68.

25. Ibid., 72.

26. Whether or not these values are actual corporate values, promulgated in employee training or business education, seems less relevant to this argument than the fact that these values are culturally recognized as corporate. Popular cultural representations of the corporate world (e.g., Oliver Stone's *Wall Street*) often portray successful companies as concerned with efficiency, delegation, organization, maximizing of profits, and the like.

27. The grounding of U.S. identity in times of war as a function of capitalism is not by any means new. Franklin demonstrates in *War Stars* that the rhetoric of capitalism has always formed a subtext to the rhetoric of war. He argues that the celebration of war and its technology is founded on the "fusion of the ideology of capitalism" with the development and use of weapons as the means to "achieve the goals of this ideology." In his first address to the nation concerning the Persian Gulf Crisis, Bush made clear that the "struggle for freedom" in this conflict was the struggle against "major threats to [U.S.] economic independence." Very early in the national debate concerning the Persian Gulf War, the concept of "democracy" was abandoned; in the videos the rhetoric of "freedom" and "human rights" is always subordinated to this new rhetoric of "corporate values."

SEEING THROUGH TOTAL TELEVISION

The War for Information Control

Television was the chief medium by which the greatest number of citizens became aware of military operations, the progress of those operations, and even what defined the operations (e.g., smart bombs, Scud missiles). Television also provided immediate feedback to policy makers, including both President George Bush and Saddam Hussein, who reportedly watched CNN for instant reports on the war's progress as well as for U.S. and international opinions about the war. More than any other medium of mass information and communication, television assumed a key role in shaping responses to the war as well as in producing a public definition of modern warfare. The essays in this section dramatize how the conditions of television production set the parameters for defining that war within a new style of corporate journalism that Tom Engelhardt calls "total television."

Total television is television news production pursued through a managerial model of sleek operating efficiency, excessive technological production, and anxiety over mounting costs and company debts. Its origins lie in the significant changes that media companies underwent in the recession of the 1980s when they increasingly collapsed, merged, or evolved into a small number of highly diversified conglomerates whose vast holdings extend throughout the entertainment and information industries. These corporations brought to television journalism the same practices they employed in the manufacture and sales of their other products and services (from real estate to electric appliances to movies/music/books to a baseball team). In other words, total television is a corporate-age invention for selling the news through well-rehearsed media marketing techniques: it shows visual spectacles rather than boring in-depth analyses; it relies upon the sexy rhythms and repetitions of television advertising; it produces journalism through marketing packages of materials rather than relying upon the unscheduled, the accidental, and the vagaries of simply responding to world events. Total television increasingly produces artificial substitutes, simulations that pass for reality, because media conglomerates can make these more sensorily appealing, more manageable within operations, more cost-effective, and altogether more profitable.

The economic base of transnational media corporations is important because, by paying attention to it, we may see why these companies are even interested in questions and issues of national identity. Although media conglomerates may superficially appear to exist in order to produce public messages for audiences, they survive *economically* because they produce audiences for advertisers. One might argue that the primary product here is not even the media message but the audience itself, packaged through demographically identifiable features and delivered to advertisers. One only has to think of the Super Bowl, an important annual media event defined publicly by its delivery of sports and entertainment. But the Super Bowl is also defined industrially by its repeated success at delivering a large, differentiated audience to advertisers. The chief means by which this audience becomes homogenized into one unified group both for the advertisers selling products and for the audience themselves is as a *national* group. In this regard, national identity becomes one important way to define and bind together large aggregates of media consumers. National identity as such provides the means by which media corporations discursively construct social coherence.

Engelhardt's essay, "The Gulf War as Total Television," shows how this model of production yielded an experience of the Persian Gulf War that promoted war as a feel-good extravaganza, an uncomplicated fantasy of nationalist pleasure. He explains how the war orchestrated on television was analogous to another modern, highly technological fantasy of cultural definition, the unified world of pleasures at a modern amusement theme park. Engelhardt argues that both are banal spectacles enveloped in a mystique of technological wizardry. In his essay, developed from a piece initially written and published in the *Nation* during the Persian Gulf War, Engelhardt speaks angrily about the persuasive power of such fantasies and how they ultimately serve only the interests of the media giants who conjure up the shows.

Although Victor J. Caldarola also examines the effects of corporate-controlled media on the dynamics of television practices, he denies the totalizing effects that Engelhardt sees produced by total television. He argues instead for the ways that total television provided new ways of imagining time and how new concepts of time reframed the world as a "global village." Yet, in this redefinition, where temporal measures of closeness defined geographic spaces as proximate, Caldarola shows how television supported a definition of geopolitical spaces within current nationalist allegiances. We have placed these two essays side by side so that different viewpoints and even disagreements will lead the readers to produce further analysis and interpretation on total television as a newly defined institutional practice in U.S. political life.

Holly Cowan Shulman moves the discussion beyond the parameters of how total television attempts to win the hearts and minds of U.S. citizens to show that the stakes also include how the

United States controls information in other parts of the world. U.S. media conglomerates have developed relationships to other media systems and governments akin to the ones established in the United States. She argues persuasively for thinking about how U.S. media domination in other countries attempted to produce the war and its meanings for other societies. Like Engelhardt's and Caldarola's essays, Shulman's piece shows how the media's propagandistic roles are more complex and subtler than the contents of their messages. By defining and then dominating an industrial structure, U.S. media and particularly CNN played an important role in engineering international war according to the goals and values of the U.S. government and military.

Finally, Mimi White offers a close reading of just what CNN produced during the key hours of their coverage of the bombing of Baghdad and the Scud missile attacks on Israel. By analyzing the formal strategies of CNN's broadcast, she shows the complex ways that image and sound relationships make meaning. Indeed, she explains how a medium that is often defined through its show(ing)—the spectacle of the visual—in fact *showed* very little during the hours when CNN claimed it mattered the most.

Tom Engelhardt

The Gulf War as Total Television

In an endless round of daily televised press conferences and briefings during the Persian Gulf War, military and civilian spokesmen commonly addressed television viewers over the shoulders of reporters unceremoniously scrambling to ask questions. These televised events made explicit and visual the sidelining of the reporter in bringing war news to the public. Unlike their military briefers, the journalists, according to one *Washington Post* reporter, looked like "fools, nit-pickers and egomaniacs . . . a whining, self-righteous, upper–middle class mob jostling for whatever tiny flakes of fame [might] settle on their shoulders." The briefings, commented spokesman Lieutenant General Thomas Kelly, were "the most significant part of the whole operation [because] for the first time ever . . . the American people were getting their information from the government—not from the press."[1]

The media (and military) assessment of the Gulf War was pithily summed up by Barry Zorthian, former chief Pentagon public affairs spokesman in the Vietnam War years: "The press lost," he told the National Press Club just as the war was ending.[2] With this assessment most journalists, editors, and media executives as well as critics of the war and the media were in agreement. U.S. government and military planning to control the media, many years in the making, and various of its techniques tested out in the invasions of Grenada and Panama, in skyjackings, and in Republican presidential campaigns were indeed impressive. On the ground in Saudi Arabia, layers of military control had been inserted between the journalist and the "action," as well as between the journalist and his or her newspaper or newscast. As *New York Times* reporter Malcolm W. Browne put it, the pool system, developed by the military, essentially turned the journalist into "an unpaid employee of the Department of Defense, on whose behalf he or she pre-pare[d] the news of the war for the outer world."[3]

Seen from the ground up, the military seemed to have won an adversarial war against the media by marginalizing the hundreds of reporters on the spot and appealing directly to the American public. In response, the media blamed journalistic defeat largely on censorship and focused on various quick fixes that would make matters better in the next war. At the executive level, editors went back into negotiation with the Pentagon in pursuit of new Defense Department media ground rules less likely than those in place to inhibit the reporting of any war to come. In this way, they renewed a fruitless process of negotiation and regulation that had gone on since the Reagan administration prevented journalists from covering the invasion of Grenada.[4]

In the meantime, journalists dreamed of techno-responses that would, in the future, circumvent Pentagon controls. Philip Shennon of the *New York Times*, for instance, commented, "[News organizations] in preparation for the next war, wherever it may be, are surreptitiously planning the technology that will make all sorts of things possible that aren't possible now. We're told that in the next two years, we'll be able to have a satellite phone that will fit into a very small suitcase. If you can get into a car and head out to where the battlefield is, you'll be able to file your story almost instantaneously. . . . I think we'll have a better war next go around."[5] "'Next time' will be different," wrote former journalist and media historian Peter Braestrup, summing up this impulse. "Improved technology will make journalists less dependent on military communications, and censorship will be harder to impose."[6]

Yet those who claimed that the media were the losers in the Gulf War—that censorship, press pools, and military handlers galore represented an epic Bush administration triumph over reportorial independence—may not have seen the screen for the pixels. What we viewed beginning on January 16, 1991, was less the death of an independent media than the birth of "total television," a new co-production process to which normal labels of media critique and complaint largely do not apply. The Gulf War can, in fact, be seen as the Ur-production of the new media conglomerate. For it, the war proved promising exactly because the boundaries between military action and media event broke down in such ways that military planning could become a new form of media reality.

Total television had its antecedents neither in traditional war reportage nor in American war mythology. It was not even the child of the Vietnam War, which was not (as is so often said) America's first television war but its last nontelevision one, at least in its inability either to adhere to precise scheduling or to achieve closure. Instead, total TV was born in certain mesmeric moments in the 1980s when the whole nation seemed to have been mobilized at couchside to stare at the same images across many channels.

Starting with the Iran hostage crisis of 1979–1981 and running through the Persian Gulf War, these glimpses of total TV generally had the theme of America or Americans held hostage—most humiliatingly in Iran, most tragically in various terrorist "planenappings" and murders, most pathetically in NASA's *Challenger* space shuttle disaster in which a schoolteacher's life was hostaged to the failure of U.S. technology, most absurdly in the ongoing drama of a little girl hostaged to the elements by her fall down a well shaft in Texas, most triumphantly in the images of U.S. students kissing U.S. soil after their ostensible rescue from the island of Grenada.

From the media's point of view, most of these events were, fortunately, quite limited: one kidnapped plane on an airport runway, one embassy surrounded by a crowd, a few film clips of an explosion replayed a hundred times—all of the above surrounded by talking heads—or one small war in a distant place with only the most minimal, government-supplied visuals. To create more expansive scenarios would have been ruinously expensive without outside help. Even Ted Turner's Cable News Network (CNN), set up for any and all twenty-four-hour-a-day media events, would have quickly felt the financial strain of total TV if left purely to its own devices. Just the attempt to recreate the "good war" on set for the miniseries adapted from Herman Wouk's novel *The Winds of War* had proved a financial catastrophe for ABC. It was not enough to mobilize an audience; new forms of sponsorship were needed.

Here what has to be remembered is the corporate context within which the possibility for Gulf War–style total television developed. On the one hand, during the 1980s media giants like Time-Warner and Rupert Murdoch's News Corporation were being stapled together, and under their roofs distinct media forms were blurring into mix-and-match TV/movie/newspaper/magazine/book/music/theme-park entities. On the other hand, just to put such entities together (as corporations gobbled each other up, merging and purging their way through the decade) was to incur incalculable billions of dollars of debt. The burden of this debt—and a crumbling advertising market by decade's end—gave rise to new pressures to downsize these unwieldy, not especially synergistic new entities. Fewer personnel and cheaper production methods were necessary to make them more financially palatable to nervous owners (or suddenly anxious potential buyers).

General Electric, Capital Cities, and the Tisch family operation, which had come to control respectively NBC, ABC, and CBS, the three dominant television networks, also faced an assault on their audiences and their advertisers from cable television and Murdoch's new fourth network, Fox. In turn, the swift erosion of network dominance in the late 1980s led money managers within each network to hack away at the prestigious but often unprofitable fiefdoms of news.

If the Persian Gulf War revealed the media's ability to mount technical operations on an unprecedented scale, it also exposed the need of these financially pressed media giants (and their upstart competitors) for sponsorship on a scale hitherto unimaginable. This is what the Bush administration seemed to offer in the Gulf War—an outside production company able to organize a well-produced, subsidized total event that could be channeled to the U.S. (and increasingly, the global) public at, relatively speaking, bargain-basement prices.

With its million or more uniformed extras, its vast sets, and its six-month preproduction schedule filled with logistical miracles (and a few fiascoes, too), the production, the Gulf War, involved intense military/media planning on a global scale. All through the winter of 1990, the production had its own built-in "coming attractions"—the many variations on "showdown in the Gulf" that teased the viewer with a possible January opening on all screens in domestic multiplexes across the nation. It had its dazzling *Star Wars*–style graphics, its own theme music, and its own logos, as well as its stunningly prime-timed first moments (Disneyesque fireworks over Baghdad).

As a production, the Gulf War relied heavily on post-1975 breakthroughs in Hollywood special-effects technology and military special-effects hardware. As a show, it was calibrated for controlled thrills, anxiety, and relief from its opening laser-guided, *son-et lumière* spectacular and its initial fears of massive U.S. casualties to its final triumphant helicopter descent on the U.S. Embassy in Kuwait. That scene was indicative of the production's carefully designed nature. Crafted for closure, it was meant to nullify in the most literal sense the final televised scene from the Vietnam War, the chaotic liftoff of the last helicopter fleeing the U.S. Embassy in Saigon in April 1975. It was as if putting that clip on rewind would not only definitively end the Gulf War production but also erase that previous televised disaster from memory.[7] In the all-encompassing nature of its planning, the Gulf War bore a striking resemblance to America's preeminent total entertainment environment, the theme park with its intense but well-ordered rides from which participants were, at an appointed moment, to descend and exit in an orderly fashion.

To succeed as a production company, however, the Pentagon had to offer the networks five things. The first was funding based on a relatively limited financial contribution from the networks themselves.

This was accomplished by a State Department/Pentagon financing team that sought out foreign investment much as any Hollywood production team might have—from the Japanese, the Germans, the Saudis, and so on; $50 billion, you might say, for "foreign rights," money that ensured a break-even point on the government side of the enterprise almost before the first missile left the ground. The Pentagon also had to offer, second, the ability to organize round-the-clock, on-location support systems across a vast theater of operations; third, a preedited flow of visuals available to all channels; fourth, control over access to the set of the production, thus limiting intranetwork competition and consequently network costs (these last two usually fall under the rubric of "censorship"); and finally, the sort of precise scheduling and closure that television craves.

At the Pentagon, much thought had already gone into matters of scheduling and closure—this, out of a post-Vietnam desire to create a Third World battlefield where maximal weaponry and minimal U.S. casualties would make public support axiomatic. In the eighties, a new wave of "smart" (and not-so-smart but highly destructive) weaponry was brought on-line or upgraded to complement an already impressive Vietnam War era arsenal. In the Persian Gulf, as a result, the preponderance and superiority of U.S. weaponry—as well as the near nonappearance of the "enemy"—made slaughter on a vast scale, at will, and with an eye to television's tight time requirements achievable.

What President Bush then could promise the nation—and the media—was a war that could be scheduled, and this promise was structured not only into war planning but also into the minds of the war makers. As Bob Woodward reported in his book *The Commanders*, "In the White House, Bush, Quayle, Scowcroft and Sununu gathered in the small private study adjacent to the Oval Office to watch television. When the sounds of bombing could be heard behind the voices of the reporters still in their Baghdad hotel rooms, Bush, visibly relieved, said, 'Just the way it was scheduled.' "8

It was lack of closure that had made the Vietnam War an event unnervingly at odds with television, just as lack of closure in the Iran-hostage crisis had destroyed whatever chance President Jimmy Carter had of winning a second term. The biggest threat to the Gulf production was exactly this pressure for closure, which was built into the very logo-ized form "The War in the Gulf, Day X" (itself a creation of the Iran-hostage crisis). Offered up twenty-four hours a day, a "war" only days old might quickly come to seem weeks or months old, as the viewer abandoned the routines of daily life (and the daily TV schedule) for vast doses of this single on-screen production. So, in the Gulf production lay the possibility—much feared at the time—of re-creating

Vietnam, more or less instantly, without the endless years of fighting. It was this anxiety about closure, or lack of it, that gave the production much of its otherwise ersatz sense of tension as well as much of its drawing power.

From all involved—network executives, advertisers, programmers, government officials, reporters, soldiers, and viewers—there undoubtedly came a longing for the relief of a return to normalcy, and for repeated reassurance on this score. Such reassurance was forthcoming from the war's first moments. In fact, one striking feature of the war was how often the viewing public was told that it was unfolding "on schedule." Nearly every military news conference included such a reminder, and the schedule being referred to was clearly television's. The public was constantly assured by the war's supporters that the war would be clean, manageable, foreseeable, endable—in short, a program as promised.

In the past, the reporting of war had often been successfully organized and controlled by governments. Generals had polished their images with the press or—like Omar Bradley and Douglas MacArthur—had whole public relations staffs to do it for them. In the post–World War II era, images of war and generalship had been re-created on-screen literally hundreds, if not thousands, of times, with the active support of and script review by the Pentagon. Moreover, the blurring of war making and image making had long been part of war, American-style, starting with the promotional self-creations of "Indian-fighters" like Davy Crockett and Buffalo Bill Cody. In the 1950s, a war hero, Medal of Honor winner Audie Murphy, became a movie star by playing himself in the screen adaptation of his autobiography, *To Hell and Back*. In the 1980s, a president, Ronald Reagan, came to half believe he had been a heroic figure in an actual war because he had spent so much time in uniform on-screen.[9] But never had generals and war planners gone before the public as actors, supported by all the means a "studio" could muster on their behalf, no less determined to produce a "program" that would fill the full day across the dial for the full time of a war.

What we have to imagine (for we were not shown it) is that behind the dark curtains that screened off the multiple daily press conferences of the various actors—each in his distinctive fashion/camouflage outfit, each wielding his distinctive sitcom quips and put-downs, each giving his distinctive impression of the Victorious General or the In-Control Press Spokesman—lay a globe-spanning network of script-writers, makeup artists, fashion consultants, graphic designers, production managers, film editors (otherwise known as "censors" or "escorts"), and even a military version of the traditional TV network

Standards and Practices department with its guidelines for on-air acceptability.[10]

Only military preediting of virtually all aspects of the Gulf War made total television a six-week-long ratings hit. Hence, despite the uneasiness of some journalists on the scene, the TV networks understandably offered no significant protest over the censoring and controlling mechanisms of the Bush administration—which were largely in their interest. In fact, no well-known media company was willing to join more marginal publications like the *Nation* or New York's *Village Voice* and individual journalists like *Newsday*'s Sydney Schanberg in a wartime legal challenge to Pentagon censorship policies. In this way, the Gulf experience that offered the media giants new possibilities in the production of entertainment also brought journalism's already tattered post-Watergate, post-Vietnam heroic self-image down to earth.

It's not surprising, then, that the approximately sixteen hundred reporters mainly camped out in high-tech hotel lounges and makeshift press centers in Dhahran and Riyadh, Saudi Arabia, watching the war on TV just like viewers at home, would see the military's media role primarily as a censorious one, but this was to miss the point.[11] More to the point would have been to compare the Pentagon to those TV production companies that, in the early 1980s, began creating a new-style children's television program. Usually done in conjunction with toy companies and their ad agencies, those shows in one quick leap eliminated the boundaries between advertisement and show by making what were essentially program-length animated catalogs for toys.

In a similar way, the Gulf production launched a major new form of the program-length commercial. It was as if the whole post-Vietnam era in the United States had built toward this forty-three-day-long ad, intent on selling both domestic and foreign markets on the renewal of U.S. qualities, as well as on the specific weapons systems that were in the process of renewing those qualities. In this sense, the Persian Gulf War can be seen as the U.S. response to the Japanese and European economic challenges in that it emphasized the leading-edge technoglories of the United States' two foremost exports: arms and entertainment.[12] It even used the simplified visual language of the eighties ad—the upbeat, brightly colored (sales) story, whose happy ending was meant to confound the darkness of the world beyond the screen with the sprightliness of the product. No one looking at the many carefully framed visuals of the Gulf War could doubt the advertorial nature of the show, segmented as it was into sets of mini-ads for various aspects of itself.

What made this program-length advertisement unique, though,

was the length of the program and the fact that its newness and its defining style unexpectedly threw into question the nature of normal television advertising. If *this* was The Ad, then what were those? Though CNN, ready-made for total TV, experienced rising advertising rates and revenues during the war, for the networks it was another story. Non-CNN advertisers were unsure of how their ads would coexist with "war" in this puzzling new version of entertainment time.[13] Of course, what they, like so many media experts, military consultants, and journalists, were imagining was a visually bloody war of body bags and body counts—exactly the war, in fact, that the military had spent seventeen years organizing out of existence. In this war, the only statistics of death were to be "weapons counts" (how many Scud missiles, tanks, or gunboats had been put out of action); the only destruction seen was to be of the inanimate (hence the repeated video footage of bridges and buildings blowing up); only tanks and airplanes were to be "killed"; and there would be no visible bags, for there would be no visible bodies.[14]

In the end, the failure of advertisers both to grasp the nature of this new media experience and to join the production team helped make total television into a financial fiasco for the big three networks. They found themselves showing a vast commercial while losing revenue from the very advertisers who felt more comfortable inside sitcoms like *Cheers* than inside the cheering framework of a war to destroy Iraq. According to media critic John MacArthur in *Second Front: Censorship and Propaganda in the Gulf War*, NBC, which like CBS ran behind ABC in the ratings, claimed losses of $55 million on its war coverage, including $20 million in withdrawn ad revenue.[15] One postwar result at CBS, at least, was a further downsizing of its news department.

This confusion over sponsorship reflected not only total television's primitive state but also the fact that "war" might not be its ultimate venue and the U.S. military not the ideal production team to develop it further. For one thing, the military, with its generally adversarial attitude toward the media, consciously inhibited the flow of fresh images that would have fed total television's voracious appetite. Though its conceptualization of the event far outstripped that of its media critics, the military itself was entrapped by a traditional vision of how journalists had to be controlled; by a deep belief in a "stab-in-the-back" theory of defeat in the Vietnam War in which the media held a central place of honor; and especially by its desire to quite literally refight that war vis-à-vis the media and win.

It is impossible to grasp the nature of military planning and behavior in the Persian Gulf without understanding the intensity of the animosity that had developed toward the media in the U.S. military command during the Vietnam War, more than twenty years ago. Mild rather than extreme was this comment by the former commander of U.S. forces in Vietnam, General William Westmoreland: "The attitude on the part of the American reporters [in Vietnam] undoubtedly contributed to the psychological victory the enemy achieved in the United States." In a fascinating study done before the war ended, Douglas Kinnard, an army general who had served in Vietnam, sent a questionnaire to all 173 other army generals who had served there. Among the 67 percent who replied, he found a startling intensity to their negative feelings about the media. Unbidden, they wrote Kinnard that, as one senior general put it, the media had conducted "a psychological warfare campaign against the United States policies in Vietnam that could not have been better done by the enemy." Eighty-nine percent declared themselves negative toward the press, 91 percent toward television. It was one of only two subjects on which they achieved near unanimity.[16]

Little surprise, then, that for junior officers like H. Norman Schwarzkopf who served under these generals in Vietnam and who, two decades later, were in charge of planning the media event in the Persian Gulf, this was a grudge match. In military eyes, the media more than the absent Iraqis had gained the look of enemy-ness, and this naturally created problems for the Gulf co-production. From lowly "handlers" to generals, many military men in the Persian Gulf were driven by a powerful desire to defeat the media this time around. In their often belligerent urge to shut down the media, they significantly retarded the Gulf production as a visual spectacular—all this despite the fact that there was little evidence that reporters freed from various military restraints would have produced anything but more fabulous visuals of American technology triumphant and more enthusiastic copy for the production.[17]

In addition, an inability to control (or even predict) all participants in the war proved an obstacle to the successful closure of the Gulf production. Even a war as managed as this one proved resistant to the sort of closure that television scheduling craves and that the war planners had taken for granted. The ground war, for instance, was carefully rounded off at one hundred hours. Although the figure was justified, in Vietnam War terms, by a lack of desire to "bog down" in a potential future Iraqi "quagmire," this cutoff point had a TV ring to it. As General Schwarzkopf has written, the one-hundred-hour figure was chosen by Bush administration officials who "really knew how to package an historic event."[18] However, this official closure of the war-as-media-production did not, in fact, close down Saddam Hussein or the Shia rebels in southern Iraq or the Kurdish rebels to the north. Within weeks, piteous images of Kurdish refugees flooded the media, forcing the U.S. administration to partially reopen the war.

This hijacking of the supposedly completed production had its analogue during the war in the unexpected intrusion of video of wounded, dead, or grieving Iraqi civilians at Baghdad's Public Shelter 25, where a U.S. missile incinerated 250 people. The missile that blasted the shelter, dubbed a military target, also blasted those bodies into a production otherwise planned for its bloodlessness. In the reaction to those images and to the reports of CNN's Peter Arnett from the Iraqi capital, it was possible to feel briefly the panic that the uncontrolled image elicited from the military. Nonetheless, the attempt to choke off anything that might have qualified as a war image as well as any visual messiness undercut the Gulf production's possible staying power as a war narrative.

Although the military production team had taken on the task of defining and delivering the range of shots that would constitute screen reality, what they actually provided, sometimes grudgingly, was largely grainy videos of missiles and bombs obliterating (nonhuman) targets; upbeat sequences of high-tech warriors doing their long-distance jobs; endless shots of planes taking off and landing; shots of magnificent penile machines firing magnificent projectiles into magnificent desert skies; and access to the outgoing-Patriots-greet-incoming-Scuds fireworks extravaganza. Though a far cry from the Grenada and Panama news blackouts, this was still visually thin stuff. There was no way to combine these isolated sequences into even a passing narrative of war.

As in the *Challenger* disaster, limited visuals forced the networks to fall back on endless replays or on the sorts of endlessly talking heads that, by the early eighties, had disappeared from all but Sunday morning public affairs programming, Ted Koppel's *Nightline*, PBS's *Mac-Neil/Lehrer News Hour*, and shrinking election-night and convention coverage (which themselves were gaining a distinctly more *Star Wars*–like look). Undoubtedly, military experts like ABC's Anthony Cordesman or CBS's forcibly retired general Michael Dugan were meant to be Monday Night War's color commentators, but if so, they seemed eternally trapped at halftime with no game to call. Although each day's show was packaged with ever more dazzling logo material and theme music, and viewers were even invited to breach computer-created versions of the (largely imaginary) "Saddam Wall," in the end, there was no war out there to be seen.[19] Except for a little oft-repeated footage from the "battle" of Khafji, itself a halfhearted ad for the fighting abilities of America's Arab allies, hardly a bit of evidence could be mustered for the war-ness of this war.

No greater problem faced the military/media production team than its inability to establish a suitably epic story at the heart of its production. From the initial "battle in the Gulf," the 1981 dogfights with Libyan MiGs over the Gulf of Sidra, through the invasions of Grenada and Panama, the Reagan and Bush administrations had engaged in a decade-long experiment in the controlled presentation of U.S. battle triumph. This attempt to reestablish a triumphant American war story via the media and in the wake of the Vietnam War ended up, in the Persian Gulf, as little more than a passing advertorial. Missing in action in this war's coverage was not so much the independent media that had seldom existed in the history of U.S. warfare (if anything, military censorship and consequently misleading reportage was more severe in World War II and, after its initial stages, in Korea, too), but any sense of what form a lasting, empathetic war narrative could take without a military struggle in which to ground itself.[20]

Offscreen, events in the Persian Gulf War were closer to a mass electrocution than a war. As a result, no Iraqi aggressors fell by the hundreds from their charging camels in the sort of on-screen battle for which our film tradition called. No armies could be discovered clashing in their multithousands, nor could tank battles—billed, before the war, as potentially the largest since World War II—be shown ranging across vast desert vistas. In fact, the crucial production number, D day renamed "G [for ground war] day," turned out to be no day at all. The penultimate event of the post-Vietnam era in which the not-Vietnamese were to be crushed in battle had to be elided because at the heart of this technically awesome spectacle was an embarrassingly plotless and unwatchable slaughter. The best that could be offered from an enemy who refused to put in an appearance were scenes of bedraggled Iraqis emerging from their dugouts to surrender and shots of Iraqi-commandeered cars, trucks, and buses turned to charred rubble by U.S. planes on the road out of Kuwait City.

In fact, only when some journalists—"unilaterals" who had evaded the pool system and consequently military controls, and others loosed by the military—dashed ahead of their escorts into Kuwait City was there a hint of an on-screen story. If the liberation-of-Paris–style crowds were sparse in population-decimated Kuwait, at least the visuals flowed and Charles Jaco, Dan Rather, and others had an opportunity to simulate the war reporter of the past down to the last safari jacket.

If the Persian Gulf War's lack of a story accounts, in part, for its remarkable disappearance from U.S. politics and culture, it was not for want of the footage of death. This was, after all, a screen war at the front as well as in the White House, the Pentagon, and at home. We know, for instance, that cameras shooting through the night-vision gunsights of Apache AH-64 attack helicopters caught graphic scenes of confused and helpless Iraqi soldiers being "blown to bits" by unseen attackers. "The Iraqi soldiers looked like ghostly sheep flushed from a pen—bewildered and terrified, jarred from sleep and fleeing their bunkers under a hellish fire," wrote John Balzar of the *Los Angeles Times,* who reported viewing the film with officers of the Eighteenth Airborne Corps at a briefing tent on the Saudi border. "Even hardened [U.S.] soldiers hold their breath as Iraqi soldiers, as big as football players on the television screen, run with nowhere to hide. These are not bridges or airplane hangars. These are men."[21] But these outtakes were never released by the military, for they would have been appropriate only to a very different production, one meant to be a horror story, not a war story.

The war to reestablish war, American-style, vaporized as a triumphant event while the ubiquitous yellow ribbons were still fluttering. The packs of Desert Storm bubblegum cards and the "kick his ass, take his gas" T-shirts that showed Saddam Hussein's forehead penetrated by a Patriot missile were quickly packed away. No major toy company bothered to produce a Desert Storm action figure, nor did a major film company produce a movie; and two years later when departing President Bush once again launched air strikes against Iraq, the story that never was proved impossible to bring back. Like some poorly done sequel, Gulf War II flickered on- and almost as quickly offscreen in January 1993. Its most dramatic videos were of missiles that missed their targets; its threadbare special effects misfired; and its plotline, unlike its weaponry, couldn't even get off the launching pad.

In the United States, Gulf War II found itself sharing a double bill with the inaugural gala of a new president, yet even the twinning of fireworks over the Washington Mall with antiaircraft tracers over Baghdad lacked resonance. In the first Gulf War, the military and the media had both acted as if the initial bombing run on Baghdad had CNN's outpost at the Al-Rashid Hotel as its target. This time even a direct Tomahawk missile hit on that hotel, captured on camera, led to neither journalistic complaint nor protest. On the other hand, this time no U.S. official or military man implied that American journalists were traitors for showing Iraqi casualties on the air. No one, in fact, seemed particularly perturbed by anything.

Admittedly, in the Middle East, missiles landed, planes were shot down, and people continued to die. But in the United States, the production was clearly over; and all that was left of that twenty-four-hour-a-day, eye-burning, blood pumping, high-tech, all-channel media-military spectacular was the promise of a new form of TV. Given its prodigious vanishing act, perhaps the Persian Gulf War will indeed have little lasting effect on U.S. society. (Its effects on Iraq and the rest of the Mideast are obviously another matter.) Total television, however, could have far more staying power, hinting as it does at possible media and advertising futures we can hardly imagine today. It points toward a world in which, increasingly, everything gets done for the media; in which the more fully meshed media systems of the twenty-first century will need to discover new, more powerful, more all-purpose sponsoring relationships; ones that, at the very least, can raise to a higher power the single-sponsor show (*The Alcoa Hour, General Electric Theater*) of a simpler corporate age.

But will the Pentagon—any Pentagon—be that all-purpose single sponsor, and is the production of war what lies in total television's future? At a global level, whether the nation (even the superpower) at war will sponsor the next century's "shows" is at least open to question. In the Gulf War, it felt like the United States went into battle in tandem with an American media, however much that media played to a global audience. It is worth remembering, though, that in the 1960s the multinational corporation also looked "American." In the Persian Gulf in 1991, the global media conglomerate still seemed at one with the United States as its sponsoring agent. Given a decade or two, it may feel far less like that, for the nature of the "national" interests of future, even more global media entities is really unknown.[22]

As a form for the long haul, total TV (and whichever media giants dominate the years ahead) must face the problem of how to pay for such global entertainment shows, what those shows can possibly be, and what stories they can be made to tell. What form they will take— whether at screen center we will see slaughter or some friendlier sport—and who will sponsor them we can hardly guess.

Notes

1. The *Washington Post's* Henry Allen quoted in Jay Rosen, "Politics, Vision, and the Press: Toward a Public Agenda for Journalism," in Jay Rosen and Paul Taylor, *The New News v. the Old News: The Press and Politics in the 1990s* (New York: Twentieth Century Fund, 1992), 22–23. Thanks to Jay Rosen, who first made this general point to me directly. Kelly quoted in Jacqueline E. Sharkey, *Under Fire: U.S. Military Restrictions on the Media from Grenada to the Persian Gulf* (Washington, D.C.: Center for Public Integrity, 1991), 129.
2. Quoted in Sharkey, *Under Fire*, 145.
3. Malcolm W. Browne, "The Military vs. the Press," *New York Times Magazine*, Mar. 3, 1991, 29. Browne's opinion, while particularly strongly expressed, was fairly typical of reportorial reaction to the Gulf experience. For instance, Carl Nolte, who covered the war from Saudi Arabia for the *San Francisco Chronicle*, later commented: "The Pentagon, in my opinion, played the news organizations, particularly television and to a lesser extent newspapers, like a

violin," quoted in *The Media and the Gulf: A Closer Look*, ed. Carolyn Wakeman (Berkeley: Graduate School of Journalism, University of California, 1991), 20.

4. See Sharkey, *Under Fire*, for a full description of these negotiations and its appendix A for the necessary documents.

5. Quoted in Wakeman, *Media and the Gulf*, 29.

6. Peter Braestrup, "Foreward," in *Hotel Warriors: Covering the Gulf War*, by John J. Fialka (Baltimore: Johns Hopkins University Press, 1991), xiii.

7. See Michelle Kendrick's essay in this volume.

8. Bob Woodward, *The Commanders* (New York: Simon and Schuster, 1991), 376.

9. On generals and publicists in World War II, see Paul Fussell, *Wartime* (New York: Oxford University Press, 1989), 160–161; Phillip Knightley, *The First Casualty: From the Crimea to Vietnam: The War Correspondent as Hero, Propagandist, and Mythmaker* (New York: Harcourt Brace Jovanovich, 1975), 279–282. On the career of Audie Murphy, see Julian Smith, *Looking Away: Hollywood and Vietnam* (New York: Charles Scribner's Sons, 1975), 65–78.

10. Military handlers sometimes made petty decisions like changing the adjective a *Detroit Free Press* reporter used to describe the mood of a returning bomber pilot from "giddy" to "proud," or refused to clear for publication the fact that Stealth pilots viewed X-rated movies before missions: "Spin Control through Censorship: The Pentagon Manages the News," *Extra!*, special issue/vol. 4, no. 3 (May 1991): 15. Such practices are certainly reminiscent of the traditional network practice of vetting shows for unacceptable language or incident.

11. Fialka, *Hotel Warriors*, 55. Fialka's figures are on the high end of estimates of journalists in the Gulf. The Pentagon estimated eight hundred to sixteen hundred journalists in Saudi Arabia. Sharkey, *Under Fire*, 128.

12. In this sense, the Gulf production was also the antithesis of the earlier *Challenger* production. Though they both shared the total TV form, *Challenger* represented the abject failure of U.S. technology. It was the anti-moon shot of post-Vietnam culture. The Gulf production was meant to free U.S. technology from O-ring disaster, from the taint of failure, just as it was meant to free the military from the "restraints" of Vietnam.

13. See Victor J. Caldarola's essay in this volume.

14. Sharkey, *Under Fire*, 28. See also Margot Norris's essay in this volume.

15. John R. MacArthur, *Second Front: Censorship and Propaganda in the Gulf War* (New York: Hill and Wang, 1992), 94.

16. Douglas Kinnard, *The War Managers: American Generals Reflect on Vietnam* (New York: Da Capo Press, 1977), 129, 132–133; see also Daniel C. Hallin's superb study, *The "Uncensored War": The Media and Vietnam* (Berkeley and Los Angeles: University of California Press, 1989), for the best analysis of the realities of media coverage of the war in Vietnam, which were at variance with both the military mind-set that developed during the war and much of the mythology about the media as an oppositional force that developed in the postwar period. On the vehemence of the military's animosity to the media in the Gulf there is much testimony. According to James LeMoyne of the *New York Times*, who covered events in the Gulf until the war began, "It was clear that the Vietnam Syndrome was deeper [among senior commanders] than I ever realized. . . . The commanders, most of whom had been in Vietnam, had a much more visceral feeling [than the soldiers and junior officers], which was that the journalists had something to do with the U.S. military's defeat in Vietnam. So I wrote a long story quoting a lot of people about this. After that it became clear to me that something had changed in my access to the U.S. military." Wakeman, *Media and the Gulf*, 33.

17. See Fialka, *Hotel Warriors*, particularly pp. 25–31, for evidence that where, as in the case of the U.S. Marine Corps, reporters were aided and encouraged rather

than shunted aside and treated as the enemy, coverage was more effusive and fuller without being faintly more investigative or oppositional.

18. Michael R. Gordon, "Schwarzkopf Says 'Hawks' Pressed for Early Land War," *New York Times*, Sept. 20, 1992, 1.
19. See Mimi White's essay in this volume.
20. See Knightley, *First Casualty*, on issues of press censorship in World War II and in Korea.
21. John Balzar, *Manchester Guardian Weekly*, Mar. 3, 1991, 10. See also Balzar's account in Wakeman, *Media and the Gulf*, 74.
22. In the U.S. context, there was another genre in the post-Vietnam era that came closer than war to meeting the needs of total TV—sports. Despite the efforts of the Reagan and Bush administrations, it was triumph in sports, not in battle, that proved the ideal media form in an age of storylessness. In the 1980s, leagues, seasons, games, and television outlets for sports expanded so dramatically that there came to be a single overlapping web of sports viewing possibilities involving multiple sports available at almost any hour of the day or night.

As an ongoing generic narrative, sports was the perfect analogue to storylessness. On the one hand, "it" was a story in its many forms at all times. On the other hand, the very nature of sports ensured that the story would be constantly forgotten and reconstituted. Sports was, then, the functional equivalent of the nonstory, the successful version of what U.S. political leaders were unable to do in the world of the traditional war narrative. Certainly, sports proved more effective in holding mobilized audiences at couchside in the long term than did the succession of one-sided, sportslike wars from Grenada to the Gulf, and thus it may offer a more reasonable place from which to project the media future of total television.

Victor J. Caldarola

Time and the
Television War

It is a disturbing irony that the global village was finally achieved during a time of terror. Television transformed the Persian Gulf War into a cultural event of extraordinary intensity—a global village at war. Time became encoded in the temporal flow of live television narrative, absorbing the real world crisis into an electronically constructed "television war" to which all subsequent actions were addressed. The resulting distortions across television time prompted a disorienting confusion among images of the "real," provoked extraordinary emotional distress among viewing publics, facilitated the war agenda on both sides of the conflict, and invited aggressive manipulation of the war story by all interested parties.

Distortion in Television Time

Although television had played a central role in the Gulf crisis since Iraq's invasion of Kuwait on 2 August 1990, few of us were prepared for the television war which began with stunning effect on the evening of 16 January 1991. News of allied air attacks reached the wired world just minutes after the first bombs fell on Baghdad, annihilating the space/time parameters of the public mind with unforeseen intensity. Anxiety at first abated by the onset of battle soon soared to new and disturbing heights as continuous real-time television coverage proceeded to distort beyond recognition the temporal dimensions

Originally published in *Public Culture*, the Bulletin of the Society for Transnational Cultural Studies, vol. 4, no. 2 (Spring 1992). Reprinted by permission. The author wishes to thank Carol Breckenridge for her comments on an earlier draft of this essay.

of a usually "cool" medium.[1] The firestorm raged uncontrolled through television time, and the viewing public responded in a fit of nervous anxiety which can only be described as stress-induced trauma. This was a war in which we would all be combatants.

Television time began its rapid disintegration as coiffed and manicured news anchors from each of the major networks made their profound announcements on the evening of January 16. "War has begun in the Mideast," intoned Dan Rather of *The CBS Evening News;* conveniently, the war began just in time for the evening news programs. As the networks scrambled for ratings during these first critical moments of the television war, the viewing public was launched into a time-distorting spectacle which kept many people glued to their television sets throughout the night, and propelled even disinterested audience members into an emotion-draining spiral of anxiety. With a suddenness not unlike live combat, "now" became encoded in the time warp of live television, and the war would proceed from moment to moment through the distorted temporal lens of this ever more intimate home appliance.

The networks responded to war by implementing contingency plans which had been drawn up prior to the Bush administration's January 15 deadline. "Wall-to-wall" coverage of the crisis replaced regular programming on CBS, ABC, and NBC, while the Cable News Network moved to an "all-war" format with exclusive live audio reports of the air attack on Baghdad. These were the first signs of distortion in television time. Viewers were stunned by the suddenness of the transformation, as the usual array of mind-dulling entertainment programs was eliminated, escape routes closed, and diversion-seeking viewers confronted with the disturbing reality of a nonfiction war.

Of course the television audience was well primed for a cathartic experience. Television had played a very significant role in the dramatic escalation of tension since the Iraqi invasion in August. But anxiety levels peaked as the January 15 deadline approached.[2] The massive allied military buildup in Saudi Arabia was progressing rapidly and with such momentum as to virtually require its ultimate use. The military buildup was accompanied by a superbly coordinated and hugely successful public opinion campaign managed by the Bush administration and designed to prepare the nation for war. Thus Saddam Hussein's threat to humanity became more heinous with every tank and attack aircraft arrayed against him. This in turn served to further heighten anxiety levels through fear of terrorism and the cruel realization that war was perhaps no longer a defensive option but in fact an offensive necessity. Thus, like a well-rehearsed stage performance, the first allied air raids into Iraq on January 16 brought about an anxiety-releasing climax, followed rather quickly by the tense uncertainties of sustained crisis, denouement withheld.

During the first 24 hours of the war, the networks struggled to fill their all-news air time in an attempt to sustain a high-definition crisis. But there was little of substance to report and so viewers watched with increasing exasperation as a battalion of military"experts" paraded across television-studio "war rooms" offering all manner of speculation about events in the Gulf. Aggressive network contingency plans degenerated into surreal desperation as psychiatrists began analyzing the mind of Saddam Hussein. But viewer anxiety peaked once again with the long-awaited missile attack on Israel on the evening of January 17, and the first dramatic "night-scope" videotape of the air attack on Baghdad the night before.

Even when the networks returned to regularly scheduled programming during the afternoon of January 18, war coverage continued with periodic updates between commercials, live coverage of military briefings from Saudi Arabia and the Pentagon, and extended network news programs. The war assumed a continuous presence on television and in most other media, with heavy continuing coverage on radio and in print. The effect on media publics around the world, wired as they are to an electronic stream of mediated consciousness, was devastating. Unsuspecting people were subjected to war as a moment-to-moment experience, inescapable even by watching television. The continuing nature of the crisis brought a sharply defined anxiety to the television experience, as many viewers became fearful of watching and fearful of not watching, compulsively turning the set on and off with varying levels of irritation, guilt, and trepidation. Many began listening and watching continuously as sales of portable radios and televisions soared.

Television time was further distorted by the unusual quality of reporting. Viewers long accustomed to the cool detachment of television news were confronted with the emotional immediacy of reporters reaching for gas masks, ducking missile attacks, and, in the case of CNN, reporting the attack live and in real time from Baghdad. The real-time format was both gripping and unnerving, as it thrust viewers into the otherwise distant war in a profoundly personal way.

Continuous moment-to-moment television coverage had compressed ordinary time into the hyperactive realm of imaged experience —like a video war game inflicting its nervous static upon the minds of novice players. As the war dragged on through its first and second weeks, public anxiety reached an exhausting plateau and television viewers began to tire of collective participation in life-and-death events utterly beyond their control. The massive air war, missile strikes, allied prisoners of war, bloodied Israeli children, and the threat of terrorism close to home had all taken up residence in our living rooms like so many uninvited guests. The real-time war raged on in the collective mind of television viewers, their sensors exposed and vulnerable to the numbing appeal of vicarious participation. Accustomed to the intimacy of far less compelling television stories and their assorted characters, viewers found it all but impossible to shut down their receptive psyches. Trauma ensued as television audiences felt compelled to dwell within the war experience, the most deeply afflicted purchasing gas masks and other military surplus equipment. Untrained in the egregious violence of combat, these spectator-participants were driven by customary practice to live day in and day out with the imminent threat of attack and the uncertainties of live combat.

Television coverage of the Gulf War distorted the medium's temporal familiarity. The first confirmed "kills" of this war were the prime-time programs which reliably populate our homes each evening. Dependent on the television experience, viewers were confronted with the reality of a distant war *and* the displacement of their most reliable escapist activity. The continuous television coverage of the first days of the war further obscured the usual temporal markers of the television day. Time became muddled and unstable as spotty, confusing, and conflicting war reports replaced the predigested and entertaining little stories which usually pass for television news.

Finally, the "real-time" quality of television war reporting elevated the live remote broadcast to a stylistic necessity while eliminating the temporal distance required for the work of journalism. The ultimate temporal distortion was the tacit but immediate denial of history with regard to the development of this conflict, as real time obliterated both past and future. What was left was a new intensity of vicarious experience defined and controlled by the television medium. These distortions in television time certainly contributed to the extreme distress and anxiety of the viewing public, which was assaulted by a "cool" medium turned aggressively "hot."[3] As the allied war machine continued its bloody rampage, public anxiety lent the critical missing piece to the television narrative—a satisfying closure—thus ensuring victory. As in an extended prime-time movie, the war was won, the enemy vanquished, the heroes returned, and the tension of climax transformed into patriotic fervor.

Real-Time Terror

The highly selective nature of real-time television reporting invited manipulations from all interested parties. These carefully orchestrated distortions thrust television into an ever more prominent role as mediator of the war story, and ensured the continuation of terror in all of its varied forms. Images and counter-images spiraled out of control as time became inexorably linked to the "real" of television experience. Precipitous actions followed in response to this electronic reality, creating in effect an image-saturated feedback loop of monstrous proportions—a window of opportunity for the Iraqi regime, a shield of moral righteousness for the American-led coalition—as the consequences of real-world terrorist actions from both sides became dangerously irrelevant.

The Iraqi missile attacks on Israel and Saudi Arabia achieved their desired effects only with the aid of live television coverage. Similarly, the dramatic but emotionally remote precision-bomb videos produced by allied Central Command served to obscure such sensitive issues as Iraqi casualties and the destruction of Iraqi civilian industries. Finally, the military briefings from Saudi Arabia carried live by the television networks served to maintain television's dominant role as mediator of the conflict and thus undermine critical journalism in the United States and abroad.

The first Iraqi Scud missiles slammed into Tel Aviv and Haifa at 2:15 a.m. local time on January 17, confirming Iraq's much-publicized threat to attack Israel in the event of war. News of the missile attacks was reported by the American television networks almost as they occurred, fueling a considerable amount of misinformation propelled by real-time anxiety: that the Iraqi missiles had carried nerve gas, that Israeli war planes were retaliating for the attack. Televisual panic ensued as correspondents donned gas masks, CNN's Jerusalem headquarters was thrown into chaos, and reporters uttered terms of apocalypse: "unthinkable," "unspeakable."

Iraqi Scuds carrying conventional explosives hit Tel Aviv again the next day, but the most serious attack came on January 22 when Iraqi missiles killed three people, injured 67, and caused extensive damage to a Tel Aviv residential neighborhood. Each of these attacks was featured prominently in "live" and tape-delayed television news reports. The images numbed the senses: a Tel Aviv mother putting gas masks on her young children, a baby sealed inside a gas-proof bassinet, and Israeli civilians being carried away from the rubble, stunned and bloodied.

As *Washington Post* columnist Jim Hoagland pointed out, these images achieved horrific status beyond their shocking literal content by reference to an obvious historical analogue. The world watched, Hoagland commented, as "a nation of Jews [was] forced to don gas masks in prime time."[4] The Holocaust imagery had been confirmed by Baghdad Radio, which boasted on January 19 that Iraqi missiles would turn Tel Aviv into "a crematorium." The communication impact was immediate and visceral throughout the Middle East, where CNN is widely available. The attacks on Israel made Saddam Hussein an enduring hero among many Arabs of the region, and in many Muslim communities from North Africa to Malaysia. But while television time coalesced around the drama in Israel, the huge allied war machine continued to inflict death and destruction across Iraq and occupied Kuwait. Thousands of people perished in the agonizing rain of terror, an extraordinary action rendered insignificant by the dense electronic silence imposed by allied forces intent on punishment, and by an Iraqi regime bent on images of victory at whatever cost to its own people.

Terrorist acts like the missile attacks against Israel are effective as a means of communication because they tend to receive immediate and sensational press coverage. But the emotional power of television images, especially in this case the sickening urgency of seeing Israeli civilians under attack, produced an intense vicarious experience that far exceeded the capacity of any other medium. Clearly the Scud attacks were carried out for their propaganda value, an attempt by Saddam Hussein to achieve a political victory where military defeat was certain, and to demonstrate Iraqi defiance in the face of massive Western power. A similar larger-than-life significance was attributed by American audiences to the Patriot missile defense system, which after January 22 mostly succeeded in countering the Scud threat as military and propaganda weapon. But both issues served the greater purpose of deflecting attention from the war's primary battlefield.

The attention-focusing power of the Iraqi missile attacks was replicated in the allied command's use of the precision-bomb videotapes. The satisfying drama, gamelike quality, and astonishing persuasive power of these nose-cone videotapes were seized upon by military authorities and used to construct an essentially duplicitous story of wartime success. The videos of electronically guided bombs dropping onto their assigned targets suggested an impossibly "clean" and bloodless war in which ultra high-tech weapons were used to destroy buildings, bridges, and other structures without, it seemed, any real killing. As cultural symbols in a war of disinformation, these computer-controlled weapons suggested Western ideals of technological prowess and high moral character. The "smart"-bomb videotapes assured guilt-prone Americans that the war was being waged in a "just" manner, that innocent lives were being properly spared, and that the massive air campaign was a kind of *selective engagement* despite its unprecedented scale. Meanwhile the gamelike quality of these images of destruction was luridly appealing to television viewers already intrigued by military adventure; the covert text confirmed deep-rooted American antagonism toward Arab and Muslim peoples, implying that it did not matter when Iraqis were killed. The precision-bomb videotapes satisfied the television demand for images of war, directly supporting the American war agenda through their prominent presence across television time.

Indications of the true destructive consequences of the conflict received little attention until after the war ended, and were thus removed from the real-time loop of war-related imagery. Among these postscripts was a U.S. Air Force revelation on March 15 that precision-guided bombs made up only seven percent of the 88,500 tons of bombs dropped on Iraq and occupied Kuwait during 43 days of war, and that the remaining "dumb" bombs managed to hit their assigned targets only twenty-five percent of the time.[5] As for Iraqi dead and wounded, post-war estimates ranged from the tens of thousands to more than a hundred thousand people, not including the estimated 170,000 Iraqi children who were expected to die from malnutrition and gastro-intestinal infections within a year of the war's conclusion.[6]

The orchestrated use of the precision-bomb videotapes was just one part of a highly successful effort by U.S. authorities—principally the executive branch and the Pentagon—to manage American and world public opinion. This was achieved largely through unprecedented information control, including overt censorship of the press, which produced and maintained the kind of information-scarce environment in which dramatic images have the greatest impact.

The military also manipulated the packaging of information so as to favor television over other news media. Military briefings at allied Central Command in Riyadh and at the Joint Information Bureau in Dhahran were always *televised* briefings, and were broadcast *live* twice each day for the first two weeks of the war. Even the precision-bomb videos inherently favored television. At the same time, military censors in Saudi Arabia often delayed stories submitted by print journalists until well past home-office filing deadlines in the U.S., thereby rendering the stories hopelessly dated even before they were set in print.[7] Thus by controlling the flow of information through time, military authorities successfully maintained television's supportive role in the conflict. The live television briefings from Saudi Arabia effectively circumvented critical journalism, and ensured that the war would be portrayed in the desired manner.

Time and Imagination

In the highly simplified and falsely dramatic world of television, the Gulf War was a rousing success. Its portrayal as a justified and necessary action found a highly receptive ideological context in American television audiences. But the television war was ultimately a work of imagination, engendered in large part by the legitimating distortions of real-time televisual mediation. In spectacular fashion, the "real war" became hopelessly intertwined with the television war so that it was all but impossible for reasoned debate to escape the ideological confines of television's narrow lens. Television infiltrated the public mind with stunning efficiency, absorbing ordinary time into the highly restrictive temporal flow of prime-time narrative—perceived as "real time" by the television audience.

The television war offered many Americans a renewal of faith in their imagined national community.[8] The experience was intensely communal and awash in "right-minded" sentiments, as symbolized by the yellow ribbons which appeared across the country in support of U.S. troops and the Gulf War agenda. For a very brief moment, America was a nation apparently free of sectarian divisions, political dissent, and the diversity of thought which marks the democratic polity. Mainstream television audiences experienced a profound sense of social solidarity while minorities and dissenting views were "symbolically annihilated,"[9] silenced, and ignored. This was a consequence of television's largely unrecognized tendency to curtail democratic expression by restricting temporal space, while positioning itself in an endless series of inherently narrow "real-time" presents.

Time is implicated as well in the perception of the Gulf conflict as a history-correcting allegory in which Iraqis came to represent the generic enemies of America's troubled past, particularly "Arab terrorists" and "Muslim extremists." Thus victory in the Iraqi desert, an image created for and sustained by television, felt like just vindication for years of perceived humiliation "at the hands of the Arabs." More important perhaps is the impression that military victory in the Gulf overcame the debilitating effects of America's defeat in Vietnam (the progenitor of television war) and returned to the United States the status of world-dominating superpower and patriarch of freedom. Of course past time is always imagined and thus continuously subject to revision. But rarely is time revamped with such startling swiftness as in the aftermath of the Persian Gulf War.

Finally, the television war served to reinforce the temporal distance separating Western society from insurgent Third World forces. While television accounts never questioned the dimensions of the conflict, a United Nations evaluation team at the end of the war concluded that allied bombing had reduced Iraq to "near apocalyptic" conditions and pushed the country back to "a pre-industrial age."[10] The destruction of Iraqi industries and civilian infrastructure reversed Iraq's impressive development gains and halted its emergence as a regional power. This served to reinstate the temporal distance separating Iraq and other developing nations from the Western world. The war was a warning to all insurgent Third World states to take note of renewed Western hegemony in the post–Cold War era, and to remain in what Fabian has called "typological time,"[11] an imagined primitive-traditional past to which non-Western cultures and peoples are consigned by their "modern" Western counterparts. Temporal distancing in this case serves to maintain the impression of hegemony in the face of the Western nations' declining real-world influence.

Thus in producing the dominant narrative of the Gulf War tragedy, television had a tremendous impact on the intrinsic shape of the conflict. Time is deeply implicated, as the war and its spectators proceeded from moment to moment in response to television's electronic reality, where time is the principal component. Constrained and manipulated by television time, the war became a conflict of images in which world public opinion was designated the prime target.

Notes

1. Marshall McLuhan, *Understanding Media; The Extensions of Man* (New York: Mentor, 1964), 268–294.
2. The Bush administration had set 15 January 1991, as the deadline for Iraqi forces to withdraw from Kuwait.
3. McLuhan, *Understanding Media*, 268–294.
4. Jim Hoagland, "Suddenly, We're Much Closer to the Mideast," *Washington Post*, 22 Jan. 1991, 13-A.
5. Barton Gellman, "U.S. Bombs Missed 70% of Time," *Washington Post*, 16 Mar. 1991, 1-A.
6. Susan Okie, "Iraqi Children Face Postwar Disease Threat," *Washington Post*, 22 May 1991, 23-A.
7. Malcolm W. Browne, "The Military vs. the Press," *The New York Times*, 3 Mar. 1991, sec. 6, 26.
8. Benedict Anderson, *Imagined Communities; Reflections on the Origin and Spread of Nationalism* (London: Verso, 1983).
9. George Gerbner and Larry Gross, "Living with Television," *Journal of Communication* 26, no. 2 (1976), 182.
10. John M. Goshko, "U.N. to Let Iraq Receive Food," *Washington Post*, 23 Mar. 1991, 15-A.
11. Johannes Fabian, *Time and the Other; How Anthropology Makes Its Object* (New York: Columbia University Press, 1983), 23.

Holly Cowan Shulman

The International Media and the Persian Gulf War: The Importance of the Flow of News

A few weeks before the Persian Gulf War broke out, an NBC producer found himself in a Baghdad government office. He was in the country overseeing NBC's Crisis coverage, and on that day he was waiting to make arrangements for Tom Brokaw to visit the Iraqi capital. When he was finally received, he walked into the minister's office—to find the Iraqi official watching CNN's *Larry King Live*.[1]

This is perhaps an apocryphal story; but its point is clear. The Persian Gulf War was a media event. Everyone tuned in, including Saddam Hussein and George Bush. The political and military authorities on both sides needed and used the media to help their causes and to sustain their war efforts. If our focus on the media diverts attention from the central diplomatic, political, and military events, it also highlights that this was a propaganda war.

The story of CNN demonstrates the importance of the twenty-four-hour, around-the-clock, international television news service. But CNN's role was more complex than that. Because the media set agendas and convey viewpoints, because information can have an impact on how and what people think, and since CNN alone of all the electronic media remained in Baghdad, CNN's role became more complicated after the fighting began. Peter Arnett, news veteran and war horse of the Vietnam War era, a former Associated Press (AP) correspondent, went to Iraq to report the war. As one of only two Western journalists to do so (the other was a Spanish journalist whose stories were rerun in the British *Guardian*), Arnett—and CNN—became the primary means by which Saddam Hussein spoke to the world.

CNN and Arnett created a firestorm. Should a United States journalist tell the story of a war from behind enemy lines if that news could help the nation's enemy speak to citizens of the United States? But to state it this way—as the press in the United States has done—is to sidestep the problem of *why* Saddam attempted to use Arnett and CNN, and to obscure any evaluation of whether or not he did so successfully. What alternatives did the Iraqi leader have? Why did he use a U.S. news vehicle to reach the West—had he no medium of his own? Why not speak through the Iraqi press, especially Iraqi radio and television?

The answer to these questions lies in the special role the Western media play in the flow of international news. What much of the world reads, watches, and hears in its foreign news—although not in its domestic news—is a product of the news services and news media of the United States and Western Europe. In this respect, the most important news media in the United States and Western Europe are the wire services and the electronic press. It is therefore important to place the story of Saddam Hussein and CNN within the context of the movement of international news generally, and the role of the international electronic media specifically.

The Wire Services

The global imbalance in the flow of news around the world starts with the wire services. Only four are important. Associated Press (AP) and United Press International (UPI) are American. Reuters is British, and Agence France-Presse (AFP) is French. These four wire services are the primary source of international news throughout most of the world and therefore exercise a great deal of control over what international news reaches people around the globe.

This is not a new problem. The channels of information have long been controlled by Western nations. In the nineteenth century and into the twentieth, this was accomplished in large measure through national ownership of the transoceanic cable lines. Thus the European wire services—which before World War II included Wolff in Germany and Havas, rather than AFP, in France—divided the world up along the lines of international politics. The United States was subject to foreign control of its own international news reporting. In World War I, for example, the British cut German cable lines and thereafter took sole control of transatlantic cable traffic. They secretly intercepted and censored all news stories filed from central Europe to the United States press in order to influence opinion in the United States. As one contemporary wrote, "The position of England . . . made it possible for her to supervise the bulk of the news of Europe destined for consumption in belligerent and neutral countries." Perhaps remembering this earlier wartime state of affairs, John Foster Dulles remarked soon after the end of World War II, "If I were to be granted one point of foreign policy, and no other, I would make it the free flow of information."[2]

Even today, the wire services set international news agendas by selecting global news items for virtually all the nations of the world. In Asia, for example, AP, UPI, Reuters, and AFP are the most important sources of Asian news for the Asian press—even when an Asian daily newspaper or radio station or television broadcaster has correspondents in other Asian news centers. In Latin America, the news organizations rely almost entirely on AP, UPI, and AFP for foreign news, despite the fact that Latin American newspapers carry about twice the number of foreign news items as do comparable papers in the United States. This same situation holds true for the Middle East and Africa. Moreover, nearly all attempts to establish competitive news services have failed; and none has succeeded to any great extent.[3]

It is perhaps not surprising, then, that many governments around the world increasingly resent this situation, which is further complicated by the preponderance of United States entertainment around the world through movies and television programs, and by Western control over communications technologies. Many governments began voicing their dissatisfaction before the United Nations in the mid-1970s. Their most visible targets were the four major wire services, plus their video adjuncts: Visnews, UPITV, and CBS. They angrily declared that world news was defined by the United States and Western Europe, which distorted, or excluded, the authentic but non-Western values of the rest of the world. As the prime minister of Guyana succinctly remarked: "A nation whose mass media are dominated from the outside is not a nation."[4]

Many governments outside Western Europe and the United States have placed increasing restraints upon Western journalists, who are seen as enemies rather than as either neutral or friendly. Foreign correspondents, as one *Guardian* journalist explained, are viewed "not as separate and diverse organizations but as elements in a system of cultural imperialism which gathers and interprets world news according to Western interests and values, and then transmits it back to non-Western societies, overwhelming their own meagre news and propaganda resources."[5]

Before the outbreak of hostilities predating the beginnings of the Persian Gulf War, Saddam Hussein probably distrusted Western European and U.S. media because they controlled the flow of news in ways that worked against his interests and those of Iraq—at least as he defined them. Within Iraq, Saddam has been able to control his own media and orchestrate them into a chorus of support for his regime. It is easy, as a consequence, to dismiss Saddam's high-handed, often threatening treatment of Western journalists as simply an outgrowth of his totalitarian politics—and clearly this is true. But it is also important to remember the concern felt in many parts of the world that the news that reaches them is controlled by the United States and Western Europe and serves Western political and diplomatic interests. What the Iraqi media say about international events, both Middle Eastern and global, over their news services—print and electronic—is in some measure a tug of war with the Western news services. It is a constant statement of what Saddam and his ministers define as within their personal and national interest—as opposed to that which is handed to them over the wire services.

International Radio Broadcasting

Shortwave broadcasting was originally seen as a means by which a nation could circumvent both the major wire services and government-run news gatekeepers. It was a way around censorship exercised by those governments that controlled the international cable lines. This was the promise of international broadcasting.

In its earliest days, radio reached a strictly local audience. But in the mid-1920s, engineers demonstrated that shortwave signals could be picked up across very long distances.[6] From the beginning, therefore, shortwave radio has been an international medium. In the late twenties, European nations began experimenting with global, external broadcasting, in part to explore and expand the new technology, but also to bind together the far-flung corners of their empires. Then, in the 1930s, Adolf Hitler inaugurated radio warfare. Benito Mussolini imitated the German effort. Britain followed suit in a measure directed toward the Arab world and in self-defense against Italian radio warfare. As former British leader Stephen Tallents noted, in a pacific tone that masked the diplomatic importance of his message, radio could allow any nation to "be truly known and understood in the world."[7]

If, for most of the world, shortwave broadcasting was a way for governments to project their international, political, and economic interests, this was not originally the case in the United States. Before World War II, shortwave broadcasting in the United States was owned and operated by the commercial radio companies, with the single exception of a private foundation (WRUL) whose goal was global harmony and cooperation.[8] In one sense, these radio operations were like CNN in that they hoped to make money from international broadcasting. But unlike CNN, they did not succeed. These efforts therefore remained small and unimportant; the basic reason they continued at all was to hold on to their international frequencies in case some technological development should render them profitable at a future date.[9]

Thus, the United States entered World War II as the only major nation in the world—and very nearly the only nation in the world at all—without a government-owned and -operated shortwave station. Only in the weeks following the entrance of the United States into the war did the U.S. Government inaugurate its own shortwave service: the Voice of America (VOA). After World War II, and especially after the escalation of the Cold War, the VOA expanded its hours and languages. It strove to "ring" the Soviet Union with maximum-strength transmitters. As the Cold War became global, the Voice began broadcasting throughout Asia, Africa, Latin America, and the Middle East.[10]

Even by World War II, it had become clear that shortwave would serve limited and specific broadcasting functions: news, information, and propaganda. The quality of shortwave reception renders it too poor a medium for entertainment. Shortwave broadcasting thus became a specialized area of the electronic media that, unlike movies and television, has not been part of the growth of the global entertainment industry dominated by the United States and Western Europe. Rather, it has remained a means by which nations could broadcast their news and information to the world.[11]

The importance of shortwave remains its ability to bypass government censors and broadcast directly overseas. But as with the wire services, there are a very few international broadcasters who dominate the international radio world—despite the fact that nearly every country maintains a shortwave station. The major players are the same countries as those with the major wire services, with the addition of Germany: the United States (VOA), Britain (BBC), France (Radio France International), and Germany (Deutsche Welle). In 1988, the Voice of America broadcast 1,159 hours a week—a total that does not include the other U.S. government stations: Radio Free Europe, Radio Liberty, Radio Free Afghanistan, and Radio Marti. Deutsche Welle was on the air 831 hours a week and the BBC 756 hours a week. The Hungarian external service, by comparison, broadcast 84 hours a week.[12]

Such an imbalance can be attributed, at least in part, to the expenses involved in external radio broadcasting operations. Transmitters need to be built and updated, and new technologies implemented. Program staffs have to be paid and news operations organized and supervised. Furthermore, to have maximum impact a shortwave radio broadcast should be rebroadcast over medium-wave AM, or over FM, or both, so that radio set owners who have neither the habit nor the patience nor the receiver to pick up shortwave transmissions can listen. It also requires a political access to far-flung spots around the world comparable to building overseas shipyards for the United States Navy. Most nations simply do not have the political power—let alone the funds—to do so.[13]

The Voice of America was, and still is, a complex operation to understand because it is a multilingual government-run station. News comes out of a central desk. The central news desk sends bulletins to the language desks, which by 1992 numbered forty-seven. The news desks translate and air them. The organization of news routines at the VOA is much like that of any other news operation in the United States. It relies on the wire services and key domestic newspapers in combination with VOA reporters and stringers. Editors choose the stories at daily meetings. They carefully follow the routines of objectivity and sources. If, as Leon Sigal says, "news is not what happens, but what someone says has happened"—and if it is required to follow this pattern in order to meet the criteria of objectivity—then the VOA follows the rules. No story may go out over the air unless it has been reported by two independent sources. This is a stringently followed regulation of which the VOA is proud.[14]

Unlike domestic news services, however, the VOA goes on the air in many languages. It speaks to the Middle East not only in English but in Arabic, a single language spoken in twenty-one countries. VOA Arabic staff must be bilingual and bicultural. The staff is largely from Egypt, Jordan, and North Africa. It is through the lens of these men and women that the United States is projected to the Arab world.[15]

People listen—as do the state-run news media and government censors. Throughout the Arab world, domestic news is government controlled. Therefore, alternative, foreign sources of news have become extremely important. Iraqi citizens, for example, bypass government censorship and listen to a wide spectrum of international radio broadcasters. This is made easy by retransmissions in medium- and long-wave AM and in FM. An Iraqi living in Baghdad during the Persian Gulf War could tune in the Voice of America while cooking, shaving, or driving to work. All she or he needed was a very ordinary, battery-run transistor radio. An Iraqi could also listen to radio from Kuwait, Saudi Arabia, and Lebanon, or dial up Kol Israel and the Voice of Palestine. Many listeners also followed the war on the French station, Radio Monte Carlo Middle East, or Deutsche Welle, or the BBC, as well as the Voice of America. In Iraq, therefore, as throughout the Arab world, international radio listening has become widespread.

"The desire to consume" foreign radio, Douglas Boyd has written, "is compelling. . . . Transborder radio broadcasting within the Arab world is almost unique" in its importance.[16]

Audience figures are difficult to measure for overseas listening, even in periods of calm. The world's expert at audience surveys, the BBC, estimates that the number of Egyptian listeners of the VOA during and immediately before the Persian Gulf War rose from 8 percent to 11 percent. In Saudi Arabia it went up to 14 percent.

Even Saddam Hussein listened. Peter Jennings of ABC television news, for example, interviewed Saddam Hussein on November 16, 1990, when U.S. soldiers were on their way to the Persian Gulf. When Saddam's interpreter gave the wrong number of U.S. soldiers in transit, Saddam corrected him. As Jennings reported, Saddam had come to the interview directly from listening to the Voice of America.[17]

These international broadcasters serve as additional news services, alongside the wire services. Arabic Ministries of Information monitor the major international broadcasters and then issue daily excerpts for their national press to use. This information is subject to censorship, but it does expand the influence of the Voice of America and the other powerful international broadcasters of Europe. Thus the Voice of America, alongside British, German, and French international radio, not only reaches audiences around the world, it adds a great deal of weight to the imbalance in the global flow of international news.[18]

By contrast, the direct impact of Radio Baghdad on listeners living outside Iraq—especially on listeners within the United States—is minimal. Very few people in the United States, an information-rich nation, tune in shortwave radio. Moreover, most adults in the United States listen to radio in their cars, which are not equipped with shortwave receivers. Shortwave stations are also more difficult to find than are domestic broadcasters, because the changing seasons and the movement of the sun requires periodic scheduling shifts.

Moreover, shortwave broadcasters from around the globe do not play an important role in bringing news of their countries to newspaper, radio, and television news editors and producers in the United States. Those editors and producers rely instead on the major wire services, their own reporters and stringers, U.S. dailies and newsmagazines, and the British press. There is no way in which Radio Baghdad can do what the VOA, BBC, RFI (Radio France International), or DW (Deutsche Welle) do: supplement the wire service flow of international news.

Furthermore, to the extent that either news editors or ordinary citizens in the United States might listen to Radio Baghdad, Radio

Baghdad's journalistic practices do not conform to Western-held beliefs about the construction of journalistic knowledge. There is no tradition of the multiple-sourced, "objective" news format that governs journalistic practices in the United States and Western Europe. One U.S. reporter, stationed during the war in Nicosia, Cyprus, described the tone of Radio Baghdad in a way that points to at least part of the chasm between U.S. news expectations and Iraqi radio. "The announcers seem to have taken voice training at the School for Drones," he wrote. But this format, which he characterized as akin to "reading hog reports over a rural Nebraska station," masks a style of broadcasts that are also "notable for extraordinary examples of personal vituperation and creative curses," carrying threats and bragging victory.[19]

If Radio Baghdad had been inaccessible before the war, by January 1991 it was hard to find on the shortwave dial, even in nearby Nicosia, where reporters and governments made it a point to listen to Iraqi radio for indications of Saddam's intentions. Its signal was jammed. Its studios had been moved to avoid coalition bombs. "There is evidence," one reporter wrote, "they are on the run."[20] Though the service continued throughout the war, the signal grew weaker.[21]

Saddam Hussein could not use Radio Baghdad to reach ordinary people in the United States or speak directly to officials of the United States. President Bush was not listening—except to the monitored reports filed by the Foreign Intelligence Broadcasting Service (FBIS)—but Bush could speak directly to Iraqi leaders and the Iraqi people. The power of international radio belongs to the governments of the United States and Western Europe.

Cable News Network

International television is a recent function of satellite broadcasting. For more than a decade, this new technology has enabled television signals to be beamed up to a satellite and returned to another point on the globe. But it does require use of a satellite, and once the war began, Iraq was excluded from ARABSAT, which is controlled from Riyadh. After the end of January, Iraqi TV could no longer transmit pictures at all, probably because of coalition bombing. If Saddam Hussein wanted to get television coverage of Iraq onto the screens of the world, he had to rely on Western European or U.S. television news, and especially on Cable News Network (CNN), to carry it.[22]

CNN first went on the air in 1980. It began its life as a domestic station, but it soon began sending its signals to the Far East. By the mid-1980s, it was transmitting programs to Europe and soon after that to Central and South America. By the time of the Persian Gulf War, CNN's reach stretched around the globe.

CNN is an around-the-clock news and public affairs operation. It has become available to viewers around the world with the necessary receiving equipment. The very nature of CNN's twenty-four-hour coverage has made it, like the premier international radio broadcasters, an important global news service, vying in importance with the big four wire services.[23]

International television differs from international radio in critical ways. Television sets are more expensive than radio receivers, so fewer people own them, especially in the less developed areas of the world. Moreover, satellite communication is only direct if one has a dish. For most overseas viewers CNN is available through the courtesy of their government, which theoretically signs a contract with CNN, although in the case of Iraq, the government pirates the station. Just as a government can downlink CNN at will, a government can also pull the plug on CNN at any time. This cannot be done with shortwave radio signals, although it can be done with government-to-government or station-to-private-station radio linkups.

CNN is distinct in other important ways. The wire services shower news around the world through local newspapers, magazines, radio, and television stations. They often set the news agenda, determining the order, context, and tone of news stories, but these news items only reach foreign audiences through the filter of a nation's news organization. The shortwave radio broadcasters, on the other hand, bypass news gatekeepers. Because they broadcast in a local language, they are unique in their efforts to speak in two languages and two cultures.

Because CNN was not set up as an international broadcaster, it has assumed that role only by a kind of accident of technology. The organization did not originally think about its importance in terms of how it projected the United States abroad, what impact its news might have on the foreign relations of the United States, or any of the myriad related questions that form the daily context for the international radio broadcasters. It is only broadcast in English. By 1991, no one in Atlanta headquarters had considered how to measure or assess foreign audiences. They did not even get BBC- and VOA-generated audience surveys that analyze foreign listening patterns.

There is almost a sense that CNN got abroad by mistake and, at least by 1991, was not quite sure what to make of it. It was, after all, a profit-making U.S. company rooted in the politics, business, and culture of the United States. Yet anecdotal evidence indicates an important overseas presence. In 1991 Bahrain TV broadcast CNN twenty-four hours a day. Jordan, Egypt, and Turkey all had contracts with CNN. Peter Arnett described Egyptian president Hosni Mubarak as a "CNN junkie." Iraq pirated it, and Tariq Aziz, the Iraqi foreign minister, reported, "We listen to American radio—and I have the advantage of seeing CNN."[24]

If CNN became a major international broadcaster by mistake, then it is perhaps not surprising that before the Persian Gulf Crisis no one in the Atlanta office considered the international implications of their new stature. Furthermore, the demands to fill up the news "holes" of an around-the-clock news and information service dictated that CNN news furnish rough footage rather than finished pieces. It was open-mike, global journalism, unedited journalism, which distinguishes it from print, radio, or the other television news operations. It therefore provided special access to news makers around the world.

Arab leaders took advantage of it. CNN played both Mubarak's press conference before the war and Jordan's King Hussein's press conference from Amman. But what was to many the most vexing of all the prewar footage was an Iraqi-made tape of Saddam Hussein patting the head of a little boy held in Iraq as a human shield. CNN anchor Reid Collins commented, when the tape had finished, "It might be added that some of the worst pages of history are replete with the images of men who loved children." But the clip raised questions about who was using whom. Was CNN using Saddam as a news maker—or was Saddam using CNN to get himself broadcast around the world, knowing that, unlike CBS, ABC, or NBC, CNN coverage would be run straight on television newscasts around the world?[25]

Both are true. CNN considered Saddam a news maker. It followed the conventions of journalism in the United States by broadcasting the opinions of important world leaders. Before the war, all the major networks were vying for interviews with the Iraqi president. But CNN had so much news time to fill that an Iraqi-produced tape was more likely to be aired in full than it would have been over the network news, whose evening newscasts contain approximately ten minutes of foreign coverage.[26]

When Arnett decided to stay in Baghdad after the outbreak of the war—and Atlanta seconded the decision—CNN leaders viewed Arnett's actions as good journalism. After all, as Arnett has argued, it was important for the citizens of the United States to know what was happening in Iraq. Furthermore, he operated out of the belief that journalists should report from as many angles and sides as they can, thus following the canons of objective journalism.

It was, moreover, a war in which the U.S. press was censored by the U.S. military. The government of the United States controlled the flow of information out of the war zone. In a context of tight censorship and of government manipulation of news and information—a manipulation that constitutes a form of propaganda—CNN news balanced U.S. government news.

These arguments may explain how Arnett understood his assignment, but they do not outline Saddam's possible motives and goals. In order to comprehend his decision to allow CNN to stay and report the war, we must understand the context for how the United States regularly reports on events around much of the world beyond Western Europe.

News in the United States portrays much of the world in terms of violence, unrest, subversion, and combat, without analysis, explanation, or cultural framework. As Peter Dahlgren has written, "disorder looms eternal," thus defining global politics as "that's just the way they are."[27] This approach heightens oppositions of "us" and "them," of civilized and uncivilized. Saddam Hussein probably recognized this too, since he was aware of the debate over these issues in the United Nations. He probably also recognized that in wartime, when he especially needed the support of his nation, it was important to counter U.S. images. How could Iraq become something more real than a totalitarian nation governed by terror? How could the people of the United States be persuaded that Iraq was more than an evil empire, that it was a nation with its own civilization, traditions, and accomplishments? The question would have been not the desirability of doing so but how to do so.[28]

Perhaps the Iraqis knew of the "Vietnam syndrome": the idea that North Vietnam had won the war on the television screens of the United States. Although there has been much debate over this among media experts and academics in the United States, it is still an article of faith for many in the United States and may have been persuasive among Iraqi leaders. The Washington correspondent for the British *Daily Telegraph* wrote on the eve of the war, "You can be certain that if saturation bombing of the Iraqi capital becomes an American tactic, stomach-churning footage of bombed-out schools and hospitals will find their way onto American screens." The fact that the war did not turn out this way does not mean that Saddam did not act in anticipation that it would do so.[29]

Perhaps Saddam hoped the United States–led coalition would bomb Baghdad and thus consolidate support for his country as victims of Western, especially U.S., aggression. In this scenario, CNN would play a critical role because it would report on the inevitable horrors that bombing raids would bring—and in turn weaken Western European and U.S. resolve. The foreign affairs editor of the BBC thus observed that according to Saddam's strategy "CNN would show the results [of such bombing] to the American people, who would put such pressure on George Bush that the air war would be called off."[30]

As it turned out, the Persian Gulf War was short and did not give Saddam time to build up support around the world—or inside the United States—as the new victim of the United States. Perhaps he had the wrong war in mind. The Iran-Iraq War was one of attrition, and such a scenario would have helped the Iraqi leader gain global sympathy.

A primary lesson of the Persian Gulf War for citizens of the United States has been a growing awareness of the ways in which news management can become war propaganda. There has already been a great deal written about the importance of balancing cooperation with the Pentagon in time of war with the need for the citizens of the United States to know what is really going on in the theater of operations—to the extent that this is ever possible. But there is little discussion about the meaning of the war in terms of international broadcasting. Yet it is important to remember that many governments around the globe regard as threatening to their own interests the control of information by the United States and Western Europe. As a former president of Finland complained, "The flow of information between states . . . is to a very great extent a one-way, unbalanced traffic." He implies that journalists and broadcasters from the United States reinforce a particular form of international order. Put another way, U.S. reporters reflect U.S. public opinion, U.S. values, and often—although not always—U.S. foreign policy.[31]

The Persian Gulf War drove home this message. It demonstrated that modern technology has augmented U.S. and Western European domination of the news. It showed that the United States, along with its Western European allies, increasingly controls the media. As Philip Taylor has written, "The idea that 'the media are American,' that Anglo-American news organizations dominate the international flow of news to the detriment of the Third World, had not only found substantiating support in the war, it had even been underlined by the coalition's media arrangements, with their Anglo-American emphasis." American technology not only won the war on the battlefield, it did so over the media.[32]

Notes

1. Dennis McDougal, "They're Watching in Baghdad," *Los Angeles Times*, Jan. 15, 1991, 1k.

2. Stuart H. Loory, "News from the Global Village," *Gannett Center Journal* (Fall 1989): 169; Oscar W. Riegel, *Mobilizing for Chaos: The Story of the New Propaganda* (New Haven: Yale University Press, 1934), 25; Dulles quoted in Herbert Schiller, "The Free Flow of Information—For Whom?" in *Mass Media Policies in Changing Cultures,* ed. George Gerbner (New York: John Wiley and Sons, 1977), 112.

3. Oliver Boyd-Barrett, "Global News Wholesalers," in Gerbner, *Mass Media Policies,* 14; Wilbur Schramm and Erwin Atwood, *Circulation of News in the Third World: A Study of Asia* (Hong Kong: Chinese University Press, 1981), 27–32; James F. Larson, *Television's Window on the World: International Affairs Coverage on the U.S. Networks* (Norwood, N.J.: Ablex, 1984), 16.

4. Schiller, "Free Flow of Information," 112; Guyana's prime minister quoted in Robert L. Stevenson and Richard R. Cole, "Issues in Foreign News," in *Foreign News and the New World Information Order,* ed. Robert L. Stevenson and Donald L. Shaw (Ames: Iowa State University Press, 1984), 6–7.

5. Quoted in Oliver Boyd-Barrett, "The Collection of Foreign News in the National Press," in *Studies on the Press,* ed. Oliver Boyd-Barrett, Colin Seymour-Ure, and Jeremy Tunstall (London: Her Majesty's Stationary Office, 1977), 26. The correspondent was Martin Woollacott.

6. Short-, medium-, and long-wave broadcasting are all characterized by amplitude modulation (AM). But the shorter waves of the spectrum are reflected off the upper layers of the ionosphere: bouncing around the globe like stones skipping across water, striking the earth at regular intervals.

   Stanley Leinwoll, *From Spark to Satellite: A History of Radio Communication* (New York: Scribner's, 1979), 114; Llewellyn White, *The American Radio* (Chicago: University of Chicago Press, 1947), 17; Michael Kent Sidell, "A Historical Analysis of American Shortwave Broadcasting, 1916–1942," Ph.D. diss., Northwestern University, 1976.

7. Stephen Tallents, *The Projection of England* (London: Faber and Faber, 1932), 11. See also Asa Briggs, *The Golden Age of Wireless: The History of Broadcasting in the United Kingdom* (London: Oxford University Press, 1965); George C. Codding, *Broadcasting without Barriers* (The Hague, Netherlands: UNESCO, 1959).

8. Andre J. E. Mostert, Jr., "A History of WRUL: The Walter S. Lemmon Years, 1931–1960," M.A. thesis, Brigham Young University, 1969; Holly C. Shulman, "The Voice of Victory: The Development of American Propaganda and the Voice of America," Ph.D. diss., University of Maryland, 1984, 81–86.

9. Holly C. Shulman, *The Voice of America: Propaganda and Democracy, 1942–1945* (Madison: University of Wisconsin Press, 1990).

10. With the Cold War the United States also entered the world of surrogate broadcasting with Radio Free Europe and Radio Liberty (RFE/RL). There are important differences in broadcast philosophy. The stated purpose of the VOA is to project America abroad; that of RFE/RL is to air news about an enemy nation into that nation. But within the context of U.S. international broadcasting, only the VOA is directed toward the Middle East.

11. Shortwave broadcasting is not an ideal medium for music or entertainment. However, shortwave stations do broadcast music to which listeners around the world tune in when they have no alternative source. Thus, Soviet citizens who were interested in jazz heard it over the Voice of America, just as people in the United States listen to the music of the Andes or West Africa over shortwave. Interview with Kim Elliott, Audience Research Officer, Voice of America, Mar. 15, 1993.

12. Graham Mytton and Carol Forrester, "Audiences for International Radio Broadcasts," *European Journal of Communication* (1988).

13. Within the last five years the Voice of America has begun placing programs on domestic radio stations and networks in a number of countries. Programs are

usually fed by satellite and retransmitted locally. Because the broadcasting systems of the Arab states tend to be government monopolies, VOA has very little of this type of program placement in the Persian Gulf region. Interview with Kim Elliott, Mar. 15, 1993.

14. For a further discussion of the VOA's practices in a comparative framework, see Donald R. Browne, *Comparing Broadcast Systems: The Experiences of Six Industrial Nations* (Ames, Iowa State University Press, 1989).

15. Interview with Mahmoud Zawawi, head of the Arabic Desk, Voice of America, Apr. 12, 1991.

16. Douglas A. Boyd, "Transnational Radio Listening among Saudi Arabian University Students," *Journalism Quarterly* (Spring/Summer 1991): 211.

17. BBC Audience Survey of Egypt, Dec. 1989–Jan. 1990, Voice of America Research Office; *Washington Post*, Jan. 10, 1991, B1; conversation with Jim Flemming, BBC Research Office, Feb. 10, 1991; memo, from Kim Elliott to Sam Hilmy et al., "Gulf War Broadcasting News," Jan. 25, 1991, VOA Research Office.

18. Conversation with Mahmoud Zawawi.

19. Kenneth Freed, "Hard-to-Find Radio Baghdad Tells Iraq's Side," *Los Angeles Times*, Jan. 26, 1991, 1k.

20. Freed, "Hard-to-Find Radio Baghdad."

21. Philip M. Taylor, *War and the Media: Propaganda and Persuasion in the Gulf War* (Manchester: Manchester University Press, 1992), 109.

22. Taylor, *War and the Media*, 109–111.

23. Since the Persian Gulf War, a number of other private and government stations have moved into international television newscasting, including the BBC World Service. Interview with Frank Cummins, Voice of America director of Program Review, Mar. 11, 1993.

24. Peter Arnett, talk given at the University of Maryland, College Park, Oct. 16, 1992.

25. Robert Wiener, *Live from Baghdad: Gathering News at Ground Zero* (New York: Doubleday, 1992), 281.

26. Wiener, *Live from Baghdad*, 18; Larson, *Television's Window*, 13–14, 145.

27. Peter Dahlgren, "The Third World on TV News: Western Ways of Seeing the 'Other,'" in *Television Coverage of International Affairs*, ed. William C. Adams (Norwood, N.J.: Ablex, 1982), 53.

28. For a brief discussion of the UN debate, see Larson, *Television's Window*, 14–16.

29. Taylor, *War and the Media*, 11.

30. Taylor, *War and the Media*, 89.

31. Urho Kekkonen, speaking at the Tampere Symposium on the International Flow of Television Programs in 1973, as quoted by Larson, *Television's Window*, 15; Dahlgren, "Third World," 62; for a discussion of public opinion and U.S. foreign policy leaders, see Daniel C. Hallin, *The "Uncensored" War: The Media and Vietnam* (Berkeley and Los Angeles: University of California Press, 1989).

32. Taylor, *War and the Media*, 266.

Mimi White

Site Unseen: An Analysis of CNN's *War in the Gulf*

A war is not any the less heinous for being a mere simulacrum—the flesh suffers just the same, and the dead ex-combatants count as much there as in other wars. That objective is always amply accomplished, like that of the partitioning of territories and of disciplinary sociality.

—Jean Baudrillard, *Simulations*

The Live History of War

On January 17, 1991, in the midst of reporting on the second day of the Persian Gulf War, the Cable News Network ran a self-promotional spot during a commercial break. The narration for this spot is striking in a number of ways, most notably for its self-conscious presentation of the network itself as the crucial global authority on a conflict—the Gulf War—that was at the time barely twenty-four hours old: "As war erupts in the Persian Gulf, the world turns to one source, as principals check the widening conflict, key figures monitor world reactions, and families look for news of hope. Now more than ever, shouldn't you be watching CNN?" (January 17, 1991). The commercial aired very nearly as soon as it was reasonably possible to put it on television. The start of the war on the evening of January 16 (EST) received continuous coverage on CNN without commercial breaks, following the common commercial-network broadcasting protocol for covering catastrophes, natural disasters, and world crises in the United States.[1] The resumption of a normal television programming structure—including advertising breaks, along with coverage of events other than the war—signaled the settling of the war into the normal flow of everyday life and everyday television.

In a crucial sense, the CNN advertisement historicizes the Persian Gulf War when it had hardly even begun, identifying the war as an event that already has an official chronicler. Indeed, the war was described by a number of news correspondents as "historic" as soon as it started, most often referring to the unprecedented scale of the air

"Now more than ever, shouldn't you be watching CNN?"

bombing assault on Iraq. This particular historic global conflict was carried live on television—covered by the news as it was taking place. The television news coverage in turn characterized itself as historic at the very moment it was occurring. A homology was thus asserted between the represented events and the mode of representation, with the war itself, and the news coverage thereof, qualified as historic from the very start. As the war developed, this homology was extended and enriched through technology, as advanced telecommunications networks constituted and guided the apparatus of both war and news.

The Persian Gulf War is widely considered the first war fought "live" on television, differentiating it from the Vietnam War, which was fought on television but on news film rather than live. It is also widely known that the news reporting that brought the historic Persian Gulf War into American—and other—homes "live" was highly managed and restricted by the U.S. government. Even before the air war against Iraq was launched, reports were made about coordinated news briefings, preselected pools of reporters gaining access to military and government officials, and restricted access for the news media to soldiers at the front. The full extent of this management of the news

by the military (or, some would say, collusion of news media organizations with the military) only emerged in the wake of the war;[2] but its
existence was part of the ongoing news reporting about events in the
Persian Gulf during the military buildup and the initiation of hostilities.

Thus, for example, many of the stories from Riyadh and other
centers of military operation in the Middle East were identified as
official government press releases, as having been cleared by the censor, or as derived from the official designated press pool reporter's account. With all of this visible "management" of the media, a result of
the cooperation/collusion between the news media and the U.S. military, the Persian Gulf War was represented in carefully preselected and
regulated terms. What, then, constitutes the war's historic "liveness?"
Just what was seen or heard on television that led to the commonplace
idea that the war was fought live for "us" in our own living rooms?
These questions are all the more pressing insofar as the lapses and ab-
sences in news coverage have been subject to substantial analysis.[3]

By way of responding to these questions, I have examined some
of the earliest live reporting of the war by CNN, self-identified (and
widely promoted) as the "one source" the world was watching precisely at this time. To examine the war coverage in this way is to perform an act of willful decontextualization. After all, the full meaning
and impact of events and their coverage are ultimately to be found in
the larger narrative they instigated. Yet it is also a process of recontex-
tualization, an effort to return to the war reporting from the very start,
reconstructing the semiotic negotiations that account for the impact
of the war coverage (and the war itself) as an event of live immediacy.

In the live sequences transmitted from the middle of the war
zone, the anomalies and contradictions of live reporting fully emerge,
with the flow of the reporting itself at the center. In the absence of direct images of the war, the voices and images of reporters in the act of
reporting come to stand as icons of liveness and historicity, at the
intersection of the telecommunications technologies carrying their
voices/images and the technologies of war. Yet even as the reporters are
seen and/or heard, the technologies of war—which centrally include
telecommunications (computers, video simulation, satellites, and so
on)—threaten the ability of the telecommunications networks to secure and present the voices and images of the reporters to the international television audience. In this context, CNN could readily claim
the status of premier source, as the cable network already devoted to
twenty-four-hour newscasting, distributed around the world, with an
extensive news reporting apparatus in place, including the fortunate
(and perhaps not fortuitous) placement of three of their reporters in a

Journalists became the focus of the news in the absence of direct war footage.

hotel in the center of Baghdad with an open phone line throughout the first evening's attack.

An examination of the first few days of reporting provides an object lesson in the struggle to make meaning in an atmosphere charged not only by the expiration of the ultimatum and the onset of the war properly speaking but also by the extreme scale and scope of coverage. This leads to extraordinary semiotic productivity (on the part of all the major networks, as well as many local stations), in the form of continuous news coverage, even at a time when it was difficult to say very much at all owing to the combination of news censorship/management and the fact that events were just getting started. In other words, the very apparatus that CNN put in place (as did the major networks) led to a profusion of information.

From the earliest war coverage on the evening of January 16, 1992 (EST), reporting strategies include extreme self-consciousness about the act of reporting and are self-reflexive in foregrounding the conditions of production and reception of the reporting as it was taking place. This coexists with an inherent inability to clarify events with certainty, as they are still in the course of happening and do not yet carry the coherence or decisiveness of a concluded sequence of events—

despite the battery of experts and on-the-spot, live reporters who are in place precisely in order to follow events with the clarity and authority of professional expertise. The news reporting contains contradictions and uncertainties that are put forth as competing truths, present in the ongoing discourse of the reporters, only to cancel each other out.[4]

This is most stunningly captured in the long haul, for the general purport of all of the initial eyewitness reports, confirmed by official military follow-up, casts the first wave of the air attack as a singular success: the bombing is represented as a surgical, strategic, tactical coup, celebrating both the high-tech machines and those who deployed them. In the aftermath of hostilities, however, the data concerning the accuracy and performance of the bombing have been substantially recast. Yet even from the earliest moments of war coverage, information is deployed in such a manner as to cast everything in terms of a fundamental uncertainty and indeterminacy, often meaningless in the final analysis except for filling television time. In this way the extensive network and local news reporting reveals itself as a semiotic machine whose primary function is to fill time on television, with information as an alibi. In some basic sense, nothing ever really meant anything in the first place, at least for certain.

For example, during the second night of the war, when Iraq launched Scud missiles at Israel, a number of CNN correspondents in Tel Aviv and Jerusalem were reporting about events as they occurred. From time to time their reports would be interrupted by the anchors in the United States, citing reports that Iraq had indeed launched Scuds at Israel. Because the U.S.-based anchors would intrude to confirm precisely what was already being reported and represented by the Israeli-based reporters, the interruptions carried the implication that the on-site correspondents were not fully in a position to know what was going on immediately around them (despite their contact with local authorities and local media, to say nothing of their direct experience of air raids). As it happens, this strategy maintains conventional journalistic standards for what constitutes "truth," sustaining the number of so-called independent sources necessary to confirm reports. Yet it also seems to challenge the authority of the on-site correspondents to describe events that immediately surround them, or to function fully as autonomous reporters and sources of information, even as the viewer may hear the air raid sirens in the offscreen background along with the reporter.[5]

The witness in the field no longer guarantees the authority of a report that must, instead, circumvent the globe in the form of an information flow, through Washington and (in the case of CNN) Atlanta, returning to the field as incontrovertible truth. Temporality is thereby distended and contracted, as the time it takes to achieve the recirculation and redistribution of information becomes the "moment" of the event. Moreover, by and large it is the reporters in the Middle East, bringing the live war coverage to us, whose reports must be reconfirmed over and over again in this way by official U.S. government reports. (The same global circuit and repetition of information *as confirmation* does not routinely occur with correspondents based at the White House or the Pentagon in Washington.) These reporters, proper white middle-class subjects, seem to have been subtly, implicitly undermined by an association with Middle Eastern "orientalism," as if their sources and their own senses and rationality were affected by virtue of their geographic location.[6]

In the end, authority is secured for the corporate entity CNN, derived as an effect of television textuality and from deploying as much information as possible, as quickly as possible, no matter how indefinite. In the process the network secures for itself the position as the "one source" to whom all others turn, defining for itself a commanding "historic" vantage on the Persian Gulf War. Simultaneously, the very fact that CNN's ongoing reporting on events is being followed around the world is an integral part of the news stories carried by CNN. This is both a self-elevating and a self-congratulatory strategy, placing CNN front and center in the information that influences world leaders and world opinion while presenting that position as already natural. This position of prominence is closely linked to the figure of the intrepid reporter, whose activities logically enable CNN to be in a position of centrality in the very events of the war in the first place. In turn the threat of the loss of the television signal is closely related to the place of the intrepid reporter, with the ever-present possibility that the correspondent may become the victim of war, a threat played out in a number of CNN locations in the Middle East during the first few days of war coverage.

The Boys in Baghdad

When the bombing began on the evening of January 16, 1991 (EST), three CNN reporters in a hotel in Baghdad were able to secure and maintain an open phone line, communicating about the war from the perspective of witnesses in the figurative, if not literal, center of the action, behind enemy lines. The fact that they occupied this position, and its unusual and unanticipated attainment, were integral elements of their reporting. With the reporters literally uniquely positioned to cover ongoing events, CNN rapidly confirmed its own position as the cutting edge of television news coverage, a position reconfirmed in the self-promotional advertisements shown the day after the first evening's bombing of Baghdad.

During the first night of bombing, Peter Arnett, John Holliman, and Bernard Shaw were located in the Al-Rashid Hotel, the major domicile of Western reporters in Iraq during the period before the outbreak of hostilities. In part the reporters tell the story of the start of the war from their perspective: the city was quiet most of the day, the bombing began at approximately 2:30 A.M. Baghdad time, and so on. But an important part of their story includes the fact that they are able to communicate at all with the outside world. At one point, very early in the course of events, one of the reporters talks to the hotel operator who is urging them to leave their room on the ninth floor to join the other hotel guests (including a number of U.S. and other Western reporters) in the basement bomb shelter. Soon thereafter, Peter Arnett notes, "It was said that once the U.S. attack started, all communications would be shut off. I don't know why we can talk to you."[7] One half hour later, the reporters have a more extended exchange about their ability to report.

> *Bernard Shaw:* Did it occur to you it is not accidental that we are still reporting to the world?
> *John Holliman:* It may not be, Bernie. I'm sure the Iraqis could pull the plug on us. I'm sure the Americans could pull the plug on us. And it's useful I hope, to our viewers around the world, to be able to hear what we have to report.
> *Shaw:* My point is this government wants word put out.
> *Peter Arnett:* This government has told us frequently that he wants the Press to stay here.

These comments are part of a larger, ongoing discourse whereby the reporters in Baghdad, and the CNN anchors in the United States, draw attention to their unique position. The spectacle of news reporting, along with the heroism of individual reporters, thus stands in for the unseen battles. The reporters' ability to provide a live, audio, and eyewitness report about the war from "ground zero" (their term, at one point, even though the hotel and its close surroundings are *not* a target of the bombing) is based on a unique, and not necessarily accidental, vantage point.

In the early morning after the first night's bombing, Bernard Shaw has Don Kirk, a reporter from *USA Today*, in the hotel room giving an eyewitness account of his experience overnight and of how Baghdad looks the morning after the attack. Kirk's story includes mentioning that he had an open phone line to *USA Today* from the U.S.

Embassy in Baghdad but that he lost it when the bombing started. He also emphasizes that currently there is no functional communication within Baghdad: no local telephone, no telex, and no outside phone lines. The anomaly of his ongoing communication is tacit but unexplored. Still later, Bernard Shaw reports that all phone lines in Baghdad are down, including in the hotel from which he is speaking, and he does not know if they were damaged in the course of bombing, or if they were shut down by the Iraqis. In this context he expresses a concern that he might lose the line he does have, noting that the hotel operator did not let them through on a phone line the previous evening. Over the course of their reporting, in the context of ongoing reports of the success of the air strike itself, the technologies of reporting and of waging war come to be closely associated, as precision bombing comes to be identified with CNN's feat of precision phoning. Like a successful bombing raid that requires precise placement of the bomb, successful news coverage requires only one phone line, as long as it is properly placed to secure the right line.

The mystery of the ability to communicate at all is counterbalanced by the reporters' painstaking verbal accounts of their position, as a way of grounding their reporting. They provide continual detailed explanations of where they are in the hotel including when they are lying down, seated, or under the bed; what direction the windows face; and so on. For example, Peter Arnett explains, "We can give this report tonight because we're on the ninth floor of the Al-Rashid Hotel which has a commanding view to the north, south, east, and west"; or Bernard Shaw announces, "I'm just crouching down here on the floor to get a better view." This scrupulous attention to the details of their orientation may be a means of providing information to the strategic experts CNN reporters in the United States will subsequently consult. It also stands in for the video image that more commonly anchors the reporter in place, within the arena of events on which she or he is commenting.

Yet something else is at work here. Although they are in the middle of the battle, the reporters cannot really see very much, and they have no access to much information beyond what they can see and hear. The CNN correspondents at the Al-Rashid Hotel can only recite what they are doing and seeing as a replacement for the sight the video image would otherwise provide. During attacks they periodically announce that they are sticking the telephone out the window in order to let the audience "hear" and experience the attack for itself—as if the sound of distant bomb explosions, carried by a long-distance telephone line, conveys significant information, or an accurate reproduction of the sound as the reporters are hearing it in their hotel suite.[8] On several occasions they refer to the presence of a camera operator who is shooting video that they hope will be made available to the network soon, including at one point asking him to describe the scene outside their window.

Television is here reduced to the dimensions of audio, and the coverage is closer to radio news than conventional television news reporting.[9] Nonetheless, the insufficiency of sound as bearer of television meaning is fully enacted by the images that accompany the reports from the Al-Rashid Hotel, as CNN mixes a range of images with the ongoing reports from Baghdad. A number of different maps are shown, including street maps, country maps, and the entire Middle East region, in different colors—beige, yellow, orange, multicolor. In between showing these maps, the photos of the reporters who are speaking are intermittently included, one at a time or all three at once. The maps in particular carry the burden of visual variety and stimulation, since there is no obvious systematic reason why the beige or yellow map appears when it does. However limited a visual repertoire is allowed by the different maps and inset photos, the fact that there is ongoing variation signals the importance of the visual image in television newscasting; it cannot remain static.

The importance of televisuality is further underscored by the references to forthcoming video images, as well as in the painstaking and labored efforts by the reporters to adequately describe their own vantage point and what they see. In the process they frequently resort to figural language. The exploding bombs and tracers are repeatedly described as looking like fireflies, sparklers, and fireworks. The sensations of the loudest and closest explosion—combining sound and physical tremors—are compared to the launching of a space shuttle. These metaphors recur throughout the evening, evoking a largely positive chain of association, with the notable exception of the space shuttle, which raises at once ideas about U.S. technological progress and the specter of the *Challenger* space shuttle explosion.[10] In a crucial sense, metaphoric power accrues to the whole situation of the reporters in Baghdad. The very presence of reporters for a U.S. cable network within the boundaries of enemy territory implies, from the outset, U.S. and allied force dominance in the war itself. Indeed, the identity of the reporters—one white American, one African American, and one white New Zealander—contributes to the self-image of CNN as a global network, casting over their reporting a veneer of multiculturalism and internationalism that is reinforced by references to the reporters' previous experiences covering wars in different places around the world.

The fact that their position is unique and unprecedented, combined with the insistent verbal literalism that characterizes their position, constitutes their reporting of events as spectacular and authoritative, even while this is intermittently undermined by the reporters' own remarks about not being able to see much, uncertainty about what they are seeing, and so forth. The reporters' previous experiences in war zones—Peter Arnett in Vietnam and Beirut, and Bernard Shaw in Latin America—are briefly referenced as a context for the authority of their interpretations of what they see. Yet both reporters stress the unprecedented—and thereby historic—nature of their current situation, which is *not* like the previous war experiences they have had.

In this general context (including what they can and cannot see, what they may or may not know relative to others, and the authority of their vision), all the talk about where they are situated in the hotel, with its sheer weight of literal description, threatens to unravel the value of what they report. At times it starts to seem like nearly all they can do is describe their own situation as the war proceeds elsewhere, around them, while they lack the clarity of vision that a different site might provide: "To paint the picture for you where we are physically, of where we are right now: we are in the hall on the floor and we can look through open doors on either side." Or, as recounted in *Time* magazine, " 'It occurs to me that I didn't get dinner tonight,' said Shaw at one point. 'There's tuna fish, Bernie,' replied Holliman, 'plenty of tuna fish.' "[11] The dead weight of such literalism is in turn contradicted by the self-congratulatory remarks by the reporters and CNN in general that characterize their position in terms of a unique, unprecedented vantage on the war.

The reporters may say anything—and indeed say almost everything—about their own knowledge and authority, promoting their superiority and expertise at one moment and challenging their own value at the next. Early in the course of reporting they note, "Our colleagues in Washington and in Saudi Arabia obviously know a *lot* more than we do." But shortly thereafter, John Holliman notes, "I think all of us—Peter, Bernie, and I—figure that since we're in Baghdad, we're the middle of the story." Later still, when Peter Arnett is referred to as a CNN expert when it comes to war coverage, he says, "I don't think anyone is an expert on this, being in the middle of a capital with an air strike going on." At another point Bernard Shaw discusses what it's like to be at ground zero during an unprecedented air attack. Peter Arnett notes that the situation is unique in journalistic history, "to have front-row seats to one of the great air bombardments in history."

In this way the air attack and the coverage of it from the Al-Rashid Hotel are equated as both unprecedented and historic, each reconstructing and supporting the other as a significant event. All of this is in turn reinforced by the CNN anchors in the United States who offer supportive evaluative and congratulatory remarks about the reporting from Baghdad: "Compelling reporting, gentleman. Thank you." "Everyone wants us to go back to Baghdad. And so do I. Where Bernard Shaw, Peter Arnett, and John Holliman have been reporting this dramatic evening." "Gentlemen, an incredible night; an incredible report. Please stay close. We'll be back with you." "We're fascinated by what you have to say there." "Thank you *very* much for your reports. We're happy to see that you're in good spirits. You have a terribly large story to report." The singular position of the reporters also situates them as experts within Baghdad for the news community, a situation they also promote in the course of their news reporting. Thus the morning after the first night's bombing they report that they "have been briefing people" about the president's address and Pentagon reports during the course of the night.

Yet for all of this expertise and successful reporting, the coverage also suggests the inadequacy of the vantage point on events from inside the Al-Rashid Hotel. While the reporters announce from the start a willingness and ability to describe what they see for long periods of time, this is fairly quickly followed by the assertion, "We can't see anything. But it looks like fireworks on the Fourth of July." During the course of the night, the reporters readily speak at length about what they see, including fairly definitive speculation about the targets that are being hit. "I think that airburst took out the Communications." "I believe we just did see a blast at the main telecommunications center." (Their discussions even include a joke about their own location: "They seem to have prearranged targets. I hope the Al-Rashid Hotel is not one of them.") Yet the next morning, despite the profusion of talk and speculation about targets and accuracy—which is in turn referred to throughout the evening's reporting by both U.S. military experts and CNN's own strategic analysts to make sense of how the attack is proceeding—and being the center of the story, they conclude, "We can't tell you the strength and number of bombs but can only describe what we experienced," even though they presented their situation in rather different terms through the course of the previous night.

The instability that informs the authority of the reporting is also played out in conversations between the reporters in the hotel in the course of the night. Very early in the evening, Peter Arnett says, "What is interesting to me is these bombs seem right on target. . . . They *seem* to be proving effective here tonight." He contrasts this with the situation in Vietnam, where bridges in the north would stand for years despite repeated bombings. Less than one hour later Bernard Shaw apparently echoes this impression as he announces, "Gentlemen, we are seeing an example of surgical bombing." Arnett asks him to explain

what he means, and Shaw obliges, only to be immediately contradicted by Arnett. "You may be right Bernie. But we won't know until
tomorrow how surgically precise these bombs were." Yet only a few
moments later Arnett says that this "seems to be a *strategic* attack on
Baghdad." In the course of individual reports and ongoing dialogue
among the correspondents in Baghdad, there are constant assertions
about what they are seeing, what targets are being hit and so forth,
offset by incidental remarks about uncertainty.

This spills over into the visual/experiential dimension. By and
large the visual description is grounded in metaphors identified with
visual pleasure: fireworks, fireflies, sparklers. Yet how this is experienced by the individual reporters is hardly uniform. On the one hand,
a sense of anticipation and fulfillment colors their presentation in a
very positive sense. They seem exhilarated by their own situation—
professionally and emotionally. This above all else, combined with
their ongoing discussion of surgical and strategic success, confers on
the war a sense of positive achievement. However, this overarching
sensibility is intermittently shattered by Bernard Shaw, who inserts a
more negative evaluation of his experience of events. Shaw's comments in this vein are in turn immediately contradicted, in a version of
experiential and emotional "good cop/bad cop" that is also being
played out in relation to the nature and accuracy of the eyewitness account the reporters provide and define, variously, in terms of information versus experience.

At one point, early in the evening, Shaw notes, "Just one comment. Obviously I've never been there, but this feels like we're in the
center of Hell." This is almost immediately followed by a response
from one of the other reporters with him, "It's a remarkable experience
to be here, ladies and gentlemen; and the night sky again lit up with
beautiful red and orange tracers." The sense of horror evoked by
Shaw's remark is immediately undermined and contradicted by a
comment that emphasizes the singularity of the event in more abstract
terms ("remarkable experience") linked to aesthetics. Shortly thereafter, during another round of bombing, one of the reporters is describing the scene with an emphasis on the "beauty" of the tracer
blasts, noting that the beautiful pictures they had taken to accompany
the sound had been confiscated by security forces at the hotel. Shaw
immediately interjects, "This is not beautiful to me." At another point,
toward morning, he suggests, "If this was surgical bombing, I don't like
being this close to the operating table." Much later as morning breaks
in Baghdad, Shaw repeats his perspective, noting, "It has been one hell
of a night here in Baghdad." Yet these moments of expressed critique
may lose their force, since they are not further elaborated and they co-

exist with ongoing description of the bombing in more evocative terms—fireflies, fireworks, and sparklers.

Yet despite Shaw's darker evaluation of his experience, he continues to participate in the reporting. There are a number of times when the reporters in Baghdad fear they will be cut off or forced to go to the basement shelter with the rest of the U.S. press corps, and they all engage in a variety of tactics to stay on the air as long as possible, including Shaw. On a number of occasions someone knocks at the door. When they think it might be a security person, two of the correspondents go to hide (under a bed, in a closet) to escape detection. Thus the image of the heroic, intrepid reporter is instated, battling the enemy figuratively by remaining on the air, even in the face of no apparent phone lines out of the country, to say nothing of the local security forces that might force them to shelter.

The image of the intrepid correspondent facing danger is repeated over and over again, with Charles Jaco in Dhahran, and on the second night of the war after the Baghdad phone connection is discontinued, in Tel Aviv and Jerusalem as Iraq launches a Scud missile attack. Indeed, for the first few nights of the war, before reporters had access to the U.S. military personnel who were waging the war, U.S. reporters seem to stand in for the human lives at risk as they report at all costs and in the face of potential, uncertain dangers.

Moreover, however much the information is cast in relative terms, it becomes the foundation for reporting on unprecedented military success. The reporters, whose nonspecific sight of bombs, flares, and tracers dominates the reporting, are cited as a source of information during the first formal military news briefing at the Pentagon during the first evening of the war. U.S. Secretary of Defense Richard Cheney directly referenced the CNN reports from Baghdad, noting that the best reporting about the air attack was on CNN. He says that it appears the operation was successful in striking targets with precision: "At least that's the reporting according to CNN." Thus the reporting on precision, pinpoint, strategic, and surgical bombing—the prevailing terms to convey the success of the air attack—itself proceeds and is substantiated from the very start in terms of impressions and uncertainties. To complete the feedback loop of information later in the course of the evening (about forty-five minutes after the press conference with Cheney), Wolf Blitzer, the CNN reporter at the Pentagon, enthusiastically summarizes the Pentagon's *optimistic* response to the bombing as it proceeds. But following Cheney's remarks, this optimism is rhetorically grounded, at least in part, in CNN reports from Baghdad. The war coverage thus enacts the colloquial phrase "what goes around comes around," as information initiated in one place on the news is then replayed and echoed by others—reporters, strategic experts, government officials—in order to be re-presented as news yet again, at another time.

Beyond Baghdad

There's a lot more to it than just putting on a gas mask and slipping on a banana peel.[12]

CNN's success in reporting in the midst of danger stands as a measure of its status as an authoritative source on the war and as a metaphor of larger U.S. success in waging war. This emerges in a variety of ways, most notably in the repeated reminders that CNN is the major source of information for everyone, from the White House, to Jordan, to Iraq and Israel. At the White House, everyone including Marlin Fitzwater is watching reports from CNN; in Israel the radio is broadcasting CNN live, and officials in the Foreign Ministry are watching CNN. Doug James reports from Amman, "We've been told that Jordanian officials, like many others, learned first about the attack on Kuwait and Iraq by watching CNN. The average person here does not get CNN and so far has not heard of the attack." James's second report from Amman similarly begins, "We understand Jordan's King Hussein is currently, like many other people, watching CNN to see the latest developments from Iraq and Kuwait." On a number of occasions, when reporters interview the families of soldiers stationed in the Middle East or informally poll popular opinion, they are in homes or bars where groups are watching CNN coverage of events as they unfold.

This contributes to the construction of a network of associations—CNN centrality as *part* of the news, the intrepid reporter, loss of video/audio signal indicating a threat to the intrepid reporter in the middle of events—and quickly instated a mythology about CNN in the course of Persian Gulf War reporting. The bravura performance of the reporters in Baghdad the first night of reporting was repeated but transformed during the second night as CNN followed reports from Israel pertaining to Scud missile attacks by Iraq. Initially the reports come as something of a surprise, since news and military analysis of the previous night's attack on Iraq concluded that all of the fixed Scud sites had been successfully wiped out. Thus, as soon as reports of the Scud attack on Israel are heard, the reporters suppose it must be from the few mobile Scud launch units that have escaped detection.

In the course of reports from Tel Aviv and Jerusalem, an interesting Dynamic emerges between the anchors in the United States and

Journalists don gas masks in Tel Aviv.

the CNN correspondents in Israel, as the on-site reporters court danger and are given orders regarding their safety from the United States. When Alex Claude in Tel Aviv reports that Israeli radio has told Israelis to put on their gas masks and go to a safe place, Lou Dobbs in the United States asks him what others around him are feeling. He responds that no one is around, since they have all followed the government's directive and gone to secure rooms. Indeed, he says that as soon as he is done talking with CNN, he is going to a secure room, noting that he hears explosions in the background. At this point, CNN anchor Dobbs announces that CNN has confirmed that the Israeli government wants people to put on masks for their own safety, adding for Claude's sake, "For your safety I have to pass this on; this is confirmed." What seems so odd about this exchange is the implication that the gravity of the situation is not serious enough to warrant concern until there is confirmation from outside Israel of events going on in Israel; Alex Claude need not take Israeli radio too seriously, even though he heard the government directive with his own ears, which is the basis of his report to CNN.

At this point—which is typical of how information gets conveyed on CNN in the course of the live war coverage—the information feedback loop seems dislocated from the sites of action that it supposedly references. The reporter's peril does not become critical until the U.S.-based experts confirm and recite the information that is already in wide circulation at the site in question. Throughout the evening, the Israeli-based correspondents convey information derived from Israeli media announcements that is subsequently confirmed from other sources, such as the U.S. State Department, which is getting its information from Israeli diplomats (who in turn get their information from the Israeli government, which is also making public announcements on Israeli radio). Often, the U.S. confirmation ends up reiterating material that originated at the same source as the Middle East–based reporter, who got the information more quickly because of being on-site.

The proliferation of information takes all reports seriously at the moment of their presentation; otherwise they would not be shown in the first place. But the accumulation of information, especially the ability to confirm and reconfirm through U.S. sources, constitutes the meaningful authority of CNN reportage, even if those sources get their information from the same place as the initial report, including the CNN reporters based in the Middle East. Recirculation and repetition of information over time constitute the truth of the material thus presented. But in the process the validity of all statements in their own right is weakened. The quantity of information flow and its international circulation—including through the center of the system (the Washington, D.C.–Atlanta axis)—combine to confirm the place of CNN in the final analysis, whereas individual reports do not carry much weight on their own.

An even more elaborate exchange involving intrepid reporter behavior and (U.S.) anchor–(Israeli-based) correspondent misunderstanding takes place between Lou Dobbs and Larry Register, CNN bureau chief in Jerusalem. Register, who is in the CNN offices in Jerusalem, explains to Dobbs that the Israeli civil defense has alerted everyone to put on gas masks and go to a sealed room: "I am ignoring that order for now." U.S.-based Dobbs asks him to point the camera outside the window, and Register protests that he does not want to open the window—which Dobbs presumably never intended in the first place. Dobbs emphatically recommends that he *not* unseal the window but asks him what he sees outside it. "Nothing unusual," is Register's reply. Dobbs persists in asking Register what he sees outside while urging him not to open the window. Register concludes that Dobbs's questioning is an interest in seeing—via camera—what is going on, even though he has already suggested that there is nothing much to see.

Register starts to put on his gas mask so that he can safely unseal and open the window; in the process he removes his earphone, so he cannot hear Dobbs insisting that he *not* open the window (which he is opening because of Dobbs's repeated questions about what is going on outside).

Over the course of the next hour, extensive time is given over to watching the Jerusalem CNN crew, including ongoing discussion with the reporters, in gas masks, in their offices. The scene of the Jerusalem newsroom also plays as the video background to discussions with other correspondents and experts in the United States. Maintaining these images on screen is a reassurance that the office in Jerusalem has not been the target of a missile attack and that the reporters are all still fine. At the same time the image, which eventually becomes familiar in its noneventfulness, also carries a reminder that Israel is under attack and that CNN is ready to jump to that story at any time. In addition, the Jerusalem news bureau, with reporters and crew sporting gas masks, is a reminder of the risk that the correspondents are taking to both *tell* and *be* the story. Perhaps more than the previous evening's live reporting from Baghdad, the ongoing transmission of the CNN Jerusalem office transforms the office itself into the site of war, displaced from the locations in Israel where Scuds have fallen.

This is underscored when, in the course of the evening's reporting, CNN's expert from the Center for Strategic Defense is adamant about the Israeli correspondents' need to follow guidelines for their own safety. "The people in Israel *must* close the window and put on gas masks. They must follow instructions. For," he notes, "if the missiles have nerve gas, it will work in a matter of seconds." This follows Register's earlier description of the protective measures at hand, including the sealed room one floor below that can be reached in twenty to thirty seconds, chemical suits, and atropine: "We can take care of ourselves." Later, the U.S. anchor affirms, "The Israeli Ministry is in a state of war alert now. CNN is the only outside source of information in Israel at the present time, we are told."

In the middle of all of this, another CNN reporter in Israel, Linda Sherzer, also participates in the ongoing discourse of reporters' bravery in the face of increasing risk and peril. She tells about hearing of the war alert by phone, and subsequently by radio, with civil defense orders to go to sealed rooms and put on gas masks. Immediately after this she arranged to have a CNN driver pick her up and bring her to work. The streets of Jerusalem were nearly deserted, and "whatever cars were on the streets were racing to get to their home and their sealed room." She is an obvious exception to this; the possibility that the people she saw on the street were also racing to work—in news, military, or medical organizations, for example—is never raised.

Without being explicit, she elevates herself for outstanding heroism, above and beyond the call of duty, in getting the story—of her bravery in flouting an Israeli government order and daring to go out on the streets during a civil defense alert—on CNN for the viewing public outside Israel.

Israeli television itself was included within the image of the CNN Jerusalem office. The place of video (and audio) transmission as the guarantee of security was thereby assured. On several occasions Larry Register turned his monitor to the CNN news camera and elaborated in some detail on what was being aired. The fact that the Israeli government video signal is intact presumably provides the certainty that whatever damage the country has sustained from the Iraqi attack is contained. The threat implied by the loss of the television signal is repeatedly played out during the course of CNN reporting, multiply embedded in the Jerusalem bureau footage that stayed on CNN for more than an hour.

Indeed, throughout the first nights of the war, frequent temporary lapses in the connections with Baghdad, Tel Aviv, Israel, Dhahran, and so on, typical of live long-distance feeds, inevitably and tacitly carry the threat of annihilation. Almost every time a connection is lost, the U.S. anchors immediately assert that "it doesn't mean anything bad has happened to those people." In other words, the immediate implicit assumption, however faulty, is that a missile or bomb has fallen and wiped out the correspondent or the apparatus of transmission, or both; this is so predictable a response that the anchors have to call attention to it in the form of a reassurance to the viewers, a reassurance that may stimulate the very anxieties it presumably aims to allay. There are multiple precedents for the connections viewers and anchors may draw between loss of signal and fatality, including the San Francisco earthquake in 1989, and Tiananmen Square in 1989, where significant killing of the demonstrators only began after media coverage was curtailed.

In this way the ongoing video signal itself assumes the weight of reassurance—even if the image is one of destructive force, or of the video/computer-simulated "bomb's eye" views that were afforded as the war proceeded. In a context in which the loss of the television signal carries the greatest cause for alarm, even images of destruction have the capacity to reassure viewers that everything is okay. The institutional authority of CNN is guaranteed by video presence, including the live on-the-scene reporters, who put their lives/images at risk in order simply to be there—in case something, or nothing, happens. The sounds and images of not much happening are precisely the security that all is going well, even as they imply the potential for something awful to happen. Live coverage is also one way that television, especially electronic journalism, establishes the historicity of events.[13] These various forces combine to explain why so much time is devoted to reporters telling us that they just came out from under the bed, describing the empty streets of a city in the dark, or explicating the slide and music being broadcast on Israeli television. Live coverage at once holds out the possibility of fatal events while sustaining the reassurance of secure lives proceeding, all in context of a larger process of ongoing historical unfolding.

In *War and Television*, Bruce Cumings writes, "The advance of American technology allowed us to sit in our living rooms and watch missiles homing onto their Baghdad targets, relayed via nosecone cameras that had the good taste to cease transmitting just as they obliterated their quarry, thus vetting a cool, bloodless war through a cool medium."[14] Yet the obliteration of the image is precisely the moment of terror for television, especially in the middle of a war, live. The site of destruction is aptly conveyed by the absence of signal, along with all the fear that generates. This is repeated through the course of CNN's early coverage, in Baghdad, Tel Aviv, Jerusalem, and Dhahran. CNN's historic success is to have remained on the air—as the war proceeded offscreen, site unseen—producing information according to the logic of simulation.[15] What is perhaps most striking about the live coverage is its fundamental banality, as reporters who were confined to rooms located within the war zone readily filled the time with news of their own activities.[16]

From the outset, CNN's coverage of the Persian Gulf War brought banality and fatality into direct identification, as audiences were treated to the banality of obsessive live coverage of the activities of the network's own reporters while, offscreen, elsewhere, the fatalities mounted. The war was no catastrophe, confirmed by the very fact of its ongoing coverage. Only the loss of signal threatened something more dire; and anchors jumped in to assure viewers that this was not necessarily an indication of fatalities occurring in the unseen site of reporting.

Notes

1. Patricia Mellencamp, *High Anxiety: Catastrophe, Scandal, Age, and Comedy* (Bloomington: Indiana University Press, 1992), especially 75–151; Mary Ann Doane, "Information, Crisis, Catastrophe," in *Logics of Television: Essays in Cultural Criticism*, ed. Patricia Mellencamp (Bloomington: Indiana University Press, 1990), 222–239.
2. Bruce Cumings, *War and Television* (New York: Verso, 1992), especially ch. 4; and John Fialka, *Hotel Warriors: Covering the Gulf* (Baltimore: Johns Hopkins University Press, 1992).

3. For example, Cumings, in *War and Television,* goes into some detail on the discrepancies between events and their reporting in print and electronic journalism.

4. In *High Anxiety* Mellencamp argues that this logic of competing truths canceling each other out is characteristic of television, and she links this with the production of anxiety on an ongoing basis.

5. At the same time, the attack also forced an immediate revision of the previous night's reports that virtually all of the Iraqi Scud missiles had been successfully destroyed, retrospectively challenging one of the key conclusions of all the reporters and official government reports from the first night of the war concerning the success of the tactical, surgical air strike on Iraq.

6. This is undergirded by more complex prejudices and stereotypes that inform the treatment of the Middle East more generally, analyzed, among other places, by Edward Said, *Orientalism* (New York: Pantheon, 1978), and *Covering Islam* (New York: Random House, 1981).

   In the live coverage of the onset of the war, some of this is also played out in the distinction in dress codes between the CNN reporters reporting live from the Middle East and those in Washington, New York, and Atlanta. The reporters based in the Middle East are dressed far more casually than their counterparts in the United States.

   This difference, and the overidentification of some of the star reporters with the quixotic instability projected onto the Middle East, may account for the inability of the correspondents to sustain their appeal/credibility (and even jobs) once the war ended. This is particularly true of NBC's Arthur Kent, dubbed "scud stud" in the midst of hostilities. He may have been a leather-jacketed icon for the duration of the war, but he has not sustained the star appeal within the news community initiated during the war.

7. Details about the reporting are based on viewing tapes of the CNN Gulf War coverage held by the Marjorie Iglow Mitchell Media Center at the Northwestern University Library. The sequences directly cited in this essay are based on viewing tapes #1, 1a, and 6 in the collection.

   A content and audience analysis of CNN coverage, and of British television coverage of the Gulf War, is offered by David E. Morrison, *Television and the Gulf War* (London: John Libbey & Company, 1992). Also see Barbie Zelizer, "CNN, the Gulf War, and Journalistic Practice," *Journal of Communication* 42 (Winter 1992): 66–81; Douglas Kellner, *The Persian Gulf TV War* (Boulder: Westview Press, 1992). In Dec. 1991 the *Chicago Tribune* ran a five-part series by Timothy J. McNulty entitled "Video Diplomacy" (Dec. 22–26); and the Jan. 28, 1991, cover story of *Time* was about the war, including a special article on CNN's coverage: Richard Zoglin, "Live from the Middle East!" 69–71.

8. Setting up a microphone to listen in on an event is one of the oldest tricks in radio broadcasting and was done often in the 1920–1922 period. This offers something on the order of a radio broadcasting of attractions, as an event plays itself out via audio representation for its duration: now you hear it, now you don't. The event is not submitted to analysis or narrative breakdown by a third party but performs as an audio "spectacle" and attraction for the listening audience.

9. Mellencamp, *High Anxiety,* in discussing the Persian Gulf War (pp. 120–128), talks about the paucity of images in the TV news repertoire. But however limited the range of images, CNN demonstrated a definite interest in deploying a range of images from the outset that her analysis does not capture. Otherwise, why would there have been any need to change the maps, alter the color of what was shown, and so forth? The variety, however apparently minimal, evinces a

fundamental concern with the image and helps define the minimum terms of "televisuality."

10. The *Challenger* explosion is discussed in both Mellencamp, *High Anxiety*, especially 103–107, and Doane, "Information, Crisis, Catastrophe," 229–232.

11. "Live from the Middle East!" *Time*, 69.

12. Yair Garbuz, quoted from Carl Schrag, "Q–Who Needs Dumb Jokes at a Time like This? A—We Do," *Jerusalem Post*, Feb. 11, 1991, on humor as a response to the Gulf War in Israel. In the quote, taken out of context, Garbuz, who edits a satirical newspaper supplement, is explaining how he uses humor to deal with the Gulf War.

13. James Schwoch, Mimi White, and Susan Reilly, *Media Knowledge: Readings in Popular Culture, Pedagogy, and Critical Citizenship* (Albany: State University of New York Press, 1992), 3–8.

14. Cumings, *War and Television*, 122.

15. Jean Baudrillard, *Simulations*.

16. Meaghan Morris has discussed the relation of banality and fatality in the work of Jean Baudrillard, with the media at the center, including discussion of an incident involving the loss of all information, including radio and television signals, when Darwin was hit by a cyclone. In the wake of this event, a number of rumors regarding the absence of information implicated the presence of a functioning radio tower on an officially unauthorized American military installation near Darwin. For elaboration of these issues, see her "Banality in Cultural Studies," in Mellencamp, *Logics of Television*, 14–43.

SEEING THROUGH
THE HOME FRONT

The War for Social Consensus

One of the necessary components of U.S. government preparation for the Persian Gulf War was the insurance of a united citizenry behind the war effort. As secretary of defense under Ronald Reagan, Caspar Weinberger stated that the United States would not enter into another war without the backing of the American people. The way that Weinberger presented this point implied that such support should preexist any military engagement. In contrast, the essays in this section suggest that current military engagements take as part of their activity the manufacture of such support, primarily through media images and narratives. In other words, the existence of a social consensus in support of a war is not assumed *before* a war is undertaken but produced *as* preparation before the war gets underway.

As the following essays show, one of the most successful means for producing such consensus is through the "other" television—situation comedies, soap operas, talk shows, sports telecasts, and personal stories within the news format. But while such seemingly supplementary discussions might seem to have been present in earlier wars through public meetings, magazine stories, theater, and other public forums, these authors suggest that the apparent division between "news" and "non-news" during the Persian Gulf War has broken down in ways that helped to make the war more acceptable to the U.S. public. These authors highlight the use of melodrama as a genre that interprets events through personalized and emotionally charged narratives; in doing so, they suggest that what might previously have been a marginalized genre—what some critics even dubbed a "woman's genre"—has become the primary means of expression in television today. Most specifically, they argue that the Persian Gulf War was portrayed to the U.S. public in the individualized, personalized, and emotional terms of the melodrama—whether "non news" or "news"—and that it was precisely this way of presenting the war that made such widespread support for the war possible. By focusing on individual feelings rather than on institutional pressures or historical influences, the war came to seem more a matter of "supporting the troops" than of debating whether the United States should continue sanctions, what role the U.S. government played in building the Iraqi military during its war with Iran, or the history of Iraq's relations to Kuwait and other Arab nations.

Ella Shohat's essay, which was written during the war, offers an overall assessment of the role played by the media in manufacturing war support. She is particularly interested in the depictions of Saddam Hussein as another Adolf Hitler and in the representations of the Jewish community in the United States as if it were homogeneous and shared only one opinion about the war. Her analysis of the media points to how "this kind of mass-mediated discourse discards political analysis in favor of melodramatic imagination of good vs. evil."

Dana L. Cloud explores one facet of this "melodramatic imagination" in her analysis of media representations of military family support groups. She shows how one aspect of social consensus was constructed through the use of military families as emblems for citizens' responses to the war. In particular, she argues that the portrayals of family and community support for troops served a therapeutic function for the nation as a whole, helping to dissipate anxieties about the death and destruction of warfare.

Robyn Wiegman takes these observations back to the news format by showing how the news programs were complicit in uses of personalized narrations of the war. Whether through the explicit focus on individual journalists' experiences or through the use of the interior space of the newsroom set in the place of actual war footage, television collapsed the public dimensions of national warfare into the realms of the personal and in so doing constructed a "narration of geopolitical crisis as private and domestic." Wiegman argues that this reconfiguration of the public and private spaces of war assisted in an overall project of redefining a masculinity that was destabilized after the Vietnam War and made it possible to "externalize the crisis of masculinity into a cosmic struggle for moral order," the kind of battle for "good vs. evil" that Ella Shohat identified.

Lauren Rabinovitz builds on the gendered distinctions made by Wiegman in her essay, but where Wiegman is interested in the reconfigurations of masculinity through the war, Rabinovitz is concerned with how television constructed a "feminized" patriotism that could be used to mobilize the support of women viewers for the war. Particularly, Rabinovitz argues that the plot elements, story lines, and stars of soap operas—a television genre generally geared toward women viewers—"became generalized to other genres as the chief means through which to understand the war." In this context, she analyzes both a "feminine" genre—the sitcom *Major Dad* and its episodes about the war—and a "masculine" genre—the Super Bowl and its 1991 halftime entertainment show. Rabinovitz argues that such feminizations of television references to the war served not only to make the war more acceptable, as

Dana Cloud suggested, but also to diminish any opportunities for the expression of dissent from the presumed popular support for the war.

Each of these essays argues, then, that the Persian Gulf War did not have a preexisting public support but that such support was produced as a form of national consensus through the use of media, particularly that media form that most pervaded the "private" space of the home—television.

Ella Shohat

The Media's War

From the very inception of the Gulf Crisis, the dominant U.S. media failed to fulfill the role of independent journalism. Instead it acted as public relations for the State Department, assimilating the language, terminology, and the assumptions of the administration, thereby undermining any critical perspectives upon the conduct of the war. Any attempt to discuss the media's coverage of the Gulf War must examine some of the ways in which it structured identification with the Pentagon's agenda, and the interests of an international elite.

Those of us who have been dealing with cultural theory and textuality know that readers or spectators have a hard time reading "against the grain" if they lack any alternative information, history, and contextualization. This is especially true since the only contextualization supplied was that provided by right-wing "experts." For example, the spectrum of "experts" interviewed on *Nightline* to discuss the Iraqi missile attacks ranged from right-wing Israeli official Benjamin Netanyahu, to right-wing former U.S. official Henry Kissinger, to right-wing columnist George Will, to right-wing Democrat Steven Solarz to right-wing military analyst Edward Lutwak. Edward Said, Noam Chomsky and the political and media analysts working for alternative media organizations such as Fair and WBAI obviously did not qualify as frequent invitable experts.

The media networks blatantly promote the goals of the war. Several wars have been evoked in connection with the war in the Gulf, particularly Vietnam, which was presented as a negative war. The right-wing hermeneutic reading of Vietnam was that now we should fight without "one hand tied behind our back," and its media corollary

This paper was delivered at a plenary session of the Socialist Scholars Conference (New York, April 1991), and later published in *Social Text*, no. 28 (1991).

was that the camera must be kept away from body bags, that reporters must be controlled, that censorship is necessary for victory.

After the "victory," Vietnam was cited even more explicitly as a disease that had been overcome. Dov Zakheim attacked the left in his article "Is the Vietnam Syndrome Dead? Happily, It's Buried in the Gulf" (*New York Times*, March 4, 1991). In a strange generational projection, he identified with the youth of the Reagan-Bush era to attack those sixties activists whose "salad days" in the antiwar movement are gone, simply because, according to him, the antiwar movement no longer exists. In this war we saw American pilots penetrate the Iraqi airspace, while their airplanes ejaculated their missiles over the unresisting land. By proving its mastery of air, sea, and land in Iraq, America imagines itself cured of its trauma of (destructive) impotence whose origin lay in another Third World country—Vietnam.

But the healthy war, or the positive war, paradigm—World War II—was cited more often, reflecting a deep nostalgia for the narrative of a positive war, a war more easily constructed by the dualism of good versus evil. This paradigm was used to structure an identification with "us" as opposed to "them," eliding all other narratives.

The glorification of our contemporary "allies" drew upon the positive connotations the term acquired in the context of World War II. The demonization of Saddam Hussein was particularly crucial for the positive war paradigm. CBS correspondent Allen Pizzey called Hussein "psychologically deformed" (January 24); entertainment magazines and television shows produced numerous voyeuristic projections about Hussein's putative sexual perversions, including still photos of his bunker bedroom and his harem and stories about his tendency to kill his lovers, especially those who could testify to his failures in bed. The cover of a *National Examiner* (March 12) featured "Saddam Hussein's Bizarre Sex Life: A Recent CIA Report Reveals" with an image of Hussein the crossdresser in a mini skirt. Geraldo's talk show (March 4) featured a series of experts' titillating descriptions of different systems of torture, all delivered up to an unsatiably repelled audience. Close-ups emphasized the responses of good Americans shocked by this dark-skinned cruel leader, compared to Idi Amin, Qaddafi, Noriega, and Stalin (the only European on the list). Hussein was nicknamed the "Butcher from Baghdad," and by Fouad Ajami, that Oriental who Orientalized the Orient, as "The Thief from Baghdad" (*The New Republic*). When one of the experts on the *Geraldo* show inadvertently mentioned that Hussein learned his methods of torture from the CIA and the Mossad, Geraldo responded that he hoped it wasn't true, and went on to engage with the fascinating perversions of Hussein.

This kind of mass-mediated discourse discards political analysis in favor of melodramatic imagination of good vs. evil, in which the presumed final physical and technological victory proves also the moral superiority of the victors. The TV anchors followed Bush in calling Hussein by his first name—"Saad'm" (the series of associations we make with this pronunciation are Satan, Damn, Sodom). How many anchors have addressed Bush as George? And if they had addressed him as George, would it not have been with friendly cues that would make him seem an intimate member of our family, perhaps our father?

Hussein was regularly compared to Hitler, and the megalomaniac occupation of Kuwait to that of Czechoslovakia. *The New Republic* went so far as to use a *Time* cover photo of Hussein, touching up Hussein's wide moustache to make him look more like Hitler. Anyone who knows anything about the style of moustaches in the Middle East knows that Middle Eastern moustaches do not look like Hitler's. And *Nightline*, of course, began a program with an image of Hussein, targeted through a gun sight, an image usually associated with police target practice.

In pointing to the ideological functions of this demonstration, I am by no means trying to recuperate the image of Saddam Hussein. To compare Hussein to Hitler, and the war in the Gulf to WWII, is to elide the fact that the Arab world, like most parts of the world (Africa, Asia and America), has been colonized by Europe, that this history and the consequences of that history are still with us. We have to remember that at the end of World War I, Britain and France divided among themselves the Ottoman empire and unilaterally parcelled up the region's inhabitants. These imperial powers decided where to draw lines in the sand in accordance with their own interests (Sykes-Picaut's Agreement)—installing monarchies and regimes which functioned as typical neocolonial powers collaborating with the interests of the old empires. They also made contradictory promises (to Palestinians and to Zionists—the Balfour declaration)—as perhaps presently the U.S. has been taking upon itself the "burden" of its "colonial motherland"— to deliver contradictory promises to different regional powers (Israel, Egypt). This crucial elision of colonial history explains why opposition to the U.S. in the Middle East could so easily be represented as the irrational, hysterical result of Islamic fanaticism. This decontextualization of events in turn helped to explain the surprise at the widespread condemnation of the bombing of Iraq, even on the part of those opposed to Hussein's regime and the invasion of Kuwait.

The analogy to Hitler enjoyed its climax with the coverage of the Scud missiles falling over Israel and the possibility of chemical warfare. Most important were stories about Holocaust survivors now forced to confront the possibility of chemical attacks, and the fact that

Hussein was armed partially by German factories. But they were always only half the story. Why was Hussein never compared to Hitler when he was armed by the U.S. and when he used chemical weapons against Iranians and Kurds? And how different was the U.S.'s use of Agent Orange and napalm during Vietnam? When TV archives provided images of the brutal consequences of chemical warfare, they used images from WWI or from the Iran-Iraq war, but never from Vietnam, where the use of chemicals continues to take its toll on both Vietnamese people and American vets.

The Hussein-Hitler analogy prolonged the historical intertext of Israeli and American imagery linking Arabs to Nazis. This link, but metonymic and metaphoric, had been a staple of didactic Israeli films (*Hill 24 Doesn't Answer, Rebels, Against the Light*) as well as of Hollywood cinema (*Ship of Fools, Exodus, Raiders of the Lost Ark*). This rhetoric has helped to delegitimize the Palestinian claims to nationhood and statehood. Hussein has thus been associated with the prospect of the extermination of the Jews. While it is true that the Scuds falling on Israel did give a certain legitimacy to this view, it remains simplistic to project the experience of Jews in Europe onto the very different context of the Middle East, where the very establishment of Israel was at least partially an exercise of power, suppressing the Palestinian counter-narrative.

The analogy insists, furthermore, on a Eurocentric approach to Jewish history. In seeing Jewish history through a Euro-American Jewish perspective, the U.S. media have presented Israel simplistically as a Western country populated by European Jews. Reading and watching media images from the Middle East, one is led to believe that there are only Euro-American Jews in Israel and only Moslem Arabs in the rest of the Middle East. One finds few images of Iraqi, Moroccan, or Ethiopian Israelis, even though Oriental Arab Jews compose the majority of the Jewish population in Israel. The elision was especially striking when the missiles hit Ramat Gan, a city well known for its Iraqi population, popularly nick-named "Ramat Baghdad," and the Iraqi-Jewish neighborhoods in the south of Tel Aviv (network reports referred to a "working class neighborhood," which is the equivalent of calling Harlem a working class neighborhood). The circulating joke in Israel was that the missile fell into the Iraqi neighborhoods because it smelled the *Amba* (an Iraqi mango pickle). This elision is especially striking, since it would presumably be wonderful propaganda for the U.S., and Israel, if Hussein destroyed those who used to be Iraqi citizens. But since Middle Eastern Jews spoil the image of Israel as a Western country, interviews were generally conducted with Israelis who speak English with American accents, and who don't look too much like Arabs.

Above all, it is the fact of Iraq's relatively good relations to its own Jews that disrupts this narrative. What was elided was the information that Iraq, until the early 50s, boasted a large and prosperous Jewish community. In many ways, Jews in Iraq had much higher positions of authority and cultural prestige, higher economic and social status, than they and other Jews from Arab and Moslem countries were ever allowed to achieve in their 40 years in Israel. The media also failed to mention contacts, in the late 80s, between three Jewish Iraqi members of the Knesset and representatives of the Iraqi government, in which one of the items under discussion was Iraqi recognition of Israel and of the Camp David accords in exchange for Israeli support in the war against Iran.

The complex histories of the Middle East, the multiplicity of ethnicities, religions, and identities, are systematically elided. As a result of the war, do Americans know more about the history and culture of their allies—the Egyptians, Syrians, Kuwaitis and Saudis? My own students seem to have only learned to read the military maps of the Middle East, at best. Colorful maps of the Middle East shown on television give an illusory sense of some overarching knowledge of the region. This political crisis led to further elaborations of the "covering the globe" trope dominant in television. On January 14, a day before the U.S. "deadline" for the Iraqi withdrawal from Kuwait, an ABC special, *A Line in the Sand*, featured Peter Jennings standing upon a colorful political map of the Middle East, as a backdrop for historical and strategic analysis. The map provided the pretext for a pedagogical tour of the recent history of the Middle East, buttressed by archival and contemporary direct transmissions from around the Middle East, in a "covering" which was both temporal and spatial. The North American narrator literally steps on, sits on and looks down on the map, thus striding the narrow world "like a colossus."

Commentary, typically, served to channel our empathies. Ted Koppel (ABC, January 21) said: "Aside from the Scud missile that landed in Tel Aviv earlier, it's been a quiet night in the Middle East." This was at a time when clearing weather allowed the Allies to increase their air attacks to 2000 missions a day. Taking sides and the structuring of selective identification, cued by the anchors' intonations and facial expressions, became instrumental in disseminating the feeling of a "just war." From the onset of the war weather reports on the Middle East employed their maps and charts to present good weather as good news, for the purpose of facilitating "sorties" (a Frenchified euphemism for carnage).

The war, presumably in the name of a victimized Arab Kuwait, has produced so much anti-Arab sentiment that most Arab grocers have taken to placing small American flags in their stores. Indian groceries

Peter Jennings "steps on" the Middle East in A Line in the Sand, *ABC News, Jan. 14, 1991.*

followed suit, since many of them are mistaken for Arabs. (I witnessed a drunk shouting at an Indian grocer next to the Staten Island ferry that the oil in the Gulf is "ours," and the Taj Mahal too. The next day the Indian grocer had a small American flag hanging from a top shelf, and a yellow ribbon was glued to the microwave door.) Jewish-Americans were also represented as more legitimate Americans than Arab-Americans. Dan Rather (CBS, January 16) interviewed FBI chief William Sessions on terrorism: "If you're an American mother who happens to be of Jewish heritage . . . do you send your child to school?" In the same interview he asked Sessions "What should our attitude toward Americans of Arab heritage be?" (Here the rhetoric of "our" includes the Jewish-American, but not the Arab-American.)

Through a series of reductions, the Jewish community has also been misrepresented by the media—only dominant Jewish organizations are assumed to be the representative of "the" Jewish position. As if there were *one* Jewish-American position, representing a homogeneity among American Jews, Susan Spencer (CBS, January 19), for example, never acknowledged American-Jewish opposition to the war. She commented "I also think from the American Jewish community that there are going to be the same kind of calls for retaliation . . . I think they're going to be absolutely united in that."

What we also saw were media reports that framed events along the lines of the war genre, thereby suturing the spectator into a familiar discourse of patriotism. News reports were introduced by logos such as "America at War," reminiscent of blockbuster movie trailers. As in ads for "soon at your local theatre," we saw a montage of scenes from the war, with the major characters (the hero/villain, and the crucial images of maps and globes). The networks clearly linked themselves to the idea of the nation in a blatant self-advertisement; they appealed to the presumably patriotic sentiments through logos of popular images from the war: soldiers with guns, "the points of light" over Baghdad, camels and Bedouins in the desert. These television logos were accompanied by martial music presided over by the classical male voice-over of authority and truth in the cinema: "America's Watching ABC . . . More Americans get their news from ABC than from any other source" and "Never is information more crucial to democracy than at times like these." These ads, which capitalize on war, promoted war and legitimized war.

Hussein as the villain, Bush as the hero, and the U.S. rescuing the victim is typical of colonial narratives. It's no accident that the metaphors of "the rape of Kuwait" were used, as were the circulating rumors about rapes performed by Iraqis against Kuwaitis or the insinuation of the possible rapes of American female soldiers by Iraqi captors. (Little has been said, of course, about the sexual harassment of American female soldiers by their male colleagues.) The rescue of white or dark women from a dark rapist is basic for most colonial narratives, whose conclusions is the assertion of patriarchal and imperial world order. The historical oversexualization of Blacks and Indians continued in the image of Saddam and the Arabs. The dark rapist must be punished and humiliated, supposedly in the name of the raped victim. The civilizing mission involves precisely teaching a lesson to the dark man who dared to disobey. Bush, as an imperial pedagogue, made an effort to "teach Saddam a lesson." (Perhaps this is what he meant when he promised to be the "Education President.") Often this order of things was sanctified by God. In the film *The Birth of a Nation*, the punishment of the Black rapist, celebrated by white supremacists, is blessed by a superimposed figure of Christ, an image echoed during the war in popular journalism. The sensationalist magazine *The Sun* (March 19) featured an exclusive report on "Desert Storm Miracle: Jesus Appears to Our Troops in the Gulf." A colorful image of Christ's appearance occupied a full page and was "anchored" with "the vision of Jesus appeared to the troops for 5 minutes when the sky was full of bright red, yellow and orange colors." (The picture is very similar to the image at the end of *The Birth of a Nation*.) According to the magazine, Pentagon sources "refused to comment on the incident," but the soldiers themselves said that "we knew after we saw Jesus that God is on our side."

Within this scenario, another victim to be defended from the "savage" was Israel. Typically, television reports used stories about specific families whose names were featured prominently—images of "rounded characters" to promote identification. We accompanied families in their sealed rooms and even learned about the psychological effects of this war on Israeli and American children. Yet how many Iraqi children, or Palestinians under curfew, received such sympathetic treatment?

Most crucial for the geopolitical narrative of rape and rescue was the low value attributed to Iraqi lives. Baghdad was seen exclusively from the air, through the gun sights of the Allies, imagery structurally similar to that of the war movie genre and the Western. Even interviews with pilots formed part of this visual heritage. Remember the CNN close-up of a grinning pilot assuring us that "Baghdad is target rich." To top it all, CBS (March 5) reported on the atrocities committed by Iraqi soldiers on animals in the Kuwaiti zoo. The camera even zoomed in on the wounded and crippled parts of the bodies. To this day, Iraqi civilian casualties have not received anything like the sympathetic treatment accorded to the animals in the zoo.

Dana L. Cloud

Operation Desert Comfort

During the Persian Gulf War, U.S. television news played a key role in domesticating dissent by rearticulating political outrage as personal anxiety and reconfiguring the will to resist as the need to "support our troops." The mobilization of the themes and language of psychological crisis and emotional support domesticated the home front, as images of military families quietly coping with the threat of war served as the key icon for the manufacturers of appropriate public response.

News stories from national magazines to CNN defined questioning and protest of the war as harmful to the U.S. social body. Protest was labeled a social disease, a resurgent epidemic of the "Vietnam syndrome." Over and over again, news stories in print and on television suggested the mystical argument that troops were killed in the Vietnam War because of a lack of unified support on the home front. Any voice of protest—and any news story covering that protest—was accused of being somehow complicit in the possible death of the troops in Desert Storm. The rhetorical cure these texts offered for the Vietnam Syndrome was silent coping and emotional unity along with support not only for the troops but for the war effort itself. The framing of responses to the war in terms of emotional support represented a therapeutic displacement of political energy, effectively cordoning off and muting the voices of opposition to the war, thereby protecting the fragile social space from the anger of protesters.

This strategy depended on a particularly gendered mapping of the home front. During this and other U.S. wars, the discourse of family support for the troops feminized and personalized the "home" front. Gender divisions in society and their reinforcements in ideological texts are deployed during wartime to mobilize uncritical support for the war effort. The maintenance of prowar interests thus depends

Family support for the troops feminizes the home front.
*(*Time, *Jan. 28, 1991)*

on a particular definition of feminine support and domestic space. As women and families are constructed within support roles, a potentially divided and conflicted country is also "domesticated."

This essay shows how a pattern of initial anxiety and critique of the war in news texts was answered by themes of comfort and consolation. Most widely watched news texts moved from reporting moments of incipient political critique to encouraging personal, emotional avenues for the expression of anxiety. This rhetorical move constituted the nation as a unified family supportive of the war. During the war, "coping," "waiting," and "healing" were the watchwords of families with members stationed in the Persian Gulf. Stories depicting families—especially military wives and children—were ubiquitous before and during the war, occurring for the most part at the end of television news broadcasts, seemingly in direct answer to anxiety-producing coverage of war technologies, tactics, casualties, and protests. Almost without exception, coverage of troops' families began with statements of ambivalence, anger, and opposition to the war on the part of the interviewed family members. By the end of each segment, however, the interviewees had resigned themselves to coping with their fears and helping others to do the same.

More than consoling the interviewees, support group news during the Persian Gulf War consoled the nation as a whole. These stories, I argue, effectively personalized the political in a therapeutic discourse that contained widespread unrest and resentment toward the deployment of U.S. troops. The themes of therapy—consolation, coping, support, and adaptation—translate political problems into personal and emotional terms. During the war, this discourse worked to moderate the antiwar edge of "harder" coverage (of danger, prisoners, protests, and the like). "Support group" stories contained and recuperated news about antiwar protest through their placement in the broadcasts and their invocation and reinflection of the history of the U.S. "defeat" in the Vietnam War. Because therapeutic themes and motifs acknowledge unhappiness and anger while encouraging personal solutions to problems, they are ideal for the expression and containment of "disease" in popular culture.[1]

Personalized News

Personalized news refers to the attempts of news producers and writers to link national and international events to the "real" lives of individuals in their hometowns. Normally this kind of news serves to "wrap up" the day's events in cheerful stories at the end of the broadcast, to leave the listener or viewer with a pleasant sense of security.[2] Personalized news is one way in which news producers structure information about opposing interests and events into narrative forms, making illegitimate any opposition to the basic assumptions of liberal capitalism.

Since its emergence in the middle of the nineteenth century, this form of news has been symbolic rather than informational, designed to achieve audience identification with certain national values in dramatic form.[3] The human interest story is a key component of "wrapping up" a news segment or broadcast featuring social discord. It can serve to restore a sense of unity and coherence, providing a "solution" to the problems posed in the text's earlier moments. The problem with this kind of news is that it suggests that the resolution of social problems lies in individuals rather than on the structural or political causes of problems. This individualistic and personal focus can work to persuade people that they do not need to work politically for social change as the solution to social problems.[4]

Personalized news was a pervasive component of Persian Gulf War coverage, portraying ordinary families coping with the stress of war and taking personal responsibility for getting through the crisis. Family support stories at the end of national news broadcasts served to "wrap up" earlier news about the war (and opposition to it) in a neat, clean package with a yellow ribbon, putting a tidy end to dissent and disunity.

Yellow (Ribbon) Journalism

Reassuring family support stories seemed like a direct response to war-induced anxiety. "24-Hour War Coverage Makes Viewers Anxious," proclaimed one headline.[5] The news described how military families sometimes avoided footage of combat and favored the suggestion that the news be totally blacked out because of fear of trauma.[6] The day after the war began, the *New York Times* interviewed marine wives. One said, "I try not to watch the news. It disturbs me too much." Another agreed: "I don't watch the news. . . . I do not pretend to understand what makes the world tick. I know only how it affects me."[7]

Around the country, support groups (numbering in the dozens in each major metropolitan or military community) sprang up to help people deal with the emotional stresses of war. While the groups themselves consoled the individuals and the families wracked with worry, news coverage of support groups and family crisis—or yellow ribbon journalism—served to console the nation as a whole. Two important patterns emerge in this coverage. First, although some men were left at home to care for children and wait for the return of the troops, the stories (except a few investigating single fatherhood as an anomaly) focused on stressed-out women (military wives) and children. Second, in the accounts of these families, a dialectic of anxiety about the war and therapeutic solutions to that anxiety plays itself out. Operation Desert Storm is answered on the home front by "Operation Desert Comfort."[8]

Many military families were critical of the war.[9] A national organization called the Military Family Support Network (an antiwar group of military families) had 136 chapters and 6,500 supporters at the height of the war.[10] While many military support networks refused disturbing political debate in favor of comfort strategies, the MFSN located blame for stress with public, political factors rather than interpersonal ones.

But the MFSN and the coverage of its particular version of "support the troops" rhetoric were not featured in the popular media. Some articles from the war pointed out that if the war were to become drawn out and bloody, support for Operation Desert Storm would wane. However, most stories were structured around the principle of ameliorating anxiety and finding ways to cope. Personal conflict over the war was the dramatic crux of military family news coverage; personal solutions made for a comforting (and rhetorically effective) denouement to the drama. For example, an account in the Baltimore *Sun* of a military support group reported initial anger toward the war but went on to say that the group was composed of both war supporters and war opponents.[11] "But whatever their differences," the article continued, "these groups share a common goal: helping people cope with the lone-liness, fear, and frustration that comes from separation from loved ones."[12] This passage marked the transition to suggested strategies for coping with the stress of war: swapping information, "getting things done for others," avoiding television, and talking about their fears. The article concluded with a list of support groups in the Baltimore area. A list of antiwar organizations was, predictably, absent.

This article was typical of most coverage of support groups in its movement from anger to coping, its emphasis on women, its plea for therapeutic unity between anti- and prowar citizens, and its assump-tion that women work through anxiety by helping other people rather than acting on their own behalf. In many of these articles, protesting the war is upheld but trivialized, on the one hand, as just another cop-ing strategy (a way to "pretend" that one has some control over events). On the other hand, protest is articulated within the context of family support news as just another source of stress.

The inclusion of war supporters and protesters under the um-brella of "support" was a common framing device during the war. Sup-port for the troops is an ambiguous construction, often becoming equated with support for the war. The rhetorical upshot of the impera-tive to community support is that we must be so careful of one an-other's feelings that politics is out of bounds at such a meeting. In other words, when political issues are framed in emotional terms, outright criticism and dissent are excluded in favor of nurturing and protecting others from potential critique. "Support"—translated to mean un-critical acceptance of existing conditions and one's ultimate pow-erlessness to do anything to change them—is the order of the day. The function of the therapeutic is to nullify anger and to silence de-bate in the context of an emotional mutuality that precludes political discussion.

The focus on women and especially children played a large part in this work. Articles on how to talk to children about war and death, respond to their questions, and deal with the absence of one or more parents proliferated in the press. In response to what was called a "na-tional collective anxiety attack,"[13] the press advised adults and chil-dren alike to do two things: unite and adapt to the situation. One psychiatrist advocated the wearing of yellow ribbons as a signifier of group identity.[14] The psychiatric discourse invoked in the popular news deployed therapeutic motifs of consolation and identification in order to encourage adaptation to the crisis rather than protest against it. In addition, readers were encouraged to find comfort in the private sphere rather than take public action. The obsession with children's needs during the war thus might be regarded as an attempt to render the entire home front docile and childlike, seeking comfort and refuge from the war. Like the press, television overall took the therapeutic advice of one reporter to "temper reality with reassurance."[15]

Television's Cure for the Vietnam Syndrome

The therapeutic went national as television news and national newsmagazines picked up and ran with coverage of families coping with war stress. *Newsweek* divided its war news into "Desert Storm" and "The Home Front," the latter devoted to news about protests, media coverage analysis, opinion polls, and—last but not least—coverage of military families coping with the war. *Time* employed a similar format, as in a story about a peace activist who had changed her mind and joined in the community "support the troops" campaign.[16]

Photographs or televised images of tearful goodbyes and anxious families huddled around the television further personalized the experience of war. Coverage of families supporting the war followed and reframed coverage of protests, emphasizing the need for emotional unity so as to avoid another Vietnam War. As Steven Roberts put it in *U.S. News & World Report,* "Vietnam etched an indelible pattern on our identity, fragmenting our families and poisoning our patriotism."[17] His article featured young prowar activists who have ostensibly gotten over the cynicism and shame of the Vietnam War era and can rally around the flag in good conscience. National pride and emotional support for the troops function in this kind of coverage as therapy against the Vietnam syndrome.

In February, *Time* covered the construction of an enormous human flag in San Diego, under the headline "Land That They Love: Patriotism and its symbols dominate the debate over the Gulf war as both sides emphasize concern for the soldiers and for the fate of the nation."[18] The reporter writes, "There is a measure of atonement in this by a country that treated Vietnam veterans with unjustified contempt."[19] This passage identifies what was so compelling about "support the troops" rhetoric: it served the therapeutic function of assuaging national guilt in the wake of the Vietnam War.

Television newscasts were blamed for reinvoking Vietnam War–related anxiety. "Just watching the war is stressful," and "War takes toll on TV viewers," rang the headlines.[20] Meanwhile, President George Bush and Vice President Dan Quayle kept insisting that Desert Storm would not become another Vietnam War.[21] Persian Gulf War presidential and news versions of the Vietnam War continually suggested that lack of support was a major cause of the "failure" of the U.S. troops in the Vietnam War. In this revised historical account, the media were partly to blame for bringing vivid scenes of the horror of war before the U.S. public. If reporters of the Persian Gulf War were to escape blame this time around, they needed to "temper reality with reassurance."

During the first week of the war, one *Newsweek* article noted the eruption of a dedicated antiwar groundswell once fighting began.[22] The article went on to say how peaceful and mainstream most antiwar protesters were, labeling the ones who did not approve even of sanctions "conspicuously more radical."[23] This strategy attempts to define the outer margins of acceptable dissent and, as in other similar stories, warmly accepts antiwar activists who still wave the U.S. flag and pay emotional lip service to the "support the troops" mantra.

The article reported that 57 percent of Americans wished that all protests would stop. To drive that suggestion home, an additional short article ran within a box inside the protest coverage with the headline "'One Big Family' in Crystal Springs."[24] Its subject was a city with 160 of its residents stationed in the Persian Gulf. The article emphasized the community's support of the troops, the administration, and the war. Despite the anxiety over the possibility of the soldiers' deaths, people in Crystal Springs bonded together for "strength and solace" and "words of consolation."[25] Crystal Springs was a town "poised to pay the price for the war in the Gulf."[26]

The juxtaposition of a unified "family" alongside the condemnation of protesters makes an implicit argument. In contrast to the "family" of Crystal Springs, antiwar demonstrators, by implication, lack "strength and solace." They are constructed as outsiders to the national community enacted in the media and are rhetorically scapegoated for the anxieties and risks attendant to the war. Such stories constitute ritual expulsion of dissent and difference. The war and discussion about its merits are subjects reserved for the domestic space of the community-family, a space in which consolation is more appropriate than dissent as a response to the crisis.

According to a Tyndall Report study, the television networks (including CNN) spent more time (measured in minutes) on "yellow ribbon" stories (focusing on domestic support for the troops) than any other war-related news stories in a ratio of almost two to one.[27] The Gannett Foundation explains this as a consequence of a similar rhetorical ploy in presidential discourse: "The President united the country under the umbrella of support for the troops [in his State of the Union speech] rather than seeking to win over skeptics to his approach."[28] Todd Gitlin and Daniel Hallin have argued that local nightly news emphasized support groups and rallying around the flag in an effort to build community morale and support for the war.[29] Between November 1, 1990, and March 17, 1991, the three primary networks (CBS, ABC, and NBC) ran a total of 115 stories about the families of troops

Family support story. (U.S. News & World Report, *Jan. 21, 1991)*

and domestic support for the war during the evening news (ABC, 36; CBS, 34; NBC, 45).[30]

These stories always ran after "harder" news about troop deployments, battle developments, casualties, and prisoners, and—most important—after news about antiwar demonstrations or criticisms of the war. For example, an NBC reporter interviewed a black soldier eating his Thanksgiving rations. The soldier criticized the racism of the military, noting that the nation's wealthy would not be fighting this war and that military service is often the only option for blacks seeking their way out of impoverished ghettos. This critical story (occurring twenty minutes into the newscast) was followed immediately by a family support story, in which a (white) military wife expressed her support for her husband via satellite video.[31] Similarly, stories about support groups, goodbye parties, and family reunions also framed stories about medical readiness for war, U.S. hostages—and Vietnam War flashbacks.

Like the other networks, CNN juxtaposed yellow ribbon therapeutic news with hard news—but around the clock in continuous newscasts that recycled story after story about support for the troops on the home front.[32] The sheer number of such CNN stories is impossible to know. According to CNN archivist John Robinson, stories with themes of family support groups and the psychological effects of the war were so numerous as to render a thorough database search unwieldy.[33]

In Every Hamlet, It's a War of Emotions

A close examination of two representative CNN slips from January 26 and 28, 1991, CNN *Headline News* introduced into its rotation a segment about a black family in Houston with thirty of its members stationed in the Persian Gulf. Pearlie Cooper, the mother of several of these soldiers, is first shown in a close-up, saying, "I really feel sad. It's just too high a price to pay." Throughout the story, family members express critical attitudes toward the war. Bettie Cooper, a young woman (presumably a sister or cousin) makes a case against the war from a black perspective:

> *Bettie:* Now they're over there in a bad fix. They're scared, wondering whether or not they might not be coming back home.
> *Andrea* (brief close-up): I wish they hadn't joined the army.
> *Bettie:* And they say they don't want to go over there and die over nothing they don't have anything to do with or know anything about. . . . We're over there fighting a war and when we come back here we're fighting civil rights! It's like we're on the front lines out there, and that's not fair.

Bettie's opposition is reinforced by the CNN correspondent who provides background in a voice-over, "Like the rest of his enlisted relatives, Ronnie Johnson and his brother Russell joined the army. They wanted a job, the money, and a free education. Their sisters . . . now regret it." During this summary, the camera pans a photograph of all the members of the Johnson clan currently serving Uncle Sam. The image of rows and rows of solemn black faces strengthens the emerging critique. (At least one woman is visible; none of the men and women are decorated as officers.)

However, three elements of the text resist the critical edge. First, there is the reference to the Vietnam War, which occurs right after Bettie's quotation. Pearlie says, "I had several family members in the

Photographs of family members in the Persian Gulf.

Vietnam War, and when they came back they got no recognition whatsoever." The correspondent says, "This war could wipe out an entire generation of men in this family. [She ignores the women in the photograph; the presumption is that troops are male, supporters are female.] It's one more reason the Johnsons are ready for the fighting to end." Next, the text appeals to unity and to religion. Sherry Hawkins (another relative) says, "We're such a close-knit, tight family. All we can do now is pray and put it in God's hands, 'cause he can take care of, he will take care of us." This verbal expression of the theme of family unity is echoed here in the visuals of the segment. There are four long shots of the entire family clustered unnaturally close together, watching CNN on television. As Sherry concludes her remarks, the camera pulls out into an extreme long shot, foregrounding a dome clock, possibly symbolizing the need to wait patiently.

The brief attempts at the end of the story to contain Bettie's clearly stated critique seem desperate. The black, working-class women refuse, for the most part, to take up the faithful supportive roles required of white, middle-class women during the war. The critique of racism offered by Bettie politicizes the personal in this story in a way that significantly injures the fragile rhetoric of support for the troops.

"Doing Something for the Emotional End of It"

More often than not, however, family support news on television resembled a segment aired by CNN on January 28, 1990. Anchor Lynn Russell introduced a story about a support group in Concord, New Hampshire. Over her left shoulder (our right), a map of New Hampshire is framed in a box. Below it, in blocked capitals, appears the word "SUPPORT," itself both a label and an implicit command. The segment cuts to a scene of the town, where, as Russell says, people are "coping with the war." The story moves from street scenes to interviews with women in a mall, back to houses bedecked with yellow ribbons and American flags against a background of sparkling snow and crystal-blue sky, back to more interviews at the mall followed by a cutaway to a rural woman alone at home and then with a group of supporters, then finally to Norma Quarrels, the correspondent, who wraps the whole thing up: "On the home front, the Persian Gulf conflict is a war of emotions—as evidenced in small towns like Concord, New Hampshire."

Unlike the January 26 segment, however, the war of emotions is one-sided. Concord, as the town's name suggests, is a place of unity and mutual support, not division, critique, or conflict. All of the people in the story are white and clearly middle- or upper-class, dressed in furs or fashionable sweaters, their hair carefully coiffed. They inhabit malls and shining white suburban homes. Dissent speaks here in a lonely voice. Coral Nieder, a rural woman with two sons in the Persian Gulf, describes her initial reaction to news of their deployment: "Oh God, I wish we weren't there. I wish my sons weren't there." Earlier in the story, a token protester (a well-dressed, young white woman) walking alone in a shopping mall provides the illusion of journalistic balance: "I think we should get the hell out of there." But these statements are subject to several strategies of recuperation. Foremost among these is the appeal in both language and imagery to rural, traditional family and community values.

Introducing the story, correspondent Norma Quarrels states, "The war in the Persian Gulf is reaching into towns, villages, and hamlets across the United States, touching many lives." The choice of nouns, "towns, villages, and hamlets," evokes a rural, small-town image of people who pull together for the common good and whose sense of community has not become a casualty of modern urban life. The text constructs such a space in its choices of images of Concord and

Bow, both towns in New Hampshire. Nostalgia for community satu-
rates the text, rhetorically exhorting viewers to emulate the supportive solidarity exemplified by these small-town residents.

In one passage, the reporter makes the following statement in
voice-over: "People in Concord, New Hampshire, are doing whatever
they can to show their support for the troops serving in the Gulf. In
addition to the flags and the yellow ribbons, there are letter-writing
campaigns, and this month, pictures are being taken and sent to the
Gulf in time for Valentine's Day." The visuals accompanying these
words are a white, spacious two-story house, crusty with glistening
snow. A man shovels the sidewalk, but the camera focuses on the yellow
ribbons adorning the house and on the flag waving in the breeze. The
segment cuts to a closer view of the ribbons, yellow on white, then to a
bumper sticker on a pickup truck: "I SUPPORT OUR TROOPS IN OPERATION
DESERT SHIELD." The segment concludes with an aestheticized low-
angle shot of the U.S. flag with yellow ribbons in the foreground. The
camera, using a starburst filter, zooms in on the flag and captures the
sun glistening on the waving fabric. Later in the story, similar shots
construct a pastoral, patriotic vision of the rural community of Bow,
New Hampshire.

When the segment moves from the quiet outdoor scene to the bus-
tling shopping mall where families gather for a photo session and
letter-writing stint, we are asked to connect the positive images of patriotic domesticity with the support group effort. The woman quoted
above who speaks out against the war is shown alone, in contrast
to framing scenes that show large numbers of community members
engaged in a letter-writing campaign to the troops for Valentine's
Day. The lone woman is young and angry, whereas the support group
members are more mature, community identified, family oriented,
and respectful. The report does not tell us her name or provide any information about her identity in or attachments to this community. In
this mythic opposition of characters, protest is defined as the willful
abnegation of community spirit and belongingness.

The iconography of the photograph contributes to this process. A
common emotional ploy of support group segments is to zoom in on or
to pan across photographs (usually adorned with yellow ribbons) of
relatives stationed in the Persian Gulf, evoking a kind of emotional
connection with the soldiers and an anxiety over their absence made
present by the photos. In this story, one woman at the mall wears a
photograph of her son pinned to her chest; later in the segment, the
camera pans across the images of Coral Nieder's four sons on a wall.
Images of those whose lives are at stake could be read oppositionally
(as I think the Johnson photograph discussed above encourages us to

The pastoral, patriotic community of Bow, New Hampshire.

do). The fetishization of the absent soldier indicates a measure of anxiety over the lives of the troops and a desperate desire to have some control over the fate of those lives. In this way, photography and death are bound up with each other.

One way in which the anxiety evoked by the photographs is channeled into support for the war is through Vietnam War references. The woman who wears the lapel photo in this segment says, "They really do need our support. I don't want them to be unsupported like the men in Vietnam felt that they were unsupported." This statement precedes the brief cutaway to the unidentified woman who speaks out against the war, as if to chastise her for potentially creating another Vietnam War with her words.

Despite her initial anger at her son's fate, Coral Nieder is lauded for channeling her energy into community support work, collecting more than four hundred names of New Hampshire families with members in the Persian Gulf and organizing letter-writing campaigns. She recalls her initial reactions: "It hit me . . . during the church service that they could die. My sons could die over there. But they chose to be there and I'll back them one hundred percent." The reference to the church service reinforces the theme of small-town values. The emphasis here on the voluntary nature of military service can be read as an implicit response to the critique illustrated by Bettie Johnson, that African Americans joined the army out of economic necessity, not out of choice. But like the Johnsons, Coral Nieder resolves simply "to do something for the emotional end of it," as she says toward the segment's end.

During the Persian Gulf War, the popular news media persuaded us to cope quietly. They told us it was all right to be clients instead of citizens. "We're a support group nation," said University of Iowa professor Kathleen Farrell. "We don't talk about whether something is right or wrong, we just talk about making it through it."[34]

The imagined interpersonal harmony and emotional unity of the family are a metaphor for an ideal national consensus. But when private-sphere virtues and spaces are constructed as models for public discussion, therapy also works to close down on the perceived desirability of public debate, conflict, and change. In the private sphere, the scope of one's power as a social agent is limited to interpersonal negotiation and, ultimately, passivity in the face of structured events in the public sphere that affect our lives.

Notes

1. In this essay I develop a broad critical sketch of the family support coverage in network news, the popular press, and CNN Persian Gulf War coverage. My method has been to engage in wide critical reading of primary news sources (including the *New York Times*, the *Los Angeles Times*, various other city daily newspapers, popular national newsmagazines, and alternative news periodicals such as the *Nation*), in addition to nearly constant viewing of mainstream news coverage (particularly CNN's *Headline News*) of the war. I also consulted with CNN archivists and scanned the Vanderbilt Archives television index and abstracts to the network nightly news over the course of the war, counting the numbers of stories related to family support groups.
2. For a review of this issue and bibliography, see Dianne Rucinski, "Personalized Bias in the News: The Potency of the Particular?" *Communication Research* 19, no. 1 (1992): 91–108.
3. Harriet M. Hughes, *News and the Human Interest Story* (New York: Greenwood, 1940).
4. Rucinski, "Personalized Bias," 92.
5. Holly Selby, "Twenty-Four Hour War Coverage Makes Viewers Anxious," *Baltimore Sun*, Jan. 23, 1991.
6. Steve Scott, "Families Favor Blackout," *Dallas Morning-News*, Feb. 25, 1991.
7. Robert Reinhold, "Tensions Crackle as Reality Invades," *New York Times*, Jan. 17, 1991, section A.
8. A phrase coined by Noam Neusner, "Operation Desert Comfort," *Baltimore Sun*, Feb. 6, 1991.
9. For example, see Alex Molnar, "If My Marine Son Is Killed," in *The Gulf War Reader*, ed. Micah L. Sifry and Christopher Cerf (New York: Times Books/

Random House, 1991). Molnar first published this piece critical of the war in newspapers across the country.

10. Jane Creighton, "War at Home," *Mother Jones*, May/June 1991, 22–23.

11. Neusner, "Desert Comfort."

12. Ibid.

13. Gerri Kobren, "War on Our Peace of Mind," *Baltimore Sun*, Feb. 5, 1991.

14. Quoted in Steve Moore, "Psychologist Offers Advice on War Stress," *Pittsfield* (Mass.) *Berkshire Eagle*, Feb. 3, 1991. In the *New York Times*, Russell Banks ("Red, White, Blue, Yellow," Feb. 26, 1991) reads the yellow ribbon phenomenon differently. He suggests, "[The ribbons signify] our desire to bring home Americans who were being held against their wills in foreign lands (which, since Vietnam, is how I have regarded enlisted men and women anyhow)." Other commentators have noted that the yellow ribbon phenomenon has roots in ancient folkloric rituals of communicating with spirits, and still others date the practice from the Civil War: "Collective Conversations," *Public Culture* 3, no. 2 (1991): 138. Banks argues that it is only when the yellow ribbon gets inextricably linked to the U.S. flag and patriotism (which he argues contradicts the motive of getting the troops home) that it becomes an unequivocal nationalist symbol.

15. Suzanne Sataline, "Kids and War: Tempering Reality with Reassurance," *Hartford* (Conn.) *Courant*, Feb. 3, 1991.

16. Nancy Gibbs, "The Homefront: A First Thick Shock of War," *Time*, Jan. 28, 1991, 34.

17. Steven Roberts, "New Generation, Old Lessons," *U.S. News & World Report*, Mar. 4, 1991, 11.

18. Nancy Gibbs, "The Home Front: Land That They Love," *Time*, Feb. 4, 1991, 52.

19. Ibid.

20. Jim Calhoun and Kevin O'Hanlon, "Just Watching War Is Stressful," *Cincinnati Enquirer*, Jan. 20, 1991; John O'Connor, "War Takes Toll on TV Viewers," *San Francisco Examiner*, Jan. 25, 1991.

21. "Transcript of the Comments by Bush on the Air Strikes Against the Iraqis," *New York Times*, Jan. 17, 1991, section A; Dan Quayle, "American Support for Desert Shield: Address before the U.S. Gulf Forces, Saudi Arabia, 1 Jan. 1991," *U.S. Dept. of State Dispatch*, Jan. 7, 1991, 4.

22. Jerry Adler, "Prayers and Protest," *Newsweek*, Jan. 28, 1991, 36–39.

23. Ibid., 37.

24. Vern Smith and Annetta Miller, "'On Big Family' in Crystal Springs," *Newsweek*, Jan. 28, 1991, 39–40.

25. Ibid., 38.

26. Ibid.

27. This research was cited in Dennis et al., *The Media at War* (New York: Gannett Foundation Media Center, 1991), 48–49.

28. Ibid., 48.

29. Todd Gitlin and Daniel Hallin, "Prowess and Community: The Gulf War as Popular Culture and as Television Drama," paper delivered at the 42d annual conference of the International Communication Association, Miami, Fla., 1992, 15–21.

30. *Vanderbilt Television News Archive Index and Abstracts*, Nov. 1990–Mar. 1991. The ratio is about five stories every six days for all networks in 137 days of coverage. This count includes only those stories containing the words *family* and *support* in the same context. The occurrence of support group stories peaked at times of crisis and stress: Thanksgiving and Christmas, 1990, as the troops celebrated holidays away from home; around news of American hostages in Iraq; around news about the failure of diplomacy; the beginning of the air war; the

beginning of the ground war; and, most notably, immediately framing news about antiwar demonstrations.

31. Ibid., Nov. 1991, pp. 1976–1977.
32. At the war's beginning, a record 10.7 million people tuned in to CNN while other stations tallied losses. Nielsen ratings showed CNN with a 19.1, ABC 14.4, NBC, 13.8, and CBS 10.9 the day after the war; see *Broadcasting*, Jan. 1991, p. 23. A *Times-Mirror* poll late in the war found that 61 percent of those questioned thought CNN had the best war coverage, compared with 12 percent, 7 percent, and 7 percent respectively for ABC, NBC, and CBS (B. Thomas, "The Bad News Bearers at CNN," *Los Angeles Times*, Mar. 3, 1991).
33. Robinson made these remarks during a telephone conversation with me on July 21, 1992. Because CNN does not index its programs (and thus information is only available by commissioning a search by the professional archivists there), numerical data on CNN family support coverage are inaccessible.
34. Quoted in Les May, "UI Professor Claims TV Dictates Opinions," *Daily Iowan* (Iowa City), Feb. 7, 1991, 3A. Farrell's comments inspired this work.

Robyn Wiegman

Missiles and Melodrama (Masculinity and the Televisual War)

As U.S. involvement in the Persian Gulf turned in 1991 from the prophylactic stage of "desert shield" to the more fully invasive "desert storm," Americans waited anxiously for TV to reveal war's palpable, life-threatening reality. But from the media's endlessly talking heads to the bombs' exquisitely filmic explosions, simulation—signs of the real, not the real itself—constituted all that we could see.[1] Saturated by the visual, the referential locus of war was decidedly displaced: war became a "theater," bound not to the scene of exploding flesh but to a vocabulary of performances where antiseptic, technologized images defined and characterized a new, politically disturbing cultural rhetoric.

For various critics of the war, this new rhetoric has been understood in the context of a historical transformation from modernity to postmodernity—from enlightened selfhood to the fragmented and disunified subjectivity produced by human arrival at its own potential for nuclear annihilation.[2] Indeed, the Persian Gulf War has been called the "first postmodern war"[3]—a phrase that turns on the ascendancy of the visual and of its frantic, continuous, and ultimately hollow deployment.[4] In this, the "postmodern" is intended to mark the substitution of a visual, highly commodified cultural terrain—what critics call spectacle[5]—for the articulation and apprehension of history and its complicating meaning. As Rhonda Hammer and Peter McLaren explain, "Spectacles do not invite situating information into a context."[6] Instead, analytical depth is exchanged for the chaos of an excessive, spectacular surface.

Perhaps it is no accident that the emphasis on the postmodernity of the Persian Gulf War is often posited within a Marxist theoretical framework, where a reliance on the transcendence of history as arbitrator of truth and liberation reinscribes Marx's own faith in the dialectical inevitability of proletarian revolution.[7] For the contemporary neo- or post-Marxist, the truth of history tends to disappear beneath the ideological mystifications of late capitalism, and it is this mystification that has come to be associated with our various technologies of visual production. For Hammer and McLaren, for instance, the visual's substitution for historical analysis in Persian Gulf War representation displaces the late-capitalism context of geopolitical realignments in the post–Cold War years. For them, the imperialist agenda of U.S. foreign policy and the organization of the domestic economy that supports this agenda are repressed so that war technology can be remarketed for a world capitalist system radically changed by the demise of the U.S.-Soviet superpower duel. The Persian Gulf War thus becomes both "a *mass advertisement*" for sophisticated war technology and a warning that such technology will be deployed to defend U.S. global rule.[8]

While this explanation of U.S. economic interests in the Middle East is both necessary and compelling, the question remains: why understand the relationship between this history and the specular deployment of the Persian Gulf War as a definitive mark of the postmodern? Is radical political praxis fully dependent on the logos of history, and is this logos inherently contrary to the visual? In other words, why define the visual as antithetical to history, and why call this antithesis the postmodern? These questions excavate the logic of opposition that resides in the critical reading of the visual during the Persian Gulf War, where history and the specular are cast not simply as inherently contradictory but as mutually excluding epistemological and pedagogical modes. Where history facilitates the neo-Marxist agenda of radical praxis and revolutionary epistemology, the visual becomes the locus of political paralysis and the historical as non-sense.

Contrary to its contenders, however, such a construction of history as primary to epistemology and of the visual as chimerical and surfacial reconvenes the very conditions of modernity that critics have declared the war to exceed. That is, the denigration of the visual recreates modernity's own anxiety over truth and representation, empirical knowledge, and the visual's partiality.[9] In this process, the complex and conflicting visual production of the Persian Gulf War is reduced to a totalized visual terrain as a very modernist reliance on history as epistemology displaces both the contents and contexts of the visual in a sweeping categorical designation. To assume the visual as antithetical to history while privileging history as epistemology is not, then, to post the modern. But it is to offer a theory of the spectacle's totalized domination during the Persian Gulf War that can focus on the technologies of the visual without attending to the contexts and contents of that visual's production.

To abandon the theoretical move to totalize the visual does not discount the specular nature of Persian Gulf War representation or its articulation of a new cultural rhetoric, though it does begin to suggest a more complicated approach to the war's concentrated visual rendering. By disarticulating the visual of the Persian Gulf War from a totalized technology—what critics termed the postmodernity of the war—we can consider other aspects of war's signification within the visual, most specifically masculinity. After all, technology and masculinity are never unconnected in war, though their relationship to each other and to the visual requires something other than an argument for the spectacle's totality. That something other emerges, in this essay, as an emphasis on the contradictions within masculinity between phallic performance (the disembodied triumph of technology) and sentimentality (the narrative situating of male soldiers in domestic space) that characterized Persian Gulf War representation. Through a focus on the visual's mutual emphasis on missiles and melodrama, I hope to intervene not only in the Persian Gulf War's drive to revive a national masculinity but in the critical discourse as well, where a fascination with the visual's totality and/as technology's abstraction ultimately ignores the contextual tensions within masculinity.

By understanding technology and masculinity as co-produced in war in ways that do not render them equivalent, we can begin to situate the visual in the context of its deployment, where the codes of television are themselves understood as conducive to the war's specular effect. For even as images of the grossly exteriorized and hypersimulated masculine body of Patriot technology may survive in our memories as most compelling, the war's representation was also marked by melodrama, that stereotypically feminized narrative and visual strategy.[10] In fact, it is through the melodramatic plottings of family trauma, separation, and loss that a reluctant citizenry ultimately distinguished between the war and its soldiery in order to align itself overwhelmingly "in support of the troops." By exploring the contradiction between the masculine's rendering as domestic on the one hand and technological on the other, we can reconsider the war's visual production, not to claim for TV some radical historicizing content, but to locate meaning in an acknowledged partiality where other configurations of history, politics, and the visual can be pursued.

The End of Nam

Much of the postwar analysis of the "Showdown in the Gulf," as CBS called it, quite astutely turned to the war's significance for appeasing a national ego still overwhelmed by the legacy of the Vietnam War.[11] As President Bush declared on March 3, 1991: "We have finally kicked the Vietnam syndrome," and it is in this kicking that a renewed masculinity was rhetorically born. In discussing this born-again masculinity, Abouali Farmanfarmaian reads the memory of the Vietnam War as "castration anxiety" for "an emasculated American manhood that could only be soothed by an open and overwhelming display of prowess in the Gulf."[12] While Farmanfarmaian too baldly posits the Persian Gulf War as an inevitable consequence of psychic castration (a "manhood that *could only* be soothed"), it is clear that one of the war's stunning effects has been to lay to rest the specter of the Vietnam War. Such an effect emerges from the Persian Gulf War's orchestration of masculine performance, where the mastery of technology recaptures the heady exuberance of military domination unavailable since World War II, reclaiming the lost phallic potential of both soldier and nation by exchanging (the Vietnam War's) failed corporeality for a new technological transcendence. In this technologically excessive revolt, in this rewriting of the male body's mutability in the form of Patriot missiles and smart bombs, masculinity renounces the corporeal altogether.[13]

This is one way, at least, of understanding the missile trajectories enthusiastically presented by General Schwarzkopf, where the wreckage of bombs, both their architectural and human toll, was effectively preempted by the technology of the visual. In this performance of masculine power predicated on corporeal displacement, the disinherited sons of the Vietnam War could be seen to reclaim their rights to generational succession. But it is a paradoxical gesture of paternity, borne of technology and corporeal disinvestment, in which the masculine body is so thoroughly linked to war, it threatens to lose its centrality to the political dimensions of the everyday. In the Persian Gulf War, this threat was held in check by a variety of representational domestications of male soldiers, demonstrating at a deeper level the pervasive contradiction within masculinity in the contemporary era. Torn between warrior models of an earlier moment and the constructs of a more nurturing "postfeminist" paternity,[14] masculinity evinces an increasing difficulty to secure a unified, noncontradictory representational domain. A September 28, 1992, *Newsweek* cover photo of Schwarzkopf displays this tension. Clad in fatigues and facing the camera, his body is spliced with the caption "Just for Kids an Election Pullout."

The master of technological domination becomes a kid-friendly paternal figure.[15]

These tensions within the masculine between the body and technological transcendence are particularly evident in the representational terrain of popular culture, where the masculine identity crisis induced by the Vietnam War has most consistently played.[16] But while the late 1970s and the 1980s witnessed an aggressive recuperation of the Vietnam War soldier, transforming his mutilated and castrated body into the hyperphallicized Rambo and other muscled men, popular representation recently has turned away from this remasculinized body toward a more sentimentalized masculinity, one that is significantly able to negotiate cultural discourses of "family" that now function as containment for post–Cold War fears. This emphasis on family shifts the locus of anxiety about national decline from the specter of Communism to an interior incursion, recasting feminism, black power, and the gay rights struggle as inherently antithetical to the familial concept of "nation." In the process, representations of the Vietnam soldier and veteran, along with the history of the war itself, have been resituated: no longer dominated by the codes of an excessive physical masculinity, the war's narration is conducted within interior and psychic space, enabling the veteran to emerge as newly aligned with the nation. As Rambo gives way to Ron Kovic, we witness the shift away from what Susan Jeffords calls the "hard body" of the late 1970s and 1980s masculinity toward a more nuanced masculine interiority, a "soft body" of emotionality, inward struggle, and familial crisis and confrontation.[17]

But such a turn is not a wholesale displacement, as the representational terrain of the Persian Gulf War begins to demonstrate. Instead, the transition from corporeal phallic performance to domestic sentimental plottings reconfigures the prevailing tensions within masculinity, shifting the emphasis while retaining the logic of extremes. By looking more closely at the contexts in which masculinity's tensions during the Persian Gulf War might be perceived, we can consider televisual relations of sexual difference as they (re)produce the contradictions within contemporary masculinity.

Domestic(ated) War

If the "wimp factor" haunted George Bush during his vice presidential and presidential years, his repeated emphasis on the family as simultaneous locus of national power and national threat participated in refiguring masculinity, drawing it away from singular equations with a phallicized body and the public geopolitical sphere.[18] Located now in the domestic realm traditionally posited as the private, masculinity was cast by this Republican rhetoric as central to the stabilization of the nation.[19] If, such rhetoric implies, men could reclaim their lost positions within the home, and if women could be made to give way, then problems of urbanization, permanent poverty, homelessness, inadequate education, and unemployment would begin to fade. This is a heady order for any masculinity, where failure is equated with the feminine and where the nation's weakness is already implicitly feminine as well. But within this equation we can understand the closing years of the Cold War as part of a broad renegotiation of masculinity's meaning, as the loss of a highly scripted narrative for masculinity's geopolitical performance shifts the emphasis inward toward the domestic private sphere.

During the Persian Gulf War, the tensions within this shift emerge as central to the media coverage, as the "hard body" that saves America from Communism (and new, equally evil and foreign incursions) and the "soft body" that repairs its internal psychic landscape are forced to exist, in contradiction and complicity, within the same representational context. Media coverage of the Persian Gulf War worked the tension between these masculine performances, moving between narrative stagings of the male soldier's interiority—his loves, fears, and tears for family and friends—and the technological armature that enables masculinity to both signify and exceed corporeality itself. In this context, technological performance defines the public, while the male soldier, as the body, signifies the private interior realm. Such a constitution of masculinity negates the traditional alignment of the private with femininity by demonstrating the masculine's ability to occupy all positions within sexual difference's spatial field. Nineteenth-century articulations of the masculine as coterminous with the public and the feminine with the private sphere thus dissolve into a more complicated gender configuration.[20]

This dissolution is highly significant in the context of the Persian Gulf War, where women, for the first time in U.S. history, entered the theater of operations as combatants, threatening to undo war as the privileged location of masculinity's performance. Female integration in the military intensified the stakes of masculinity's articulation by raising the specter of a national feminization at the scene of battle, thereby undermining, at least potentially, this war's revision of the Vietnam War's failed masculinity. But it is precisely in the context of women's presence that the exteriorization of the masculine body as technology most effectively functions, enabling the fetishization of masculinity that heightens, even as it displaces, the warrior symbolics once solely attached to masculine bodies. The technological abstraction through which masculinity can now be written inexorably separates the phallus from the penis, making possible the recuperation of the domestic as more than femininity's privileged domain.[21] Interspersed between scenes of technology's Fourth of July display, media coverage presented stories of soldiers in their repetitious (and as they say "boring") domestic routines. Images of male soldiers shaving, decorating their quarters, or gazing en masse at a TV normalize the theater of phallic aggression, linking the soldier to that singular context in which civilians knew the war: the living room and television screen.

As this last comment suggests, women's integration into military service is not the sole factor in the shifting gender alignments of the domestic in the Persian Gulf War, because the deployment of the war as predominantly a televisual affair moved war itself into the domestic and located the most public performance of masculinity within the rhythms and spaces of the home. The orchestration of the United States' entrance into war on January 16, 1991, reveals the military's overt awareness of the apparatus of cultural reception: the first bombs were dropped over Baghdad at 4:50 P.M. Eastern Standard Time, thereby poised not only for coverage by the evening news but also for the full panoply of aggression to occur during prime time. As the social space in which this war was enacted and represented, the domestic sphere enclosed the so-called theater of war, becoming war's most interior and intimate space, not simply a stage for war, but the theater (albeit a private one) in which war-as-theater was played.[22] Television, then, functioned as both the simulated realm of war and the medium through which war's public machinery was interiorized, relegated to the home.[23]

By figuring the domestic in terms of both social and psychic space, the catastrophic temporality of war is emphasized through narrative interruptions of the repetitions of the everyday. For instance, the media's reliance on a domestic discourse of familial bonding repeatedly featured the soldier being torn from the fabric of cultural normalcy, family production, and heterosexual coupling, thereby marking the domestic as the primary social space in which the war was being played. In the later stages of the war, the media lingered on the family's routine, organized now around the absent figure whose potential loss defined a new, horrifying psychic possibility. How many images did we see of tearful women and children amassed around TV screens, or the less frequent, though no less important, stories of fathers maneuvering alone in the domestic scene? Through such images, familial tears and fears served as the emotional texture of war, a striking embodiment of sentience that contrasted the emptiness of technology's abstraction.

The domestic thus surfaced as locus for both loss and human reunion, the realm of death and its transcendent figuration.[24]

Given this arrangement of sexual difference in relation to the domestic, the often accepted mappings of masculine/public and feminine/private need to be rearticulated. As Persian Gulf War representation reveals, the masculine can take its place in both public and private space, thereby making definitional claims on what feminists, among others, have identified as the interiorized, feminine sphere.[25] In this context, the domestic emerges not as the difference of an "other's" interiority but as the psychic content of masculinity itself. Such a fashioning of masculinity has significant implications for feminist theory, where woman's body often serves as the sole methodological route for figuring the structure and function of sexual difference. Tania Modleski's *Feminism without Women*, for instance, understands the presence of woman as definitive to any feminist cultural criticism, thereby tying feminist resistance and theoretical analyses quite literally to the bodies of women.[26] But the refiguration of sexual difference in media coverage of the Persian Gulf War demonstrates, I think, the necessity of feminist investment in tracking the cultural delineations of masculinity, that symbolic tracing of the male body that ironically has come, in the wake of feminism, to fulfill feminism's own demand for a domestic(ated) masculinity.

Missiles and Melodrama

The implications for melodrama of this cultural discourse of masculinity are perhaps already apparent, given my suggestion that the domestication of the male soldier, physically and spatially, mobilizes a nationalist fervor and a nurturing passion for the troops. By offering the family and the crisis of its potential disruption and loss as the contextual means for evoking soldier subjectivity, melodrama writes the war for American television screens. In this, as Thomas Elsaesser explains, melodrama demonstrates a cultural refusal "to understand social change in other than private contexts and emotional terms."[27] Experience emerges as epistemologically central, relying for its truth on the emotional texture of lived extremes. For this reason, melodrama privileges the psychic contexts of suffering, fear, and the tragedy of the unforeseen. A genre critics have often traced to the social convolutions of the French Revolution, melodrama encodes an implicitly bourgeois social organization, dependent on interiority and individualization.[28] In the cinema, these bourgeois encodements give rise to strategies of visual saturation—an emphasis on facial expression and the body's movement—to mark emotional degrees. During the

Persian Gulf War, these representational strategies of melodrama became routine as a complicated process of individual and familial tragedy defined and characterized war's emotionality.[29]

But the deployment of melodrama was not limited to an emphasis on the kind of familial domestic intimacy I have discussed above, and we would be wrong to assume that such an emphasis is the only way the bourgeois dependency on the psychology of "home" can be narratively or visually wrought. In Persian Gulf War representation, the narration of geopolitical crisis as private and domestic was also figured in the nearly claustrophobic containment of action to interior spaces, as the lack of live war footage accessible to the media engendered television's subsequent, often frantic quest for visual simulation and live "feed." A key example here is the coverage offered by CNN correspondent Larry Register reporting from a hotel room in Jerusalem while air raid warnings sounded there and bombs dropped in Tel Aviv. Within a short two-minute stretch, the camera moved from a focus on Register's neck (where his gas mask met the collar of his shirt) to a cluttered desk to a mirror that reflected Register's silhouette. Then the camera turned abruptly to the window where indiscernible lights moved in the distance, and the camera operator appeared briefly, a faint image moving across the glass, which was for us another embedded TV screen. As he disappeared, the camera zoomed in on a car winding down city streets, and then, seemingly indiscriminately, it returned us to Register, his gas mask now removed while a talking head behind him mouthed inaudibly on the TV.

In this frantic movement of the camera, in this quest for some kind of visual feed, in these TV images of multiple TV screens, the fragmented overemphasis on the objects of interior space seeks to effect emotional intensity. But whether focused on the night sky or located in military briefing halls, hotel rooms, or network soundstages, television cameras more often than not could only connect us to their own—however makeshift—interiors, those spaces quite distinct from the public performance of war, those spaces where the war could only be lived (especially in its early stages) through talking heads, maps, graphs, computer terminals, television monitors, and dramatic musical crescendos accompanying network advertising themes (such as CBS's "Showdown in the Gulf" or CNN's "War in the Gulf"). As fetishes that filled the gap of our visual loss and substituted for the censored "real" of the war, these items punctuated the emotional narrative set forth by news anchors and reporters, highlighting their own panic and latent hysteria through the excessive and frequently useless reiteration of material and narrative detail.[30]

Such focus on detail, particularly the details of interior space, emotional context, and displaced visual excess, reiterates the conventions of melodrama. This is especially so as the tension between public and private finds its articulation, discursively and spatially, in the domestic realm where social and political issues are reduced to the personal and its breeding ground of the family and the familiar. As Elsaesser writes, dramatic conflict is signified by "decor, colour, gesture and composition of frame," and it is this "acute sense of claustrophobia in decor and locale" that characterizes melodrama's elaborate plotting of the interior domain.[31] But, of course, this is melodrama with a difference: for unlike the focus on the feminine often attributed to it, melodrama here revolves around the masculine and its crisis of socio-symbolic location.[32] As such, we might understand the contradictory regime of Persian Gulf War representation—where the masculine embodies the tension between public and private and serves as its primary figure of signification—as an extension of melodrama's broader deployment within the televisual regime.

In an important reconsideration of melodrama, Lynne Joyrich argues that TV fragments and proliferates melodramatic conventions, extending the focus on domestic relations into programs once considered quite far removed from melodramatic form. In particular, she cites the news, which increasingly frames its narratives in personal and individualistic terms, thereby "avoiding the larger institutional, political and ideological issues" the stories might begin to raise.[33] Through a focus on family—"the news 'family' and the families investigated," news programs "achieve the emotional intensification and moral polarization associated with dramatic serials."[34] Such an infiltration of melodramatic modes into media reportage not only underscores the logic in Persian Gulf War representation but also points to the way melodrama must be understood as a "contaminated" genre: cutting, mixing, and otherwise transforming the representational strategies often associated with it from the study of cinema.

But while TV melodrama differs by virtue of a heightened fragmentation of the genre's encodements, its central focus—figuring, as Joyrich writes, "social turmoil in the private, emotional terms of self and experience . . . reject[ing] the psyche as a realm of inner depth . . . [and externalizing] psychological conflicts . . . so that they may be clear as fundamental forces"—is nonetheless everywhere to be seen.[35] In the rhetoric of the Persian Gulf conflict, where the public performance of war found its articulation within a domestic discourse aimed at repairing the damaged masculinity of the Vietnam War, now understood at the level of the individual male soldier, we confront the overarching narrative design of a moral struggle between fundamental forces. The clear-cut marking of Bush and Saddam Hussein as good and evil and the evocation of that clarity in a discourse overwritten by sexual difference (Saddam becomes Sodom and Kuwait is "raped") demonstrate the use of the melodramatic to externalize the crisis of masculinity into a cosmic struggle for moral order. That this external-ization is wrought through conventions that rely on the psychological and spatial privileging of domestic interiors is as paradoxical as it is self-evident. Masculinity, through the melodramatic, turns inward to achieve the transcendence that defies and negates the contradictions of interiority.

One of the best examples of the Persian Gulf War as a confronta-tion with cosmic moral forces is NBC news anchor Tom Brokaw's dra-matic January 15 commentary. As the United Nations' deadline for Iraqi withdrawal from Kuwait passed unheeded, Brokaw provided the narrative of melodramatic excess that was echoed in various quarters during the opening stages of the war:

> The night has passed here in the East. So the fuse is lit. How quickly it burns toward the explosion of war will be determined by two men, Saddam Hussein and President Bush, and neither appears likely to step forward and extinguish it at this late hour. So now we await the sound and the consequences of bombs, missiles, tanks, artillery, gre-nades, and guns unleashed. We await the price of war with the combi-nation of emotions: determination, fear, sadness, confusion. We've never been through anything like this before. . . . The instant buildup of a massive force in a distant desert, the public and, ulti-mately, failed diplomacy, an extraordinary alliance of unlikely part-ners on one side and a solitary and ruthless figure on the other. This is the stuff of Tom Clancy or Frederick Forsythe novels, and at this hour it still has that quality, a feel of fiction. . . . Once the shooting starts, reality will take over. And while in fiction we can look ahead to see the tidy ending, here we cannot. We are about to experience the ter-rible truth and unknown consequences [of war].

Brokaw here offers a narrative born of melodrama, a paradigmatic in-stance in which the purely oppositional forces of good and evil come to play in a context now more fictive than real. Like all good melodrama, his narrative acts as witness to the emotional texture of war as both vision and sound, as we await the "consequences" and their promised audiovisual feed of guns and bombs. In this, he gives us the essential and noncontradictory truths that melodrama functions to secure.[36]

It is in the process of securing a stable moral order that the use of melodrama in Persian Gulf War representation can most effectively be viewed, especially as the melodramatic achieves its reassuring effect not only by collapsing the public into the private but by negotiating that collapse through the figuration of the masculine and its crisis of socio-symbolic location. The televisual war becomes *the* symptomatic moment of the complex instabilities of gender relations as they now inflect, and are inflected by, the public-private split, since it is here, in the province of war's technologically abstracted yet excessively melodramatic deployment, that the crisis of the masculine is most revealed. It is here as well that the televisual text displays its own generic instability, its reconfiguration of the elements of genre that were initially defined in light of the cinematic regime. These, then, are two of the crucial aspects of the war's structure of representation: the breakdown of the public/private shape of sexual difference and the televisual proliferation of melodramatic codes. Taken together, they are powerful means for addressing masculinity's contemporary instabilities, making possible the very contradictions of "domestic soldiers" on the one hand and "televisual war" on the other.

Persian Gulf: Take Two

When the U.S. military began bombing Iraqi civilian and military targets early in 1993, nearly two years after the outbreak of Desert Storm, the American media's interest in the story was characterized by an incredible lack of both emotional and visual intensity. Instead, U.S. attention was turned to its upcoming, homegrown visual extravaganza, Bill Clinton's inauguration, and the melodramatic import of the Persian Gulf was no longer to be seen. No doubt some critics will interpret this as another sign of the postmodernity of the Persian Gulf encounter, as the fluidity of First World interest in the region moves dispassionately between the surfacial encounters of our many consumptive, visually excessive national routines.

But there is something here that speaks not to the issue of the visual as a purported postmodern totality but to masculinity and the contents—and contexts—of its contemporary visual performance. For part of the success of Bill Clinton's candidacy (and of the Democratic campaign more broadly) emerges in its ability to refocus national attention away from the geopolitical sphere to the violence and chaos of its interior realm, where the nation's masculine performance might be said to have most failed. In this, the man who refused to support the Vietnam War—who continues to refuse to apologize for that earlier, youthful refusal—is an important emblem in the national project of reviving U.S. masculinity. Most crucially and perhaps most paradoxically, Clinton benefits from the Persian Gulf War's recuperation of a military masculinity by mobilizing for himself the cultural rhetoric of family that serves in the contemporary era to anchor masculinity to the body in the context of that body's technological abstraction. He benefits, that is, from the tensions within masculinity: the renegotiation of public and private space as well as the sentimentality attached to the masculine in the context of the everyday.

In this regard, it is quite significant that Clinton's use of the discourse of family has tended to pluralize the scope of that rhetoric's inclusion instead of functioning along the lines of the Republican right, which deploys family as a vehicle for constructing exclusions and limits. Whether we understand this pluralization as evinced by platform speeches at the Democratic Convention (where even the gay and lesbian coalition can be applauded for serving as its own deeply bonded family) or by the racial and gendered diversity of his cabinet, Clinton offers himself more as an older brother than a father figure, one who seeks, at least at the level of representation, to govern according to the new laws and rites of "postfeminist" paternity.[37] It is finally this—this incursion into the realm of interiority and the family's domestic drama—that defines the emergent cultural rhetoric of masculinity and marks the negotiatory function that the Persian Gulf War played. And while the events in the unfolding weeks of 1993 may prove me wrong, I am doubtful that U.S. masculinity needs to play again the Persian Gulf as a theater of performance with such a massive, specular display. That is an old story, one whose rearticulation of a framework for masculinity, at least for now, has been won.

Notes

1. Jean Baudrillard defines the concept of simulation as a "liquidation of all referentials" in *Simulations*, trans. Paul Foss, Paul Patton, and Philip Beitchman (New York: Semiotext(e), 1983), 4. In this framework, we might understand media coverage of the Persian Gulf War as simulating the real of the war, offering images that can only refer us to television's production of the war and never to the war itself. In this, the war "itself" becomes impossible to conceive.
2. I don't adhere to this notion of postmodernism as pivoting on the potential for nuclear annihilation, though Joyce Nelson does, in *The Perfect Machine: TV in the Nuclear Age* (Toronto: Between the Lines, 1987).
3. Robert Hanke, "The First Casualty?" *Public 6: Violence* (1992): 135. Others who cite the Persian Gulf War as postmodern or who understand the war's visual representation as the ultimate evidence of the postmodernity of contemporary culture include Rhonda Hammer and Peter McLaren, "The Spectacularization of Subjectivity: Media Knowledges, Global Citizenry, and the New World Order," *Polygraph* 5 (1992): 46–66; Rob Wilson, "Sublime Patriot," *Polygraph* 5 (1992): 67–77; Jochen Schulte-Sasse and Linda Schulte-Sasse, "War, Otherness, and Illusionary Identifications with the State," *Cultural Critique* 19 (Fall 1991): 67–95. For an important counterpoint to those who identify the war in terms of a totalized visual terrain, thereby making the theorization of resistance difficult, if not impossible, to imagine, see David Tomas, "Polytechnical Observation: An Artistic and Popular Response to Political Events in the 'Age of the Smart Bomb,'" *Public 6: Violence* (1992): 141–154.

4. The "visual" refers to the many forms of cultural representation that rely not only on a visual mode of signification but also on a visual technology, including TV, film, video, and advertising.
5. The concept of spectacle has been used within media studies in a variety of ways, from Laura Mulvey's notion of woman as spectacle to the panoramic imagery on which epic and war genres depend. What links these versions is primarily an emphasis on visual signification as the central encodement of meaning (as opposed, say, to narrative). As such, spectacle marks a reliance on visual excess. See Mulvey, "Visual Pleasure and Narrative Cinema," in *Feminism and Film Theory*, ed. Constance Penley (New York: Routledge, 1989), 57–68; Susan Jeffords, *The Remasculinization of America: Gender and the Vietnam War* (Bloomington: Indiana University Press, 1989), 1–53; and, for a consideration of spectacle as constitutive of completely alienated subjectivity within capitalism ("Everything that was directly lived has moved away into a representation" [1]), see Guy Debord, *The Society of the Spectacle* (Detroit: Red and Black, 1983).
6. Hammer and McLaren, "Spectactularization," 50.
7. As Robert Young points out in *White Mythologies: Writing History and the West* (New York: Routledge, 1990), "History" as the logic of revolution derives from the Hegelian trajectory of Marxist theory, initiated by Lukács's *History and Class Consciousness* in 1923. See Young, *White Mythologies*, 21–27.
8. Hammer and McLaren, "Spectacularization," 50.
9. Barbara Maria Stafford, in *Body Criticism: Imaging the Unseen in Enlightenment Art and Medicine* (Boston: MIT Press, 1991), reinforces the point that modernist epistemologies privilege logos over the visual by reading the relationship between the rise of modern sciences and theories of visual representation. "Optical demonstration and visualization were central to the processes of enlightening. Yet from a conceptual standpoint, images, paradoxically, were reduced to misleading illusions without the guidance of discourse" (2). For Stafford, the use of visual observation (increasingly enhanced by technological extensions of the limitations of the eye) as the hallmark of modern science pivots on the attending narrative that scientists construct to render the visual's meaning. The ocularcentrism frequently linked to modernity nonetheless demonstrates a reliance on the discursive to frame and support the visual's meaning, and, in this, modernism demonstrates a denigration of the visual as epistemology that the conversation on the postmodernity of the Persian Gulf War replicates.
10. For discussions of melodrama's relationship to femininity, see Tania Modleski, *Loving with a Vengeance: Mass-produced Fantasies for Women* (New York: Methuen, 1982); Janice Radway, *Reading the Romance: Women, Patriarchy, and Popular Literature* (Chapel Hill: University of North Carolina Press, 1984); and Robert C. Allen, *Speaking of Soap Opera* (Chapel Hill: University of North Carolina Press, 1985).
11. See, in particular, John Carlos Rowe, "The 'Vietnam Effect' in the Persian Gulf War," *Cultural Critique* 19 (Fall 1991): 121–139.
12. Abouali Farmanfarmaian, "Sexuality in the Gulf War: Did You Measure Up?" *Genders* 13 (Spring 1992): 2.
13. See Michelle Kendrick's essay in this volume.
14. "Postfeminism" is used here not as a term demarcating a social reality, but as part of a cultural rhetoric that feminists are invested in rejecting.
15. The "good daddy" image of Schwarzkopf is emphasized again in his photo just inside the cover. Here he sits on a child's twin bed smiling in a pair of shorts, an American-flag shirt, and Birkenstocks and holding two teddy bears clad in fatigues.

16. No study more thoroughly details the gender implications of Vietnam narration in popular culture in the 1980s than does Susan Jeffords's *The Remasculinization of America: Gender and the Vietnam War* (Bloomington: Indiana University Press, 1989).

17. See Susan Jeffords, *Hard Bodies: Hollywood Masculinity in the Reagan Era* (New Brunswick, N.J.: Rutgers University Press, 1993).

18. George Mariscal, "In the Wake of the Gulf War: Untying the Yellow Ribbon," *Cultural Critique* 19 (Fall 1991): 97–117, offers a reading of the "wimp factor" that moves in the direction of my essay. "[S]ome degree of 'wimpiness' (i.e., tenderness, sensitivity) was an essential component of the kind of masculinity figured during the [Persian Gulf] crisis. . . . One of the president's favorite stories from the war was the one about the U.S. soldier who gently said to the surrendering Iraqi: 'Don't worry. You're OK now'" (104). By reading the symbol of the yellow ribbon in the context of changing definitions of masculinity, Mariscal demonstrates the tie between a domestic masculinity and the phallic aggression of the Persian Gulf War.

19. I am not suggesting that masculinity was not or has never been situated within a rhetoric of family (for that is surely not true) but that this renewed emphasis during the late 1980s has to be understood as part of a broad cultural renegotiation of the contours of masculinity. It is not, then, that masculinity simply flips from one end of the spectrum to another but that its imbrication in the public/private shifts the very terms of that duality itself.

20. It is not clear, in fact, that the binary inscription of social space via gender in nineteenth-century popular discourses was ever adequate to understand the complexities of sexual difference. This is especially the case when the category of race is taken into account, as Maxine Baca Zinn, Lynn Weber Cannon, Elizabeth Higginbotham, and Bonnie Thornton Dill briefly discuss in "The Cost of Exclusionary Practices in Women's Studies," *Signs* (Winter 1986): 290–303.

21. Much has been made in feminist critical discussion of the Lacanian distinction between the penis and the phallus, where the phallus functions as signifier of the symbolic order. Jane Gallop, in *The Daughter's Seduction: Feminism and Psychoanalysis* (Ithaca, N.Y.: Cornell University Press, 1982), for instance, has pointed out the impossibility of a final separation of the terms, even as she explains the conceptual framework through which Lacan draws a distinction. In *Between Men: English Literature and Male Homosocial Desire* (New York: Columbia University Press, 1985), on the other hand, Eve Kosofsky Sedgwick finds the distinction crucial to antipatriarchal struggle, since it allows for a more nuanced approach to masculine sexualities by marking an important fissure within male homosocial bonds. For if the concept of the phallus designates the law of the father and the patriarchal symbolic more broadly, its difference from the penis makes possible political resistances on the part of men for whom having a penis is not the same as wielding the phallus. Contemporary work on masculinity often forges this distinction to avoid the essentialist equation between being male and perpetuating patriarchal power. See also Juliet Mitchell and Jacqueline Rose, eds., "Introduction," *Feminine Sexuality: Jacques Lacan and the École Freudienne* (New York: Norton, 1983).

22. But as those of us working on television well know, the metaphorics of the theater as a way of defining and describing televisual consumption ultimately eludes a crucial distinction necessary for any understanding of this apparatus: that it is precisely television's nonpublic reception that marks its technological specificity. See Lynn Spigel, "Television in the Family Circle: The Popular Reception of a New Medium," in *Logics of Television: Essays in Cultural Criticism*, ed. Patricia Mellencamp (Bloomington: Indiana University Press, 1990), 73–97.

23. Obviously, the deployment of the war in the domestic sphere is not unique to Persian Gulf War representation, since the national backlash against the Vietnam War was tied, however intimately, to the circulation of images presented on TV. But, as many others have noted, it is crucial to recognize the difference between the sanitized version of war offered by the military personnel in the Persian Gulf and the raw (though no less representationally complex) footage signifying the Vietnam War. For a further discussion of the precise means whereby the Persian Gulf conflict represents a new deployment of television, see Mark Poster, "War in the Mode of Information," *Cultural Critique* 19 (Fall 1991): 217–222.

24. See Dana L. Cloud's essay in this volume.

25. While not the project of this essay, it is also the case that the feminine reconfigures along the fault line of public and private as well, though this reconfiguration is adumbrated by asymmetries, since the public continues to function within the symbolics of phallic power. As my discussion here begins to suggest, the loosening of the public for woman's admission carries the loss of the domestic as her seemingly privileged sphere. The implications of this loss may be more significant than feminists are willing to admit, as the rhetoric against abortion, for instance, becomes more strenuous as women seek to relocate themselves within the public sphere.

26. While I am sympathetic to Tania Modleski's fears in *Feminism without Women* (New York: Routledge, 1991) about the seeming primacy being accorded to masculinity in contemporary popular culture—to which this essay is certainly a response—I do not share her skepticism that poststructuralist theory, as it has been taken up by feminists, amounts to a negation of women.

27. Thomas Elsaesser, "Tales of Sound and Fury: Observations on the Family Melodrama," in *Imitations of Life: A Reader on Film and Television Melodrama*, ed. Marcia Landy (Detroit: Wayne State University Press, 1991), 72.

28. See Elsaesser, "Tales of Sound and Fury" and Peter Brooks, *The Melodramatic Imagination: Balzac, Henry James, Melodrama, and the Mode of Excess* (New Haven: Yale University Press, 1976).

29. During the bombing of Tel Aviv, U.S. media increasingly turned to melodramatic strategies to capture the fear of the Israeli population, focusing on families in their gas masks, especially the often hysterical responses of young children. The Iraqi, on the other hand, were routinely depicted as isolated and unemotive, a kind of pure body of excess whose interiority failed to signify. In the last stages of the war, the images of the road leading to Kuwait City, with Iraqi bodies strewn across a burning landscape, often seemed to lack in narrative and detail the kind of emotional pitch achieved by the reportage of familial contexts.

30. See Mimi White's essay in this volume.

31. Elsaesser, "Tales of Sound and Fury," 76.

32. For a discussion of work that challenges the singular association of melodrama with femininity and women, see Ellen Seiter, "Men, Sex, and Money in Recent Family Melodramas," in *Imitations of Life: A Reader on Film and Television Melodrama*, ed. Marcia Landy (Detroit: Wayne State University Press, 1991), 525–537; Jackie Byars, *All That Hollywood Allows: Re-reading Gender in 1950s Melodrama* (Chapel Hill: University of North Carolina Press, 1991); and Sasha Torres, "Melodrama, Masculinity, and the Family: *Thirtysomething* as Therapy," *Camera Obscura* 19 (Jan. 1989): 86–106.

33. Lynne Joyrich, "All That Television Allows: TV Melodrama, Postmodernism, and Consumer Culture," *Camera Obscura* 16 (Jan. 1988): 132.

34. Joyrich, "Television Allows," 133.

35. Joyrich, "Television Allows," 138.

36. See Brooks, *Melodramatic Imagination.*
37. Do not mistake me here for supporting or celebrating this "postfeminist" paternity. As we have been learning for quite some time, the ability of masculinity to shift cultural significations rarely aligns it with the political interests of feminism, and it is not yet clear how Clinton's mastering of contemporary tensions within masculinity will affect the national discourse on feminism.

Lauren Rabinovitz

Soap Opera Woes: Genre, Gender, and The Persian Gulf War

Over the years, countless combat-action films have appeared about soldiers in World War II, the Korean War, and, in the last two decades especially, the Vietnam War. Even though singular films may occasionally have followed the women left behind at home—their pain, suffering, and their participation in the war effort (e.g., *Since You Went Away* in 1944 or *Coming Home* in 1978)—war fought in the domestic, private sphere is hardly the way that war has been generally historicized in the United States. At least since World War II, war has been narrativized in those entertainment genres associated with muscular action. Yet, in the Persian Gulf War, war appeared on television in a different way, utilizing the storytelling conventions, icons, and expressiveness of such feminine genres as soap opera and family melodrama. The result was a new way of characterizing war through a generally feminized media.

Indeed, one feminist critic has already argued that the feminine genres of television became so pervasive during the 1980s that their codes, conventions, and formulas subsequently infiltrated all of television's programming, time slots, and even the rhythms and vocabulary of televisuality.[1] By the beginning of the 1990s, television had generally come to depend upon those characteristics associated with feminine genres—the establishment of personal intimacy between characters; the abundant spectacle of interiors, props, costumes, and objects as consumer goods that symbolize characters' interior state of mind; and the organization of social groups, issues, and places according to rules that govern the domestic, familial realm—rather than upon the characteristics of masculine genres—the visuality of fast-paced action and plots centered upon the resolution of problems through physical confrontation and force. The production of a more feminine war occurred not only within individual television shows, programs, or segments but across types of materials and channels during any given period of viewing. It occurred in both traditionally feminine and masculine genres.

During the Persian Gulf War, the live war was on television around the clock. It infiltrated and colored the rhythms and idioms of all television programming, whether or not the individual show was directly related to the war. The process of feminization through which the Persian Gulf War was defined, therefore, can only be understood by examining the ways in which war was narrativized in both traditional masculine and feminine genres in addition to straightforward news or journalistic programming. The implications are important both for the ways that television binds national interests through the very dynamics of the medium itself and for the ways that television especially addresses its most important and broadest market of viewers, adult women consumers. During the Persian Gulf War, a more pronounced feminine agenda served a dual purpose: it sustained the normal ideological routine of television entertainment during a period of crisis, while it remade the idea of women's political opposition into feminized registers of emotionality, personal therapy, and family loyalty.

A Feminine Genre: Talk Shows

Certain television genres (soap operas, talk shows, sitcoms) and time slots (daytime) traditionally address women as a category of feminine viewers. During the Persian Gulf War, for example, the talk shows—consistently labeled "women's shows"—all featured programs with individuals who had relatives in the Persian Gulf. These covered such topics as the life of the military wife, the challenges to husbands whose wives were in the military, and dual-career military couples. During January and February 1991, *The Oprah Winfrey Show*, *Donahue*, and *Sally Jessy Raphael* allowed and even solicited angry antiwar statements, thereby holding up the talk show itself as a modern construction of the town meeting, a media performance of democratic discussion in the public sphere. Whenever a guest or audience participant made an antiwar statement on any of these programs, the show repositioned the statement in one of two ways: (1) the host or hostess immediately shifted to a discussion led by therapy experts on the importance of expressing and coping with one's personal emotions during periods of crisis or family loss, or (2) an audience member, the host or hostess, or a guest responded to any terms of *political* opposition by nevertheless asserting the importance of supporting the troops on an *emotional* level. In this manner, public debate and discussion became reconfigured within the limits of the personal, the emotional, and the ideal of a woman's nurturing role in the family.[2]

Feminizing the News

Local and national newscasts brought the highly feminine narrative of family disruption, emotionality, and therapy typical of soap operas to a conventionally nonfeminine genre. Repetitive journalistic coverage of the war offered numerous interviews with individuals who had family members in the Persian Gulf—individuals differentiated only by their geographic or regional proximity to the television spectator, by their race, or by the size of their family. Close-ups of the interviewee generally emphasized the individual's face as a visible record of struggle and emotions, often including a rolling tear or two and a tremulous voice. The individual was always located as a family member—through shots of accompanying children, siblings, and parents, or through pans or cuts to family photographs, often featuring the military enlistee—so that the war itself became repetitively defined as a melodrama of family life.

Once such parameters were established for each individual family—serving as a personalized stand-in (or synecdoche) for the national family—interviewers elicited descriptions of personal and family hardship due to the absence of the military family member. Whether or not there was explicit criticism of the war during this portion of the interview, these structured narratives always moved from introduction of a happy family to a description of loss and threat to that family to a final reconciliation—the individual being interviewed would restore temporary unity and cohesion to the disrupted family unit.

In this portion of the interview, the subject usually described local support groups of other military families; religion and the church; letter-writing campaigns, fund-raisers, buttons, yellow ribbons, and other symbolic displays of communication that signify community and the importance of supporting the troops. The interviews frequently incorporated footage of support groups, local prayer services, or other visual references to this individual's social forms of therapy. The implication was that there is a supportive community—remarkably like the fictional ones daily depicted in *All My Children*, *As the World Turns*, *The Young and the Restless*—and that individual fear, loss of control, and anger could be redirected into familial and communal groups that serve as therapeutic narrative agents for family stability.[3]

A Masculine Genre Example: The Super Bowl

Feminization of nonfeminine genres was so pervasive during wartime that it even invaded that bastion of masculine address: the Super Bowl. (This is not to say that only men watch sports and women soap operas. Quite often, the opposite is also true. But the modes of address have come to be characterized as masculine and feminine, and the commercial advertisements intertwined with these genres speak to a highly specified, idealized audience of either male or female consumers.) Unlike the soaps, televised professional and college basketball and football games were quick to incorporate the Persian Gulf War. The juxtaposition of new emblems of flags and yellow ribbons on the teams' uniforms signified that these were the warrior-heroes not only for school or geographic community but also for the state. The singing of the national anthem (already a part of sporting events but now accompanied by standing ovations and announcers' voice-over commentaries as well as team prayer huddles) brought patriotism, God, and country together into new ritualistic elements. The Twenty-fifth Anniversary Super Bowl telecast, whose January 27, 1991, broadcast coincided with the first crisis-ridden days of the Persian Gulf War bombings, especially became repositioned as a feminized spectacle by linking football and warrior glory to the family. Preparing a live telecast that would generally address the United States' war effort no matter what were the timely details of the war's events, the Super Bowl producers feverishly rehearsed the pregame and halftime entertainment in the weeks between the U.S. bombings of Baghdad and the Super Bowl for a patriotic extravaganza.

The Super Bowl's two-hour pregame ceremonies showed fans waving small U.S. flags in the stands while the players were individually introduced running onto the field through a gauntlet of leggy cheerleaders. Their individual features obscured by football helmets and padded uniforms, the players were individually marked only by the numbers emblazoned across their chests as they jerked their thumbs up in the "we're number 1" gesture seen earlier in the week when individual pilots garbed in military helmets and baggy flight uniforms returned from bombing sorties. The visual action condensed the symbols of athletic style into one iconic image: male warrior-heroes jogging through the frame of the field and recognizing the camera eye and the nature of the spectacle with a jubilant gesture of victory. Their individual identities were covered by and subsumed within that of the team uniform—here the football team uniform echoes that of the U.S. soldier. Team members were on display not only for the camera and the home audience but for an inscribed audience of

Whitney Houston at Super Bowl halftime show, Jan. 27, 1991.

enthusiastic flag-wavers, and the space or boundary between them and the audience was literally marked by a chorus line of scantily clad female beauties. In this fashion, the otherwise all-male spectacle also incorporated an idealized white, youthful female sexuality. It defined structural relations between masculinity, femininity, and patriotism while simultaneously identifying gender as the sole division along which roles should be separated and differentiated. As Susan Jeffords has argued, such a popular representation "re-establish[es] the social value of masculinity and restabilize[s] the patriarchal system of which it is a part" at a time when women's entrance into the military threatened the identity of the warrior as a means for proving manhood.[4] This spectacular organization linking traditional definitions of gender to the war occurred at precisely the moment when women's highly publicized participation in the Persian Gulf military operation was blurring and threatening traditional gender boundaries.

The explicit linkage of soldier patriots and football heroics was repeated at the end of the pregame ceremonies when pop singer Whitney Houston, dressed in a red, white, and blue sweat suit and headband, sang "The Star-Spangled Banner." Her appearance was crosscut with a montage of U.S. flags and athletic-looking, young male representatives of U.S. combat units (Marines, Army, Navy, Air Force) who stood at attention in salute. An African-American female celebrity enacted patriotism through her theatrical performance and costume, while it was the gesture and costume of interchangeable military personnel that signified their status as warrior-citizens. Whitney sings for the troops who fight for Whitney. Her singing indicated her support while it also articulated her role in the war, "to smile and sing," just as the formal portraits of soldiers standing at attention indicated their readiness, their loyalty as citizens, their physical preparedness. They were as ready for their game as the football players were for the Super Bowl. Linking the war to the beginning of the Super Bowl as an event that was offered up as spectacle for the fans in the stadium and at-home viewers repositioned the battle from the gore of the battlefield—with its destruction, dead, wounded, and displaced victims—to the allegory of a football game of equally matched masculine superheroes who meet for the glory of the game, hefty paychecks, and the spectacle of individual and team accomplishment.

The troops themselves became more than just a rhetorical figure within the spectacle by being included as the spectatorial object of ad-

U.S. soliders watching Super Bowl televised in Saudi Arabia, Jan. 27, 1991.

dress as well. For the first time, football spectatorship itself became identified as patriotic and heroic. The Super Bowl halftime "show" began with a news summary and live satellite-fed interviews of U.S. male and female soldiers gathered at Saudi Arabia base TV rooms to watch the game—even though it was 3 A.M. in Saudi Arabia. The coverage emphasized both the importance of this momentary leisure activity for their psychological well-being and their statements that the Super Bowl telecast showed them that those "at home" cared about them.

After the interviews—which were marked at beginning and end by the logo "The Gulf War/Super Bowl"—the pageantry resumed at the stadium with a blond boy in a football uniform singing "You are my hero." His song accompanied a slow-motion montage of U.S. troops in the Persian Gulf. Occupying the same spot as Whitney Houston did in the pregame ceremonies, the boy reappeared midsong accompanied by marching flag bearers behind him. On the field, an unseen narrator announced the two thousand sons and daughters of Persian Gulf military personnel who then marched onto the field. Each wore a yellow ribbon and carried a small U.S. flag. Well scrubbed and groomed, they filed past the camera, and the camera cut to close-ups among them, stressing their racial and ethnic diversity.[5] They were literally identified as family to the soldiers, and their faces answered the ones beamed via satellite from the Persian Gulf, thus uniting mothers and fathers with sons and daughters in a television multicultural family of faces. Families broken by the war were made whole by the television apparatus.

As if that were not enough to make a point, President and Mrs. Bush then appeared in medium shot in a White House domestic setting. They dedicated the Super Bowl to the soldiers in the Persian Gulf and thanked the U.S. people for having them in their *homes*. The chain of connotations of family already set into play became realigned in a chain linking family to home and home to the aesthetic and psychological expressivity of domestic space. The halftime pageant reached its pinnacle as a high-angle extreme long shot showed the marchers on the football field spelling out the letters *USA*. Behind them was a Disney World Magic Kingdom castle, the final representation of "home," but now posited as a fantastic one that further confuses the place of home with North American leisure, commodified tourism as family unity, and the exoticized elements of Disney's turrets (borrowed from Islamic architecture)[6] as belonging to and property of U.S. families.

U.S. culture already purveys conventionalized, interchangeable sports/war iconography and metaphors. Drawing on the shared language of warrior combat and competition, patriotism has always been an easily entered arena through masculine terms. But for most women, as Cynthia Enloe remarks, the traditional and only way into the patriotic realm has been "through those narrow doorways marked 'motherhood' and 'wife.'"[7] The coverage of the Super Bowl—especially its halftime show—constructed through its simultaneity, liveness, and spectacle a "national family" of viewers, specifying the soldiers' places in the family as sons and daughters, brothers and sisters. Being a loyal family member became synonymous with being a patriot. So, what seems most interesting about the Super Bowl spectacle is how another discourse doubled over the masculinist one and allowed the entry of the feminine, which functioned to position both male and female viewers as *feminized* patriots. While some viewers may have had, perhaps, more ambivalent identification with the family discourse, the way that the Super Bowl offered up a feminized, disciplined arena (particularly intense in its pregame and halftime segments) is a notable example of how the meaning of war itself became narrowly feminine in television's production of the Persian Gulf War.

A Feminine Genre Example: The Sitcom *Major Dad*

Within the constraints of advance production and the possibility of political changes before air date, prime-time fiction admitted the Persian Gulf War in ways that allowed the war's containment both in episodic formats that provided closure to the problems posed and in segments that could easily be excised without disrupting the overall narrative sense. For example, in the precredit opening sequence of *L.A. Law*, the law firm's partners mentioned the Persian Gulf War while they were seated around a table at a meeting. They presented opposing positions on the war—liberal characters were opposed; conservative ones were for the war. But their "pro" or "anti" stances—all announced within a sixty-second segment—did not instigate any in-depth discussion, nor did it figure again in the rest of that week's or future episodes. If the war momentarily invaded the boardroom as a reminder of the national preoccupation, it neither materially affected the partners' lives nor affected the development of any plot trajectories already set in motion.

Among situation comedies, a few series offered individual episodes that addressed fears and tensions about the Persian Gulf War, thereby linking the political, national sphere to the highly personalized and familial communities of sitcomdom. In *A Different World*, nonregular characters—college students who were not part of the show's featured "family"—were called up for military duty. Their military obligation was a crisis not for themselves and their future but for Whitley, the regularly featured character marked as "class privileged." Whitley had to come to grips with the classed and racialized components of who has to fight and why. Even though her crisis—a temporarily disturbing realization that racism and class inequality structures the military as well as U.S. life—raised interesting issues for resistance to the U.S. support of the war, it only posed a momentary crack in her psychological well-being. By the end of the episode, her faith was restored through the fraternal love of her college chums and housemates even though their bandages of comfort could not literally solve the social and political problems that the episode raised.

Because the very format of the half-hour sitcom requires some closure, problems initiated within the narrative must be resolved. Any sitcom narrative could not really resolve the kinds of complex problems posed by the Persian Gulf War, and any attempt to refer to the war would have to pose only those war-related problems that could be contained by the end of the episode, most notably with stock sitcom resolutions of emotional therapy and family togetherness. *Major Dad*'s February 4, 1991, episode was exemplary for how a sitcom handles such disturbing issues and tensions of the public sphere through their textual reorganization in the private sphere. Both the amount and type of publicity predating and postdating the show (on television and in *TV Guide*) emphasized and exceptionalized *Major Dad* among all prime-time fare as a fictional show "going to war."[8]

Major Dad's single episodic "going to war" story was framed as a flashback through U.S. marine wife Polly's voice-over narration to her diary: "I heard my children laughing this morning, and, for a glorious split second, there was no war. Although it has only been three weeks, I know the events surrounding January 15, 1991, will be with me forever." Her words are spoken as the camera dollies into a long shot of Polly seated in her window while her children laugh offscreen. The camera cuts to a long shot of her three daughters playing in the yard. Within the boundaries of the show itself, the episode begins by marking itself as doubly exceptional, since wife Polly has never before been given the authority of narrational point of view and since it is highly unusual for a fictional situation comedy to make such pointed references to the troubled politics of the real world outside the fiction— "war," "January 15, 1991." This doubling, however, also effectively places a maternal frame around the crisis right from the outset.

When the series first aired, Polly's character served as the politically liberal opposition to her husband's militaristic, hard-line politics. But now that there is an acute political issue inscribed in the episode about which they *would* disagree (perhaps all too disturbingly

*Polly's flashback about the Persian Gulf War. (*Major Dad, *CBS)*

as a metaphor for the national family), Polly's politics are softened to an antiwar view represented only in an initial scene as "support for peace." She says that she will attend a "peace vigil," but the picketing, as she characterizes it, takes place offscreen and without any further inscription in the episode.

Indeed, Polly's prior definition as a professional journalist and liberal political activist necessarily undergoes an overhaul here to remake her from an active, possibly resistant figure involved in the public sphere into one solely defined by the image of a more passively constructed maternal vigilance—which only requires watching, waiting, and worrying.[9] Even the term *peace vigil* negates, through its very language, the possibility of war protest, opposition, or resistance. By relying on its connotations of a prayer ritual or of waiting (keeping a vigil by a sickbed), the term as well as the unseen event replaces the active outward anger of antiwar protests with a passive, nonexpressive response. Although such passivity is a different strategy than the talk shows' displacement of anger with therapeutic terms, it serves a similar purpose of rerouting antiwar expression.

The sitcom narrative, however, works hard to figure her husband

Major MacGillis's emotional support for the war as active rather than passive. Major Dad MacGillis and his co-workers at the U.S. Marine base in Virginia act as iconographic rhetorical support in their service uniforms. They discuss the situation with uncharacteristic solemnity and gravity for a comedy. They are given a narrative means for applauding patriotism when they interact with three comic old-timers who have arrived at the base because they wish to reenlist.

Major Dad's and his co-workers' patriotic loyalty and volunteeristic enthusiasm are repetitively interjected without putting them in any physical danger. Major Dad, along with his co-star co-workers, does put in for Saudi duty but will stay stateside because his colonel explains that he will reject all transfer requests. Yet their wartime contribution is represented as equally as important as the marines in the Persian Gulf in three ways: (1) the colonel's rejection of transfer requests comes only after Gunny, Major Dad's female marine secretary, makes a speech about the importance of stateside marines; (2) repetitive cutaway shots to warehouse activity as well as verbal references to the shipment of supplies they are readying for Saudi delivery reinforce the domestic role of the military; and (3) the labor of getting the shipment ready becomes a chief narrative referent for the remainder of the episode. Thus, Major Dad is a model hero not because he is a good warrior but because he is a good manager, and the military itself—at least its stateside location—becomes heroicized through its service and managerial skills. Such a theme has been present in the series from the beginning, which figures the office (furnished with a female secretary, a lovable but irascible male boss, and a handsome male junior executive type) rather than the battlefield or barracks as the military workplace.

It is also important that Major Dad's decision to apply for a transfer to the Persian Gulf occurs not at the base with his office buddies but while in bed with his wife. The marital bed, more conventionally linked to adult heterosexuality and sexual relations, is established early in this episode as the site for family closeness, not adult sex, when the children come to the bed for nurturing and comfort from both parents. In this way, the issue of soldiering as a disruption of family and romantic relationships is articulated as a primary concern of the show. The point is visually reinforced when the three children enter the bedroom and spontaneously jump into bed with their parents after Major Dad's announcement to his wife that he is requesting a transfer to the Persian Gulf. Major Dad ends this scene by telling Polly, "You have to understand that I've got two families" (whereas she has only one), thus enabling, on one level, the position of family and country as dualistic. He simply makes explicit the structure of the sitcom itself—the doubling of domestic and professional families. But for Polly, who has assumed the privileged position of narrator in this episode, the war is now repositioned from abstractions of war versus peace to become configured in her final reaction shot to Major Dad surrounded by her children as a crisis threatening her only family.

The episode, however, relieves the threat of Polly's "problem" in two ways: first, by making soldiering an individual's *choice*, and second, by reneging on the issue of how family members will cope. Although Major Dad feels morally and ethically committed to go to the Persian Gulf (as expressed through his simple characterization of marine family loyalty), he is just as quickly provided a deus ex machina that relieves him and his family of the consequences of his decision. Polly never has to deal with a situation beyond her control. Indeed, the episode never interrogates its underlying assumption throughout that soldiering is, indeed, a choice.

As if that isn't enough, Polly is given a situation that she does control—through her *feelings* about the war. By displacing the issues of the Persian Gulf War onto an allegorical subplot wherein two of the daughters fight over the territory of their bedroom, war itself can be

Family unity around a dented globe. (Major Dad, *CBS*)

simplified and Polly can control events through maternal mediation. If resolution regarding the war could not be achieved, then reconciliation can—at least on the home front. The issues alluded to and raised by an episode timely relating to national tensions and fears are reconciled through a family sitting down, likening the daughters' fight to "the line in the sand" of the Persian Gulf battlefield, and agreeing on the importance of family unity while they gather around the dented globe of the world that had served as an object of battle in the children's fight.

The Feminine Genre That Refused to Speak about War?

In order to teach a feminized patriotism, *Major Dad* and the numerous other TV genres relied on the tropes, thematic values, and melodramatic conventions usually associated with soap operas. It was surprising, then, that war did not come to Pine Valley or to Llanview or to Port Charles or to Bayview or to any other soap town. The soap operas, the premiere *feminine* television genre, conspicuously refused to speak about the war or to allow that staple of soap opera expressive vocabulary—emotional coping—any outlet in war-related stories or references. No one in *All My Children*'s Pine Valley even seemed to remember that a character had been conveniently written out of the show in August when he joined the marines and shipped off to Saudi Arabia. Now, in February, his brother, best friends, foster mother, and former girlfriend were so preoccupied with personal and local problems that—unlike many U.S. citizens sporting yellow ribbons—they forgot their marine. Only one other soap opera similarly shipped a character off to war, only to forget him, too, once he departed.

Soap producers contended that, unlike live sports events like the Super Bowl, their schedule of taping productions up to six weeks in advance made it difficult to comment directly on changing world events.[10] Their conditions of production, however, are similar to those of prime-time companies who were able to prepare special war-related segments and episodes even though the possibility of unfolding events might render their productions untimely or dated.[11] But, unlike prime-time shows, soap operas can less easily react to changes in world events by changing the chronological order in which they air shows or by reediting a single episode if necessary. They depend upon both a fixed order of broadcast in relation to production and a rapid, efficient, economical production schedule that can yield a much larger output of shows than that of prime-time companies. Soap operas remained mute on a vital social subject although they have a long-standing tradition of participation in social issues (e.g., alcoholism, drug abuse, AIDS, date rape) even if they only address those topics that become social managerial problems because they threaten the fundamental stability of the family.

It even appeared that daytime news coverage was helping to recover the fantasy element of the soap operas and the soaps' silence about the war. Networks, CNN, and CNN *Headline News* were all quick to mark graphic logos and signature theme songs as flags of specific time slots for Persian Gulf War news and updates. This effectively both regularized and routinized war coverage in record time (rather than the more crisis-oriented method of "interrupting" daytime programming with "news bulletins"). In the days immediately following the January 16 bombings of Baghdad, daytime soaps as well as talk shows and sitcom reruns were interrupted less often by the Persian Gulf War, as coverage quickly became assigned to the top of each hour. *TV Guide* and *Soap Opera Digest* even featured stories promising that the networks were trying to keep the soap operas on their regular daily schedules.[12] The soap towns that had not been narratively invaded by the war now became even more impervious as the fictional worlds themselves became less prone to shattering, disruption, and lost gaps.

But, maybe it was not necessary for the soaps to reference the war in order to teach women patriotism, since they provided the vocabulary and parameters that determined the discussions in so many other texts. Soap opera provided the context and the backdrop, an explanatory model for understanding the wartime ideological operations of such disparate genres as television news, football games, and situation comedies. Perhaps audiences could identify with the melodramatically constructed soldiers' families of the evening news because they already knew how to identify with the multiple, ever-shifting families of daytime dramas, their good mothers, and their regularized problems of family disruption, emotional loss and anger, and communal therapy. If both sports events and sitcoms could posit the rewards of women's wartime roles in images of maternal fulfillment, perhaps their arguments hinged on the fact that maternal and romantic self-sacrifice has been the backbone for women's movies, radio and television soap operas, and romance novels for most of the twentieth century. If this war was also about bringing the alienated, unappreciated male Vietnam War veteran back into the national family, the narrative of the lost or abandoned son is one already familiar and even comfortable to soap viewers. The very qualities of soap opera became generalized to other genres as the chief means through which to understand the war.

If soap operas themselves did not "speak" the war, there was ample coverage in fan magazines and supermarket tabloids about the "patriotic" activities of the soap stars. One article repeated in more than one magazine featured *All My Children* star Kate Collins (who is granted an abundance of ready-made patriotic stature as the daughter of astronaut-hero Buzz Collins) sharing the poems she regularly received from a fan stationed in the Persian Gulf and describing the diligent pen pal relationships she maintained with Persian Gulf soldiers. Other tabloids featured stories about soap opera stars making public appearances at shopping malls in order to spearhead letter-writing campaigns to military personnel in the Persian Gulf. Star discourse thus contextualized favorite soap opera characters as "patriotic" friends and family even when the shows' narratives could not.

If soaps themselves did not "speak" the war through ongoing plot lines and character relationships, they did offer an occasional image that connected their domestic scenarios to the ones being played out elsewhere in television. One of the most eloquent images of the war was one such visual signature. It appeared on a normal day in Pine Valley (*All My Children*)—well, as normal as things ever are in soap opera towns—but it was also well into the Persian Gulf War in late February, and the scene was the living room of the Martin family. The Martins represent one of the most all-American families of soap operadom and one of the best loved among fans. Someone, it does not matter who, opened the Martins' front door to let in a visitor, and there nailed up on the front door was one of the biggest, fullest, most oversize yellow wreaths anyone has ever seen. The visitor came in, and the scene went on. That was it. Without saying a single word, *All My Children* signaled in no uncertain terms that its model family was also a loyal, patriotic family.

It may have taken the Martins more than a month to sport a big yellow wreath on their front door and to learn that patriotism, in feminized terms, simply signified what they had held dear and practiced all along—family loyalty. But, as Cynthia Enloe said, "In tying a yellow ribbon 'round an old oak tree—or car antenna, porch pillar, or shop sign—most women probably do not see themselves as endorsing something as grandiose as a new world order."[13] Television ameliorated these implications by locating and relocating women's battlegrounds in the private, domestic sphere and by discursively constructing the battle itself as one of melodramatically constructed emotions won over with weapons of personal and family therapy—nowhere better symbolized than in the yellow ribbons, bows, and wreaths that appeared *everywhere* (even in otherwise mute soap operas). Television authorized the limits of discussion not simply through the contents of news coverage and political analysis but by structuring the war as a discourse for feminine pleasure across programming: it wrapped the war in buttons and bows and soap opera woes. For U.S. women, already socially conditioned not to talk or be concerned about governmental politics and military maneuvers, the television feminization of patriotism served as a disciplinary effort to eschew open political debate and discussion about military and governmental policies during the Persian Gulf War months.

Notes

1. See Lynne Joyrich, "All That Television Allows: TV Melodrama, Postmodernism, and Consumer Culture," *Camera Obscura* 16 (Jan. 1988): 129–153.
2. There were, of course, other avenues on the talk shows through which war-related issues were remade into the purely personal. One of the most outrageous was the Jan. 22, 1991, *Sally Jessy Raphael* show, which featured as its topic beauty makeovers for the stateside spouses of the U.S. military personnel serving in the Persian Gulf. For an example of how talk shows reconfigured war-related issues of racism and demonized Arabic cultures, see Therese Saliba's essay in this volume.
3. See Dana L. Cloud's essay in this volume.
4. Susan Jeffords, "Women, Gender, and the War," *Critical Studies in Mass Communication* 6 (Mar. 1989): 86–87.
5. Chuck Kleinhans and Julia Lesage, "The Gulf War Superbowl, January 1991," *Jump Cut* 36 (Spring 1991): 8.
6. Ibid., 9.
7. Cynthia Enloe, "Tie a Yellow Ribbon 'Round the New World Order," *Village Voice*, Feb. 19, 1991, 37.
8. See, for example, Monica Collins, "Humor vs. War: It's a *Major* Conflict," *TV Guide*, Feb. 9, 1991, 27; Ileane Rudolph, "Stateside Duty for *Major Dad*," *TV Guide*, Jan. 26, 1991, 33–34.
9. Executive producer Rick Hawkins claimed that this was a deliberate move made by the producers, who were contending with increased monitoring from CBS's broadcast standards department; Collins, "Humor vs. War," 27.
10. "Why Aren't the Soaps Dealing with the War?" *Soap Opera Digest*, Mar. 5, 1991, 38.
11. Collins, "Humor vs. War," 27.
12. See, for example, "How the War in the Gulf Affects the Soaps," *Soap Opera Digest*, Mar. 5, 1991, 40.
13. Enloe, "Tie A Yellow Ribbon," 37.

SEEING THROUGH PATRIOTISM

The War
for National Identity

Much of the production of social consensus during the Persian Gulf War was formed around the idea of what it meant to be "American" during the war. In addition to making comparisons between the Persian Gulf and Vietnam wars, the media used the example of the Vietnam War to "prove" the supposed consequences of "un-

American" antiwar protests, as ʿany in the government and military argued that it was antiwar demonstrations that at worst lost
the Vietnam War and at best destroyed the lives of returning veterans. This historical specter was used to place pressure on U.S. citizens during the Persian Gulf War to rally around *American* troops
and *American* policies. One of the most severe consequences of
this pressure was that the definition of what constitutes "American" became narrower and more coercively enforced.

Certainly previous wars have created similar pressures to be
"American"; we have only to think of the internment of Japanese
Americans during World War II to realize this. But there are specific
reasons why such pressures would be present in 1990–1991 and
why they would take the shape of "American-ness." Because the
United States is going through an anxious period of redefining its
population—owing to multiculturalism, changing racial distribu-
tions, immigration, and more severe class separations—the war
functioned to offer an illusion of unity through support of the
troops. While the shift to an all-volunteer military in 1972 yielded
more women and a disproportionate number of African Americans,
Hispanics, and Asian and Pacific islanders in the military, their joint
participation in Operation Desert Storm made it seem as if there
were some core of "American-ness" that drew them all together as
representatives of a coherent nation.

A national identity—what it means, for example, to be "American" —cannot be cohesive and can only be made so through the kinds
of deliberate genocide practiced in 1940s Germany and in 1990s Bos-
nia. But while genocide is practiced in the twentieth century largely
through the military and through science, the mainstream media have
their own form of "genocide" in their elimination or redefinition of
groups or entire populations of people whom their government does
not wish to be seen or whom their audiences do not wish to see. In
order to create the image of a coherent and united nation, people who
don't fit the national self-image have to be ignored, marginalized, or
recategorized in a way that makes their "unfitness" unobtrusive.

In an essay written during the war, Cynthia Enloe shows the
ways in which women were both ignored and redefined to shore up
U.S. government views of the war. Non-U.S. women were ignored
in discussions of the effects of the war and of U.S. support of
Kuwait. As Enloe points out, the lives of Philippine and Sri Lankan
women domestic workers were ignored both in discussions of the

effects of the Iraqi occupation of Kuwait and in the abuse many received on a daily basis from their Kuwaiti employers. At the same time, principally white U.S. women, presumably harder to ignore, were redefined as the war proceeded. As Enloe states, whereas pictures of women as wives, mothers, and soldiers were widely popular during the buildup to the war, "in the midst of the ground war . . . women suddenly had become invisible." Enloe notes the pressure on U.S. women to conform to an image of "supporting the troops" that is simultaneously an image of being American: "Governments encourage women to imagine that being a loyal family member is synonymous with being a patriot. For women in wartime, the nation becomes a family."

Leonard Rifas focuses on another group of people who were marginalized during the war—war protesters. In his examination of supermarket tabloids, Rifas concludes that support for the war was shaped largely through the depiction of celebrity spokespeople who were shown to support the U.S. effort against Iraq. More specifically, Rifas argues that, by maligning Hollywood celebrities like Woody Harrelson who opposed the war, the tabloids created an environment in which their readers would hesitate to express similar opinions out of fear of receiving similar reprisals.

Venise T. Berry and Kim E. Karloff take a different approach in examining the construction of national identity for a group that was, unlike the war protesters, foregrounded during the war—African Americans. The mainstream press celebrated the "color-blindness" of the war in the way that African-American and white troops worked together or in the way that African-American families supported the war effort through their support for the "troops." In contrast, Berry and Karloff argue, popular black magazines performed a distinct function from that of the mainstream media in their emphasis less on a U.S. national identity than on a black community identity. What makes Berry and Karloff's argument so important for any consideration of the formations of war support and national identity is that they show how support for the war in popular black magazines, in contrast to war support in the mainstream media, was used as a mechanism for dissenting from a unified national identity: "The repetitive emphasis on *our* (meaning black) men and women in the Persian Gulf . . . consistently distinguishes communal identity from national identity." Such arguments insist that since national identity is neither unified nor coherent, the means for constructing that unity—patriotism and war support—can be used in different ways and toward different ends. They can be used, in fact, to work against coercive pressures to construct such a unified nation.

While Enloe's essay emphasizes the ways in which images of women are used in media differently than are images of men to show how national identity is gendered, Therese Saliba examines how representations of different groups of women are used to create categories of national identity in which only certain women are able to participate. By focusing on how Arab women were portrayed during the Persian Gulf War, most frequently as contrasts to the "liberated" U.S. woman, Saliba shows how Arab women are "present but only for the purpose of representing [their] invisibility or silence in order to serve as a subordinate to the Western subject of the scene," thereby "granting white women a presence at the expense of brown women." By examining fashion advertisements, the *Donahue* show, and *Time* magazine articles, Saliba argues that the racist representations of Arab women served not only to reinforce already existing patterns of U.S. anti-Arab racism but also to silence the dissenting voices of Arab women in their efforts to resist constructions of Saudi national identity.

The most deafening silence of the Persian Gulf War, and one that offers clues about the violence of national identity construction, was the silencing of the voices of dying Iraqi citizens. Margot Norris's essay shows how military censorship policies effectively shielded the U.S. public from any images of Iraqi deaths and war casualties, thereby making the war less "real." At the same time, such "unreality" made way for the media to construct out of whole cloth the kinds of images of a "real" war the essays in this volume have cited—bomb's eye views, Patriot missiles, journalists in gas masks, veiled Saudi women, and yellow ribbons. Significantly, Norris notes that one of the unintended consequences of this "unreality" was that when the war was declared over, large segments of the U.S. public seemed to forget it, as if in fact it had been as unreal as its images implied, thereby failing to "register as a significant and lasting political credit for the administration."

What this observation suggests is that the pressures to construct a coherent national identity for the purposes of war support through the marginalization, silencing, and redefining of populations of people cannot finally be controlled in their effects or determinations. Instead, like the pressures to define national identity, such efforts are incomplete, creating possibilities for articulating alternate identities and political communities, even, as Berry and Karloff suggest, using the very tools designed to create unity and coherence. Such spaces, however, are not innocent. If the Persian Gulf War could not carry George Bush into a second presidential term precisely because the national identity forged during the war could not contain anxieties about jobs, geographies, and international futures, this failure was nonetheless achieved at the price of more than 100,000 dead Iraqi soldiers and civilians and the demolition of a national infrastructure. Bill Clinton will be long out of office before the bodies of the Iraqi people—those the media ignored during the war—will cease to suffer the deaths, diseases, and dismemberments that Americans call the Persian Gulf War.

Cynthia Enloe

The Gendered Gulf

Most of us still are trying to make sense of the Gulf War. Its meanings are as multilayered as a Mesopotamian archeological dig. For instance, I realize now that I know nothing—nothing—about Kurdish women. This means that I have an inherently faulty understanding of how Iraqi Kurdish nationalism is being conceptualized; nor do I know how either the Peshmerge guerrilla force or the non-combatant refugee communities are organizing their lives. The three essays that follow, therefore, are best read as incomplete, time-anchored attempts to bring a feminist sensibility to bear on what was initially described as the "Gulf crisis" and later was labeled the "Gulf War." The first attempt was written in mid-September 1990, only a few weeks after returning from my first visit to the South Pacific.

I was in the Cook Islands when I heard the news of the Iraqi military's invasion of Kuwait on the BBC World Service. The South Pacific was teaching me to imagine this world in new and surprising ways. I was seeing Australia as an emerging and militarizing regional power, New Zealand as not only an anti-nuclear renegade but as a former colonizer; small islands no bigger than pin pricks on a world map were turning out to have dynamic and complex international relations they barely had the resources to monitor, much less control; women's relationships to men in each one of these small societies—Fiji, Vanuatu, the Cook Islands, Tahiti—were as much the stuff of political myths, alliances, and anxieties as they were in any other society. So when I head the news of what was instantly called the Gulf crisis, I tried not to slip back into my natural world-as-seen-from-Boston mode. I tried, not always successfully, to sense what the invasion and its

Parts I and II of this essay were originally published in the *Village Voice*, September 25, 1990 and February 19, 1991, respectively.

ripple effects meant for Cook Islanders, Australians, and Fijians: higher petrol and kerosene prices, drops in tourism, further rationales for expanding Australian military presence—each with its own distinctively gendered causes and consequences. Perhaps it was this mental aerobics exercise that pushed me a month later, now back on the American east coast, to set off on my trial run at analyzing the crisis by imagining it from the vantage point of one of its apparently least significant participants, a Filipina working as a maid in Kuwait City. Although I didn't have all the analytical ends neatly tied together, I had been taught by feminists over the last twenty years to be very wary of presuming that the political actors with the most power—and the most media coverage—were the most useful starting points when trying to figure out exactly how politics works. I might get back to George Bush, François Mitterrand, King Fahd, and Saddam Hussein eventually, but coming to their ideological outlooks and uses of state power via particular groups of women, via the relationships of those women to each other, would prove, I had learned, far more fruitful than taking the lazy masculinist short cut of presuming that those men in and of themselves revealed the most about why this crisis had developed and why it was following its peculiar course.

The second essay in this trilogy was written almost five months later, in February 1991. The Bush administration and its allies—including Australia's Hawke administration—had launched their massive air bombardment of Iraq and were in the opening stages of what would be an alarmingly short ground war. I had been following the elite Saudi women's driving protest, watching for the consolidation of military prostitution policies which would rely on Third World women, and scanning the European press (more promising than the U.S.) for any signs that the feminist, pro-democracy Iraqi Women's League would be recognized in the exiled opposition coalitions. But in February, I felt compelled to turn my puzzlement directly toward women closer to home. Yellow ribbons were sprouting like dandelions in spring. They seemed to be spontaneous expressions, especially expressions by women; only later did the press and Washington officialdom make efforts to impose their own meanings on them.

To this day I am not at all sure I know what each woman who put a ribbon on her winter coat lapel or on her secretarial in-tray or on her hospital staff association noticeboard was saying. That is something we still had better be curious about. But in the midst of the ground war I felt that women suddenly had become invisible. At least during the tense months of the "pre war" autumn, women—as familiar wives, soldiers, girl friends, mothers, as alien veiled women—had served as valuable "human interest" stories. Now that the serious business of combat had begun, women had slid further off the page; only their yellow ribbons caught the public eye. Yet it seemed clear that the yellow ribbon phenomenon (which occurred to a lesser degree in Canada and Britain) was drawing U.S. women into the Bush administration's larger global scheme in ways we needed to understand—not just because any new or old world order would affect women, but, more radically, because any configuration of international relationships can only be fashioned by government leaders if they can devise ways to harness women's compliance.

The final essay was written in June 1991. The British and U.S. troops were being pulled out of northern Iraq, where they had been protecting Kurdish refugees.

The Bush and Major governments wanted the refugees to return to their homes in Iraq less because the Kurds were now secure than because a lingering American troop presence might remind voters back home of a Vietnam-like "quagmire." Also, if Iraqi Kurds stayed in southern Turkey they might destabilize that less-than-ethnically harmonious NATO partner. Oily smoke continued to hang over Kuwait City, though only the most committed of environmental investigators were charting the spills threatening Persian Gulf marine life or the after-effects of the bombing of Iraq's chemical plants. There was no date set, no list of invitees agreed upon for an Israeli-Palestinian peace conference, and meanwhile new Soviet Jewish immigrants were being settled on the disputed West Bank. Arms salesmen were doing a brisk business in the Middle East; disarmament seemed to have few genuine advocates. Yet, even with Saudi Arabia and Israel as showcases for its Patriot missiles, Raytheon was laying off hundreds of women and men in recession-hit Massachusetts. Wearing yellow ribbons and hosting the president back in February hadn't saved their jobs in June.

Yet with all these signals that the war—wars, actually—had not ended, most North Americans and Europeans were acting in early summer as though they were living in a "post-war" era. Those who had come, however reluctantly, as had a majority of women, to support the U.S.-led warmaking went to parades. Those who opposed the warmaking went to conferences. Post-war periods are dangerous times. They are times when lessons—often the wrong lessons, often lessons right for some but harmful to others—are hammered out. Post-war is a time for feminists to keep their eyes wide open, for it is now when masculinity and femininity will be reconsidered, and perhaps reconstructed, by warmakers and war resisters alike.

I. September 1990: Womenandchildren

In the torrents of media coverage that accompany an international crisis women typically are made visible as symbols, victims, or dependents. "Womenandchildren" rolls so easily off network tongues because in network minds women are family members rather than independent actors, presumed to be almost childlike in their innocence about the realpolitik of international affairs. Rarely are women imagined to reveal any of the basic structures of a dangerous confrontation.

If there is an image that defines television's Gulf crisis, it's a disheveled white woman coming off a 747, an exhausted baby on her shoulder. States exist, this media story implies, to protect womenandchildren. U.S. intervention in the Gulf would be harder to justify if there were no feminized victim. The real diplomatic wives, the British and American women who in the last decade have created formidable lobbying organizations to press their interests, don't fit this scenario.

It follows that the Gulf crisis story must also ignore the female attaché at the U.S. embassy in Kuwait, negotiating with the Iraqis for the release of these very same womenandchildren. Passing over State Department women's organizing, which opened up the previously masculinized foreign service, the media treats her merely as an honorary man: capable, able to take care of herself—and others. Her existence is not allowed to disturb the womenandchildren-protected-by-statesmen scenario.

Though you don't see them on the evening news, there are an estimated 17,000 Filipino women today working as domestic servants in Saudi Arabia. Thousands of others have been cleaning, washing, and minding children in Kuwait and the United Arab Emirates. Together, there are over 29,000 Filipino domestic servants in the Middle East. Government officials not only in the Philippines but in Sri Lanka, Indonesia, Jamaica, and Ethiopia have been counting on the paychecks that maids send home to lessen their nations' imbalance of payments and to keep the lid on politically explosive unemployment.

These Asian women, now trapped in occupied Kuwait or crowded into Jordanian refugee camps, have been crucial players in reducing global tensions generated by international debt.

After the 1970s oil boom, Kuwaiti and Saudi women became employers in their homes. But their relationships with their Sri Lankan or Filipino maids had to be devised in ways that met with their husbands' approval and kept the foreign workers at least minimally content. As stories have filtered back home of the abuse that some—not all—Asian domestic servants experienced, the Sri Lankan and Philippines governments have been pressed by their own women's advocates to take steps to protect their nationals working abroad. The regimes have acted ineffectually, in part because they have been afraid of offending Gulf states on whom they depend for oil, in part because they have rebellions and other worries closer to home diverting them, and in part because they have concluded that they need to satisfy the men from the International Monetary Fund (IMF) obsessed with balance-of-payments more than they need to win the support of their own domestic women's movements.

Caryl Murphy, the *Washington Post* reporter who sent out clandestine reports from Kuwait in the days following the Iraqi invasion, has described how some Filipino maids were taken by their Kuwaiti employers to the Philippines embassy so that they would have some modicum of protection. Other Kuwaitis, she reports, fled in front of the invading troops, leaving their Filipino employees to fend for themselves. Filipinas in Kuwait City told Murphy that they had heard stories of Iraqi soldiers raping other domestic workers. Rape in war is never simply random violence. It is structured by male soldiers' notions of their masculine privilege, by the strength of the military's lines of command and by class and ethnic inequalities among women. If you're a rich Kuwaiti woman you have less chance of being raped than if you are an Asian maid.

To make sense, then, of the Iraqi occupation of Kuwait we have to talk about soldiers' ideas of manliness, middle-class women's presumptions about housework, and the IMF's strategies for handling international debt. Debt, laundry, rape, and conquest are understandable only in relation to each other.

Though we have a hard time understanding it, to many Jordanians, Palestinians, and other Arabs Saddam Hussein is a potent symbol of nationalist aspirations, which are fueled by a resentment of European and U.S. attempts to impose their values and their priorities on the societies of the Middle East. To many Arab men, women are the people most vulnerable to Western corruption and exploitation. This conviction has infused debates over women's attire and women's education with political passion.

But Middle East women haven't been mere symbols. First, they are diverse, distinguished by ethnicity, ideology, class, and nationality. Second, since the turn of the century many have been active participants in their countries' freedom movements. Arab feminists have criticized many of their male compatriots for trying to fashion a nationalism that camouflages male privilege under the legitimizing mantle of "Arab tradition." Being an Arab nationalist feminist is a risky enterprise (one might say that being a nationalist feminist in any community is a daunting project). A women's-rights advocate always is open to nervous men's double-barreled charge that she is succumbing to alien western bourgeois values, while splitting the nation at a time when it needs unity above all else.

The current Gulf crisis, defined largely by massive U.S. military posturing, has radically complicated local feminists' task. Arab women activists walking a tightrope between male nationalists' patriarchy and Western policymakers' cultural imperialism have the most to lose when an international crisis polarizes internal debate. Western male officials who claim their policies are supporting "civilized" politics are, in fact, painting Arab women into an oppressive corner.

But many observers nonetheless are portraying wartime mobilization as good for women. Saddam Hussein, a secular not a religious nationalist, has made wide use of women in his military buildup. During the Iraq-Iran war, Saddam encouraged the Iraqi Women's Federation (an organization quite separate from the exiled Iraqi Women's League) to channel women into non-traditional jobs in order to free men to fight.

A Saudi feminist stationed with the United Nations in Baghdad during that war has even wondered aloud whether it didn't further Iraqi women's emancipation. The more devastating the war became, she recalled, the more Saddam's all-male Revolutionary Council called on women to lend their efforts to the nation (though never forsaking their primary responsibility of producing more children). Her puzzle would sound familiar to many U.S. feminists. The U.S. government followed the same course during World War II. Of course, the Iraqi cousins of "Rosie the Riveter" also discovered, once the war ended, male government officials—and their fathers and husbands—expected women to return to the more restricted domestic feminized roles that bolstered male egos and made space for the employment of demobilized male soldiers.

Today there is evidence that once again the Iraqi Women's Federation is being called upon to mobilize women, this time to put in place the consumer-rationing programs that will be the key to the Saddam regime's ability to withstand the UN embargo. It would not be surprising if many Iraqi women activists saw in the crisis yet another opportunity to use wartime mobilization to demonstrate their public capabilities. Now, however, in search of Muslim allies, Saddam is beginning to refer to his campaign as a holy cause. The more he couches his brand of Arab nationalism in religious terms, the less likely even the exigencies of wartime mobilization will produce long-term gains for Iraqi women.

There are reports out of Saudi Arabia this week that King Fahd has instructed his ministries to encourage Saudi women to volunteer for war-related jobs until now closed to them. Saudi women nurses who have been restricted to caring only for women patients are now to be permitted to attend male patients. Though the western media is heralding this announcement as evidence that the wartime mobilization may benefit "benighted" Saudi women, there has been scarce curiosity about the history of current thinking of those women.

In fact, U.S. coverage of the Gulf crisis has been framed by a contrast between the liberated American woman soldier and the veiled Arab woman. It is striking how consistent this current media preoccupation is with the western tradition of "Orientalism," that package of often-ambiguous ideas about the presumed backwardness, yet allure of Arab culture. The harem was at the center of western writers' preoccupation. In the past it was the daring Victorian lady traveller who posed the stark contrast with the secluded Arab woman. The former's presence served to reassure the self-satisfied western man that his society was the more "civilized" and thus within its natural rights in colonizing the Middle East. The European woman traveler also tempted many of her homebound sisters to imagine that they were a lot more emancipated than they really were: Even if they were denied the vote, couldn't control their own reproduction, and couldn't divorce a violent husband, at least they weren't pent up in a harem. The imperialist enterprise relied on both western women and men feeling superior to the patriarchal Arabs.

Today, many television and print journalists are substituting the U.S. woman soldier for the Victorian lady traveller, but the political intent remains much the same. By contrasting the allegedly liberated American woman tank mechanic with the Saudi woman deprived of a driver's license, U.S. reporters are implying that the United States is the advanced civilized country whose duty it is to take the lead in resolving the Persian Gulf crisis. Women of both countries are being turned into the currency with which men attempt to maintain the unequal relations between their societies.

Yet Arab women, even in the conservative societies of the Gulf, are more than passive victims of *purdah*. There are Saudi women who have university educations, who have founded women-only banks, who practice medicine in women-only hospitals, earn wages in newly established garment factories. One need not overstate the political and economic freedom of these women to argue nonetheless that Saudi women are diverse and have authentic analyses of their own.

There are Kuwaiti women who have organized neighborhood-level protests against the occupying Iraqi army. Susan Shuaib, a Kuwaiti-British feminist writing in the latest *New Statesman and Society*, puts this surprising news in the broader context of Kuwait's changing political relations between women and men. Just this July, according to Shuaib, women had become more visible as activists pressing for parliamentary government. They organized petition drives and took part in public rallies.

The second problem with the neo-Orientalist interpretation

adopted by so many U.S. reporters is that it treats U.S. women soldiers' "advances' outside any consideration of militarism. There are daily stories now about women soldiers coping with life in the desert. Approximately 6 percent of all U.S. forces in Saudi Arabia are women, a little more than half their proportions in the military as a whole. In the U.S. and British media, the woman flying a giant C-141 transport plane is portrayed as the natural descendent of Susan B. Anthony.

It is true that many women in the military do see themselves as feminists, breaking down formidable sexist barriers. For them, the Persian Gulf operation is not part of Middle East political evolution, with its volatile mix of imperialism and nationalism. Rather, it is part of a political struggle that began with the American women in Vietnam, and was carried into the U.S. invasions of Grenada and Panama. Each U.S. military intervention has provided a chance for women to hone their bureaucratic skills, perfect end runs around chauvinist field commanders, and turn up the heat on Pentagon officials still dragging their feet in opening up military career opportunities to women soldiers.

If, however, winning "first-class citizenship" depends on American women gaining full acceptance in the military, what does that suggest about the very meaning of citizenship? In all the coverage of American women soldiers' advances, there is the implication that the military defines citizenship.

The always artificial categories of "combat," "near combat," and "non-combat" may indeed be crumbling in the desert. But few women are talking yet about what sorts of sexual harassment they are likely to experience as the weeks pass with male soldiers having none of their usual access overseas to foreign women. Which country will play host to the thousands of American soldiers on "R & R"? Not Saudi Arabia. Whichever government agrees to serve as a rest-and-recreation site will make agreements with the Pentagon to ensure that American male soldiers have direct access to local women without endangering the men's health. Buried in the fine print of government-to-government R & R agreements are stipulations about public health and police authority that directly affect local women's relations with GIs. According to the Pentagon's own recently released study, 64 percent of women in the military say they have been sexually harassed. A woman soldier who won't pay attention to a male colleague is always vulnerable to lesbian-baiting. But this is made doubly intimidating when the Pentagon persists in its policy of forcing suspected lesbians out of the service.

The Persian Gulf crisis has not been built out of relations between ungendered presidents, kings, foreign ministers, oil executives, and soldiers. If we pay attention to the experiences and ideas of the women involved, two realities come into sharper focus. First, this international confrontation, like others before it, is played out in part by governments attempting to confine women to roles that, even when they briefly shake conventional social norms, nonetheless serve those governments' interests. Second, those government attempts are not always successful. Third, men's sense of their own masculinity, often tenuous, is as much a factor in international politics as the flows of oil, cables, and military hardware.

II. February 1991: Tie a Yellow Ribbon Around the New World Order

On the eve of the Gulf War, polls revealed a startling gender gap: American women were far less likely than American men to support going to war with Iraq. As recently as one week before the fighting began, the ABC News/*Washington Post* poll showed that only 58 percent of women surveyed, compared with 82 percent of men, thought war was the best way for the U.S. government to respond to Saddam Hussein. For pollsters, a 24-point spread is a gender gap of monumental proportions. Then on January 16, U.S. bombs began falling on Baghdad. As the bombs rained, the gender gap began to shrink. It wasn't men who were changing their minds. It was women. By January 20, the gender gap had shrunk to a mere 10 points, 71 percent to 81 percent.

George Bush has justified using force against the Iraqis to protect a "New World Order." Whereas under the old order, East was pitted against West, in the new post-1989 order, North is pitted against a South personified by Saddam Hussein. Yet this allegedly "new" order remains stuck in the old presumption that military power must be the principal tool for wielding international influence.

Bush's world order depends on its own kind of gender gap: George Bush, Colin Powell, John Major, Saddam Hussein, Yitzhak Shamir, the Iraqi Republican Guards, and British Tornado and American B-52 pilots remain state elites, their masculinities unquestioned. The wives of each of these men, as well M-16-toting American women soldiers and Saudi women driving protesters, are of course discussed as women, but consequently treated as trivial. Yet, as feminists have revealed in the last decade, every public power arrangement has depended on the control of femininity as an idea and of women as workers, carers, and sexual partners. We cannot make sense of any government's hoped-for world order in a gender vacuum. The post-August U.S. gender gap, and its recent dramatic shrinkage, must be explained precisely because the not-so-new militarized Pax Americana won't work unless women cooperate.

The current world order is "orderly" only if national-security officials can imagine their responsibilities to be manly, if diplomats can be served by unpaid diplomatic wives, if nationalist men can count on their women to pay homage to the nation's gendered culture, if multinational corporations can feminize and thereby cheapen labor, if indebted governments can send maids overseas to mail home remittances, and if technocrats can celebrate supermoms as models of modernity.

A militarized world order needs women to find rewards in a militarized femininity. Wives who refuse to behave like self-sacrificing "military wives," mothers who reject military service as their sons' avenue to manhood, young women who will not see enlisting as a guarantor of "first-class citizenship" jeopardize Bush's global design. For the United States to wage a war successfully in the Gulf, the gender gap had to be closed. A lot of women had to be persuaded to move across the opinion divide, without throwing overboard their notions of femininity.

Turning U.S. soldiers into "our troops" seems to have been the key. It was when U.S. soldiers in the Gulf were subjected to the dangers of actual combat that the gender gap collapsed. In tying a yellow ribbon 'round an old oak tree—or car antenna, porch pillar, or shop sign—most women probably do not see themselves as endorsing something as grandiose as a new world order. They probably see themselves as providing moral support to particular sons, daughters, neighbors, and friends. But, for the U.S national security elite, they are voluntarily constructing a feminized "homefront" to complement— thousands of American women soldiers notwithstanding—a masculinized battlefront. As well-meaning and as profoundly humane as every ribbon-tying gesture may be, each one makes it harder than ever to preserve that earlier distinction between caring for particular soldiers on the one hand and objecting to the Bush policy on the other.

Patriotism always has been an arena into which it's especially difficult for women to enter. It has always been easier for an Oliver North to gain entrance than for a Betsy North. For many women, the only path is through the narrow doorway marked "mother" and "wife." If a woman cannot become a recognized patriot on her own merits, then she may try to become one by becoming a patriotic mother or a patriotic wife—real or vicarious. Governments encourage women to imagine that being a loyal female member of a family is synonymous with being a patriot. For women in wartime, the nation becomes a family.

The Gulf War makes this myth of the wartime family even more potent. The U.S. military today has daughters as well as sons, husband-soldiers married to wife-soldiers, single parents. Yet the spiritual soul of the institution, male-only "combat," remains intact. So long as the allies continue to rely on air war, the image of American global power will be of male top guns, not female ground mechanics.

At the same time, the military's reliance on 200,000 women in uniform has given the U.S. military a new cloak of legitimacy. The institution doesn't seem such an anachronism. It even can claim to be a means for women to achieve full political status as people who can "die for their country." To many American women, whether or not they themselves are considering signing up, today's military is no longer the "Other." The military looks every day more like General Hospital. That makes it all the better an instrument for building and entrenching a U.S.-designed not-so-new world order.

Not only American society, but Saudi, Egyptian, Kuwaiti, Israeli, Iraqi, British, Japanese, and German societies are waging this war at a sexually specific historical moment. For instance, this war has sparked new debates amongst Saudi men about just what constitutes Saudi nationalism: can Saudi nationhood withstand dependence on other countries' men to fight its battles? Thus news of a Saudi fighter pilot's first victories in the air has consequences for women. The wartime coalition between American senior partners and Saudi junior partners may create a new, more militarized form of Saudi nationalist masculinity. In post-war Saudi Arabia will Saudi women, just now reaching out for political rights, be faced with not only religiously sanctified patriarchal barriers, but militarily blessed ones as well?

Likewise, Americans have named the gender gap only during the past two decades—as women have developed their own perspectives on many public policies, have become more organized in articulating those perspectives, and have voted into office more women willing to give authoritative voice to those perspectives. Furthermore, this war has been launched by a president who nervously wielded masculinity in his 1988 electoral campaign at a time when U.S. collective manliness appeared to be jeopardized by the country's slide in global economic competitiveness.

The Gulf War furthermore is being waged by Americans still living in the shadow of the sexual politics of another war. The Vietnam War has left a cultural legacy of gendered guilt: the betrayed male vet. He has taken fifteen years and a lot of celluloid and paper to create, but today he is a potent figure inspiring complex emotions. While there are at least 7,500 female American Vietnam veterans, it is the unappreciated, alienated male Vietnam vet whose image looms over the present war. It is for him as much as for the soldiers actually in the Gulf that many women seem to be tying yellow ribbons around their trees and antennas. This war is about masculinity, just as all wars have been; but it is a historically and socially specific masculinity. Without the feelings of guilt inspired by the image of the betrayed Vietnam male vet, without a public discourse that permitted the stories of male soldiers to blot out discussions of government policy errors, perhaps it would have been much harder to convert January 15th women against a war into January 20th women supporting it.

III. "Post-War" Patriarchy

As I walked home yesterday in the 100-degree heat of a Somerville, Massachusetts, June afternoon, I noticed yellow ribbons still tacked up on my neighbors' front porches. They drooped now in the heat, their color almost drained by months of rain and wind. Most of the houses that had proudly flown American flags had taken them in, but somehow the yellow ribbons seemed best left to age naturally in the New England elements.

We are now officially in the "post-war era." Though the fate of Iraq's Kurdish minority hangs precariously undecided and wartime embargos are causing, medical experts report, scores of infant deaths among other Iraqi communities, we have adopted a post-war emotional and political stance. We are thinking retrospectively. We are generating lessons.

The Gulf War lasted less than a year, but this post-war period is as fraught as that following on the heels of longer conflicts. Just as atheism is defined by reference to a god, so any post-war era is marked by its relationship to the war is succeeds. In that sense this is a militarized time, not a time of peace. And thus it is a time for vigilance, not just introspection. Many of those horrified by their inability to have prevented the massive use of military power, or perhaps even by their inability to withstand the seductive attractions of technological wizardry and post-Vietnam patriotism, will use these post-war months to take a close look at the failings of their country's peace movement. But it is at least as crucial that we watch how other players in the Gulf War are using this post-war era to fashion "lessons." For what lessons are presumed to have been taught by the war against Iraq will become the basis for militarizing the next international conflict. Many of those lessons are specifically about the relationships between women and men.

After every war, governments—on the losing, as well as winning side—take stock of how gender served or undermined their war efforts. The Crimean War offers a striking example of the post-war politics of gender. Every government involved in this mid-nineteenth-century conflict came away unhappy about its performance. The British military command and its parliamentary masters, for instance, were convinced that British soldiers had been ill-equipped to fight in the Crimea. Just like military strategists today, they devoted their post-war energies to pinpointing what ensured that male soldiers had high morale and optimum physical well-being. And just like their counterparts today in Washington, London, Riyadh, and Baghdad, they paid special attention to masculinity—and to the ways different groups of women might be controlled so that they could not jeopardize the sort of manliness deemed best suited for waging the government's military campaigns. In practice, this meant that British officials sparked two fierce debates: 1) over whether rank-and-file men should be allowed to marry (Were women as wives a drag on the military as long supposed or were they a potential insurance against venereal disease and debt?) and 2) over whether the rampaging venereal disease among male soldiers was controllable (Was it more effective and honorable to impose police restrictions on women in British garrison towns than to humiliate military men by making them undergo compulsory genital examinations?). Britain's first women's national political campaign—the Anti-Contagious Diseases Acts Campaign—was prompted by the nineteenth-century post-war lessons devised by worried military planners.

Marriage, morale, sexuality, discipline—these are the arenas for lesson-forging that still produce post-war attempts to refine the relations of women to the government's mostly male soldiery.

The first post-Gulf War attempts to change the American military's relationship to mothering already has been concluded: The military won. Representative Barbara Boxer, a progressive California Democrat, was dismayed by the stories published during the war of dual-military families having both parents called up and deployed far from their very young children. For several weeks the media had been full of pictures of infants being tearfully left behind with relatives while their mothers and fathers donned their fatigues and headed for the Gulf. No one should have been surprised. The military during the past decade had been relying more and more on the reserves in their global planning. The Pentagon deliberately had been using women to compensate for the decline in the pool of eligible (high-school graduate, drug-free, non-felon) young men; and, after an initial reluctance, it had come to see dual-career military couples as promoting re-enlistment and deepening whole families' loyalty to military service. But for the media, much of the public, and Congress it came as a rude shock to see this military-personnel strategic formula being translated into the apparent abandonment of infants.

Barbara Boxer thus saw as one lesson of the Gulf War the need to put limits on military deployment: Parenting of very young American children must take priority over the Pentagon's need for soldiers. Yet her bill barely survived its initial hearings. Defense Department officials, not surprisingly, raised immediate objections. In the Bush administration's vision of the New World Order, the U.S. military would have fewer overseas bases and reduced numbers of soldiers in its active-duty force while continuing to carry global responsibilities. In personnel terms, this combination will be possible only if the military can have absolutely free rein in calling reserves and moving those reserves and active-duty soldiers anywhere any time at a moment's notice. Mobility: It always has been the *sine qua non* of an effective military. And it always has required military commanders to have control over some women as service workers, as wives, as mothers, and as girlfriends. Bush's conception of the New World Order makes this need for control over women (so that they will in no way slow down mobilization) acute.

Barbara Boxer's bill was a very real threat to optimum mobility. But in the 1990s U.S. political scene the politics of parenting—especially of mothering—are at least as potent as the strategic imperative for a mobile military. So why did the Boxer bill never get off the ground? It would appear that it was killed not just by the Pentagon's opposition, but by the cool reception it received from many women military careerists. They, perhaps rightly, feared that while the bill sought to restrict deployment of "parents" of young children, if passed, it would be used to restrict the deployment of mothers in uniform. The Boxer bill, many canny military women lobbyists predicted, would create a militarized "mommy track."

"Women in combat" achieved an even higher post-war profile than military mothering. What lessons did the Gulf War generate about women's capacity to engage in combat and militaries' willingness to use them for combat? The Canadians had carried on this debate for several years before their government sent women and men to fight Iraq: As the result of a court case brought by women's-rights advocates under the country's new Charter of Rights, women soldiers as a class no longer could be excluded from combat. But neither they nor Dutch women, also theoretically eligible for combat, actually served in officially designated combat roles during the Gulf conflict. The British and Australian forces ban women from whatever they deem to be "combat" (the definitions are arbitrary in any military). But observers in both of these countries watched as the much larger and more visible U.S. contingent became the site for this latest in a long series of debates over femininity, masculinity, and the changing landscape of high-technology warfare.

Again, it was women members of the House of Representatives who took the lead in raising this post-war issue. Patricia Schroeder, Democrat of Colorado, and Beverly Byron, Democrat of Maryland, interpreted the Gulf War as proving that the nature of contemporary warfare made the conceptual divide between combat and non-combat irrelevant. Despite the U.S. ban on women in combat, 13 U.S. women soldiers were killed in Gulf action and two were taken prisoner by the Iraqi forces. "Women returning in body bags" turned out not to have seriously undercut the legitimacy of the Bush administration's war policy. The Pentagon itself was divided over the political and logistical wisdom of ending the combat ban. According to astute Pentagon watcher Linda Grant De Pauw, editor of the journal *Minerva*, older military professionals didn't conclude that the Gulf operations had proved that allowing women access to combat roles would not jeopardize the fighting morale of men in the now masculinized infantry, armor, fighter plane and bomber units. Morale always has been the sticking point. A military cannot afford to take any step that undermines the morale of its mainly male force; and morale among men is dependent to a large measure on esteem derived from their sense of manliness.

But a younger generation of Pentagon officials, civilian and uniformed, had come of age professionally since 1973, the start of the military's deliberate efforts to compensate for the end of the male draft by recruiting large numbers of women. These officials were willing to let the post-war lessons be honed by public representatives. If the U.S. public would legitimate women in combat, the military would have even more flexibility in deploying personnel according to its own needs. Women officers who made their views known backed the Schroeder and Byron legislative initiatives. They had become convinced that the combat ban was a major stumbling block on their path towards senior promotions.

According to Linda Grant De Pauw, however, the actors most notable for their silence in this post-war debate were organized feminists. When the legislation reached the Senate in May 1991 (sponsored by Bill Roth, R-Delaware), no feminist organization submitted testimony. Although during the war, the National Organization for Women had issued a declaration calling simultaneously for support of women in the Middle East and an end to all forms of sexism in the U.S. military, they, like other women who had spent years working for the Equal Rights Amendment, still remembered how anti-ERA forces had wielded women-in-combat anxieties to defeat the amendment. As in the past, too, many U.S. feminists, even those who adopt a liberal-feminist approach which assigns priority to equal opportunity, were profoundly ambivalent about making women's access to combat jobs a political priority. The debate, coming as it did in the wake of a war that frustrated many women whose feminist activism had been devoted to unsuccessful peace campaigning, seemed to leave no space for a more complicated dialogue about women's relationship to a militarized state.

So it was without an active civilian feminist organized presence that on May 22, 1991 the overwhelmingly male House of Representatives passed the 1992/93 Defense Authorization Bill as amended by Byron and Schroeder to permit for the first time the civilian secretaries of Navy and Air Force to assign women soldiers to fly combat aircraft. The amendment—which formally repeals the combat-exclusion Section 512 (the Army's combat-exclusion policy is not dictated by law but by the service's administrative policy)—is expected to pass the Senate later this year.

At the same time, further away from the floors of Congress and from the public limelight, Defense Department officials were assessing how well they did in ensuring that military wives and girlfriends stayed supportive not only of their men in uniform but of the military cause at large. This war provided the department with a chance to try out their revised family strategies. Since the early 1970s, in part in response to increasingly vocal military wives, the military had taken a far more activist and interventionist role in military-family affairs. The once-autonomous Military Family Resource Center, run by the YMCA, was integrated into the Pentagon. Child abuse and wife abuse became issues to be discussed administratively inside the Defense Department. Men's anti-violence groups reported being asked to come on bases to give training sessions to men returning from Operation Desert Storm, men likely to have inflated expectations of wifely homecomings, men likely to be too quick to resort to physical abuse when confronted with the messier realities of ordinary domestic life. Military social workers and military spouses learned that, if they could show that dysfunctional families threatened "military readiness," they could get even Under Secretaries to sit up and take notice. During the Gulf War, the Pentagon authorized the creation of family support groups for girlfriends and parents as well as spouses. Despite officers' wives during the 1980s becoming more resistant to pressures to perform unpaid labor on military bases, many of these groups relied on women married to senior male officers to serve as the hub of supportive networks. While many family members found the authorized groups helpful in everything from sharing fears to figuring out how to deal with creditors, others who took part said the groups seemed to be intent upon ensuring that women stayed supportive of the Bush policy and that they poured their energies into reducing soldiers' worries, not their own.

Even further from public attention, Allied militaries thought about the lessons of a war fought without prostitutes. The Saudi regime of King Fahd had made a no-brothels policy a stipulation of his acceptance of foreign forces. As his harsh suppression of the apparently modest women's driving protest later revealed, the regime was being challenged by male Islamic fundamentalists. Each group of men—the monarchy's supporters and the emergent opposition—used its respective abilities to control Saudi women as the litmus test of political legitimacy. We still know almost nothing about what the consequences of this prohibition were for militarized masculine sexuality. In Central America, Vietnam, the Philippines, South Korea, Japan, Puerto Rico, mainland United States, Germany, and Italy the Pentagon has operated as if prostitution were a necessary and integral part of U.S. military operations. It has not always, it is true, been easy to control that prostitution: It has been connected to the spread of AIDS; it has produced marriages not wanted by the military; it has caused friction between local police and military police; it has exacerbated tensions between Black and white soldiers; it has threatened the morale of American women in the services. But not until this war did the U.S. Defense Department believe it could sustain the masculine morale needed to ensure motivated, disciplined soldiering without prostitution. Perhaps the intensity and brevity of the Gulf conflict will make the absence of prostitution merely an anomaly, generating no institutional policy revisions. Or perhaps there have been delayed negative results, male sexual behaviors only known to awaiting girlfriends and wives back home or to Thai women working as prostitutes who greeted some of the first U.S. ships returning from the Gulf to Japan. We don't know yet. What we do know, based on years of experience, is that somewhere in the military someone is trying to figure out whether this war provided lessons for a better way to control sexuality for the sake of more effective warmaking.

Women's relationship to their government's military remains one not fashioned primarily by broadly based women's organizations in large part because that relationship sows such confusion. Is the military chiefly a public institution that distributes valuable benefits (pride, skills, salaries, influence, independence)? Or is the military best understood as a vehicle for state violence? What should feminists' stand be if it has become *both?* The hanging of yellow ribbons and the push to end the exclusion of women in combat seem to be intimately connected in the United States of the 1990s.

Women inside and outside the country's military are insisting that they have their own thoughts, their own aspirations. But long as women have so little control over the terms of debate, even their genuine efforts to voice those ideas and press for those aspirations are likely to produce short-term gains (more media coverage, more military promotions) without changing the basic ways in which public power is used. For their part, many men working in peace movements have barely conceded that the issue of women's relationship to state power, confusing as it is, is worthy of serious political attention. Few men asked women exactly what thoughts they were expressing when they put a ribbon on their secretarial in-tray; few monitored with genuine concern the congressional debate over women in combat. In this sense, many male peace activists have yet to recognize that militarization cannot be reversed until the politics of femininity's relationship to both masculinity and to the state are taken seriously.

It may be that the U.S. military—and other NATO militaries—has learned how to absorb just enough of the changes in women's expectations and influence to permit it to use women without drastically altering its own political mission. Maybe the U.S. military has come out of the Gulf War more thoroughly integrated into the social structure than it ever has been in the last two centuries. If so, the end of the Cold War will not mean the end of the militarization of women's lives.

Leonard Rifas

Supermarket Tabloids and Persian Gulf War Dissent

Supermarket tabloids do not carry political news, but this did not stop them from covering the Persian Gulf War. "Making the war seem amusing, entertaining, heartwarming, patriotic, or in other ways perfectly continuous with ordinary, upbeat programming" was, as James English has pointed out, not regarded as "political."[1] The estimated fifty million readers of the seven tabloids being published at the time of the Persian Gulf War—the *National Enquirer, National Examiner, News Extra, Globe, Star, Sun,* and *Weekly World News*—saw a version of the war that was sometimes silly or incredible but always supportive of the U.S. military intervention.[2] Tabloid war stories did not appear as lumps of hard news but were thoroughly interwoven with all the ongoing concerns of these weeklies, including health, diet, the British royal family, romance, country music, wrestling, Hollywood, psychics, and UFOs.[3]

In the seven supermarket tabloids, from February 5, 1991, through April 23, 1991, approximately four hundred stories and column items related, in various ways and at various distances, to the Persian Gulf War.[4] These two and a half months of stories begin with evangelist Billy Graham's sermon marking the beginning of the war and end with his summation of the war's lessons.[5] The politics of tabloid entertainment come most visibly to the surface in those stories about protest and dissent: representations of celebrity activism in the antiwar movement, tabloids' failure to present the arguments for "peace," and their explicit and implicit recommendations for responding to the peace movement.

Celebrity Activism

The tabloids can be read both as journalistic evidence that dissenters were being intimidated and as a potentially intimidating force for conformity in their own right. Elisabeth Noelle-Neumann's theory of a "spiral of silence" argues that an apparent majority can intimidate those with unpopular views into keeping their opinions to themselves.[6] The dissenters most reported on and most subject to the policing power of tabloid gossip were celebrities.

The role of film and television actors as political spokespersons, fund-raisers, and activists has become formidable.[7] During the Persian Gulf War, many celebrities received friendly tabloid attention for their expressions of support for U.S. troops. Vanilla Ice and Alice Cooper were photographed wearing red, white, and blue.[8] One columnist reported that Dr. Ruth Westheimer had chatted with troops at a Patriot missile base near Tel Aviv and noted Arnold Schwarzenegger's donation of fifty tons of workout equipment to "our boys in the Gulf."[9]

However, the tabloids depicted celebrity opponents of the Persian Gulf War less respectfully, as locked in struggle, not with government policies, but with their own families and co-workers. The tabloids emphasized that the protesters were economically endangering those around them. The *Star's* February 5, 1991, article "Lynn Redgrave blasts sister Vanessa over pro-Iraq rantings" introduces the theme of intrafamily conflict in the headline and lead, while the possibility of career reprisals follows closely:

> Shocking pro-Iraqi comments by actress Vanessa Redgrave has [*sic*] outraged everyone around her—including her own sister, Lynn.
> The controversy could cause ABC-TV to pull the plug on an upcoming movie starring the Redgrave sisters—*Whatever Happened to Baby Jane?*[10]

The article also quoted "an insider" as reasoning: "If a lot of U.S. blood is spilled in the Gulf War it seems unthinkable that the American people would welcome into their homes—on TV or in any other form—someone who has publicly sympathized with the madman Hussein and his vicious policies." (The show was eventually broadcast as scheduled.)

The article encouraged sympathy for Lynn Redgrave, giving an example to support her fear of economic reprisals: "In April 1978, Vanessa's pro-Palestine Liberation Organization statement at the Academy Awards ceremonies caused canceled seats for sister Lynn's performance in the play, *St. Joan.*" The verbs *could cause* and *caused* suggest a natural, mechanical response, neatly absolving the influence of such additional factors as the inflammatory article itself. Vanessa

Redgrave made the "pro-Iraqi comments" in a peace rally speech in Barcelona on January 13, before the outbreak of the war. The *Star* article presented Redgrave's speech with one short quotation ("We have to unconditionally defend Iraq against American, British and Israeli aggression") and one brief paraphrase ("The 53-year-old British actress claimed that the U.S.-led coalition had been trying to sabotage a peaceful solution to the Gulf crisis.")

The *Star* report uses about as many words to characterize Redgrave's speech as it does to summarize it. The reporter and those quoted in the article describe Redgrave's statements as "pro-Iraq rantings," "shocking pro-Iraqi comments," a "bizarre declaration," "inflammatory remarks," public sympathy for "the madman Hussein and his vicious policies," and "radical political views."

U.S. daily newspapers used the same brief quotation to encapsulate Redgrave's speech. Redgrave believed that her position had been so badly mischaracterized that she paid for a half-page advertisement in the February 8, 1991, *New York Times* to clarify that although she was in "unqualified" opposition to the war, she was also "unconditionally" opposed to the Iraqi invasion of Kuwait (p. C-5). Her first argument in her own defense was: "In context, the statement fully supported a peaceful, negotiated settlement of the crisis; a position taken by all the American church organizations, twelve American trade unions, His Holiness Pope John Paul II, Cardinal Hume, Crown Prince Hassan of Jordan, and millions of peace-loving individuals throughout the world." The supermarket tabloids failed to follow the story when Vanessa Redgrave's "shocking comments," as they were reported in the daily tabloids of London and New York, led to her being fired from the starring role in an upcoming national tour of a Broadway play, *Lettice and Lovage*.

Actors' Equity filed a grievance against the producers of *Lettice and Lovage* on Vanessa Redgrave's behalf, charging that firing her was a violation of an agreement that expressly prohibits discrimination against any actor on the basis of political persuasion or belief. The arbitrator sided with the producers, who argued that they had not blacklisted Redgrave because of a political disagreement. Instead, according to the *New York Times*, "the producers had said that their decision not to hire Ms. Redgrave was based on their belief that public reaction to statements the actress made in January about the situation in the Persian Gulf eliminated any possibility that a national tour starring her would be financially successful."[11]

Although Vanessa Redgrave might seem to be a poor example of a protester who could be intimidated into silence, in fact, Redgrave had decided on a policy of refusing to be interviewed about politics.

Whereas the tabloids stereotyped her as a "leftwing loudmouth," accounts in the mainstream press emphasized Redgrave's refusal to discuss politics.[12] Vanessa Redgrave's career exemplifies the economic price that can be exacted from an actor because of unpopular views. After her comments at the 1978 Academy Awards ceremony, which were interpreted as anti-Semitic, she was virtually banned from the U.S. stage for the next decade.

The tabloids found "shocking" but unworthy of investigation Redgrave's idea that the U.S.-led coalition had tried to sabotage a peaceful solution to the Persian Gulf Crisis. They spared their readers any evidence that might lead them to agree with such a conclusion.[13]

The same basic formula that introduced the story on the Redgrave sisters—family conflict and fear of economic reprisals against the protester's innocent partner—recurs in the February 26, 1991, *National Enquirer* story "Ted Turner Tells Jane Fonda: Keep Your Mouth Shut About the War":

> CNN boss Ted Turner has ordered bride-to-be "Hanoi Jane" Fonda to keep her mouth shut about the Persian Gulf War—and now she's having second thoughts about marrying him.
>
> The cable TV mogul has told America's most hated Vietnam War protester not to speak out against this war because any controversy could hurt his network and his political ambitions—and earn her a new label as "Baghdad Jane," say sources. (36)

Most of Jane Fonda's statements in this *Enquirer* article concern her relationship with Ted Turner, but, in the middle of the piece, there is a brief statement of her political views:

> Jane told a close pal, "I resent that Ted doesn't trust me. Does he think I'm going to pose on a scud missile with a bunch of Saddam look-alikes? What I did in Vietnam was stupid and I wouldn't do it again. I'm an older and wiser woman.
>
> "I'm still against war. But I'm for America and our troops. I just don't want them dying so gas moguls can gouge us at the pumps."

In this case, the pressure to remain silent was represented as successful: "Pals say she had planned to speak out against this war too—until Turner stopped her."

As in other tabloid stories about protest, supporting "our boys" is contrasted with opposing American troops and supporting Saddam Hussein's policies. The tabloids usually allowed antiwar celebrities only enough space to deny that they were anti-American or supporters of Saddam Hussein, but never enough space to clearly explain how they squared this with opposition to the war.

Although the article had warned that "their wedding plans [were] in big trouble," they did go on to marry. Tabloid predictions in these

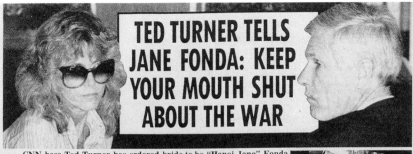

TED TURNER TELLS JANE FONDA: KEEP YOUR MOUTH SHUT ABOUT THE WAR

CNN boss Ted Turner has ordered bride-to-be "Hanoi Jane" Fonda to keep her mouth shut about the Persian Gulf War — and now she's having second thoughts about marrying him.

The cable TV mogul has told America's most hated Vietnam War protester not to speak out against this war because any controversy could hurt his network and his political ambitions — and earn her a new label as "Baghdad Jane," say sources.

As a result, Jane and her billionaire boyfriend — who'd made plans for a June wedding — had their first fight ever, say insiders. But surprisingly, the outspoken actress has followed orders by canceling TV talk show appearances and refusing interviews — even though she's fuming inside.

"One of the things I appreciated most about Ted is that he let me be me — no matter what I said, or did," Jane told a longtime friend.

"But now he's asking me to be a different kind

She's furious and their wedding plans are in big trouble

of woman. I'm not sure I want to marry a man who wants to dominate me.

"The first time we ever had a fight was when he told me, 'If you love me you'll shut up. Everybody hated you when you were Hanoi Jane. I don't want you to become Baghdad Jane.' "

Jane infuriated millions of Americans when she protested the Vietnam War by going to Hanoi, attacking the U.S. in propaganda speeches and even having her picture taken on a North Vietnamese antiaircraft gun. Pals say she had planned to speak out against this war, too — until Turner stopped her.

Now the first cracks have appeared in the couple's relationship — after nearly two blissful years together.

Jane told a close pal, "I resent that Ted doesn't trust me. Does he think I'm going to pose on a SCUD missile with a bunch of Saddam look-alikes? What I did in Vietnam was stupid and I wouldn't do it again. I'm an older and wiser woman.

"I'm still against war. But I'm for America and our troops. I just don't want them dying so gas moguls can gouge us at the pumps."

Ted — who supports liberal and conservative causes — is worried about what his fiancee says because he doesn't want to fuel controversy. That's important so his CNN reporters appear impartial while covering the news from Baghdad, Riyadh, Amman, Tel Aviv and Washington, said an insider.

Added one of Turner's friends: "Ted's tried to be neutral in public statements on the war, but privately he supports the allied action

INSULT: When Jane Fonda posed on an enemy antiaircraft gun during the Vietnam War, America was outraged. Ted Turner wants no such controversy.

'Does he think I'm going to pose on a SCUD missile with a bunch of Saddam look-alikes?'

against Saddam 100 percent."

Ted's also careful about what he says because he plans to launch a political career that could eventually land him in the White House, say sources. And he realizes Americans aren't likely to elect a President whose First Lady is blasting the government.

Jane's spokeswoman Pat Newcomb insists the actress has recently canceled interviews about her new workout video because she "doesn't feel it's appropriate to be discussing videos when

there's a war going on."

But the real reason Jane's keeping an unusually low profile is her promise to Ted, say pals.

"Jane loves Ted, but above all, she's a fiercely independent woman," said a source. "She doesn't like taking orders from anyone.

"She told Ted, 'I'll hold my tongue for now. But don't expect this to go on forever — because hiding your beliefs isn't much better than lying about them!' "

— *LYDIA ENCINAS, ROGER CAPETTINI and ALAN BRAHAM SMITH*

YOU READ IT HERE FIRST

'Guns N' Roses' star ends marriage after 9 rocky months

Rowdy rocker Axl Rose, of the heavy metal group Guns N' Roses, has had his marriage secretly annulled — because he says his wife wouldn't stay home and r___

FLASHBACK to January 14 ENQUIRER.

Newspapers, TV and radio stations across the country flashed the "news" recently about the annulment of rowdy rocker Axl Rose's marriage —

but it was an old story to ENQUIRER readers.

We revealed in our issue that went on sale January 14 that the star of the heavy metal group Guns N' Roses had his marriage to Erin Everly secretly annulled in Reno, Nev., on January 3.

In an exclusive interview, Rose told The ENQUIRER that he called it quits with Erin — daughter of Don Everly of the Everly Brothers — after only nine months because she wouldn't stay home and raise a family.

"In that nine months we

By CLIFF BARR

spent about two months together," he said. "So obviously I didn't have a wife."

Weeks later, the other news media finally caught up with The ENQUIRER's scoop.

In early February People magazine published a report about the annulment. The story also went out on the United Press International wire which serves newspapers, radio and TV stations.

But once again, The ENQUIRER was the first to break the news!

Popularity comes from allowing yourself to be bored by people while pretending to enjoy it. — Karol Newlin F

Ted Turner tells Jane Fonda, "Keep your mouth shut about the war."
(National Enquirer, *Feb. 26, 1991*)

articles are a consistently poor guide to the future, but they all serve to build an association between dissent and loss.

If all the tabloids cared about were sensation and scandal per se (rather than as weapons in the war effort), they might have characterized differently Jane Fonda's years of protest. They could have quoted internal FBI documents, released through a Freedom of Information

Act suit, which show that in 1970, FBI director J. Edgar Hoover personally authorized an agent to send an untraceable letter to a Hollywood gossip columnist in which the agent falsely claimed that he had heard Jane Fonda exhort a crowd at a Black Panther Party fund-raiser to chant "We will kill Richard Nixon and any other motherfucker who stands in our way." For the tabloids, though, newsworthy scandals include antiwar protest but not illegal government harassment of protesters. (The gossip columnist who had received that unmarked FBI letter did not use the item.)[14]

The article on Ted and Jane also failed to clarify that much of Jane Fonda's work against the Vietnam War had been done in support of the GI movement.[15] The tabloids' dichotomy between "supporting our troops" and "opposing the war" would have been damaged if they had acknowledged that some troops opposed the war. The only Persian Gulf War "protest" within the military that the tabloids recognized was the griping of two enlisted women who were ordered to the Persian Gulf while in labor.[16]

A third example of celebrity activism varies the formula by substituting co-workers for family. After Woody Harrelson, an actor on the TV series *Cheers*, was caught by news cameras at a public antiwar meeting, he became the topic of several tabloid articles.[17] The *Enquirer* published a full-page report on February 19, 1991, "They're calling him . . . 'Baghdad Woody.'" From the beginning, the article describes the protest in terms of interpersonal conflicts: "'Cheers' bartender Woody Harrelson is under furious attack from outraged members of the cast and crew because of his opposition to the war. They've tagged him 'Baghdad Woody'—and some have even branded him a traitor to America" (36). The article focuses particularly on Harrelson's coworkers' insults and pranks against him. Deep into their story, the reporters add that Harrelson's employers also opposed his protest:

> Series execs are terrified Woody's actions will send the hit show into a ratings slide, said the source on the set. They hauled Woody into a meeting and read him the riot act. He was defiant—but producers finally pressured him into releasing a statement saying his presence at the rally had been misinterpreted. In that statement, he said: "I join the people of this country in unanimous support for the lives of our young men and women in the Gulf. I certainly do not support Saddam Hussein or his actions."

The tabloids suggested that Harrelson not only economically endangered his co-workers but that his protest might also be exposing them to physical danger. The *Globe* reported that Harrelson's *Doc Hollywood* co-star Michael J. Fox, who had already been "terrified of Arab terror

"*Baghdad Woody.*" (National Enquirer, *Feb. 19, 1991*)

ist activity in Hollywood," was now also frightened of "retaliation from war supporters."[18]

Reprisals against the protester himself are also featured: "TV cameras caught Woody enthusiastically applauding [Ron] Kovic—and the star was immediately dumped as grand marshall of this year's Mardi Gras parade in New Orleans."

In the February 19, 1991, *Star* article "Cheers uproar as Woody waves the white flag—Kirstie Alley: Shape up and back our boys in the Gulf," Woody Harrelson explains how he felt about losing his position as grand marshal:

> Woody responded: "As far as I'm concerned, Mardi Gras has nothing to do with politics. I'm not a bad guy. I have no animosity toward anybody.
>
> "I just wanted to come down there, meet a lot of people, hang out and party."
>
> Harrelson said he supported the U.S. troops and "will be the first in line to greet them when they come back."
>
> But he said he wished President Bush had given the sanctions against Iraq more time to work. "I wasn't alone in that belief," he said. "Nearly 48 percent of Congress agreed with me. Seven of the last nine chairmen of the Joint Chiefs of Staff agreed with me."
>
> He also charged that the decision to drop him from the New Orleans parade made him "a victim of something opposite to democracy," and said it harkened back to McCarthyism. (5)

Woody Harrelson's comments in the *Star* as well as Vanessa Redgrave's ad in the *New York Times* gave high priority to listing some of the people and institutions that had agreed with their respective antiwar positions. They insisted, in effect, that the papers were overstating their isolation.

Much of the power in these three cautionary celebrity stories is in their reduction of political conflicts to a very intimate scale, one in which fear of rejection is keenly felt. Communication researchers Charles T. Salmon and Kurt Neuwirth have observed that "fear of ostracization is more likely to occur in a community setting, in which individuals interact on a face-to-face basis, than in a more ambiguous national setting, in which a holder of a minority opinion might not actually be ostracized."[19] Salmon and Neuwirth argue that people do not live within a monolithic, national climate of opinion. They suggest that dissidents' fear of ostracism may be tempered by the awareness that there are people in other communities who agree with them. An isolated antiwar tabloid reader might take heart from knowing that some communities were organizing protests. The tabloids, however, did not acknowledge the existence of diverse, local communities of opinion about the war. They depicted only a "tidal wave of pride . . . washing over the nation" as "from sea to shining sea, . . . Americans of every age [took] to the streets to salute the men and women who [were] putting their lives on the line."[20] Opponents of the war were shown as isolated and ambivalent.[21]

The case of Hollywood celebrities, though, is not directly comparable with the issue of climates of opinion intimidating ordinary readers whom Salmon and Neuwirth and other "spiral of silence" researchers have investigated. For one thing, historically, gossip has had an especially intense power over Hollywood actors. Richard Schickel remembers, "[A]s we did not discover until some years later, the columnists, the whole shabby show biz press, were used as enforcers, whipping wayward players into line by the threat of printing damaging stories if they refused to abandon bad habits, or even if they became rebellious over roles or salaries."[22] Even if the direct effect of tabloid coverage on dampening dissent could be shown to be negligible, the indirect effects—through silencing celebrities, the symbols through which much of the public grasps issues and events—might be significant.

The tabloids managed to associate heroic protest with *support* for the war rather than opposition to it. They did this with stories of noncelebrity, patriotic Americans who defied rules and ordinances in order to fly the U.S. flag. There were several variations. In two cases, parents of Desert Storm airmen defied their condominium associations' bans on flag displays.[23] A firefighter was fired for sewing a flat patch onto his uniform, while another beat a similar ban by having his hair cut and dyed to resemble a flag.[24] "Persian Gulf War opponent" Jessica Lange's drivers refused her demand to "remove all patriotic decorations from their cars."[25] The only tabloid story naming a noncelebrity opponent of the war was about an actor, fired from his job waiting on tables, allegedly for arguing with patrons about the war.[26]

The Emptiness in the Word Peace

The tabloids' stories of celebrity activists seem well suited to stir whatever fears of public condemnation that a pacifist tabloid reader might harbor. Salmon and Neuwirth, however, argue that fear of standing against the crowd may not be the central issue: "[I]f individuals are refraining from engaging in political discussion out of fear, the nature of the fear may be 'fear of appearing ignorant' rather than 'fear of isolation' as hypothesized by Noelle-Neumann."[27] In this connection, it is relevant that the tabloids failed to supply their readers with sufficient information to challenge the government's war policies.[28] Even if they had, because some tabloids admittedly scramble fiction and fact for the sake of entertainment, their stories cannot be taken seriously as documentation.[29]

By not fleshing out the reasons for the opponents' positions, tabloids reduced opposing the war to a role or adjective. *Star*'s February 5, 1991, article about Hollywood activist-actor Ed Asner, entitled "Ed Asner's secret obsession: Sex toys," begins by drawing attention to his opposition to the war:

> Ed Asner's secret has been revealed—the former *Lou Grant* star and anti-war activist frequents a Hollywood sex shop in search of erotic adult toys.
> The 61-year-old Asner, an outspoken opponent of the Gulf War, is a regular customer at the Pleasure Chest, a Santa Monica Boulevard store that stocks everything from edible panties to torture devices. (9)

It would be an unusual tabloid reader who would ask at this point, "What are Asner's arguments against the Gulf War?" The story leads the reader's attention in a more salacious direction and adds nothing further about Asner's political opinions.[30] This article seems a throwback to the old method of discrediting radicals by linking them with scandalous sexual behavior.[31]

Unique among the articles, "Why I'm fighting this war" by Pfc. Alexander N. Porter allows the powerful word *peace* to be associated with opponents of the government's policies.[32] Usually the peace movement was defined less positively as an "antiwar" movement. However, this article mentions the peace movement only in passing, once in a headline ("GI's letter inspires his town, silences peace protestors and moves Cher to tears") and again in the introduction to Porter's letter: "Army Pfc. Alex Porter, 22, explains why he is proud to serve his country—and even die for it. The moving testament, first read by his mother, Clo, on a Southern California radio station, brought a tremendous outpouring of patriotism, silenced peace demonstrators and even brought Cher to tears."[33]

In the absence of a reasoned argument for opposing the war, the Orwellian identification of President Bush as a great seeker of peace (and of the war as his means for seeking peace) became possible. This was brought out most forcefully during the first week of tabloid war coverage in both the *Enquirer*'s article "Billy Graham: Why we have to fight for peace" and the *Star*'s "How Billy Graham brought light to George Bush's darkest hour." These articles quote extensively from Graham's sermon "A Service for Peace," delivered to government and military leaders assembled in the Memorial Chapel at the Fort Myer, Virginia, army base. In the sermon, Graham calls on all Americans to recognize the ethical necessity of war and to pray for peace. As if to foreclose the argument that it is logically inconsistent to "fight [a war] for peace," Graham emphasizes: "The issues . . . are complex and diffi-

"How Billy Graham inspired George Bush to go to war." (Star, Feb. 5, 1991)

cult. . . . [T]here are some spiritual forces at work—both good and evil—that are beyond our comprehension. . . . Let us pray that God will intervene and bring peace to that troubled region." As it turned out, then, the most extensive call for "peace" in the Middle East that the tabloids reported during this period was also the most explicit call to support the war.

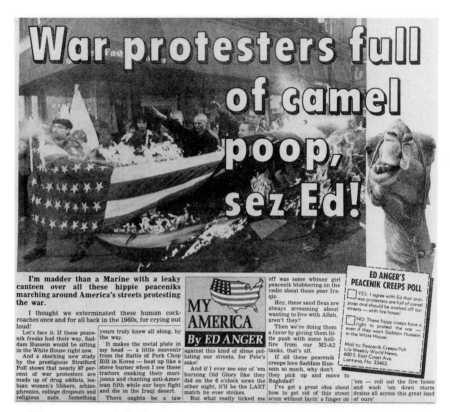

"War protesters full of camel poop!" (Weekly World News, *Mar. 5, 1991*)

What to Do about Dissent

The tabloids' most extensive comments on noncelebrity protest were in Ed Anger's parodic editorial "War protesters full of camel poop, sez Ed!" In brief:

> I'm madder than a Marine with a leaky canteen over all these hippie peaceniks marching around America's streets protesting the war.
> I thought we exterminated these human cockroaches once and for all back in the 1960s, for crying out loud!
> . . . I've got a great idea about how to get rid of this street scum without layin' a finger on 'em—roll out the fire hoses and wash 'em down storm drains all across this great land of ours![34]

Ed Anger has a reputation in tabloid circles as a classic liberal who writes 180 degrees away from his own opinions to make his column amusing.[35] The point remains, though, that this satirical column merely exaggerates the actual tabloid prescription for dealing with dissenters. The tabloids suggested to their readers that they were in personal danger from Iraqi terrorists in the United States, that war opponents were Iraqi-sympathizers, and that force might be the only language these protesters can understand.[36]

A brief gossip column item in the March 12, 1991, *Enquirer* presented, in miniature, the tabloids' suggestions for coping with dissenters: "Feisty 87-year-old *Bob Hope*, who's braved more war zones than most generals, stood up for America during a shopping stroll through LA's Century City when he spotted antiwar protestors—and when one heckled him, he flung Gatorade in his peacenik puss!" (14).

The *Enquirer* article "Baghdad Woody" approvingly quoted insiders on the *Cheers* set as saying: "'With American troops fighting and dying thousands of miles away, many of the cast and crew believe Woody's anti-war activities are downright unpatriotic. Some are so livid they're even talking about pounding some sense into him!'" The excuse that Louisiana officials gave when they withdrew Harrelson's invitation to be grand marshal was:

[T]hey were worried about protecting him from people angry over his political views.
"I don't think anybody could have ensured Mr. Harrelson's safety if he had come to New Orleans," said one organizer.

The *Enquirer* hinted at violence in its caption for a photograph of a white pinup model with a red top, a bare midriff, and blue cutoffs, standing in front of a flag: "Nobody'd better try burning the flag around Ava Fabian—she's not only a patriot, she's a kick-boxer!"[37]

The most violent fantasies for suppressing anti-U.S. sentiments were those made in response to wrestling villain "Sgt. Slaughter's" pro-Iraqi posturing. In the February 19, 1991, *Examiner*, readers responded to a poll asking whether to throw "Sgt. Slaughter" out of the World Wrestling Federation "for hiring Iraqi General Adnan and pledging allegiance to the hated Iraqi flag" by proposing "hanging" him, "blowing him apart," "blow[ing] him away," having him shot, dropping him "into the middle of the ocean," and deporting him and stripping him of his citizenship (8).

Although the articles about Jane Fonda and Vanessa Redgrave did not mention violence, one item did suggest that protesters forfeit their civil rights:

Left-wing loudmouth Vanessa Redgrave is raising a helluva stink because she claims she's been electronically bugged by British security agents. That's kinda funny, isn't it—she's been bugging everybody else by squawking that Saddam Hussein is a good guy who has been persecuted by us nasty Americans and our allies.[38]

Taboids fostered confusion between opposing government policies and acting as an enemy operative. One "intelligence agent" revealed to the *Sun:*

> [T]here is concern that certain anti-war groups would be willing to
> help Saddam hide in the United States.
>   The CIA reportedly is already monitoring certain individuals
> and groups who may be sending assistance to the Iraqis.
>   "The vast majority of Americans favor our deployment in the
> Middle East," says one source.
>   "But there are some wealthy men and women—as well as some
> fanatical groups—who will do their best to sabotage our interests."[39]

Although the tabloids included suggestions that dissenters could
be handled by yelling at them, playing tricks on them, throwing Gatorade on them, turning fire hoses on them, burying them alive, banning
them, and spying on them, there was one simple option that they never
mentioned: reasoning with them.

Judged by the standards of serious journalism, the war coverage
in the tabloids was horrifying. The intellectual tradition of professing
horror at the sensationalism of popular newspapers is as old as popular newspapers themselves, and yet, some of the excesses of tabloid
war coverage were of historic proportions.[40] Judged from the viewpoint of the tabloids, the standards of serious journalism are a preten-
tious bore.[41] However, the mythic standoff between mainstream
propriety and tabloid sensationalism is out of date. The former boundaries between news and gossip, respectable and trash information,
have decomposed beyond repair.[42]

Perhaps the tabloids are horrifying for what they reveal as a parodic reflection of the themes in the mainstream coverage: the demonization of Saddam Hussein, the indifference to Iraqi lives, the great
shows of support for the military. The reflection, though, was very un-
even. Military technology was infrequently celebrated and military
activities were rarely reported.[43]

Besides fear of ostracism and reprisals, fear of appearing stupid,
and lack of visible protest leaders, there is an additional factor suppressing dissent. Chomsky argues that "the huge slaughter preferred
by the Bush administration" was made possible because U.S. citizens
were "isolated, deprived of the kinds of associations that might [have
led] to independent thought and political action."[44] In his analysis, the
crucial problem is the institutionalization of a "murderous totalitarian culture" that reduces people to spectators and consumers. Tabloids have been relentless in encouraging such isolation. P. J. Corkery
recalls that when writing for the *Enquirer* in the late 1970s, he submit-

ted a story idea on how to give a simple house party. His boss, Generoso Pope, Jr., grimaced over the proposal and killed it. Corkery explains: "The Boss never wants the reader to feel bad about his or her life. The job of the paper, aside from getting people to buy it each week, The Boss says, is to entertain. And to ameliorate. Never to make our readers feel as if they're missing something. Like parties."[45] Judging from recent content, this policy has not changed.

Until Chomsky's arguments, and others like his, are widely available in the easy-to-read, personalized, dramatic, scandalous, popular, and exciting language of the tabloids, the fear that we are spiraling into totalitarianism cannot be safely dismissed.

Notes

1. James F. English, "That's Entertainment," *Lies of Our Times,* Apr. 1991, 5–6. English argues that "it may be far more important, in assessing the public impact of media representations of this or any future war, to consider all the 'non-political' programming that is to one degree or another parasitical of the war story itself. And the first step in such a consideration would have to be a close look at the very category of 'non-political' programming and of the way it sustains itself in our media."

   English's point of departure in this article is that actress Margot Kidder's participation in an antiwar press conference, as dramatized by the mainstream press, quickly resulted in "a call from Plan International USA informing her that if she continued questioning the wisdom of the war, they 'could not afford to have someone so "political" representing them.' "

   In an interview conducted by Claudia Dreifus published in the *Progressive,* June 1991, actor Tim Robbins refers to Margot Kidder as one of "several outspoken and political figures" who "were publicly mugged for their dissent." Robbins explained the reluctance of actors to speak out against the war by saying, "I think a point was made with Margot Kidder. People *did* jump down her throat. And that sent out a clear message. This is nothing new. The same thing happened in previous wars. All you need to do is shut down one person to get to many."

   The supermarket tabloids ignored Margot Kidder and her antiwar activities.

2. Elizabeth S. Bird cites the estimates of fifty million supermarket tabloid readers and ten million copies weekly paid circulation in *For Enquiring Minds: A Cultural Study of Supermarket Tabloids* (Knoxville: University of Tennessee Press, 1992), 7.

3. Some memorable examples include Nick Patrick's "Combat duty in Middle East cures arthritis," *Sun,* Feb. 5, 1991, 35; Cliff Barr's "Outpouring of love from Gulf heroes inspires girl who got AIDS from dentist," *Enquirer,* Mar. 5, 1991, 21; "Saddam's sickening mania: 'Iraq Butcher' tortures and kills cats, dogs—for fun!" *Examiner,* Mar. 5, 1991, 6–7; "Di steals soldier boy's heart," *Globe,* Apr. 2, 1991, 7; and "Captured UFO flown—by U.S. Navy," *Weekly World News,* Mar. 19, 1991, 46–47.

4. The issues of the *Weekly World News* are postdated two weeks, rather than one week. The issues dated Feb. 12 through Apr. 30 were included in the research sample.

This essay is based on the author's personal research collection of super-market tabloids. Unfortunately, this collection does not include issues published between the Iraqi invasion of Kuwait and the beginning of Operation Desert Storm. One pertinent clipping from this crucial period that I chanced to have saved is "You don't have to jeopardize one man," published in the *Star*, Dec. 4, 1990, 5. The opening paragraph is: "Rambo yellow? A pacifist wimpo? Could be. Sylvester Stallone is urging President Bush: Bring back our troops from the Persian Gulf."

Stallone warned that a battle with Iraq could cost thousands of American lives; "he adds[, however,] that if the United States has no other option then it should, as a last resort, nuke 'em. 'That way,' he says, 'no American would get hurt." The reporter warned that Stallone's pacifistic remarks against President Bush's Mideast policy "could lead to an outcry similar to that over Jane Fonda's antiwar stance during Vietnam—one that still haunts her today."

Rebecca Sturm Kelm has described the difficulties that librarians' indifference or hostility to tabloids has posed for historical research: Kelm, "The Lack of Access to Back Issues of the Weekly Tabloids: Does It Matter?" *Journal of Popular Culture* 23 (Spring 1990): 45–50.

5. Ed Susman and Dan McDonald, "Billy Graham: Why we have to fight for peace," *Enquirer*, Feb. 5, 1991, 6; Norma Langley and Leon Frellich, "How Billy Graham brought light to George Bush's darkest hour," *Star*, Feb. 5, 1991, 6–7; Dan McDonald and Ed Susman, "Billy Graham: How peace will make America stronger," *Enquirer*, Apr. 23, 1991, 33.

6. Elisabeth Noelle-Neumann, *The Spiral of Silence: Public Opinion, Our Social Skin* (Chicago: University of Chicago Press, 1984).

7. Ronald Brownstein, *The Power and the Glitter: The Hollywood-Washington Connection* (New York: Pantheon, 1990); Richard Schickel, *Intimate Strangers: The Culture of Celebrity* (Garden City, N.Y.: Doubleday, 1985).

8. "Pizzazz at the American Music Awards," *Enquirer*, Feb. 19, 1991, 42.

9. Peter Wilde, "Extra Hot Gossip," *News Extra*, Mar. 12, 1991, 19; Feb. 26, 1991, 19.

10. "Lynn Redgrave blasts sister Vanessa over pro-Iraq rantings," *Star*, Feb. 5, 1991, 21. See also "Hot Stuff!" *Globe*, Feb. 5, 1991, 3; and "Lynn Redgrave boiling mad at sister Vanessa," *Weekly World News*, Apr. 23, 1991, 13.

11. Mervyn Rothstein, "Redgrave Rebuffed on 'Lettice' Tour," *New York Times*, Aug. 20, 1991, C11.

Alan Dershowitz had argued when the grievance was filed, "[H]er performances on stage generally receive rave reviews, and she does fill the theaters in which she performs. The decision to cancel her tour cannot be justified as a purely economic one. It is primarily a political decision based on disapproval of her politics. Those who canceled her tour will argue that there were economic considerations as well. But that is always the argument in such cases." Dershowitz editorialized in favor of Redgrave's right to perform in a manner that made his personal contempt for her political views unmistakable. "Defending a Theater for the Absurd," *New York Times*, Feb. 24, 1991.

An article in *Variety* reported that the arbitrator's opinion "almost certainly denie[d] Redgrave $540,000 she would have earned for the proposed 36-week tour": Jeremy Gerard, "Redgrave loses 'Lettice' Appeal," *Variety*, Aug. 26, 1991.

See also "Actors' Equity to File Grievance for Redgrave," *New York Times*, Mar. 26, 1991, C15; Jeremy Gerard, "'Lettice' tour wilts: Redgrave's war comments apparently shocked backers," *Variety*, Feb. 25, 1992, 249ff; "Patriot Fallout," *Nation*, Mar. 11, 1991, 291–292; Lloyd Grove, "Vanessa Redgrave Bites Her Tongue," *Washington Post*, June 23, 1991, G5.

12. Vanessa Redgrave's refusal to be interviewed about politics was mentioned in Elaine Warren's "Lynn Redgrave opens up . . . but whatever happened to sister Vanessa?" *TV Guide*, Feb. 16, 1991, 18, and Sally Ogle Davis's "Redgraves Close Ranks," *Boston Herald*, Feb. 13, 1991; and her contract for interviewers formalizing this condition was published the previous year by *Harper's:* "Any Questions?" Feb. 1990, 23.

13. The mainstream press also underplayed evidence that the United States and Britain deliberately sabotaged a peaceful solution to the crisis. See Noam Chomsky's Jan. 30, 1991, speech at Bates College, Lewiston, Maine, published in Westfield, N.J., as Pamphlet #6 of the Open Magazine Pamphlet Series under the title *The New World Order*.

14. Bill Davidson, *Jane Fonda: An Intimate Biography* (New York: Dutton, 1990), 5–7; James Kirkpatrick Davis, *Spying on America: The FBI's Domestic Counterintelligence Program* (New York: Praeger, 1992), 120–121.

15. Thomas Kiernan, *Jane: An Intimate Biography of Jane Fonda* (New York: G. P. Putnam's Sons, 1973), 329, 338–342.

16. "Angry protests: Moms in labor ordered to Gulf," *Examiner*, Mar. 12, 1991, 4.

17. Ella Taylor cited the *Cheers* show in passing as an example of situation comedy "work-families" in *Prime Time Families* (Berkeley and Los Angeles: University of California Press, 1989), 157, 177.

18. "Michael J. Fox blows top over peacenik Woody bomb scare," *Globe*, Feb. 26, 1991, 35.

19. Charles T. Salmon and Kurt Neuwirth, "Perceptions of Opinion 'Climates' and Willingness to Discuss the Issue of Abortion," *Journalism Quarterly* 67 (Autumn 1990): 669.

20. "The true voice of America tells our troops we're right behind you: America's Pride and Glory," *Star*, Mar. 15, 1991, 2–3.

21. One example of antiwar ambivalence appeared in the gossip item "Mick can't get satisfaction with new anti-war song": " 'The song only expresses the ambivalent feelings that many people have about the war,' says Jagger, who's in Atlanta making a movie. But the BBC has already banned it." *Star*, Mar. 5, 1991, 15.

22. Schickel, *Intimate Strangers*, 82–83.

23. "We're at war, but . . . Old Glory is Banned," *Examiner*, Feb. 12, 1991, 16; and "Mom fights to fly flag as sons go off to war," *Star*, Feb. 5, 1991, 18.

24. Bob Temmey, "Fireman axed—for wearing an American flag on his sleeve," *Enquirer*, Feb. 19, 1991, 2; and "Fireman's star-spangled haircut beats ban on flag," *Enquirer*, Mar. 26, 1991, 38.

25. Janet Charlton, "Star People," *Star*, Mar. 26, 1991, 15. One of her drivers yielded to the demand.

26. Dave LaFontaine, "Woody's ex-roomie fired for backing Saddam," *Star*, Mar. 12, 1991, 8. The lead stated: "Cheers star Woody Harrelson has outraged his co-stars again by rallying behind an Arab ex-roommate who was labeled an Iraqi sympathizer and the 'Son of Saddam.' "

27. Salmon and Neuwirth, "Perceptions of Opinion 'Climates,' " 576. Noelle-Neumann's book makes a related point: "The media provide people with the words and phrases they can use to defend a point of view. If people find no current, frequently repeated expressions for their point of view, they lapse into silence; they become effectively mute." *Spiral of Silence*, 173.

28. One item did inform readers that the war's constitutionality had been challenged. In its entirety, the item reports: "The loneliest, wackiest politician in America just might be *Henry Gonzalez*, a Democrat House member from Texas. On January 16 Gonzalez made this astonishing statement: 'Mr. Speaker, it is with great sadness, yet with great conviction, that I introduce today a Resolution of Impeachment of *President Bush*.' "

"Gonzalez believed the Prez violated the principles of the Constitution by going to war with Iraq. Back in the '80s he tried the same finagle on the Gipper. If at first you don't succeed . . . —Special to *Weekly World News.*" John Hannon, "World's Hottest Gossip," *Weekly World News*, Mar. 26, 1991, 13.

29. In 1990, the *Sun* published a photograph of an old woman with the caption "Pregnancy forces granny to quit work at age 101." The woman sued. The lawyers defending the *Sun* claimed that all their stories were "fiction and fantasy and not meant to be taken as news" and insisted that the *Sun's* readers understood that most of the newspaper is fantasy. According to Robert S. McCord, "They [the *Sun*] get away with it, almost never winding up in court because their victims usually are movie stars who settle out of court for small amounts because they don't want to submit to humiliating discovery or have skeletons come rattling into the courtroom." McCord, "The '101 Year-Old-Woman' Wasn't Pregnant—So She Sued," *Washington Post*, Feb. 2, 1992, C7.

30. Ed Asner may have been an outspoken Gulf War opponent, but the Newsbank and Infotrac databases reveal no evidence of it. In an interview published on Apr. 1, 1991, in the *Kansas City* (Missouri) *Star*, which focused on Asner's politics, the Gulf War was not mentioned. In that interview, Asner said that the result of his liberal activism in the 1980s was, in the reporter's words, "that he ha[d] worked less in the last decade than he might have if he had kept his mouth shut. He [knew] of at least four cases in which he was turned down for roles because of his politics." Robert Trussell, "High School Walk-on Is Now a Star," *Kansas City* (Missouri) *Star*, Apr. 1, 1991, Newsbank: PER 64:C5.

31. Upton Sinclair gives many examples in *The Brass Check: A Study of American Journalism*, self-published in Pasadena, California, in 1920, including that of "Mother Jones," who was described as a former keeper of a house of prostitution in a "fly-by-night" scandal sheet, a charge that was then read into the *Congressional Record* (180).

Frank J. Donner notes that the FBI files on the New Left movement against the Vietnam War were "roiled by an undertow of sexual prurience," and FBI agents sent reports based on "sexual snoopery" to parents, spouses, school authorities, and the local press. Donner, *The Age of Surveillance: The Aims and Methods of America's Political Intelligence System* (New York: Alfred A. Knopf, 1980), 232–240.

After the suicide of actress Jean Seberg in 1979, the FBI admitted that its agents had used a Hollywood gossip columnist to besmirch Seberg's reputation in 1970, spreading a false rumor that Seberg was pregnant with the child of a prominent Black Panther Party leader. The action was intended to discredit her support for the Black Panther Party. Seberg's former husband charged that the FBI had destroyed her life. "F.B.I. Admits Planting a Rumor to Discredit Jean Seberg in 1970," *New York Times*, Sept. 15, 1979, 1.

32. Pfc. Alexander N. Porter, "Why I'm fighting this war: GI's letter inspires his town, silences peace protestors and moves Cher to tears," *Star*, Feb. 26, 1991, 3.

33. If peace demonstrators were indeed silenced, it may have been more because they were stunned by how low the debate on the war had sunk rather than because they were overcome by the logic of Porter's analysis (Porter saw his role as to protect American freedom, fight terrorism, but especially to maintain the American tradition of bleeding in battle.) Porter writes: "Just know that I'm also going for the many Americans who have gone before me for 200 years. They paid for my freedom and yours with their blood. Their sacrifice has made it possible for me to choose my own course, and that means more to me than anything else. So, if I should fall in battle in an attempt to preserve those freedoms so the rest of our nation . . . so Aemily's [sic] children . . . don't have to live and

grow in a terrorized America, it will be well worth the sacrifice" (ellipses in original).

34. Ed Anger, "War protesters full of camel poop, sez Ed!" *Weekly World News*, Mar. 5, 1991, 17.

35. Bird, *For Enquiring Minds*, 194–195. Bird mentions that some readers do tend to agree with Ed Anger's editorials.

Another Ed Anger column, "Pro-Iraq Newsmen Oughta Be Tried for Treason!" proposed that "blubbering, America-hating camera hounds like Bernie Shaw, Dan Rather, Bryant Gum-ball and this whining idiot Arnett ought to be treated just like any other deserters in the face of the enemy—thrown into the brig and brought to trial!" The column was illustrated with a photograph of "Hanoi Jane Fonda" and her "left-wing pro-Iraq wimp" fiancé, Ted Turner. *Weekly World News*, Mar. 19, 1991, 17.

36. "Jitters" over the threat of Iraqi terrorist attacks was a common theme in tabloid war coverage. Stars of TV, film, music, and sports took precautions. See, for example, Mike Walker's "Behind the Screens" *Enquirer* columns, Feb. 12, 1991, 14–15; Feb. 19, 1991, 14; and Mar. 5, 1991, 14; Glenn Troelstrup, "Call out the Secret Service—Bush wants to eat dinner," *Examiner*, Feb. 12, 1991; 33; Bruce Honick, "Country Capers," Feb. 26, 1991, 35; Glenn Troelstrup, "Boomer's miracle: Kitten abandoned in box survives when Army blows it up as terrorist bomb," *Examiner*, Feb. 26, 1991, 47; "Ring Talk," *Examiner*, Mar. 12, 1991, 36; John Turner and Mark Carlisle, "Charles Manson begs Saddam: Let me help you destroy America," *Examiner*, Mar. 19, 1992, 6–7; "Saddam puts $1M 'bounty' on Stormin' Norman," *Examiner*, Mar. 26, 1991, 19; Thomas Maxwell, "Madman Saddam targets Diana for death!" *News Extra*, Feb. 19, 1991, 11; Kathleen Tracy, "Sally Field targeted by Arab terrorists," *Globe*, Feb. 5, 1991, 27; "Fear grips Hollywood," *Globe*, Feb. 12, 1992, 17; and "Security beefed up as stars guard against Saddam Hussein's merchants of terror," *Star*, Feb. 5, 1991, 20–21.

37. Mike Walker, "Behind the Screens," *National Enquirer*, Feb. 19, 1991, 14.

38. "Hot gossip," *Globe*, Mar. 26, 1991, 3.

39. "Saddam has a secret fortress in the Rockies," *Sun*, Mar. 5, 1991, 33.

40. One of the tabloid's most prominent themes was that Saddam Hussein is a sex monster who wants to "destroy the world." See Patrick Wilkins, John South, and Alan Braham Smith, "The shocking secret life of smiling killer Saddam," *Enquirer*, Feb. 12, 1991, 6–7; John Harris, "Saddam's love child: I love America and hate my father—I will kill him!" *Examiner*, Feb. 12, 1991, 14–15; John Turner and Mark Carlisle, "I was the love slave of the most terrifying, hated man in the world," *Examiner*, Feb. 26, 1991, 14–15; "Saddam has AIDS," *Examiner*, Feb. 26, 1991, 16; "Saddam's a sex pervert: performs unspeakable crimes against girls—and young boys," *Examiner*, Mar. 12, 1991, 4–5; Vic Kristol, "Saddam's secret past as a gigolo," *Sun*, Mar. 12, 1991, 7; and Laurel Bowie, "Saddam's gay lover tells all!" *Weekly World News*, Mar. 26, 1991, 37.

Jim Hogshire, a former reporter for the *National Examiner* tabloid, rightly claims that paper's demonization of Saddam Hussein "rivaled German baby-eater stories of World War I for both grotesqueness and mendacity." "Supermarket Tabloids: Propaganda in the Check-Out Lines," *Extra!*, April/May 1992, 26.

Hogshire reveals that the stories were fictitious and then asks "so what? They're no less real than some of the stories put out by the U.S. government, which the mainstream media dutifully transmitted. Both types of stories encourage war hysteria. And by the time anyone gets around to debunking them, they're just atrocity stories from the last war."

Hogshire also reveals that President Bush sent a note thanking *Globe*

Communications—publisher of the *Globe, Examiner,* and *Sun* tabloids—for their support of the war.

41. Billy Burt, editor of the *National Examiner,* explained in 1988, "Most [American journalists] are corrupted by journalism school into dreary, humorless utopians out to save the world. They are Puritans who should stay on Plymouth Rock. Ghosts? The occult? We don't say these stories are true; we just report them." Quoted in Martha Smilgis, "In Florida: The Rogues of Tabloid Valley," *Time,* Aug. 15, 1988, 13–14.

42. Patricia Mellencamp connects the dissolution of the old categories to the rise of women's issues. Mellencamp, *High Anxiety: Catastrophe, Scandal, Age, and Comedy* (Bloomington: Indiana University Press, 1992), 180.

43. For exceptions, see Peter Fenton and Wayne Grover, "Zap! Video games turned America's kids into today's top-notch pilots," *Enquirer,* Feb. 19, 1991, 26, and "Take that, Saddam!" same issue, 28–29, which shows "awe-inspiring photos" of the Tomahawk cruise missile's "pinpoint accuracy." The only military maps published during the war illustrated John Harris's "Incredible psychic pinpointed vital targets for the U.S.," *Examiner,* Feb. 5, 1991, 17–18; and "Flipper goes to war," *Examiner,* Feb. 19, 1991, 6–7.

44. Noam Chomsky, "U.S. warns Third World: 'Don't raise your heads,'" *Guardian,* Apr. 3, 1991, 18.

45. P. J. Corkery, "Exclusive! Inside the National Enquirer," *Rolling Stone,* June 11, 1981, 18ff.

Generoso Pope, Jr., was the individual most responsible for the current supermarket tabloid formulas. Before buying the *Enquirer* in 1952, Pope had spent a year doing propaganda-related work for the Central Intelligence Agency. Pope's reason for quitting the CIA was, "I really got fed up with the government bureaucracy. You'd spend weeks trying to get things done, and then you couldn't do it." Quoted in George Bernard, *Inside the National Enquirer . . . Confessions of an Undercover Reporter* (Port Washington, N.Y.: Ashley Books, 1977), 281.

Pope's purchase of the paper had the backing of racketeer Frank Costello, but Pope denied that Costello had ever "bankrolled" the *Enquirer.* Leonard Katz's biography of Costello, *Uncle Frank: The Biography of Frank Costello* (New York: Drake Publishers, 1973), claims that the racketeer had loaned Pope ten thousand dollars each week to meet the paper's operating expenses. Frank Greve, "Exclusive! Now It Can Be Told . . . ," *More,* July 1974, 1, 16–19.

Venise T. Berry and Kim E. Karloff

Perspectives on the Persian Gulf War in Popular Black Magazines

One ever feels his twoness; an American, a Negro; two souls, two thoughts, two unre-
conciled strivings; two warring ideas in one dark body, whose dogged strength alone
keeps it from being torn asunder.
—W.E.B. Du Bois, *The Souls of Black Folk*

As early as 1948, W.E.B. Du Bois recognized the cultural importance of
black media by noting that black newspapers and magazines were
read by every literate Negro in the nation and that they offered a new
kind of coverage independent of distortion and suppression by the
white press.[1] The black press, which today enjoys circulation in the
hundreds of thousands, has historically served this purpose in two
ways. First, it has been a vehicle for cultural assimilation, where mainstream ideals and value systems are reproduced and spread in the
black community through a variety of news and feature stories.
Second, and more important, the black press has at the same time
fostered a communal voice of resistance to black cultural exclusion.
Former *Emerge* magazine editor Roberto Santiago explains, "When
writing about the black community, look first to the political and cultural tends in the white community. Then, ask yourself—what is the
black angle of this? How does this impact black people? Why is the
mainstream press ignoring the black angle?—That is an *Emerge*
story."[2] Santiago's comments suggest that resistance works within the
black print media in the twentieth century in complicated ways. According to Gunnar Myrdal, the black press has indeed been "the greatest single power in the Negro race." But it has offered historically
something of a paradox for constructing resistance, since Myrdal
claimed that the black press serves as both a "safety-valve" function for
"boiling Negro protest" and a true voice of cultural leadership.[3] Any
concept of black media resistance here is dependent upon the ways

that the press addresses and responds to Du Bois's concept of a Black American dual consciousness, a split identity that takes into account beliefs and values defined as "white" while simultaneously critiquing them from an outsider's position.

Such racially formed dual consciousness in the United States is further defined in the writings of bell hooks, who rethinks the important notion of dual consciousness through an identity spatialized in terms of the locations of center and margins. She explains that "it is crucial to radically revise notions of identity politics, to explore marginal locations as spaces where we can best become whatever we want to be while remaining committed to liberatory black liberation struggles."[4] Hooks calls for a process wherein one constructs radical black subjectivity—radical in the sense of determining one's own legitimacy—by *choosing* the margins. The margins of the larger cultural formation thus may serve as the location for a unified black identity that derives from the conscious rearticulation of the separation of center (or mainstream) and marginality that has historically defined African-American experience.

Hooks says there is a difference between structural oppressive marginality that is imposed from without and the marginal site of resistance *chosen* by a culture or individual. It is within the *chosen* marginal site, she adds, that resistance is enabled: "Cultural criticism has historically functioned in black life as a force promoting critical resistance, one that enabled black folks to cultivate in everyday life a practice of critique and analysis that would disrupt and even deconstruct those cultural productions that were designed to promote and reinforce domination."[5] In this way, she illustrates how Santiago's comments effectively promote a black resistance that is the creation of radical black subjectivity, one that involves a process of self-identity as oppositional and liberatory. *Emerge, Black Enterprise, Ebony, Jet,* and *Essence*—all of which have culturally conventional formats and widespread availability and are popular in the black community—present a viable case in which to better understand the dualistic nature of black identity. Despite their assimilationist style and look, the ability of these black magazines to continue the political struggle for identity, community, and culture through resistance if of particular interest.[6]

During the Persian Gulf War, the struggle of the black press as a struggle at the margins is particularly important for a community that was identified nationally as against the war. For example, most Black American politicians went on record as against the war. Twenty-four members of the Congressional Black Caucus voted against President Bush's call for arms in the Persian Gulf, with only one member voting in support.[7] Additionally, when an *Ebony* readers' poll in January 1991 asked for opinions on the president's position on Kuwait, a majority of the respondents (66.9 percent) reported serious reservations about the U.S. government's Persian Gulf policy and the deployment of U.S. troops. Only a small 17.9 percent supported the action.[8] In operating from a marginal position, the black press redefined concepts like patriotism, nationalism, and racism within the ongoing cultural criticism of the black community that has always functioned as a form of resistance.

Selected Magazines

Black Enterprise. Black Enterprise focuses on blacks and the social value systems as well as the economic structures in which they live, from "Buppies" (Black Upwardly Mobile Youths) to big (and small) business networks. First published in 1970 under the direction of Earl G. Graves, *Black Enterprise* set out to chart the progress made by blacks within U.S. corporate structures. The magazine emphasizes businesses, job and career opportunities, and black entrepreneurship as well as political and social awareness in the black community. Still under the eyes of Graves as editor and publisher, *Black Enterprise* is one of the largest black publications in the United States, and black media historians credit it with promoting multicultural development in the world of business.[9]

Ebony. Fresh from his publishing success with the *Negro Digest* in 1942, John H. Johnson published the first issue of *Ebony* in 1945. *Ebony* built on the *Negro Digest's* success at reproducing and excerpting stories and comments about black life taken from mainstream publications by constructing its own stories of successful blacks in all avenues of U.S. life. Profiles of success range from sports figures to entertainment stars, from elected politicians to political activists. With its slick graphics and production values, *Ebony* posits a positive view of blacks in the United States as seen through individual success stories. Through repeated stories of individual achievement and rewards, *Ebony* implicitly emphasizes interracial understanding as a winning strategy.

Emerge. Wilmer C. Ames, Jr.'s four-year-old magazine advertises itself as "Our Voice in Today's World." This voice is a mixed bag of topical black features and news stories for the most part devoted to entertainment, music, dance, and the other arts as well as to politics, international news, policy, and conflict (including war). The magazine attempts to maintain a "news" edge through its focus on recent current events.

Essence. "The Magazine for Today's Black Woman" is what the founders called it. Others call it a black version of *Cosmopolitan*.[10] *Essence* does indeed focus on women—black women—and their concerns. First published in the 1970s by Jonathan Blount and Clarence Smith, the monthly periodical does not explore black issues as such. Rather, it emphasizes topics associated with the conventionally feminine—like fashion, feelings, and fitness. It is one of the largest black publications. Although it is not a newsmagazine, it still gives cursory attention to timely issues like the Persian Gulf War, elections, and politics within a framework of concern for their relationships to the magazine's generally female audience.

Jet. Comic Redd Foxx once called *Jet* the "Negro's Bible," and a character in one of Maya Angelou's plays said: "If it wasn't in *Jet*, it didn't happen."[11] Started in 1951 by John H. Johnson, *Jet* is "a weekly news magazine in [a] handy, pocket-sized form."[12] The top black magazine in circulation figures, *Jet* focuses on the wide range of social, political, and economic life in Black America. It claims that it wants to "see and feel" what blacks see and feel, thereby setting itself up as a representation of African-American cultural life in all its manifestations.[13]

War and the Black Press: A Historical Perspective

During World War I, the black press for the most part consisted of more than two hundred weekly newspapers and a half dozen monthly magazines. Many of these publications called for equal rights, a call linguistically seen as evenhanded.[14] This topic has an important history, since blacks had systematically been denied the vote in the southern states where most of them lived even though such denial was against the law. By 1910, the denial of voting rights had been socially extended to more complete racial segregation, accomplished legally in the South and through daily practices in the North. When Woodrow Wilson was elected president, his Democratic administration sanctioned such segregation at the national level in 1913 by legalizing segregation of federal employees in the workplace. Widespread acts of violence against black people further helped to maintain white supremacy. An average of sixty-five blacks were lynched annually between 1910 and 1919.

It should have come as little surprise, then, that when President Wilson declared war "to make the world safe for Democracy," few in the black press supported him. An example of such reservations by the black press included editorials calling for a new patriotism that did not "condemn massacres and lynchings in Germany and condone them in its own country."[15] After all, an international call for democracy seemed hypocritical to those who were not experiencing democracy at home.

The black press's efforts are all the more notable because new governmental legislation enacted during World War I, like the Espionage and Sedition acts, attempted to suppress dissent during wartime. By late 1918, the U.S. government's efforts to suppress opposition to the war were effective on the black press, since, as Mark Ellis notes, the black press may have continued to sound the call for equal rights and "evenhandedness," but its tone and language were greatly diminished.[16] By the end of the war, however, the call for equality became louder. As Du Bois, editor of the National Association for the Advancement of Colored People's journal, *The Crisis*, wrote in May 1919, "We return. We return from fighting. We return fighting."[17]

During World War II, the black press—which had become one of the leading black industries—was again subject to intensive governmental scrutiny. As Patrick Washburn notes, the government's reasons for such special scrutiny of the black press were its expressed concerns that Communists or the Japanese would enlist black support for the enemy through growing criticism of discrimination in the United States.[18] Attempts by FBI director J. Edgar Hoover and others to indict the oppositional press for its "un-American" views were unsuccessful.

Even amidst government regulation and intensified press restrictions, however, the black press reported on such stories as the army's confinement of black soldiers to four units, the navy's inclusion of blacks only as mess boys, and other armed forces units where blacks were restricted from service. Other coverage during World War II included stories on education and job discrimination, police violence, and lynchings. Even the issue of black patriotism as a critical practice from the margins was itself a subject taken up at that time by the black press. As columnist Cliff MacKay wrote in 1942:

> One gathers . . . that some white people would like to read "sedition" and "subversive activity" into the determination of Negroes to achieve democracy here and at the same time they are called upon to fight for its preservation abroad. Nothing could be further from the truth, as these FBI agents were told on both occasions of their visits (to black newsrooms). The Negro, in fact, is the most American of all Americans. He has proved this over and over again. He has no split loyalties, no ties with other countries, no relatives "across the pond." He is all American, first, last and always.[19]

In the Korean and Vietnam wars, the black press continued its dual roles of perpetuating both assimilation and resistance. Again and again, coverage included not only military issues but societal ones as well. Calls for equality and the language of "evenhandedness" persisted, especially during the civil rights movement of the 1950s and 1960s. Black leaders continued to point out the irony of fighting for so-called democracy overseas when they all too keenly knew the domestic shortcomings of U.S. democracy. Dr. Martin Luther King may have best stated Black Americans' concerns in this regard in a speech about U.S. involvement in Vietnam delivered in New York City on April 4, 1967. King expressed his concern for both young blacks and whites who "kill and die together for a nation that has been unable to seat them together in the same schools."[20]

Black editors also noted how this war and U.S. history generally have been shaped by the U.S. history of wars against the American Indian, Mexican, Philippine, Cuban, and Korean peoples. The editors of *Freedomways* magazine wrote: "This is not the first racist war in which the American people have been dragged by their political leaders."[21] They argued that the U.S. government could "so arrogantly violate" the rights of the Vietnamese people because the United States had "a tradition of never having upheld and defended the right of the black people . . . to choose the kind of government they wish to live under, by guaranteeing to them the ballot and free elections."[22]

The Persian Gulf War

The historical perspective that the black press maintained in evaluating U.S. participation in past wars remained prominent during the Persian Gulf War even though it was a perspective not widely asserted elsewhere in U.S. society. The April 1991 *Emerge* noted, "We [blacks] have always died in U.S. wars," and summarized black participation in every U.S. war since the Revolutionary War.[23] An earlier article in the February 1991 *Ebony* traced the paths of various black soldiers, sailors, and spies as unsung heroes during the Civil War.[24] In its subsequent issues, *Ebony* presented photographs of black World War II heroes, including a black sailor honored for bravery during the attack on Pearl Harbor and members of the first class of black army pilots at the Tuskegee Institute in 1942.[25]

A critical piece in *Emerge* took a different and more international approach. A comparison was made between the dual consciousness of black soldiers in an African film, *The African Soldier's Story*, which examines the demobilizing of African troops coming home from service in Europe during World War I, and in such U.S. movies as *Glory* and *A Soldier's Story*. The author used the movie comparisons to make a statement about the historical project of black participation in war:

You go off to fight in the White Man's war thinking it's a fight for your democracy too. Meanwhile, folks back home are catching color-coded abuse that makes the White Man's war seem a remote cause. You come back expecting a hero's welcome and greater freedom in the country you have loyally served, but instead before you have even taken off the White Man's uniform you meet with the old discrimination, contempt, and even lynching.[26]

In this pointed example, arts criticism becomes a means to confront the historical problem of black patriotism within the formations of racism.

Jet, Emerge, and Black Enterprise all addressed the issue of Persian Gulf War patriotism as black patriotism. Emerge, in the April 1991 issue, opened with a full-page promotion saluting *our* (meaning black) men and women on duty in the Persian Gulf and wishing them a speedy and safe return home. A story in Jet pointed out a recent survey by the National Opinion Research Center that found that 51 percent of white respondents believed that blacks were less patriotic.[27] But, in the same manner that Emerge editor Santiago suggested, Jet went on to take a black angle to the reported white opinion by claiming that the high numbers of black soldiers in the Persian Gulf demonstrated patriotism by virtue of their bodily inscription.

Several articles were also quite adamant about the need for support of black troops when they returned from the Persian Gulf, often contrasting the situation to the negative atmosphere that Vietnam War veterans faced. One such story specifically focused on a hero's welcome home, with yellow ribbons, flags, and banners waving.[28] On the publisher's page in the April Black Enterprise, Earl Graves called for full support from all people back home. He urged his readers to make sure soldiers were appropriately honored and compensated for their work in the Persian Gulf. Graves, however, also recognized in his editorial the need for a more equitable United States where Black Americans would select black military service as a matter of choice and not of economic necessity.[29]

Numerous articles as well as photographs addressed the impact of the Persian Gulf War on black families. Jet, in particular, ran several pictures of GIs and their families hugging one another and crying.[30] In another issue an article addressed the controversy over sending black mothers to war and discussed the difficulties children encounter when their mothers are pulled away to war, saying, "We are winning the war, but losing the family."[31] In this way, the article set the difficult position of blacks struggling to maintain traditionally defined families against military service in the Persian Gulf. It further made claims for the difficulty of achieving a traditionally defined family within black culture as well as of maintaining any family during wartime when parents are called into service by citing statistics of the high numbers of black mothers raising their children alone. Authorities like pediatricians, counselors, the president of the Children's Defense Fund, and even mothers themselves were used as evidence. The same story also offered a partial governmental solution to this dilemma by supporting a bill that would exempt single parents from combat duty.[32]

Several articles also voiced concern over the high percentage of blacks in the Persian Gulf War as a potential threat to black family life in general and to the state of black communities in the United States. The large number of blacks in the military was an important issue in every magazine except *Ebony*, which generally contained fewer articles on the Persian Gulf War. Blacks compose 12 percent of the total U.S. population but made up 30 percent of the active troops in Operation Desert Storm. Blacks accounted for 30 percent of the army, 21.3 percent of the navy, 17 percent of the marines, and 13.5 percent of the air force.[33] Magazine articles in *Essence* and *Jet* cited that 31,000 out of 513,000 soldiers deployed in the Persian Gulf War were women and, of these women, 48 percent were black.[34] In one brief summary, military analyst Martin Binkins estimated that 35 percent of all qualified black men between the ages of nineteen and twenty-four were in the military, as compared with 17 percent of all qualified white men in the same age range. Binkins speculated that this high percentage could have serious repercussions in Black American communities if significant numbers of lives were lost. Binkins based his argument on the statistics that 95 percent of black soldiers were high school graduates and 53 percent were married.[35] He included in a discussion of war the ongoing problem of losing black fathers, particularly productive black fathers.

Over the four-month period of war combat activity, all black magazines ran recruitment advertisements for the U.S. Marines, West Point, Army, Navy, Army National Guard, Army ROTC, Army Military Police, and Air Force. (The ongoing push for blacks to join the military has been well documented by sociologists.) But between January and April 1991, each magazine averaged at least one military ad per issue, and recruitment even extended to articles in which, for example, a story on job possibilities for blacks included the military as a prime career opportunity, listing annual earnings, the ability to become commissioned officers, job security, eligibility for retirement, and a variety of skilled positions that are transferable to the civilian workplace.[36]

To some Black Americans the effectiveness of these recruitment campaigns and the resulting high numbers of Black American soldiers represented a milestone in the history of the military, but to others they were an atrocity. In *Jet*, the Reverend Benjamin Chavis presented a negative case for the large numbers of blacks in the Persian Gulf War. He suggested that many black soldiers did not join voluntarily but were drafted by poverty, unemployment, and the lack of opportunities for blacks in this country.[37] Another *Jet* article on the same topic that summarized General Colin Powell's testimony before the House Armed Services Committee implicitly offered in Powell's statements authoritative support for Chavis's position. Powell told the committee that the military offers minorities opportunities denied to them in other areas of society: "I wish that corporate America . . . the trade unions around the nation, would show the same level of openness and opportunity to minorities that the military has."[38] Yet, in a third *Jet* article that followed both Powell's and Chavis's, President George Bush's top-ranking business adviser Joshua Smith talked about contracting and other job opportunities for minorities in the reconstruction of Kuwait and promised that a nationwide canvas of minority businesses had already begun.[39]

In a different article in *Essence*, Chavis raised questions about the priorities of the U.S. government, pointing to a relationship between the evolving crisis in the Persian Gulf region and the deterioration of many black communities across the country.[40] An *Emerge* article also posited this relationship by stating that Black Americans faced a bleak outlook for 1991 with the recession, high unemployment, a hostile racial environment, and the Persian Gulf War. The article quoted Coretta Scott King, who said that it is important to make preparing for education a greater priority than preparing for war.[41] But, like *Jet*'s response to Chavis, *Emerge* also provided a possible answer to King's call in a piece that talked about special military recruiting programs in Florida and California that train minorities for careers in education by making the skills they learn in the military applicable to the classroom.[42]

As a whole, these articles exemplify the problematic nature of black dual identity as represented in the black press. They all argue that blacks have been afforded opportunities in the military, but they simultaneously ask at what price. The magazines continue to figure the military as well as its extended economic benefits—skills applicable to careers in education, enabling more job opportunities—as a double-edged sword.

Musicians and actors were consistently in the news for their good deeds in relation to Persian Gulf War troop morale. Quite a few articles reported on the activities of stars like LaToya Jackson, Whitney Houston, and James Brown, who performed for the troops.[43] Houston was mainly recognized for her dedication of "The Star-Spangled Banner" to the GIs at the 1991 Super Bowl. Proceeds for her single and video of the song were donated to the American Red Cross Gulf Crisis Fund to benefit military families. This story, however, appeared only in *Jet*, even though she received much mainstream press coverage for the event. There are two possible explanations. First, one of the major roles embraced by the black media has been to present otherwise unavailable information to the black community. Second, many of the mainstream articles involved a negative report of Houston's national anthem debut concerning whether or not she lip-synched the song. *Jet*'s piece ran as a counterarticle disputing those indictments.[44]

Two stories featured a recording session in which close to one hundred celebrities came together to show their support for the troops in the Persian Gulf. The group "Voices That Care" was also much discussed in the mainstream press. But here the *Jet* story prominently discussed only the role of black participants like Mike Tyson, Luther Vandross, L.A. Raiders running back Marcus Allen, Whoopi Goldberg, Denzel Washington, and Al Jarreau.[45]

Even in stories about black entertainers' unproblematic patriotic contributions to the Persian Gulf War, the selectivity and contextualization of such stories in black magazines still emphasized the dualistic nature of black experience. These stars may have been patriotically in support of the war, but they were also presented as having "made it" in a system that is considered against them and maintaining ties with the black community through their achievements as well as through their performances. When the black press wrote about Whitney Houston or James Brown showing support for the troops, they figured them not as individual patriots or nationalist stars defined through their national identity, but they claimed them as representatives of the black community.

The primary topic of black leadership featured General Colin Powell. Several articles in *Jet* included coverage of him as a celebrity—Powell's withdrawal from the Martin Luther King parade in Atlanta, Powell's demonstration of his basketball skills to the Harlem Globetrotters, Powell's meeting with the Black Caucus on Capitol Hill, and a movement in the Senate to award Powell the historic fifth star.[46] General Powell graced the 1991 cover of *Emerge* in January 1991 and headed the magazine's list of "Top 10 Persons of 1990." *Emerge* called Powell a "new-breed soldier and politician" and praised him as the first black man in charge of a U.S. war.[47] Not to be outdone, *Ebony* featured in its February 1991 issue a portrait of General Powell as part of a historical story on the United States' black leaders.[48]

Stories on other individuals as black role models and leaders ranged from inculcating the authority of leaders of the past as well as of new celebrities produced by the war itself. *Ebony* ran a piece speculating on Dr. Martin Luther King's position concerning the Persian Gulf War.[49] King's widow, Coretta Scott King, felt that he might have opposed military retaliation stressing instead the need for patience and restraint to resolve the crisis. U.S. Representative John Lewis said he believed that since Dr. King was against U.S. involvement in the Vietnam War, King would not shrink away from speaking out against the moral dimensions of our foreign policy in the Persian Gulf War. *Jet* featured black journalist Bernard Shaw for his heroic coverage in the Persian Gulf War.[50] *Jet* also ran a story expressing pride in black navy officer Robert Goodman, who had been held as a hostage for thirty days after a Syrian attack in Lebanon and was returning to the Persian Gulf War.[51]

Finally, a Dateline U.S.A. section in *Emerge* featured a dialogue with Kwame Ture (formerly civil rights activist Stokely Carmichael) concerning his views on the Persian Gulf War. Ture was radically opposed to the war. He called the U.S. government the most barbaric government on the face of the earth. He quoted the Malcom X philosophy, "Whoever the enemy is for, you must be against; whoever the enemy is against, you must be for," and he called General Colin Powell a traitor because of his role in the war.[52] Ture is the exception among all of the black leaders in these articles because he alone was credited as the only radical leader who did not achieve his position by "making it" within mainstream U.S. culture. Whereas the other leaders interviewed or profiled had created a space for black existence through assimilation, Ture remains oppositional and continues to question the kind of black success that the others represent.

Even when the articles themselves do not espouse a practice of critique, they function, as hooks argues, to confirm a sense of identity within the black community, offering a black perspective as a form of resistance to dominant culture. The repetitive emphasis of *our* (meaning black) men and women in the Persian Gulf (as in the *Emerge* ad) consistently redefines communal identity as distinct from that of national identity (as in the mainstream press). Another example is the article examining whether or not mothers should go to war, focusing specifically on black mothers.

That distinct identity formation implicitly addresses and exposes issues of classism and racism in the United States, as in those articles that discuss how a career in the military for blacks may not be a chosen path but rather one of economic necessity (and perhaps the only accessible way to achieve some class mobility). While this path is hailed through descriptions of the military as one of the most integrated institutions in the United States, other articles attack it as structural racism that allowed a disproportionate number of blacks to fight in the Persian Gulf War.

The recurring theme that blacks should not fight for democracy abroad when they have yet to realize true democracy at home is a more explicitly resistant critique of mainstream ideology. An especially pointed example is Kwame Ture's defamation of the U.S. government as barbaric and his assault on General Colin Powell as a traitor to the black community.

In conclusion, all of the articles and advertisements involving the Persian Gulf War offered readers a distinctive perspective rooted in some level of black identity. They represent a marginal site of *chosen* resistance to mainstream ideology and, as a catalyst for change, make black voice the empowered voice.

Notes

1. W.E.B. Du Bois, *The Souls of Black Folk* (New York: Dodd, Mead and Company, 1961), 95.
2. Roberto Santiago, "Close-up," in *1993 Writer's Market: Where and How to Sell What You Write*, ed. Mark Kissling (Cincinnati: Writer's Digest Books, 1992), 375.
3. Gunnar Myrdal, *An American Dilemma* (New York: McGraw-Hill, 1964), 910, 924.
4. Bell hooks, *Yearning: Race, Gender, and Cultural Politics* (Boston: South End Press, 1990), 20.
5. Hooks, *Yearnings*, 3.
6. Monthly circulation figures range from *Emerge*'s 200,000 and *Essence*'s 900,000 to *Ebony*'s 1.8 million readers in 1993. Kissling, *Writer's Market*, 374, 693.
7. "Ticker Tape U.S.A.," *Jet*, Feb. 11, 1991, 10.
8. "Readers Poll Responses," *Ebony*, Apr. 1991, 16–18.
9. Jannette L. Dates and William Barlow, eds., *Split Image: African Americans in the Mass Media* (Washington, D.C.: Howard University Press, 1990), 375–377. For further discussion of this matter, see Walter C. Daniel, *Black Journals of the United States* (Westport, Conn.: Greenwood Press, 1982), 21–175.
10. Dates and Barlow, *Split Image*, 375.
11. "Backstage," *Ebony*, Mar. 1991, 14.
12. Ibid.
13. Ibid.
14. Mark Ellis, "America's Black Press, 1914–1918," *History Today* 41 (Sept. 1991): 20.
15. A. Phillip Randolph and Chandler Owen as quoted in Ellis, "America's Black Press," 26.
16. Ellis, "America's Black Press," 27.
17. W.E.B. Du Bois as quoted in Ellis, "America's Black Press," 27.
18. Patrick Washburn, "J. Edgar Hoover and the Black Press in World War II," *Journalism History* 13 (Spring 1986): 32–33.
19. Cliff MacKay, "Now Just Who Is Subversive?" *Birmingham World*, July 10, 1942, as quoted in Lee Finkle, *Forum for Protest: The Black Press during World War II* (London: Associated University Presses, 1975), 9.

20. Nancy Zaroulis and Gerald Sullivan, *Who Spoke Up? American Protest against the War in Vietnam, 1963–1975* (New York: Holt, Rinehart and Winston, 1984), 108.
21. Anonymous, "The War in Vietnam," *Freedomways* magazine (Spring 1965): 229.
22. Ibid.
23. Marc Crawford, "We Have Always Died in America's Wars," *Emerge*, Apr. 1991, 17.
24. "Black, Blue, and Gray: The Other Civil War," *Ebony*, Feb. 1991, 96.
25. "From the Ebony Files," *Ebony*, Mar. 1991, 130.
26. Clyde Taylor, "Ousmane Sembene's Proud Epic: African Soldier's Story," *Emerge*, Jan. 1991, 59.
27. Simeon Booker, "Black Participation in the War," *Jet*, Feb. 25, 1991, 4–9.
28. "Yellow Ribbons, Flags Greet First U.S. Troops Returning from Gulf War," *Jet*, Mar. 25, 1991, 4–9.
29. "After the War: Support Our Troops," *Black Enterprise*, Apr. 1991, 7.
30. "Family Reunion," *Jet*, Jan. 7, 1991, 37; "Tearful Fairwell," *Jet*, Feb. 4, 1991, 10; "Showing His Support," *Jet*, Mar. 4, 1991, 13.
31. Richette Haywood, "Should Moms Go to War?" *Jet*, Mar. 4, 1991, 6–10.
32. Ibid.
33. Booker, "Black Participation in the War," 7.
34. Richette Haywood, "Did You Know?" *Essence*, Apr. 1991, 96.
35. "Blacks in the Gulf," *Black Enterprise*, Apr. 1991, 12.
36. "Boom Careers for the 90s," *Black Enterprise*, Feb. 1991, 72.
37. "Poverty, Racism 'Drafted' Blacks into Army: Chavis," *Jet*, Feb. 4, 1991, 8.
38. "Powell Testifies That Blacks Join Military for Those Opportunities That Are Denied Elsewhere," *Jet*, Mar. 4, 1991, 34.
39. "Drive Launched for Black Input for the Rebuilding of Kuwait," *Jet*, Apr. 8, 1991, 15.
40. Benjamin F. Chavis, Jr., "Speaking on the Gulf Crisis," *Essence*, Jan. 1991, 100.
41. "Fighting Wars Abroad: Losing the Battle at Home," *Emerge*, Apr. 1991, 17.
42. "Soldiers-to-Teachers: A Post–Cold War Mission," *Emerge*, Mar. 1991, 24.
43. "True Patriot," *Jet*, Jan. 7, 1991, 16; "Whitney Houston Welcomes Home U.S. Troops in Live HBO TV Special on Easter," *Jet*, Apr. 1, 1991, 37; "James Brown Gets Release from Work Center to Entertain Troops in S.C.," *Jet*, Jan. 14, 1991, 52–55.
44. "Whitney Houston Did Not Lip-sync National Anthem," *Jet*, Mar. 18, 1991, 60.
45. "Stars Sing for GIs on 'Voices That Care' Record," *Jet*, Mar, 4, 1991, 54.
46. "Gen. Powell Withdraws as Grand Marshal [in] King Parade," *Jet*, Jan. 7, 1991, 18; "General Control," *Jet*, Apr 4, 1991, 46; "General Powell Visits Black Caucus on Capitol Hill," *Jet*, Mar. 18, 1991, 5; "U.S. Sen. Kasten Pushing Effort to Award Powell with Historic Fifth Star," *Jet*, Mar. 25, 1991, 8.
47. "Emerging Persons of 1990," *Emerge*, Jan. 1991, 24–25.
48. "Black History in Words and Pictures," *Ebony*, Feb. 1991, 50.
49. "What Martin Luther King Would Do Now About: Drugs, Poverty, and Black-Jewish Relations," *Ebony*, Jan. 1991, 27–28.
50. "Black Journalist Report First Bombing of Baghdad: 'Feels Like Center of Hell,'" *Jet*, Feb. 4, 1991, 4–6.
51. "Former Hostage Goodman Back in Battle in Gulf," *Jet*, Mar. 4, 1991, 13.
52. "Dateline U.S.A.: A Dialogue with Kwame Ture," *Emerge*, Apr. 1991, 12.

Therese Saliba

Military Presences and Absences: Arab Women and the Persian Gulf War

Looking for the "Nile River," according to the fifteenth century Portuguese notion, is someone's joke. For all that pre-Columbian "explorers" knew about the sciences of navigation and geography, we are surprised that more parties of them did not end up "discovering" Europe. Perhaps, from a certain angle, that is precisely all that they found—an alternative reading of ego.

—Hortense Spillers, "Mama's Baby, Papa's Maybe"

Despite the many changing appearances it has taken through the years, the image of the white colonial savior seems more pernicious than ever since it operates now via consent.

—Trinh T. Minh-ha, *When the Moon Waxes Red*

In the postmodern era, news media, with their subservience to corporate advertisers and government interests, have come to emulate the disinformation of fashion magazines, popular films, and talk shows, suggesting that the discourses of fashion and politics are not so disparate. U.S. political discourse on the Persian Gulf War created an illusion of consensus to a fashionable war with "picture-perfect" bombing assaults that were supposedly "saving" Iraqi lives.[1] The specifically *gendered* representations of demonized Arab men and captive or absent Arab women fed a revival of colonialist attitudes and heralded George Bush's new world order to reassert U.S. dominance in the Middle East.

The absent Arab woman has been deployed within the U.S. media both as a resonant and as an efficient signifier of so-called Western cultural superiority over the Arab world. By the *absent Arab woman*, I mean two notable forms of absence: the first, a literal absence, when the Arab woman is not present or is entirely missing from the scene; the second, a symbolic absence, when she is present but only for the purpose of representing her invisibility or silence in order to serve as a subordinate to the Western subject of the scene. She is also granted moments of presence when her actions and speech are manipulated and exploited to serve the interests of her Western interpreters. In all these instances, the *absent* Arab woman is objectified and contrasted to the "liberated" Western woman, who often serves as a representative for Arab women. The white woman is granted agency to speak for Arab women, usually on behalf of their liberation. In *Women and Gender in Islam: Historical Roots of a Modern Debate*, Leila Ahmed defines this form of "colonial feminism" as "feminism used against other cultures in the service of colonialism,"[2] a "feminism" that is racist in its assumptions and exploitative of both "native" and Western women in its appropriation of feminist language to serve imperialist/patriarchal interests. In the case of the Persian Gulf War, the neocolonialist rhetoric of Western intervention to save Arab women from Arab men mirrored "colonial feminist" strategies in its attempt to discredit Arab culture as universally oppressive to women. The U.S. media's predictions of Saudi women's liberation, exemplified in "Images of 'GI Jane' fuel Saudi Women's advance on tradition" (Chicago *Tribune*, September 19, 1990), juxtaposed U.S. military women in camouflage to Saudi women in their *abayahs*, to depict Arab women as the agents of Western influence. However, in contrast to its anticipated liberatory effect, U.S. military presence in the region did nothing but reinforce the invisibility of Arab women within Saudi Arabian society. In particular, Saudi women were sacrificed by their government for the preservation of a culture that seemed to be deteriorating under the growing threat of Western influence.

This relentless absenting of Arab women, from its most banal forms in U.S. fashion magazines and talk shows to U.S. news reports on the Persian Gulf Crisis and War, I argue, supports the neocolonialist interests of the new world order and the U.S. media's repressions of the war's destruction. The double invisibility imposed on Arab women, not only by the U.S. media/military (which became virtually indistinguishable during the war) and by Arab government leaders, but also by U.S. women and feminists who served as "stand-ins" for absent Arab women, effectively stripped Arab women of agency and disallowed their "illegitimate voices" to be heard, voices that might have disrupted the racist stereotypes of Arabs used to justify U.S. military actions.

The Fashionable Contrast of East and West

The Autumn 1990 catalog for Tweeds, a mail-order fashion company for the young and upwardly mobile, evokes the colonial fantasy of exploring the Nile River in order to exoticize Tweeds's fairly staid and conventional yuppie attire. The catalog cover alludes to Sir Richard Burton's adventures portrayed in the 1990 box office hit *Mountains of the Moon*. In the center of a "Map of the course of the Nile," a rugged Burtonesque Anglo-American holds a young Egyptian girl in his arms, his "conquest" of her represented by her clothing, because she is dressed in a man's oversized dress shirt and sweater that hang to her feet. The goal of Tweeds's "less extensive" journey along the Nile is explicit: "We wanted to rediscover our clothing in the context of a different culture" (2). In other words, we in the United States discover ourselves, our clothing, against a backdrop of otherness.[3]

To make Egypt a viable context for U.S. fashion, the magazine focuses primarily on its exotic colors: "the rose tint of the Pyramids at sunset, the desert's stark beige, the verdant green of the Nile valley" (2). For a taste of cultural flavor, the second paragraph introduces the phrase "Inshallah," which, as the catalog explains, "literally means 'God willing', but the Egyptians use it so often, it's simply taken to mean 'perhaps', 'we'll see,' 'who knows?' " (2) Tweeds, in effect, secularizes the term "Inshallah" for its U.S. audience. Perhaps it does so because one of the greatest obstacles to rapprochement between the Arab East and the West—a division that is a construct of imperialist ideology—is Islamic religion, which is most often cast by the U.S. media in terms of "Islamic extremists," "jihad" or "holy war," presumably against the West. While Tweeds emphasizes the *color* contrast of the landscape, it simultaneously downplays *cultural* contrasts that would upset its constructed colonial fantasy or expose the political tensions and contradictions between the two worlds.

The *color* contrast of Egypt's landscape, against which "splendid things gleam in the dust" (12), points to the racial contrast of its inhabitants, the backdrop of darker peoples against which the colonizer is highlighted. Throughout the catalog, Arab men and boys form an out-of-focus background for the white U.S. models. The text and the pictures present the reader/consumer with conflicting messages: we are reminded that "Egyptians are naturally courteous, friendly and hard-working people" (57), lest we forget their natural "humanness," because any photographs of Egyptians without Americans are done in black and white, making the Arabs drab in comparison. Arab women are noticeably absent from the catalog, except for one woman in a long black dress, who is identified as "lead[ing] a gypsy's life" (60). While the U.S. male models are made to look decidedly Anglo, the U.S. female models are alternately cast in the role of Western colonialist and the role of the exotic yet absent Egyptian woman, with straight dark hair hanging down or wrapped in deep-colored scarves. In the opening pages, the U.S. female models appear as the colonialist tourists in pleated skirts and oxford shirts, travelers, as the text suggests, accustomed to

Tweeds's "journey to the Nile." (Tweeds catalog, Autumn 1990)

"Egyptians are naturally courteous, friendly and hard-working people."
(Tweeds catalog, Autumn 1990)

the comforts of home: "To Western travellers of half a century ago, staying at one of the venerable colonial hotels scattered along the Nile
must have felt like finding an oasis in the middle of the desert" (46).
However, in the center section, they form a "centerfold," standing in
for the absent Arab women, with bare bellies, sashes around the waist,
and lines around the eyes to make them more almond shaped (40). The
final pages restore the U.S. models to colonialist adventuresses, with
sunglasses, camera, and other desert paraphernalia, standing in the
desert sands with camels in the background.

Though many of the same models are used in all sections, the
darkest one appears exclusively in the central section as the exoticized
other. The positioning of the female models suggests Western women's
dual role within a colonialist/capitalist structure, casting them alternately in positions of dominance and submission, as agents and objects of imperialism. The U.S. women appropriate the Arab woman's
exoticized sensuality as a transforming act that empowers their otherwise repressed sexuality. In these advertisements, the female body

U.S. models standing in for absent Arab women. (Tweeds catalog, Autumn 1990)

"both stands for the 'Other' culture and provides the negation of its Otherness."[4]

Another, perhaps more blatant example of commercialized representations of Western and Arab women is exhibited in a Jerry Hall swimwear ad that appeared in the winter of 1989. The advertisement depicts Jerry Hall in a red two-piece bathing suit, with bangles on her wrists and a transparent scarf draped over her shoulders, her thinly clad body highlighted against a backdrop of veiled Arab women. The text reads, "Jerry Hall's swimwear may have raised a few eyebrows in Morocco. But no one's really sure." Playing on images of concealment and exposure, the advertisement employs cultural contrast to exoticize the white woman and her expressive feminine sensuality. The suggested spectators of Hall's exhibitionism, however, are not men, but the othered, supposedly oppressed and sexually repressed Moroccan women who seem to gaze enviously at the Western woman. The women, not visible except for their eyes (even their eyebrows are not seen), stare at the camera—they see but are not seen. Jerry Hall, in contrast, looks away from the camera—the object of the camera's gaze—as she stands towering above the squatting or standing women, one hand on her hip, the other threading its fingers through her long blond hair. In order to stage this cultural contrast, the advertisement blatantly misrepresents Moroccan women, suggesting that all women in Morocco wear the veil, when, in fact, most women in Morocco who attend schools or hold jobs outside the home today are unveiled.[5] Even the form of the veil is incorrect,[6] but most Westerners are not concerned with the subtleties and variations of veiling, rather with veiling as a monolithically oppressive practice. Still the point of the advertisement is clear: Western women are more sexually expressive and liberated. Ironically, the ad reveals how both Western and Arab women are held captive by patriarchal practices that cast them as sexual objects, either fetishized or repressed. Jerry Hall's central position further accentuates the narcissism of Western culture, which pursues "contact" with other cultures merely to find an alternative reading of the self, in this case an exoticized version of the self that fulfills the colonial fantasy.

The Arab woman remains absent from this discourse of fashion, except as a backdrop against which to highlight the Western woman, or in the case of Tweeds, as a little girl cradled in the arms of an Anglo man superimposed on the colonial map. As Gayatri Spivak argues, "to buy a self-contained version of the West" such as that sold by Hall or Tweeds "is to ignore its production by the imperialist project."[7] Replacing British imperialism with U.S. capitalism, these advertisements exploit the imperialist project as a fashionable ideology. This is

**Jerry Hall's swimwear
may have raised a few eyebrows in Morocco.
But no one's really sure.**

Jerry Hall's swimwear advertisement. (New York Times Magazine,
Nov. 19, 1989)

an ironic comment on Third World/First World relations under late capitalism, in which the development of multinational corporations based on the economic exploitation of Third World peoples mirrors colonialist strategies of exploitation. The Arab East is marketed for the U.S. consumer in this celebration and revival of colonialist ideology. Coincidentally, this ideology merged neatly with tactics used to sell the Persian Gulf War to U.S. audiences.

The Perverse Sexuality/Morality of the Orient

With Saddam Hussein's August 2 invasion of Kuwait, "Arabia" instantly fell out of fashion, yet the Arab world remained at the center of U.S. media attention. According to mainstream news media, which operated in unquestioning synchrony with U.S. government policy, Saddam's "rape" of Kuwait had to be avenged. Even the liberal *Nation* described the sanctions against Iraq as "a kind of ritualistic foreplay to the violent penetration of an entire region of the globe" (December 24, 1990). While sexual metaphors pervade the language of U.S. military conflict and conquest, the emphatic gendering of Persian Gulf War relations was characteristic as well of representations of the East/West relationship, which Edward Said argues have always been defined in sexual terms: these exotic, secretive, feminine regions were thought by Orientalists to "invite" Western "penetration and insemination" with its knowledge and civilization.[8] During the Persian Gulf Crisis, Orientalist depictions of the perverse sexuality of the Middle East pervaded the U.S. media, which implied that these cultural perversions would be morally righted by the "forces of good," in this case, the U.S. military.

"Lifting the Veil," reads the title of an article in *Time* magazine.[9] Beside these bold letters, a Saudi woman wrapped from head to toe in a black *abayah* stands over a crate of tomatoes in the marketplace. The subtitle reads, "A secretive and deeply conservative realm, Saudi Arabia suddenly finds itself on the sword edge of change." The image of the veil serves two purposes here. First, the rather Freudian imagery of the lifted veil and the sword suggests not merely the problematic liberation of Arab women but also a new "intimacy" in U.S./Saudi relations. The Gulf Crisis, the article claims, has "ripped the veil off Saudi Arabia's closely shrouded ties with the U.S." This rhetoric assumes that veiling always operates as a form of oppression, so that this veil, whether it veils a country or a woman, should be ripped off by the West. Second, it assumes that the veiled Saudi woman, who serves the popular media image of Arab women, has no rights and no opinions of her own. Because the veil is often read by Western audiences as a form of absence, the purported purpose of imperialist intervention is to rip off the veil and thereby to create a presence for the Arab woman.

Within U.S. imperialist ideology, the veiled Arab woman is effectively transformed into an object of imperialist rescue. As a "captive body,"[10] she captivates U.S. media attention, in both the forms of an absent subject position and as an irresistible sensuality, the deferral and multiplication of desire that results from the veil. In a Western context, the veil has traditionally been viewed as a signifier of inaccessibility, associated with the hidden, forbidden woman shrouded in mystery, masked in a cloak of purity, underneath which lies unbridled sensuality. In the Arab world, the veil takes many forms and may signify piety, class differences, or even a radical fashion statement against Western influence, particularly in those countries where women have the choice of veiling.[11] French and British colonialists of the nineteenth century saw the veil as a major obstacle to the modernization [read *Westernization*] of the Arab world and sought to abolish the practice of veiling. With the rise of colonialism, the discourse on women and the veil came to the forefront of nationalist debates both in the West and in the Middle East, where the veil allowed women a private space within public spheres but did not necessarily negate their presence. But the U.S. media interpret cultural practices such as veiling as captivity and powerlessness. Furthermore, war propaganda and colonialist discourse construct the Arab woman as captive to Arab patriarchy rather than a captive to imperialist forces, or to both. The dominant discourse's emphasis on the Arab woman's body and her position within an alleged despotic family structure therefore allows external forces of racism and imperialism to continue unquestioned.

In his 1981 *Covering Islam*, an analysis of media representations of the Middle East, Edward Said prophetically predicted the U.S. "reoccupation of the Gulf region" to secure U.S. oil interests, a move justified by supposed Islamic barbarism as the threat to Western civilization.[12] The consensus manufactured in the days leading up to the Persian Gulf War relied heavily on the conflation of all Arab groups under the "barbarism" of Islamic fundamentalism. Saddam, however, was somewhat belated in taking up the expected war cry of *jihad*, and the Iraqi state's generally secular policies were far from the conservative, fundamentalist policies of Saudi Arabia, whom the United States was defending.[13] Said attributes U.S. consensus in this anti-Islamic battle to a rejection of medieval theocracy, but a major appeal was made in the name of women's rights, with repeated images of silent, shrouded Arab women.

The film *Not without My Daughter*, released one week prior to President George Bush's January 15 deadline, reinforced U.S. notions of the brutality and "primitivism" of Muslim men who confine and op-

press women and children in the name of their religion.[14] Although the
film takes place in postrevolution Iran, media propaganda succeeded
in creating a monolith of Islam and associating it with the war effort.
(More than a year after the war, I was listening to a radio talk show in
Los Angeles in which a woman called in and made reference to the
film. The deejay then said, "Oh yes, I saw that movie. Didn't it take
place in Iraq or Saudi Arabia?" "Yes, that's right," the woman said, as if
both could be right. The specific geographic and historical context of
the film becomes irrelevant, making its racist propaganda more effective). In media representations during the Persian Gulf Crisis, the
twentieth-century "civilizing mission" to avenge the rape of Kuwait
and to unveil Saudi women was performed symbolically in the name of
women's rights. The Saudi women's struggle for autonomy was distorted by U.S. media to portray them as dependent on the white cultural savior. Ironically, much of the destruction in Iraq, which
included the deaths of tens of thousands of women and children, was
justified by the "barbarism" of Arab sexism from which the United
States was purportedly "protecting" Arab women.

Gendered Culture Clash: Or, "We Want to Respect You (But We Don't)"

A postinvasion episode of *Donahue* entitled "American Wife/
Saudi Husband: Culture Clash" (October 23, 1990) examined the "volatile" relationship between Arab men and their U.S. wives.[15] The producers of *Donahue* thought it "no bad idea for us," as Phil says, "to take
a look at just some of the features of the culture of the Middle East, . . .
with specific reference to those countries which are a part of and surround our Persian Gulf effort." The feature Donahue proposes to
examine is the "sexism" of Arab Islamic culture. The underlying assumption: if the United States could understand the marital relationships and problems between a U.S. wife and an Arab husband, then we
might decipher the Persian Gulf Crisis. The guest panel consisted of
one Palestinian-American man, Dr. Hassan El-Yacoubi; Dr. Amar El-
Yacoubi, his U.S. wife (who is consistently addressed as "Dr." while
Donahue refuses to recognize her husband's equal title); Laurie Ko-
fahi, who "loves being a Jordanian wife"; Kristine Uhlman, who lost
her children when she divorced her Saudi husband; and "Shelly," who
divorced her Kuwaiti husband and cannot see her children. While the
panelists discussed their varying attitudes toward Arab men, there
was only one Arab man present as their representative; and while the
predominantly white female audience joined in bashing Arab men,
Arab women were absent from the scene.

The talk show's investigation into the ills of Arab culture is

couched by Donahue in terms of cultural tolerance: "We do not pre-
sume to stand above you, look down upon you, and we want to respect
your religion." He says this just after saying to the panelists, "In our
audience, you're all members of the Communist Party." The identification of Arabs, or even Americans who ally themselves with Arabs, as
Communists exemplifies the transference of the Evil Empire label
from the Soviet Union to the Arab world in the post–Cold War equation of cultural dominance. After this comment, Donahue says, "I hope
a little humor is permitted within your culture." But what kind of
"Western" humor is this? The joke is hardly humorous, nor is the fact
that each time Donahue addresses Mrs. El-Yacoubi, he repeats her entire name, "Amar Jane Biddle Merritt El-Yacoubi," even though she insists three times, "You can call me Amar." Donahue, it would seem, is
playing with identities, mocking them in his guise of cultural tolerance while insisting on Arabs' absolute otherness, particularly when a
U.S. woman adopts Arab cultural customs such as the veil.

The title of the show, "American Wife/Saudi Husband: Culture
Clash," subsumes gender relations under a Saudi model, which is the
most conservative of all Arab countries in its treatment of women. In
fact, there are no Saudi Arabians on the panel; the only Arab man on
the panel is Palestinian, and only one woman on the panel was married
to a Saudi husband. The avowed purpose of the program, that of cultural understanding, is undercut by assumptions of a particular "Arab
character," one represented exclusively by its men. Edward Said explains such characterizations: "While it is no longer possible to write
learned (or even popular) disquisitions on either 'the Negro mind' or
'the Jewish personality' it is perfectly possible to engage in such research of 'the Islamic mind' or 'the Arab character.'"[16] The proliferation of articles on the "Arab mind" during the Persian Gulf Crisis and
War attests to the racism inherent in what passed for political
analyses.

In the context of this *Donahue* show, Dr. Hassan el-Yacoubi represents, like Saddam Hussein in media reports of the war, the "Arab
mind." He is portrayed as a man who got a good deal, having married a
"good Western . . . upper-middle class, Philadelphia debutante" with
a Ph.D. All of her superior qualifications are foregrounded from the
opening of the show, and not until the final minutes is he presented as
anything other than an Islamic fanatic with "a devoted wife." Finally,
when Donahue asks him what he does for a living, we learn that he is a
professor, and he says, "I wrote about eight books. And I have a book
coming called *The Arabic Koranic Islamic Paradigm*. And we want the
Americans to understand this." Yet discussion of this book, which
might allow the audience some understanding of Arab Islamic culture,

is never broached, because it would present Dr. Hassan El-Yacoubi as more than a religious fanatic who has seduced his intelligent wife into the veil and because it might allow for an analysis of cultural difference outside specifically gendered relations.

Dr. El-Yacoubi is positioned on the show as the stereotyped representative of Arab men. As he voluntarily teaches the audience an Islamic prayer and responds to Donahue's questions by repeating religious phrases, the women in the audience boo and hiss at El-Yacoubi's responses. Shelly, one of the panelists, says of him, "This man is a very poor example, in my opinion, of what a good Muslim should be. He is making a spectacle of himself." However, as the only Arab male in a show about Arab sexism, he has already been positioned as a spectacle, an oddity, the thing we must fight against, on an individual or national level. The U.S. audience can assume that if he is a poor representative, then so are all Arab men, because they engage in spectacles of terrorism, religious fanaticism, and sexism, while they keep their women hidden under veils, especially their U.S. women, who are obviously superior to them in every way. The absent Arab woman is replaced by the U.S. woman who takes up the veil but is obviously more articulate about her position, because she can speak from beneath this covering.

The notable absence of Arab women both on the panel and in the audience suggests one of the many ways that U.S. women serve as stand-ins for invisible Arab women. The veiling of these U.S. women enables them to "put on" an Arab identity, suggesting that the fashionability of "Arabia" might be merely a matter of dress. This manipulation of female agency accords Anglo-American women the right of representing, or speaking for, as well as "re-presenting," or acting as a fashionable semblance of, the Arab woman. Although the U.S. women panelists say much in defense of Arab culture, their words are often subsumed by the culture clash dramatized on stage. Donahue (himself ironically enough married to an Arab-American woman, Marlo Thomas) becomes the Burtonesque liberator of women, another example of what Gayatri Spivak terms "white men saving brown women from brown men,"[17] or better here, saving white women from brown-skinned Omar Sharifs turned religious fanatics. Furthermore, this transfer of cultural relations to the sexual realm of Arab man/white woman relationships reverses the colonialist model of Western "penetration" and rescue of the Arab East and violates imperialist terms of domination. The only way to excuse the U.S. women's activities is through a purported "seduction" by an Othello or an Omar Sharif. Phil's presence, however, reminds us, despite the Arab man's "theatrical" attempts to be heard, who, in fact, is running the show. Ms. Amar

El-Yacoubi and the two divorced women are there to remind us that miscegenation is a dangerous game, and Mr. El-Yacoubi is publically emasculated to remind us of the supremacy of the white man, who assumes "a reasoned position towards both the white and non-white worlds."[18]

In examining representations of Arab culture within U.S. popular culture, I want to emphasize the repetition of similar performances being played out within the U.S. news media: the veiled Arab woman embodies the powerlessness of Arab countries, even as Saddam Hussein, the despotic ruler and "terrorist" (whose forces were greatly exaggerated), represents the Law of the Father out of control. Saddam has been adequately described as prey to the "cult of virility,"[19] and I do not wish here to defend his invasion of Kuwait or subsequent actions. However, in these consistently gendered representations of Arab men and women, little attention has been given to the fact that women in Iraq have equal opportunity and pay as well as the rights to vote, drive, and dress as they wish; rather, Iraqi women, who purportedly "sing the praises of Saddam," have been portrayed as the hysterical followers of a madman. Media representations of the Saudi monarch, King Fahd, also emphasized the sensuality/sexuality of the Orient, depicting him as a "tamed playboy" who had "engaged in myriad liaisons with women"[20] yet who manages an "exquisite balancing act" between modernity and the feudalism of his kingdom. In contrast to Saddam, King Fahd's sexual escapades are cast in notably Western terms, as the playboy who "still has an eye for women," and his reign is depicted as a benevolent monarchy, despite the position of women within Saudi society. But the media's obsessive imaging of Arab male sexuality alongside exclusively veiled women (which represent approximately half of Arab women)[21] reinforces the supposed perversion of Arab gender relations and the absenting of Arab women. In effect, the veil itself stands in for Arab women and covers over the contradiction of the U.S. military's crusade to protect and liberate women when the U.S. administration has consistently supported those regimes, such as Saudi Arabia and Kuwait, that have been the most oppressive to women.

The Driving Demonstration: Driven Further into Invisibility

While details of the war's potential destruction were covered up, the Saudi women's driving demonstration of November 6, 1990, was highly dramatized by the media as an event that exemplified the gender politics of Islamic fundamentalism to stress the West's superior treatment of women. On November 6, 1990, forty-seven Saudi women dismissed their drivers and drove through the *suq* (marketplace) in Riyadh, many with the support of their husbands and brothers who watched. The women insisted that the protest was a practical matter, that they feared the war would leave them without drivers; they wanted the right to drive, especially in the event of an emergency. Despite Saudi women's insistence to the contrary, U.S. reports emphasized the connection between U.S. military presence in the region and the Saudi women's struggle, depicting these women as agents of Western influence. The significance of the driving demonstration was evident from the number of groups that participated in the debate over this issue: the Saudi *mutawa* (religious leaders), the Saudi royal family, the U.S. media/military, and even the National Organization for Women. The assumption that women's rights were a Western rather than an international value fed into the ideology of the new world order, which demanded respect for the Western values of liberation and democracy that the U.S. was purportedly in the region to defend. Reports of the demonstration were framed by displays of U.S. weaponry to suggest to U.S. audiences the vulnerability of the Persian Gulf and the chivalry of U.S. troops sent in to protect these feminized regions. Yet to cover over the contradiction of U.S. support of the repressive Saudi regime, the reports also fairly consistently ended with claims that the Saudi royal family and King Fahd supported women driving and that "by all indications" were moving slowly toward more liberal policies concerning women's rights.[22] Another embarrassing fact to U.S. media predictors, however, was King Fahd's punishment of these women who had achieved a momentary presence in the U.S. media, his deference to the conservative religious leaders, and his use of the incident to reassert his control over his kingdom, which many Saudis felt had fallen under spreading Western influence. These facts were subsequently covered up by the media, and Saudi women slipped once more back into invisibility when they no longer served U.S. propaganda needs.

Whatever happened to Saudi women in the Gulf War, particularly those who participated in the driving demonstration? Although the mainstream media abandoned them for more picturesque bombing displays, reports have appeared in alternative presses (including *Middle East Report* and *Ms.* magazine). The women, among them university professors, businesswomen, housewives, students, and teachers, were detained for twelve hours, interrogated, and released to their closest male relatives. They were denounced by fundamentalist leaders as "corrupters of society," and their "immoral behavior" was rebuked in a song recorded in a chorus of children's voices and broadcast on children's television. According to an anonymous Saudi woman writing to *Ms.*, "The women's phones were tapped; they were fired from their jobs, and stripped of travel papers. Their families were threatened. They have lived for a year in terror."[23]

With the "modernization" of the Persian Gulf region, as well as other parts of the Arab world, Eleanor Abdella Doumato asserts that Arab women are forced to bear the burden of traditional culture and to serve as emblems of "moral values of the community."[24] In Saudi Arabia, where "the public invisibility of women has become a visible sign of the monarch's piety," the driving demonstration occurred at a fortuitous time for the monarch, when "oppositional voices to Western presence were nearing a crescendo." To silence these voices and restore his power, King Fahd sacrificed these women to the *mutawa* in the defense of Islamic tradition. According to American newspaper accounts in mid-October 1991, "thanks to King Fahd" the demonstrators have had their passports returned and have received financial compensation for their lost income when they were forced to quit their jobs. Yet one Saudi woman writing anonymously in *Ms.* insists that the government's reimbursement was an attempt to break the women's solidarity and their support network, which had provided financial aid from local businessmen. Although some Saudi women are hopeful that their action will spark a greater women's movement, Doumato predicts that "in the absence of open institutions to express political dissent, women will remain a reliable barometer of stability in the kingdom" and the means by which Saudi rulers will reassert their faltering authority.

White Women Saving Brown Women

After the driving demonstration, the National Organization for Women (NOW), which had been outspoken against the war since the early days of the crisis, joined in the battle to free Saudi women from the hands of Arab Islamic patriarchy. In a "Resolution on Troop Buildup in the Persian Gulf" passed by the NOW board of directors on November 18, 1990, NOW elucidated five points of opposition to U.S. involvement in the Gulf:

1. Bush's military buildup as protection of U.S. oil interests and as a distraction from the U.S. economic crisis and the savings and loan scandal;
2. Saudi Arabia's and Kuwait's subjugation and sytematic oppression of women;
3. the billions spent in military mobilization means cutback in social services, for which women, the poor, and people of color will disproportionately bear the economic burden;

4. the deadly nature of today's conventional and biological weapons and their catastrophic effect on people and the environment;
5. Saudi Arabia and Kuwait as despotic clan-run monarchies complicit with Western oil interests.[25]

NOW's opposition to U.S. military presence in the Persian Gulf was appropriated by the media, which focused almost exclusively on NOW's statement against the subjugation and oppression of women within Saudi Arabia, the assumption being that NOW, as a women's group, had the right to speak, and be heard, on women's issues alone. The revision of NOW's protest in the media served the "off-loading of women from the realities of social and political activity"[26] and relegated them exclusively to the realm of gender relations.

However, NOW capitalized on the media attention it received. On November 27, 1990, NOW came out with a statement "denouncing Saudi Arabia for its attitude toward women—both its own citizens and female U.S. troops based there." According to a *USA Today* article entitled "NOW blasts Saudis for treatment of women," NOW president Molly Yard connected Saudi Arabia's oppression of women with South Africa's apartheid policies, saying, "We would be outraged if the administration sent American troops to defend South Africa from invasion, ordering black soldiers to 'respect the culture' by bowing their heads in the presence of white racists." Yard's analogy conflates racial and gender apartheid, thereby privileging gender oppression over racial oppression. In doing so, she fails to account for the complex and contradictory positionings of Arab women within the existing imperialist structure, or for the ways in which Arab women have defined their struggle. In the discourse of war, as in the discourse of fashion, gender often functions as a category that denies other forms of difference, including race and class.[27] NOW further failed to see how gender issues were being invoked by the U.S. military/media to support not only a racist agenda but, in fact, the massacre of Iraqis, including women and children. This strategy of using feminist rhetoric to support imperialist interests exemplified Leila Ahmed's definition of colonial feminism: "Feminism on the home front and feminism directed against white men was to be resisted and suppressed, but taken abroad and directed against cultures of colonized peoples it could be promoted in a way that admirably served and furthered the project of the dominance of the white man."[28]

Although NOW consistently denounced U.S. military presence, and later U.S. military actions, its denunciation of the war was subsumed in its attack against Arab patriarchy. In the *USA Today* article, for example, NOW's call for the withdrawal of U.S. troops is briefly mentioned; but in its statement against gender apartheid in Saudi

Arabia, NOW set itself up to be appropriated by the media as a mouth-
piece for the war. Although NOW's concern for Saudi and Kuwaiti
women is viable, within the existing racist structure, NOW's position
was predictably treated by the press to reinforce anti-Arab racism in
this country and the absenting of Arab women. NOW's purported solidarity with Arab women actually had the opposite effect in a way that
is so predictable that it calls into question what NOW had intended by
the statement. Like the U.S. wives and converts to Islam on *Donahue*,
NOW stands in for the seemingly absent Saudi woman. In taking this
position, the organization denies Arab women subjectivity and reinforces notions of the West as their cultural savior. In formulating a feminist antiwar agenda, NOW might have more effectively attacked the
U.S. military for posing as liberators of Arab women and for their
treatment of U.S. military women, rather than targeting Saudi Arabia
and Kuwait as the seats of patriarchal oppression.

*The juxtaposition of Arab women and western women. (*Austin Chronicle,
Fall 1991)

This tendency among U.S. women and feminist groups to position themselves in contrast to Arab women recurred in a postwar advertising campaign for Planned Parenthood marketed by the Hollywood Policy Center.[29] The advertisement depicts a veiled Arab woman and is captioned, "Abortion is illegal in Iraq. But at least they're not trying to pretend it's a free country." Reminiscent of Jerry Hall's swimwear ad both in its juxtaposition of Arab and Western women and in its phrasing of this contrast, this advertisement simultaneously equates the repressions of the U.S. antiabortion movement with the suppression of democracy and human rights in Iraq, a country now infamous in the United States for such violations. Once again, the ad blatantly misrepresents Iraqi women and, by suggestion, Arab women in general. For example, Iraqi women are not bound by law to veil, and there are conditions under which abortion is permitted in Islam.[30] Although the ad purports a kind of solidarity between U.S. and Iraqi women "who never had a chance to fight for their rights," it depicts Arab women as the silent recipients of injustice at the hands of the Iraqi government. Arab women are represented in the ad to suggest the hypocrisies of U.S. claims to democracy only as they reflect on U.S. women's rights to abortion. Ironically, the advertisement, which describes the United States as "the greatest democracy on earth," obscures the hypocrisy of such claims in light of U.S. military destruction of the lives of Iraqi peoples.

In negotiating the complex and often contradictory positionings of Arab women, particularly within the context of the Persian Gulf War, I have tried to show how female subjects, both Arab and Western, are manipulated within the discourse of war to limit greatly their forms of resistance. U.S. media representations of the Persian Gulf War substituted a concoction of colonialist fantasies and heroic myths similar to those found in popular culture for factual information on the events of the war. These cultural "fashion statements" follow a general trend within U.S. society in which news is more and more fabricated and shaped in the interests of the military industrial complex, obscuring the relationship between consumer capitalism, which markets sexuality and power, or sexuality as power, and the new world order, which presents its own sexual and gendered relations as well "ordered" under the law of a more benevolent father. The repeated imaging of the absent Arab women in the U.S. media reinforced racist stereotypes of Arabs and Western cultural superiority by denying Arab women's agency and by silencing their "illegitimate voices." Many of the U.S. women who operated as the "legitimate speakers" or stand-ins for Arab women played their roles too well, reinforcing racist assumptions and aiding in the further oppression of Anglo-American women.

In its photojournalistic display entitled "Images of 1991," *Time* included several pictures of heroism, technological wizardry, Iraqi defeat, and U.S. homecoming celebration, all of which featured men. One photo depicts a male sergeant returning home to his wife and children, captioned, "The women are waiting and the beer is cold."[31] Women, it would seem, did not exist in 1991 except as commodities, like beer, to be shelved. *Time's* photo repertoire forgot not only the veiled Arab women and female victims of war but U.S. military women as well. Although much of the "foreplay" of the Persian Gulf War relied on gender issues and "women's liberation" in order to mask its racist intentions and to prove the superior morality/sexuality of the United States, once the bombing began, both U.S. and Arab women were effaced or commodified by a myriad of masculine signifiers.

Saudi women, pushed further into invisibility by U.S. performances of "liberation," served as a "visible sign" not only of the Saudi monarch's piety but also of the U.S. military's supposed antichauvinism. The U.S. military's visible performance of liberation, however, stands in stark contradiction to the invisible events censored from the U.S. media—bomber pilots watching porn movies, rampant sexual assault of U.S. military women, Saudi women under house arrest, and tens of thousands of Iraqi women and children killed by U.S. bombs and in the aftermath of the war's destruction. These contradictions remind us that war, while often justified in the rhetoric of liberation, is rarely intended to liberate anyone—least of all women.

Despite the influx of U.S. businesspeople and oil interests into Saudi Arabia, the country has in many ways resisted internationalization in its adherence to a fundamentalist interpretation of Islamic law, a reactive form of resistance that has placed the burden of culture on women and is represented most saliently to a Western audience in the guise of the veiled woman. The Saudi women's driving demonstration and its repressive results exhibit the ways in which Third World women's resistance is often bound within the limits of global capitalism, the military industrial complex, and cultural or nationalist movements. The tragedy of the Persian Gulf War should give us pause to question how the gender debate is invoked in the name of war. It is, afterall, not surprising that NOW's attacks against Arab patriarchy were so readily appropriated to serve military interests, a problem due in part to the inability of many U.S. feminists to understand Western women's role within the legacy of colonial power structures and to distinguish between a feminism that serves the interest of *all* women and "colonial feminism," which serves imperialist and patriarchal interests by granting white women a presence at the expense of brown women.

Notes

1. The *Newsweek* cover for Feb. 18, 1991, read "The New Science of War/High-Tech Hardware: How Many Lives Can It Save?" Cited in "Gulf War Coverage: The Worst Censorship Was at Home," *Extra!* May 1991, 7.
2. Leila Ahmed, *Women and Gender in Islam: Historical Roots of a Modern Debate* (New Haven: Yale University Press, 1991), 151.
3. Otherness may be best defined here as a constructed *absolute difference* that is set in opposition to the self. In *Orientalism*, Edward Said explains how the Orient, the Arab East, has been a source of Europe's "most recurring images of the Other" (New York: Pantheon, 1978), 1. In the process of othering, Third Word peoples, women, and other subordinate groups are represented through stereotyped images that tend to say more about the Western interpreters than about the "other" peoples they purportedly represent. In the case of Tweeds, it is always the Western self one rediscovers in different cultural contexts, a point emphasized in the catalog's unenlightened attempts to explain Arab culture.
4. Judith Williamson, "Woman Is an Island: Femininity and Colonization," in *Studies in Entertainment: Critical Approaches to Mass Culture*, ed. Tania Modleski (Bloomington: Indiana University Press, 1986), 109.
5. Fatima Mernissi, *Beyond the Veil: Male-Female Dynamics in Modern Muslim Society* (Bloomington: Indiana University Press, 1987), 144. Mernissi rejects the tendency to compare Western and Muslim women, an argument that lapses into debates about cultural superiority. Rather, she asserts that a desegregated society that grants women equal rights both economically and sexually would be "an authentic Muslim society" (9).
6. Personal reference; Monia Laraqui, a Moroccan woman, told me the veil depicted in the Hall advertisement was not commonly, if ever, worn in Morocco.
7. Gayatri Chakravorty Spivak, "Can the Subaltern Speak?" in *Marxism and the Interpretation of Culture*, ed. Cary Nelson and Lawrence Grossberg (Urbana: University of Illinois Press, 1988), 291.
8. Said, *Orientalism*, 209.
9. Lisa Beyer, "Lifting the Veil," *Time*, Sept. 24, 1990, 38–40.
10. In her essay "Mama's Baby, Papa's Maybe: An American Grammar Book" (*Diacritics*, Summer 1987), Hortense Spillers uses this term to discuss the "captive body" of African-American women as a legacy of slavery. In borrowing the term, I do not mean to conflate black women's experience under slavery with Arab women's experience under Western imperialism. Her theory, however, explains how women of color are represented as captive to an "interiorized enemy," namely the men of their own culture, rather than to the external forces of the dominant Western culture.
11. The debate among Arab scholars and feminists regarding the history and socio-religious significances of veiling is complex. For more information on the practice of veiling, refer to Ahmed, *Women and Gender in Islam;* Mernissi, *Beyond the Veil* and *The Veil and the Male Elite: A Feminist Interpretation of Women's Rights in Islam*, trans. Mary Jo Lakeland (New York: Addison-Wesley, 1991), and Malek Alloula, *The Colonial Harem*, trans. Myrna Godzich and Wlad Godzich (Minneapolis: University of Minnesota Press, 1986).
12. Edward W. Said, *Covering Islam: How the Media and the Experts Determine How We See the Rest of the World* (New York: Random House, 1981), xiii.
13. The ruling Ba'ath party in Iraq is "secularist in its sensibilities" and has promoted "land reform and the provision of free social, educational and medical services." Michel Moushabeck, "Iraq: Years of Turbulence," in *Beyond the Storm: A Gulf Crisis Reader*, ed. Phyllis Bennis and Michel Moushabeck (New York: Olive Branch Press, 1991), 30. Saddam Hussein, however, has used

violent repression to destroy his opposition whom he accused of using "religion as a cover for politics" (32).

14. Ann Norton discusses the sexualization of the Middle East and the demonization of Saddam Hussein in "Sexuality and the Gulf War," *Middle East Report: Gender and Politics*, Nov./Dec. 1991, 27.

15. Unfortunately, I was unable to view this show, which was brought to my attention by a friend who described much of its visual contents to me. All of my analysis, therefore, is taken from the episode's transcript, which at times recorded the audience's verbal responses, such as booing, hissing, or laughter, but does not include any visual cues. All quotations are taken from *Donahue* transcript #3061, "American Wife/Saudi Husband: Culture Clash," Oct. 23, 1991.

16. Said, *Orientalism*, 262.

17. Spivak, "Can the Subaltern Speak?" 296.

18. Said, *Orientalism*, 227.

19. Fawwaz Trablusi, "The Harvest of War," *Middle East Report*, July/Aug. 1991, 31.

20. George J. Church, "An Exquisite Balancing Act: Onetime Playboy King Fahd Tries to Mingle Modernity and Feudalism," *Time*, Sept. 24, 1990, 45.

21. Although it is difficult to find exact statistics on the practice of veiling, Saudi Arabia is the only Arab country in which veiling remains compulsory. In Algeria and Libya, for example, most women veil, whereas in Tunisia, Egypt, Syria, and Lebanon few women veil. See Joni Seager and Ann Olson, *Women in the World: An International Atlas* (New York: Simon and Schuster, 1986), 3.

22. See the *New York Times*, Nov. 7, 1990, and AP reports. It is also significant to note that the Saudi women who participated in the driving demonstration were from the upper echelons of Saudi society. Their struggle for driving privileges hardly compares to the sufferings of the women guest workers, from the Philippines, Sri Lanka, etc., who have been abused and raped by their masters in both Saudi Arabia and Kuwait. The plight of these women was conveniently omitted from the U.S. media until after the war had ended.

23. "Saudi Arabia: Update on Women at the Wheel," *Ms.*, Nov./Dec. 1991, 17.

24. Eleanor Abdella Doumato, "Women and the Stability of Saudi Arabia," *Middle East Report*, July/Aug. 1991, 36–37.

25. For the sake of brevity, I have paraphrased these resolutions, adhering closely to the original wording. For the resolutions in full, refer to "Resolutions on Troop Build-up in the Persian Gulf" passed by the National Organization for Women Board of Directors, Nov. 18, 1990. National Organization for Women, Inc., 1000 16th St. NW, Suite 700, Washington, D.C. 20036–5705.

26. Williamson, "Woman Is an Island," 110.

27. Susan Jeffords explains the dynamics of gender, race, and class within the discourse of war in *The Remasculinization of America: Gender and the Vietnam War* (Bloomington: Indiana University Press, 1989), 179.

28. Ahmed, *Women and Gender in Islam*, 153.

29. *The ADC Times: News and Opinions of the American-Arab Anti-Discrimination Committee*, Nov. 1992, 13. The ADC Times report explains how the ad appeared in a number of newspapers in late Oct. 1992. The ADC asked the Hollywood Policy Center to pull this advertisement from its campaign because it misrepresents Arab and Muslim women in order to promote a political cause and is offensive to peoples of Arab decent. The center agreed to pull the ad, to consult with the ADC on any new ads regarding the Middle East, and to include an Arab-American woman in future coalition meetings.

30. For an explanation of attitudes toward abortion within Islam, see Leila Ahmed's "Arab Culture and Writing Women's Bodies," *Feminist Issues* (Spring 1989): 41–55.

31. "Images 1991: A Turbulent Year in Pictures," *Time*, Dec. 30, 1991, 42.

Margot Norris

Only the Guns Have Eyes: Military Censorship and the Body Count

The unprecedented Pentagon censorship of the press during the Persian Gulf War not only limited what North American viewers learned and saw of the conflict: it altered the sense of the "reality" (or "unreality") of the war itself. The military censorship was patently aimed both at concealing and at making the extent of the dead—both U.S. and Iraqi, and particularly the numbers of dead Iraqi soldiers and civilian casualties—unknowable. But in answering the question of why national conflicts are settled by the killing and injuring of the human body, theorist Elaine Scarry argues that it is precisely the dead body that lends the sense of "reality" clinging to its own empirical materiality to the issues and ideologies over which war is fought. The dead body is therefore needed less for what it accomplished while still alive than as a sign or signifier that makes winning and losing *real*:

> That is, the outcome of war has its substantiation not in an absolute inability of the defeated to contest the outcome but in a process of perception that allows extreme attributes of the body to be translated into another language, to be broken away from the body and relocated elsewhere at the very moment that the body itself is disowned. . . . The force of the material world is separated from the fifty-seven thousand or fifty million hurt bodies and conferred not only on issues and ideologies that have as a result of the first function been designated the winner, but also on the idea of winning itself.[1]

Necrology, or knowledge of the dead, is therefore central to the phenomenology of war. Censorship that conceals the body, like that imposed by the Pentagon during the Persian Gulf War, makes war *both more and less real* to the public at home—making it seem more like a "real" war than the military adventurism or packaged media event it was, yet less historically significant, less humanly meaningful, and therefore less politically consequential than other wars. To explore this relationship between censorship and the phenomenology of war, I make use of some postmodern theory, particularly Jean Baudrillard's concept of "hyperreality,"[2] to explore the strange perceptual effects that Pentagon censorship of the body and the body count produced.

The Pentagon's censorship policy resulted from news industry protests of the total press exclusion in the Grenada "war" of 1983. Malcolm W. Browne reported, "Their [news reporters'] employers objected so strongly that the Pentagon convened a commission headed by Maj. Gen. Winant Sidle, retired chief of Army Information, and made up mainly of military and Government public-affairs officials. It recommended that future wars be covered by pools of news representatives —selected, controlled and censored by the military."[3] The censorship policy produced by the Sidle Commission differed from that governing previous wars (World War II, the Korean War, and the Vietnam War) because it constituted "pre-censorship," as Walter Cronkite called it in his testimony before the Senate Committee on Governmental Affairs. "I'd rather have post-censorship, where you could argue it out after you get your story," Cronkite told the senators.[4] Precensorship allows the Pentagon to determine in advance what will be seen and not seen, known and not known, shown and not shown, of the war. The effect is that the military is able to program history in advance of preediting its possible narratives. The result is what theorist Jean Baudrillard calls "hyperreality"—that is, history scripted in models, maps, and simulations before its events occur, producing a reality *preceded by its own simulacra:* "It is the generation of models of a real without origin or reality: a hyperreal. The territory no longer precedes the map, nor survives it. Henceforth, it is the map that precedes the territory— *precession of simulacra*—it is the map that engenders the territory."[5] The new military censorship policy creates, in effect, the map that precedes the territory: the map of U.S.-waged war as a technological miracle marked by the unlocatability of the dead. When *Newsweek* writes the story of the Persian Gulf War under the headline "A Textbook Victory,"[6] the trope, marred only by its technological anachronism, functions as a tautology and a redundancy. The Sidle Commission's censorship policies would make all future U.S. wars prewritten or scripted events by definition, since the unprogrammable experiential residue or excess—unpredictabilities, irregularities, mistakes, accidents, costs, atrocities, gratuitous destructions, uncontrollable consequences—would all have been preedited from the model text that writes its history in advance.

Within the machine of this hyperreality, the role of the press becomes especially problematic. Censorship allowed "Operation Desert Storm" to be offered to the public as a media extravaganza—a public relations stunt intended from the outset to recover the military image damage from the Vietnam War, in which the Iraqis were destined from the start to serve as conscripted props and involuntary extras. At the same time, censorship seemed to guarantee that behind the media hype lay a secret reality and a dreadful truth—say, the materiality of 100,000 dead Iraqi bodies. Was this censorship's "real" job, to lend a patina of "real" war of superpower status to a trivial conflict that even *Newsweek*'s tame and obsequious reporting characterized as colonial adventurism, like "the use of air power by colonial forces in the 1930's; Italians beating up on defenseless Ethiopians," or "as if, one Marine put it, Rhode Island had taken on the United States"?[7] Both facts required the press to be neutralized, something the news industry's harshest critics, like John R. MacArthur in his book *Second Front: Censorship and Propaganda in the Gulf War,* called administration "collaboration."[8]

By making the press narcissistically preoccupied with its own oppressions and forcing it to write in a journalistic mirror, the Pentagon preempted an effective adversarial function that might have demanded to know how many Iraqis were being killed, how the military justified burying them alive, why they were buried in unmarked graves, and how this violation of the Geneva Convention was countenanced by an American public obsessed with the return of its own Vietnam War MIAs. None of these issues became matters of national interest because, throughout the war, the press was locked into the self-reflexive maneuver of protesting and reporting its own victimization. The result of the Sidle Commission censorship policies was a press (at best) ingested by the military ("Some reporters, hiding out in American Marine and Army field units, are meanwhile working in the guise of mascots, given G.I. uniforms and gear to look inconspicuous, enjoying the affection [and protection] of the units they're trying to cover.")[9] At worst, reporters had copy delayed and rerouted ("[O]ur stories have been sent instead to officials at the Tonopah Test Range in Nevada—the home base of the Stealth fighters"),[10] prose altered ("Even adjectives were edited: Frank Bruni of *The Detroit Free Press* wrote that pilots were 'giddy' on returning from early missions. Officers changed the word to 'proud'; they compromised on 'pumped up' "),[11] and discipline inflicted on them for infractions of the "guidelines" ("I was spread-eagled across a Humvee [military vehicle] and searched and blindfolded").[12] Stripped of its adversarial function ("In effect, each pool member is an unpaid employee of the Department of Defense, on whose behalf he or she prepares the news of war for the outer world," Malcolm Browne wrote),[13] the press was left to describe its own impotence and report its own failures ("I cannot tell you much about Army aviation at any price").[14]

Academic journalism failed even more embarrassingly to offer any meaningful resistance to military censorship. The *Columbia Journalism Review*, journalism's most respected academic organ, assigned its war correspondence to a writer who camouflaged himself in name and persona as the protagonist of Evelyn Waugh's satirical *Scoop*: "William Boot is the pen name of Christopher Hanson, the Washington correspondent for the *Seattle Post-Intelligencer*. He will be reporting on the gulf war from Saudi Arabia in the next issue."[15] In place of a serious analysis of press options for eluding censorship (to report,say, Iraqi casualty figures to the U.S. public), Boot gave the press either comic self-parody or what can only be described as mock-heroic advice drawn from the Hemingwayesque school of war correspondence —"they should get in their Land Rovers or onto their motorcycles and go where the action is. The public might hate them. The Pentagon might expel them. The Iraqis might even kill them. But at least they shall have acquitted themselves with honor."[16] Boot's metaphor ("journalists accredited to the allied command in Saudi Arabia are, in effect, prisoners of war, trapped behind the barbed wire of reporting curbs")[17] was eventually enacted by CBS Middle East correspondent Bob Simon and his crew, who were captured by Iraqi patrols in an unauthorized zone near the border intersection of Iraq, Saudi Arabia, and Kuwait on January 21, 1991. But the result of this maverick action was only self-reflexive news—the press reporting on itself—"Iraq Frees Captured CBS News Crew; Network Credits Soviet Intervention."[18]

When that mirror in which censorship imprisoned journalism cracked only a little (and then after the fact), the truth it revealed—of what was censored and why—was no surprise: it was killing, and the image of the violently killed, that the Pentagon's elaborate press-control mechanisms sought to keep out of sight. This is John Balzar's story of why his crew failed to get their story on army aviation: "Maybe it was because of the stories two of us filed before the ground war began. The stories described vivid videotapes taken from Apache gun cameras during early patrols into Iraq. The video images were the first of the conflict to show, close up, the killing of individual soldiers."[19] The army was not ashamed of killing but only of *being seen* killing. But by squelching knowledge of what the guns "saw," the Pentagon was shown trying to neutralize a stunning bit of new technology with the potential to once again make soldiers, and the citizenry that puts the guns in their hands, take responsibility for individual killings in warfare.

Guns with camera "eyes" could reverse the "blind," impersonal, anonymous, and nonhuman killing made possible by the telekinesis of the big guns, missiles, and bombs in modern mass warfare. Giving guns "eyes" so that we see what they "see" makes it possible to reintroduce a "witness" into mass warfare, that obliges those who pull the trigger to "see," literally and visually, those human beings they kill. By extension, if such video clips of close-up kills were shown on television, the viewer would find himself or herself ocularly in the position of the gun and its operator and would have to recognize himself or herself as occupying the position of the agency of killing. Instead of the thrill of the pyrotechnics of the Patriots bursting Scuds in midair, the viewing public would have had to recognize itself as the killer of individual Iraqi men during the Persian Gulf War. By censoring Balzar and his crew and refusing to let them tell the public what they saw on the camera eye video, the military drove the peril of this self-recognition "underground" (in a cultural sense) and transformed the video into a secret, obscene, and taboo "snuff film"—the name of pornographic film of a killing that turns out to have been "real" rather than merely staged. This is why when footage of close-up carnage became available to the U.S. public—for example, in the images of charred bodies and killing obtained by Bill Moyers from *Newsday* and British television— the "truth" felt disturbingly embarrassing and transgressive to the viewer, who was placed in the position of a media voyeur.[20]

The crack in the mirror of censorship revealed only ghosts—John Balzar reporting stories he could not tell about scenes he did not see— whose residue is a rumored knowledge of classified army footage of close-up killing that no one ever saw except the guns. But even the most aggressive investigative reporting to ferret out the censored enemy casualty figures seemed doomed to entrapment in the "precession of simulacra." In one of the most significant pieces of reporting on the Persian Gulf War, John H. Cushman, Jr.'s story in the February 3, 1991, *New York Times* announced, and analyzed for the public, why there would be no Iraqi body count during this war. But his best suggestion for reconstructing this information relied on electronically inferred and produced data that owed their chief instruments, methods, and procedures to the very war college apparatus that produced the "textbook" in the first place. After speaking to Joshua Epstein, a military analyst at the Brookings Institution, Cushman reports:

> But other analysts noted that the Pentagon has a great deal of information, including photographs taken by satellites and aircraft, and complete lists of targets hit and bombs dropped, that would allow it to make a reliable estimate, perhaps within a margin of error of several thousand. . . . [A] formula could be constructed based on a list of targets struck, estimated population densities at and near the targets,

the lethal radius of the explosives dropped, and the accuracy of similar weapons in tests.²¹

But as an aspect of BDAs (bomb damage assessments), the censored enemy dead return to their origin as ghosts in the electronic simulators that engendered them theoretically at the war college in Leavenworth, Kansas:

> Each of four battalion commanders sits at an oversized computer screen, giving directions to a keyboard operator who executes the order. The display shows a contour map of the battlefield. U.S. forces are blue markers; the enemy is red. The software replicates the soldier's weapon and its range. When a shot is fired, the computer gives a mathematical result based on the probability of hitting the target, and if hit, of killing it.²²

War is literally preceded by simulacra, and the enemy dead are both before and after the fact figures of theory, hypothetical objects before and statistical folds or margins of error afterward. What they are *not* are figures of phenomenology, actual beings (subjective or objective), or, in their mortality, figures of empiricism, material objects of sufficient individuality to be either counted or represented. *Time* magazine reported in June 1991, "[T]he Defense Intelligence Agency last week released an internal estimate of 100,000 Iraqi soldiers killed, 300,000 wounded. But DIA said those figures had an 'error factor of 50% or higher'—to a statistician, a grotesque number. The Pentagon has little wish to refine its figures either."²³ Which 50,000 Iraqi are the phantoms that live in the dimension of unknowability and unlocatability and in the rhetorical carelessness of the "more or less" of a margin of error of 50 percent on a figure of 100,000 lives?

When censorship reduces the dead to phantoms of speculation, it shifts them from one language to another. Instead of objects of *destruction*, "evidence" (in empirical language) capable of serving as the locus of ethical debate, the dead become objects of *deconstruction*, figures impossible to verify and locate and therefore incapable of serving in any intellectual operation other than that of the impossibility of determining their reality. Censorship makes possible the implementation of the conscious philosophical shift in military theory that shaped Pentagon policy during the Persian Gulf War. Colonel Harry G. Summers, Jr. (a retired military specialist who wrote theoretical military analysis for the *Los Angeles Times* during the war), traced the historical roots of the Pentagon's abandonment of the "body count" (a practice common to the Vietnam War) to a shift from one Napoleonic war strategist to another, from the empirical approach of Baron Antoine Henri Jomini, who urged understanding war in terms of mathematics, to the more psychological theories of Carl Von Clausewitz, who emphasized the role of perception and morals in the achievement of victory.[24] The Pentagon's own philosophical moves between the Vietnam War and the Persian Gulf War appear crudely to mirror as well the large shifts in academic social theory in the late twentieth century away from scientific positivism toward a more subtle grasp of the significance of institutional control over the production of knowledge of the sort described in the theories of Michel Foucault. By substantially increasing Pentagon control over information and knowledge, censorship allows the military to determine how its newly increased technological firepower will be discussed, interpreted, and understood. Press censorship joins the arsenal of the Pentagon's metaweapons as a rhetorical and discursive "smart bomb"—a weapon for focusing public attention on, and limiting discussion to, the military's own interests and aims. The Persian Gulf War was not exempt from even the crudest propaganda —"Journalists can only cringe as MacArthur recounts the widely reported story of Iraqis throwing infants out of incubators in Kuwait hospitals. Stories of baby massacres have served propagandists for centuries. Like most, this was a complete fabrication," Christopher Dickey writes in *Newsweek* on June 8, 1992.[25] But when the issue is lying or deceit, as in propaganda, there remains faith in a recoverable "truth" in war. Pentagon censorship makes possible the far more troublesome specter of war presented through state-of-the-art strategies of image control.

Enabled by censorship to control the deployment of knowledge selectively, the Pentagon invests its lethal activity with the intellectual legitimations of empiricism and the social authority of science while suppressing the representations of killing and destruction that would make its effects recognizable. The daily military briefing and press conference on C-SPAN during the Persian Gulf War became a theater of intellectual domination, a space where warrior-scientists became pedagogues imparting to the public a knowledge "hard" and authorized because it was invested in the symbolic-truth status of the empirical "facts" of quantifications and the occultations of a new technical language. This discourse was simultaneously supported with an apparatus of demonstration designed to confound representation and simulation in a performance of the indeterminate status of the "real." Thus the video clips of target hits were selected to replace the close-up killing in Balzar's "snuff film" (that is, a photographic or video image or representation) with the simulatory images of electronic gaming, the miniaturized and abstracted dots and lines inside the cross hairs, that made Schwarzkopf's "luckiest man in Iraq,"[26] the tiny vehicle just safely crossing the exploding bridge, a Pac-man. Schwarzkopf's video of an actual bombing and an actual potential killing cannot be distinguished as a representation with a "real" or actual reference from a simulacrum or pure model of the same event. The "Nintendo" character of the Persian Gulf War merely signified the public's attempt to name its perception of the conflict's hyperreality, its sense that it was seeing models and diagrams—abstract figures—rather than representations (photographs, films, video) of violent events. Censorship, then, has come to play a crucial role in the phenomenology of modern warfare by allowing the military to manipulate codes of the "real" for the purpose of controlling public perception and response.

Because of the power of the dead body's materiality to signify an excess of "reality" in its massed and accumulated effects, military discourse has historically developed conventions to simultaneously display and hide, acknowledge and disavow its presence. One of these strategies is a rhetorical convention that is described by Scarry as the abstracting of the body of the individual soldier into a collectivized metaphoric corpus that transforms the army itself into an embodied colossus. The features of this army-as-giant come especially into focus in the anatomical personification of the unit's injury and disablement (the severed "arteries" of ruptured supply routes, "decapitation" by destroying command headquarters, the maneuver of "outflanking" battalions by skirting their sides, and so on). Scarry sketches the ideological consequences of this "convention which assists the disappearance of the human body from accounts of the very event that is the most radically embodying event in which human beings ever collectively participate."[27] By replacing necrology with technology, contemporary censorship allowed the Pentagon to shift the trope of the army as a colossal body onto the cybernetic machine, transforming the enemy into a robotic body whose injury is best calculated by BDAs (bomb damage assessments) undistorted by body counts. "In military terms," John Cushman explains, "the number of dead is not considered as important as the number of hits against command centers, communication links, airfields, and major weapons,"[28] targets whose translation reconstitutes them as the vital sites of a cybernetic robot: brain (command centers), speech (communication links), feet (airfields), and arms (major weapons). The logic of translating the enemy army into a giant robot evoked, in the Persian Gulf War, precisely those popular cultural formations that we recognize as simulacra (computer-generated "special effects" rather than representations) of futuristic warfare—"Robowar"[29] and "Star Wars" ("Buck Rogers and Luke Skywalker would be at home in the Gulf War").[30]

Metaphorizing the soldierly body as a collectivized robot not only disembodies the killed body twice over—materially and rhetorically—as Scarry suggests, but further transforms it into a postmodern figure that no longer represents the product of a humanistic scenario. The dead enemy body becomes the product of chance and accident—as much a form of "collateral damage" as the civilian dead—and it thereby becomes noninstrumental, nonreferential, formally irrelevant, and meaningless. The operation of censorship, which implements the dead enemy body's institutional irrelevance by denying the need to see it or know it or count it or commemorate it, colludes with its marginalization as a material excess or surplus, as garbage, as bombing debris ("After bombing, they were moving this debris with shovels. . . . While [doing so], they see dead bodies—some legs, some heads. They remove these things"),[31] as technological detritus. This marginalization was confirmed in the aftermath of the Persian Gulf War, when for a time the only attempts to produce or learn an official Iraqi body count were made by conservation agencies: Greenpeace had its director of military research produce an estimate, and the Natural Resource Defense Council used the Freedom of Information Act to compel an estimate from the Defense Intelligence Agency. Their efforts suggest, in addition to a humanitarian concern, the logic that the Iraqi dead may end up mattering chiefly as a potential pollutant and contaminant whose effect—the decay and degradation of 100,000 largely formally unburied corpses—upon a fragile desert ecosystem may be as serious as that of the long-uncapped oil fires. The minimal eyewitness journalism permitted after (but not during) the ground war on the highly localized highways inscribed in the timing of its utterance the effects of time and nature on the material degradation of the recently dead: "At one spot, snarling wild dogs have reduced two corpses to bare ribs," Bob Drogin wrote on March 10, more than a week after the fighting stopped. "Giant carrion birds claw and pick at another; only a boot-clad foot and eyeless skull are recognizable."[32]

These journalistic accounts of the carnage on the highway, the only graphic necrological accounts to come out of the Persian Gulf War in the United States, demonstrate how shrewdly the military controlled not only what it concealed but also what it permitted to have revealed. Virtually every report expended considerable prose on an inventory of looted consumer goods strewn about at the site ("new television sets and videocassette recorders; shirts in plastic wrappers; unopened bottles of Chanel perfume; children's bikes and baby strollers")[33] to tacitly suggest that the carnage signified the justice of a criminal execution meted out to looters whose rupture of the capitalistic compact—that Western consumer products (particularly luxury items like Chanel No. 5) must be bought and not stolen by Third World countries—constituted a capital offense.[34] The new style of war correspondence inaugurated by contemporary military censorship contributes to a cycle of ideological consumption. The media's outrage over the Iraqi looters' violation of the consumer economy ironically mirrors journalism's own unacknowledged allegiance to that same economy. The censorship policy allows the Pentagon to use journalism to package the news of war as other political news (campaigns, summit conferences, diplomatic travel, televised hearings) is packaged—for politically profitable purchase and consumption. The U.S. economic interests served by the Persian Gulf War exceeded mere oil: the war itself was transformed into a Western consumer commodity policing the Third World theft of other consumer commodities.

The easy selection of domesticated martial images of the war's aftermath—Norman Schwarzkopf in signature "camies" with stuffed bear in hand, tearful reunions of soldier families, yellow-ribboned parades—made the Persian Gulf War's assimilation to the genres of television entertainment smooth and seamless: Schwarzkopf's talk show interviews with Barbara Walters and David Frost, Jonathan Winters's parody of his briefing style for America West advertisement, Schwarzkopf's entry into the Disneyland logo, the made-for-television movie (*Heroes of Desert Storm*), the *TV Times* discussions of Peter Arnett's celebrity. In a piece titled "Antihero: On the Gulf War's First Anniversary, Danny Schechter Looks at an Unreported Casualty—the Death of a Free and Objective Television Press," *Spin* magazine brutally indicted the television networks for the crass commercial exploitation of the war aftermath:

> New [sic] organizations ran promo after promo, pimping off the war's popularity. *Time* and *Newsweek* pumped out souvenir editions; the line between news, entertainment, and merchandising began to disappear. In New York City, a daily newspaper helped pay for the "victory parade." . . . ABC tried to cash in one last time with a prime-time movie of the week salute to "the heroes of Desert Storm," complete with President Bush as the MC. Footage of the real events and dramatized material were intermixed. In a sense, this lack of distinction between fantasy and reality was consistent with the way network news treated the war.[35]

The curious effect of the military censorship's transformation of the Persian Gulf War into a hyperreal event is that, while it spared the U.S. public the trauma of contending with a "real" war, it also failed to register as a significant and lasting political credit for the administration, as Desert Storm's failure to sustain George Bush's election campaign a year later shows. "Hyperreality" cuts both ways: if it removes historical information from the realm of referentiality into the realm of illusion that the electronic game machine industry has named "virtuality" (from "virtual reality"),[36] its success in making the dead bodies and the suffering generated by the massive destruction "unreal" deprived the war of what Elaine Scarry calls the "anchor" for its issues (*The Body in Pain*, "The End of War: The Laying Edge to Edge of Injured Bodies and Unanchored Issues," 108). Precensorship's preediting of representation places not only the phenomenological events of the fighting but also the political and historical significance of the enterprise under a kind of erasure. The war passed through the public imagination and memory like a video phantom, unable—in the absence of any national pain or suffering—to imprint a lasting inscription on either the national conscience or the national self-image.

The result has been a political revisionism ("The Day we Stopped the War . . . Did the fighting end too soon")[37] that precisely misses the point. The argument that the war is unfinished because Saddam Hussein remains in power fails to grasp the metaphysics of military winning and losing. Wars are not won or lost because this or that political objective is realized; they are won or lost because the killing and destruction that is the military activity of war has lent those military objectives their own peculiar code of empirical reality. According to this logic, even a significant change in Iraqi leadership or political power— bought at the cost of, say, a doubling of allied and Iraqi casualties— would not have made the outcome more "real" if press censorship and information control would have continued to render it "virtual" (in the optical sense). Or was that precisely the hidden point of the revisionary criticism of the war's aborted aims? By retrieving the suppressed violence made visible by the ground war—a violence articulated in the conventional language of carnage, slaughter, and massacre ("The way Colin presented it, to have pursued the campaign beyond where we did would have been just a massacre")[38]—did the revisionary recriminations against the prematurely ended ground war attempt to make the "clean win" produced by censorship retroactively appear less hyperreal for the media blip of its first anniversary celebration? However, in his recent book, *It Doesn't Take a Hero*, Norman Schwarzkopf both concedes and deplores the military's inability to control media coverage of the killing in the ground war as producing a politically motivated premature cease-fire:

> What had happened, of course, was that journalists were now interviewing Air Force pilots who'd been hitting the convoys fleeing Kuwait. And as soon as we'd liberated the area around Kuwait City, reporters who had once been part of the media pools had taken pictures of Highway 6, where we'd bombed a convoy Monday night. It was a scene of utter devastation that they named the "Highway of Death." Powell and I both knew that wasn't the case. Though many

Iraqis in the convoy had died, most had jumped out of their vehicles and run away. I felt irritated—Washington was ready to overreact, as usual, to the slightest ripple in public opinion. I thought, but didn't say that the best thing the White House could do would be to turn off the damned TV in the situation room.[39]

Schwarzkopf does not concede that reporters were not permitted to film what U.S. soldiers called their "turkey shoot"—their killing, with rifles, of individual Iraqi soldiers fleeing the bombed convoy.[40]

In the end, the Defense Intelligence Agency estimates that 100,000 Iraqi soldiers were killed, give or take 50,000. The number is unknowable because every effort was made to prevent the dead from being counted, including U.S. complicity and activity in burying the dead in mass and unmarked graves, a violation of the Geneva Convention.[41] The relationship between censorship and the burial of the enemy in unmarked graves is not merely one of analogy or metaphor— the mortuary concealment of the dead repeated by the media. In the case of the Persian Gulf War the relationship was causal, censorship permitting the mass burial of the uncounted dead ("U.S. journalists have reported seeing American and British troops shovelling the dead into shallow graves without identification and registration").[42] Indeed, censorship made possible the burial of the living as well, as *Newsday* (whose repeated groundbreaking information suggests the help of a Pentagon informant) reportedly disclosed, according to a September 1991 *Los Angeles Times* piece: "Using plows mounted on tanks and combat earthmovers, the U.S. Army division that broke through Saddam Hussein's defensive front line buried thousands of Iraqi soldiers—some still alive and firing their weapons—in more than 70 miles of trenches, according to U.S. Army officials. . . . No Iraqi body count was possible after the assault."[43] Would this assault by the First Mechanized Infantry Division have been countenanced by the U.S. public had journalism reported it in narrative and pictorial form on the evening news? Until the leak through *Newsday*, censorship made it possible for the administration and the Pentagon to conceal the incident (which had no journalistic witness) even from Congress ("Defense Secretary Dick Cheney made no mention of the 1st Division's tactics in a recent interim report to Congress on Operation Desert Storm. . . . The Pentagon has withheld details of the assault from both the House and Senate Armed Services committees, according to committee officials").[44]

Military censorship should place the mark of skepticism on all news information and official announcements received by the public in time of war, and could thereby stimulate an intense interrogation of governmental and military policy. Instead, it seems to have translated history into hyperreality, with the effect of making warfare unreal to the point of blunting apprehension, conscience, and memory along with criticism. The juxtaposition of official and journalistic discourse that at the time of the Vietnam War provoked protest and debate was as potentially ruptured and dissonant in the Persian Gulf War, yet blurred by censorship. "Americans treat human life as our most precious value," Marlin Fitzwater stated in the official White House response to the bombing of the Baghdad shelter on February 13, 1991.[45] But the unedited CNN feeds shown in the United States could have been supplemented by far more detailed and graphic footage of the bombing impact, obtained by Jordan TV, "most of which the world's public—including Jordanian viewers—has never seen," according to Laurie Garrett, the medical reporter for *Newsday:*

> This reporter viewed the unedited Baghdad feeds the following day; they showed scenes of incredible carnage. Nearly all the bodies were charred into blackness; in some cases the heat had been so great that entire limbs were burned off. Among the corpses were those of at least six babies and ten children, most of them so severely burned that their gender could not be determined. Rescue workers collapsed in grief, dropping corpses; some rescuers vomited from the stench of the still-smoldering bodies.[46]

Garrett quotes Rabah Rousan, the anchor for the English-language broadcast on Jordan TV, remembering the footage, " 'I saw a young child's body, completely charred, clothes and hair all burned off, and there was still smoke coming off him.' "[47] Children are, of course, particularly sentimentalizable icons in propaganda, as the Kuwait incubator stories showed. But the dead bodies of children are evidence, like any other, of the real costs of war. They should be neither concealed nor exploited but represented like any other "collateral damage." Their representation as victims of U.S. bombing in the Persian Gulf War might, at any rate, have mixed some shame into Marlin Fitzwater's pious cant about the sanctity of human life. Later admissions forced by disclosures from the *London Independent* confirmed that the Pentagon—aware that the Ameriyah facility had been used as a shelter during the Iran-Iraq War[48]—believed it was bombing the families of the Iraqi military elite.[49]

Although the U.S. public apparently widely supported military censorship during the Persian Gulf War—"The survey found that a majority of nearly 2 to 1 felt that military censorship is more important than the media's ability to report important news"[50]—its consequences require exploration and critique. A number of news organizations, including the *Nation, Village Voice,* and *Harper's,* sued the

Defense Department in U.S. District Court in New York for "imposing unconstitutional restriction during the gulf conflict." But as Michael Massing pointed out, "In the current climate, the outcome of any contest between *The Nation* and the nation would seem foreordained."[51] Indeed, the suit was dismissed. The Pentagon press guidelines have since been revised: "After eight months of negotiations, it recently agreed to new guidelines for future war coverage, endorsing the principle of 'independent' reporting and limiting the use of controlled pools," Christopher Dickey writes. "But it still insists that stories must pass a 'security review,' which is still censorship with a censored name."[52]

Notes

1. Elaine Scarry, *The Body in Pain: The Making and Unmaking of the World* (New York: Oxford University Press, 1985), 124.
2. Jean Baudrillard, *Selected Writings*, ed. Mark Poster (Stanford: Stanford University Press, 1988).
3. Malcolm W. Browne, "The Military vs. the Press," *New York Times Magazine*, Mar. 3, 1991, 27–45.
4. Thomas B. Rosenstiel, "Senators Told of Press Curb Problems," *Los Angeles Times*, Feb. 21, 1991, A5.
5. Baudrillard, *Selected Writings*, 166.
6. John Barry and Evan Thomas, "A Textbook Victory," *Newsweek*, Mar. 11, 1991, 38–42.
7. Ibid., 42.
8. Christopher Dickey, "Not Their Finest Hour: Did the Press Fail during Desert Storm?" *Newsweek*, June 8, 1992, 66.
9. Chris Hedges, a *New York Times* reporter, used the term *unilaterals* to describe reporters who managed to escape the pool system. "By this time I had my hair cut to military regulations, my jeep marked with the inverted 'V' that was on all military vehicles, and a large orange cloth tied to the roof," he described his camouflage before the ground war. With the ground war, unilaterials were outlawed, "no reporters were allowed to wear military dress, to use cellular phones to file stories, or to mark their vehicles." *Columbia Journalism Review* 30 (May/June 1991): 29.
10. Browne, "Military vs. the Press," 44.
11. Jonathan Alter and C. S. Manegold. "Showdown at 'Fact Gap,'" *Newsweek*, Feb. 4, 1991, 61–62.
12. Douglas Frantz, "Restrictions—and MPS—Have Journalists on Defensive," *Los Angeles Times*, Feb. 11, 1991, A15.
13. Browne, "Military vs. the Press," 29.
14. John Balzar, "No War in Sight—Flying Blind to Report on Army Aviation," *Los Angeles Times*, Mar. 3, 1991, A8.
15. William Boot, "The Press Stands Alone," *Columbia Journalism Review* 29 (Mar./Apr. 1991): 23–24.
16. Ibid.
17. Ibid.
18. Mark Fineman, "Iraq Frees Captured CBS News Crew; Network Credits Soviet Intervention," *Los Angeles Times*, Mar. 3, 1991, A8.

19. Balzar, "No War in Sight," A8.
20. In an interview on the Bill Moyers special, *After the War*, the Jordanian writer Fadia Faqir said of seeing the violence, "It was like watching pornography. You felt guilty watching it, but you can't help but watch it." *Special: After the War*, Public Affairs Television, June 27, 1991.
21. John H. Cushman, Jr., "Pentagon Seems Vague on the Iraqi's Death Toll," *New York Times*, Feb. 3, 1991, K10.
22. Duncan Moore, Jr., "A Graduate School for Warriors," *Los Angeles Times*, Feb. 21, 1991, A9–10.
23. "How Many Iraqi Soldiers Died?" *Time*, June 17, 1991, 26.
24. Harry G. Summers, Jr., "Body Count Proved to Be a False Prophet," *Los Angeles Times*, Feb. 9, 1991, A5.
25. Dickey, "Not Their Finest Hour," 66.
26. John Balzar noted that U.S., British, and French military briefers all made use of aircraft-gun camera video "hits," but occasionally to very different effect. "The French also showed laser-guided bombing videos but went a step further and showed the destruction of an air base hangar just after a car or truck raced inside, presumably for shelter. Observers quickly entitled the driver the 'unluckiest man in Kuwait.'" *Los Angeles Times*, Feb. 12, 1991, A5.
27. Scarry, *Body in Pain*, 71.
28. Cushman, "Pentagon Seems Vague," 10.
29. Gregg Easterbrook, "Robowar," *The New Republic*, Feb. 11, 1991, 17–19.
30. VADM R. F. Dunn, USN (Ret.), "Early Gulf War Lessons," *Naval Institute Proceedings* (Mar. 1991): 25.
31. Mark Fineman, "Refugees from Iraq Describe Hellish Scenes," *Los Angeles Times*, Feb. 5, 1991, A10.
32. Bob Drogin, "On Forgotten Kuwait Road, 60 Miles of Wounds of War," *Los Angeles Times*, Mar. 10, 1991, A1.
33. Bob Drogin, "Images of War: Carnage, the Last Push, Nightmares," *Los Angeles Times*, Mar. 2, 1991, A1.
34. Sergeant Mike Ange, whose National Guard unit followed the Twenty-fourth Mechanized Infantry Division into Basra, reported in an interview on the Bill Moyers special that he examined some of the vehicles that had been "taken out" on the road, and found that they appeared to belong to fleeing refugees, loaded down with furniture, suitcases, and household goods.
35. Danny Schechter, "Antihero," *Spin*, Jan. 1992, 54. See also Michelle Kendrick's essay in this volume.
36. John Schwartz and Phyllis Brasch Librach, "Entering the Virtual Zone," *Newsweek*, Jan. 20, 1992, 45.
37. "The Day We Stopped the War," *Newsweek*, Jan. 20, 1992, 16–26.
38. General H. Norman Schwarzkopf, book excerpt from *It Doesn't Take a Hero*, in *Newsweek*, Sept. 28, 1992, 62.
39. Ibid.
40. Moyers, *Special: After the War*.
41. Holly Burkhalter, "Some Bodies Don't Count," *Los Angeles Times*, Mar. 12, 1991, B11.
42. Ibid.
43. Patrick J. Sloyan, "U.S. Tank-Plows Said to Bury Thousands of Iraqis," *Los Angeles Times*, Sept. 12, 1991, A1.
44. Ibid.
45. "Fitzwater's Remarks: 'Loss of Civilian Lives Is Truly Tragic,'" *Los Angeles Times*, Feb. 14, 1991, A6.
46. Laurie Garrett, "The Dead," *Columbia Journalism Review* 30 (May/June 1991): 32.

47. Ibid.
48. Melissa Healy, "One Thousand Iraqi Civilians Died in Illegal Attacks, Rights Group Says," *Los Angeles Times*, Nov. 17, 1991, A4.
49. Allan Nairn, "When Casualties Don't Count," *Progressive*, May 1991, 16–19.
50. Thomas B. Rosenstiel, "Americans Praise Media but Still Back Censorship, Postwar Poll Says," *Los Angeles Times*, Mar. 25, 1991, A9.
51. Michael Massing, "Another Front," *Columbia Journalism Review* 30 (May/June 1991): 23.
52. Dickey, "Not Their Finest Hour."

Susan Jeffords

Afterword: Bringing the Death-World Home

One of the striking things about the Persian Gulf War, and one of the consistent themes of the essays of this volume, is the extent to which the war, with the cooperation of the media, reconfigured the relationship between bodies and war. War historically and ontologically depends for its enactment upon the presence of bodies, most particularly as sites for the articulation of war's concrete existence and, as Elaine Scarry notes, its concrete achievement—victory. The fullness of this logic became most apparent during the Vietnam War, when parts of bodies "counted" as enemy "kills" and seemed thus to signify a U.S. victory. The failure of this strategy either to "win" that war or to persuade the U.S. public that the war was worth continuing indicates that the relationship between bodies and wars is not simply, then, one of numbers but instead has more to do with a distinct interpretation of bodies as nationally defined.

In her deeply interrogative book about "man-made mass death," *Spirit in Ashes*, philosopher Edith Wyschogrod argues that the relationship subjects hold to their bodies and their culture's positioning of those bodies altered drastically with the introduction of consciously planned, scientifically engineered, and culturally sanctioned systems of mass-produced death actualized during the Second World War through the Holocaust. Such a system produces what Wyschogrod calls a "death-world, a sphere of life in which the living are forced to exist as if already dead," in which "the annihilation of persons as an end in itself is the aim not only of the death-world but also of contemporary warfare, thus transforming war into a death event."[1] Because of the global potential of the technological means for the production of mass-produced death, made possible principally through nuclear weapons but through chemical weapons as well, the death-world has become a part of contemporary self-perception and of self-determinations of the body.

Wyschogrod suggests that the death-world is an extension of what she calls "technological society," of which technique, quantification, logic, and efficiency are its chief features. Quite simply put, without the inventions of technological society, the death event could not be produced. While the aims of technological society, according to Wyschogrod, are commensurate with the production of the death-world, they are not coterminous with it. This is necessarily the case because the single goal of the death-world—the elimination of life—is at base antithetical to the system of meaning of the technological world, in which efficiency of production requires the ongoing existence of the society's members. The key distinction between the two worlds, for Wyschogrod, is the presence of terror: "The apparatus created by the technological society provides the means through which terror is achieved. But the point and purpose of technological society is the increase of technique, whereas the raison d'etre of the death-world is the proximate or delayed death of its inhabitants" (26).

What I would like to suggest is that, by examining the configuration of bodies in the Persian Gulf War, a configuration that was fundamentally dependent upon media representations of those bodies, we might recognize a significant shift in the way in which U.S. wars are fought, a shift that is indicative of broader changes in the determination of bodies in U.S. culture. It is important in this context to recall that this is the first overt war fought by the United States after the end of the so-called Cold War, in which the prevailing parameters for warfare necessarily included considerations of widespread nuclear destruction, if not nuclear annihilation. It is, then, the first superpower war fought outside the parameters of the death-world. Conventional wars, such as those fought in Grenada or Panama, were not participants in the death-world because they deliberately did not risk escalation to nuclear war by involving Soviet allies (it is why, for example, the U.S. government was willing to invade Panama to oust a "corrupt dictator" but not Cuba; why it was willing only to sponsor a "rebel" army in Nicaragua rather than invade with U.S. forces). These conventional wars remained, for all of their death and destruction, limited in their use of technology and widespread annihilation.

The Persian Gulf War presents a different story, precisely because it was able to be fought outside the threat of superpower nuclear confrontation. Consequently, the U.S. military could, as it were, pull out all the stops, utilize, as it did, all the facets of its military "toolbox," as Colin Powell fondly referred to U.S. weapons, and in so doing it could reintroduce mass-produced death—the death-world—into the realm of conventional, technological warfare. The Persian Gulf War shows us how the death-world and the technological world can be combined in a post–Cold War, postsuperpower era of warfare. It shows us, in other words, how the mass annihilation of human bodies can become a functional and acceptable part of a U.S. technological society.

As John W. Dower's *War without Mercy* makes clear, the one-dimensional portrayal of enemy bodies is an elemental part of the production of war.[2] Such portrayals, what Michael Rogin calls the "demonization" of the enemy,[3] were a fundamental part of the Persian Gulf War, in which Saddam Hussein was Hitlerized,[4] labeled a madman, a "monster,"[5] and the "beast of Baghdad."[6] But more than such characterizations, which have been a part of U.S. wars since the Puritan rhetoric about the American Indians, the Persian Gulf War figured Iraqi bodies as well. As Margot Norris's essay shows, those bodies were necessarily absented from mainstream media depictions of the war, whether through deliberate censorship on the part of U.S. military authorities or through the complicitous behavior of U.S. journalists, who made no real efforts to make such images accessible to U.S. audiences (though they were available through journalistic reports from other countries, particularly England's ITN network). The U.S. government absented U.S. bodies as well, prohibiting any coverage of the arrival of U.S. soldiers' coffins at Dover Air Force base, the receiving point for military dead. While U.S. audiences were treated to elaborate pictures of weapons, ranging from video records of "smart" bomb maneuvers to two-page colorized newspaper and magazine displays, those same audiences were prevented from seeing the bodies these weapons killed.

But the use of technology to commit mass death during warfare is nothing new; it has, in fact, been the purpose behind the introduction of technology into warfare since the invention of gunpowder. Nor has the use of mass-death technology been justified in substantially different ways: President Truman's use of the atom bomb in Hiroshima and Nagasaki was designed, as was the use of the devastating air war against Iraq, both to save U.S. lives by eliminating the need to defeat the enemy through the meeting of armies, and to terrorize the enemy population into surrendering or downscaling the war (as well as to terrorize spectator countries, such as the Soviet Union or Syria, to prevent them from engaging in war with the United States). What distinguished the Persian Gulf War from earlier instances, though, is that the strategies of terror that are part of the death-world were used, not at the end of an already long and brutal war (as in the use of the atom bomb, the firebombing of Tokyo, the conflagration of Dresden, the carpet bombing of Hanoi, or the massacre at Wounded Knee), but as its initial strategy. In this way, the U.S. engagement in the Persian Gulf War moved warfare in the post–Cold War era into a distinctively different and more terrifying phase: the combination of the death-world and the technological world as a philosophy of war.

This means not only that the techniques of efficiency, productivity, and performance that are hallmarks of the technological world are now parts of the production of the death-world through war (the Nazis certainly sought for and achieved increasingly efficient means of killing masses of people); it means as well that the death-world has become a part of the social production of technological war. The invention and manufacture of the nuclear bomb was a product of an elite and tiny cadre of researchers at Los Alamos, and the decision to use that bomb and the mission to drop it were performed by similarly small groups of isolated individuals. In contrast, both the manufacture and the use of Gulf War military technology are more widely distributed throughout the United States. The military-industrial complex that manufactures weapons and weapons-support systems such as the Stealth bomber, the Patriot missile, the AWACS plane, the Trident nuclear submarine, the Tomahawk missile, and so on is a fundamental part of the U.S. economy, constituting parts of some of its largest and most powerful corporations, such as IBM, Boeing, General Electric, ITT Corporation, United Technologies, McDonnell-Douglas, and Westinghouse. In 1985, fully 85.3 percent of the shipbuilding industry was devoted to defense work, 62 percent of the aircraft industry, 84.2 percent of the space industry, and 49.6 percent of communications equipment industries.[7] Figures from that same year show that 3,207,000 people were employed in defense-related jobs in private industry, 2,151,000 in the armed forces, and 1,322,000 in federal employment.[8] The strategy for using the armed forces in the Gulf War extended warfare into less overtly military sectors of society as well through the use of reserve forces, thus further extending the military into nondefense industries and homes.

This means that the technology and production of the death-world in warfare have more deeply permeated the economic, social, and familial network of U.S. society than during the Cold War. While certainly everyone in the country was vulnerable to nuclear attack and therefore subject to its potential death-world during the Cold War, nuclear war existed for most Americans (excluding principally those Japanese Americans whose families were killed during the bombing of Japan) at an abstract, psychological level. (The reality of the death-world existed, of course, for survivors of the Holocaust and families of Holocaust survivors, as well as for many Jews who feel that such genocide is not unrepeatable.) What the Persian Gulf War achieved was the more efficient and pervasive intermingling of the production of warfare and the reproduction of U.S. social culture, implicating broader sectors of U.S. society in the manufacture of the death-world.

Such a process necessitated, then, not only the reconfiguration of Iraqi bodies as absent but the reconstruction of U.S. bodies as carriers and purveyors of the technological death-world. This is one of the reasons for the reconstruction of the military body as both female (in the many images of female soldiers that became popular during the war) and familial (as mothers went to war), simultaneously distancing the family from and inserting the family into the death-world through the presence of the life-giving mother. The extent to which increasing numbers of U.S. citizens became participants in the production of war changes significantly the culture's relationship to the military, to warfare, and to the production of the death-world. As H. Bruce Franklin's history of war photography suggests, the video images of smart bombs conveyed quite literally this shift, by placing each viewer in the eye of the bomb on its way to killing Iraqis.

The media is thus instrumental in conveying this altered relationship to the production of war, as citizens participate in the visualization of war through media representations. To the extent that those representations are limited—censored—they enable viewers to maintain the apparent separation between the technological world and the death-world. In other words, "clean" images of war—images without dead bodies, charred remains, or devastated environments—reinforce the technological side of U.S. society by underscoring the sense of war as efficient, organized, even "tidy." What these images hide is the production of the death-world that is the product of that technology.

Media made possible, in other words, the illusion that conventional warfare was still the limited warfare that had typified nonnuclear engagements during the Cold War. It enabled citizens to identify their participation as being only in the technological world and therefore not responsible for the production of the death-world. More than simply saying that the media kept people from seeing unpleasant images that they wouldn't like, I am suggesting that media masked the transition of limited conventional warfare into massdeath warfare and thereby protected U.S. citizens from recognizing their direct relationship to the propagation of this war. This separation was all the more necessary because of the permeation of the defense industry and military work into the daily lives of so many Americans. The illusion of separation therefore serves both to mask the actual product of this specific war and to maintain the continued efficient industrial production that is so fundamentally a part of the U.S. economy.

If such is the case, as I believe it is, then it is all the more important to study the devices of the media and its collaboration with the military in the production show "The Persian Gulf War." Only by seeing through the media can we begin to alter our own relationships to the production of this and future death-worlds.

Notes

1. Edith Wyschogrod, *Spirit in Ashes: Hegel, Heidegger, and Man-Made Mass Death* (New Haven: Yale University Press, 1985), 34, 40.
2. John W. Dower, *War without Mercy: Race and Power in the Pacific War* (New York: Pantheon Books, 1986).
3. Michael Rogin, *Ronald Reagan, the Movie, and Other Episodes in Political Demonology* (Berkeley and Los Angeles: University of California Press, 1987).
4. This was most pointedly accomplished in *The New Republic* cover that airbrushed Saddam Hussein's mustache to make him resemble Hitler. A Gannett Foundation study found 1,170 examples in print media and television of Saddam Hussein as Hitler. Dennis E. Everette et al., *The Media at War* (New York: Gannett Foundation, 1991), 42.
5. Mary McGrory, *Newsweek*, Oct. 20, 1990.
6. Mary McGrory, "Bush and the Beast of Baghdad," *Washington Post*, Aug. 7, 1990, A2.
7. Cited in Ann Markusen et al., *The Rise of the Gunbelt: The Military Remapping of America* (New York: Oxford University Press, 1991), 21.
8. Ibid., 20.

A Persian Gulf War Chronology

In order to understand the historical meaning of the Persian Gulf War, we need to go at least as far back as World War II and the British reconfiguration of territorial boundaries of the nations of the Middle East. But since this book is devoted to the Persian Gulf Crisis and the ensuing war, we felt it important to begin the chronology at the moment at which a crisis was defined in the Persian Gulf, which is August 2, 1990, and to note that even the mark of crisis itself is a U.S. construction. We did, however, think that it was important within that construction of crisis to incorporate the July 25 meeting between Saddam Hussein and the U.S. ambassador to Iraq, since it has figured in so many discussions about the war and in so many essays in this volume as a contradictory element to the way the United States cast the crisis. We see this crisis as being initiated by the United States rather than as an Iraqi action.

1990

July 17:
- Saddam Hussein accuses the U.S. and the Gulf states of conspiring to cut oil prices.

July 25:
- Saddam Hussein and U.S. ambassador April Glaspie meet in Baghdad, at which meeting Glaspie allegedly tells Saddam, "We have no opinion on the Arab-Arab conflicts, like your border disagreement with Kuwait."

July 27:
- OPEC raises oil target price.

August 2:
- Invasion of Kuwait at 0200 local time. Emir Sheik Jabar Ahmed al-Sabah flees to Saudi Arabia. Iraq installs a provisional government to replace Kuwaiti regime.

- UN Security Council passes Resolution 660 by a vote of 14–0, demanding immediate Iraqi withdrawal.
- The U.S. and Great Britain freeze Kuwait and Iraqi assets.

August 3:
- Puppet government set up in Kuwait; Iraq asserts it is aiding popular uprising. Iraqi troops assemble on Saudi Arabian border.
- President Bush orders U.S. Navy to Persian Gulf.
- The U.S. and the U.S.S.R. call for an arms embargo against Iraq.
- The Council of Foreign Ministers of the Arab League condemns the Iraqi invasion and calls for immediate and unconditional withdrawal of Iraqi troops from Kuwait.

August 4:
- Saudi Arabia begins mobilization of forces.
- The European Community announces broad sanctions against Iraq.

August 5:
- President Bush declares, "This will not stand"; he calls Saddam Hussein the "moral equivalent of Hitler."

August 6:
- The UN passes Resolution 661 by a vote of 13–0, imposing a trade embargo against Iraq minus humanitarian aid.
- Saudi Arabian government requests U.S. troops to help protect the country from an Iraqi attack.
- Iraq begins to move Westerners in Kuwait to Iraq.

August 7:
- 4,000 U.S. troops from 82d Airborne Division sent to Saudi Arabia.
- Turkey turns off Iraqi pipeline.

August 8:
- Iraq formally declares Kuwait annexed.
- President Bush gives televised address delineating objectives. He announces that the U.S. will send ground forces, probably about 50,000, to Saudi Arabia.

August 9:
- UN Resolution 662, passed by a vote of 13–0, nullifies Iraqi declaration of annexation.

August 10:
- In Cairo, the Arab League votes 12–9 to send Arab coalition to Saudi Arabia.
- Iraq orders foreign governments to close their embassies in Kuwait.

August 11:
- The first Egyptian troops arrive in Saudi Arabia.

August 12:
- President Bush orders U.S. naval vessels to stop Iraqi oil exports in addition to the cargo ships embargoed by UN Resolution 661.
- Saddam Hussein connects Iraqi withdrawal from Kuwait with Israeli withdrawal from Occupied Territories, Syrian withdrawal from Lebanon, and U.S. withdrawal from Saudi Arabia. This becomes known as the issue of "linkage."

August 13:
- First press pools arrive in Saudi Arabia.

August 14:
- King Hussein of Jordan arrives in Washington, D.C., in a failed effort to mediate a settlement.

August 15:
- Iran-Iraq War formally ends.

August 16:
- Iraq announces use of "human shields."

August 18:
- In response to Iraqi threats of using foreigners as human shields, the UN passes Resolution 664 by a vote of 15–0, demanding that all foreigners be allowed to leave Iraq and Kuwait.
- First shots are fired by U.S. naval vessels across the bows of Iraqi tankers attempting to pass the UN blockade. Iraqi tankers turn back.

August 19:
- Iraq offers to release all foreign nationals if the U.S. will withdraw all forces from the region.

August 20:
- Iraq places foreigners as human shields in critical areas. President Bush denounces Iraq's actions.

August 22:
- President Bush announces that 40,000 reserves will be called to active duty.
- Jordan closes its border with Iraq.

August 23:
- Saddam Hussein meets with hostages; the meeting is televised.

August 25:
- The UN passes Resolution 665 by a vote of 13–0, authorizing enforcement of embargo via naval blockade.
- First BBC and CNN crews arrive in Baghdad.

August 26:
- Pentagon disbands press pools.

August 27:
- 80 Austrian hostages are released.
- OPEC votes 10–1 to increase oil production.

August 28:
- Saddam Hussein modifies his hostage policies in allowing women and children to leave Iraq.

August 29:
- U.S. defense secretary Richard B. Cheney appears on ABC's *Nightline* and assures journalist Sam Donaldson that the U.S. is not in Saudi Arabia "in an offensive capacity, we're not there threatening Iraq."
- Syrian troops kill pro-Iraqi demonstrators expressing support for Saddam Hussein.

September 1:
- 200 British women and children are released.

September 6:
- Iraqi foreign minister Tariq Aziz leaves Moscow after an unsuccessful attempt to rally support for Iraq.

September 9:
- At the Helsinki summit, Presidents Gorbachev and Bush call for immediate Iraqi withdrawal from Kuwait; Gorbachev stresses a diplomatic approach; Bush stands by military commitment.

September 10:
- Iran and Iraq announce the reestablishment of diplomatic relations.
- Iraq offers free oil to developing nations.

September 11:
- President Bush addresses the Congress on his actions.
- ABC obtains and broadcasts Iraqi transcript of a July 25 meeting between April Glaspie and Saddam Hussein.

September 13:
- The UN passes Resolution 666 by a vote of 13–0, authorizing international relief organizations to distribute emergency humanitarian aid shipments.

September 14:
- Iraqi troops enter the Belgian Embassy and residences of the French and Canadian ambassadors to Kuwait.
- Britain sends 7th Armored Brigade to region.

September 15:
- France sends 4,000 French troops to the Persian Gulf.

September 16:
- UN Resolution 667 condemns Iraqi raids of embassies in Kuwait.

- Iraq televises President Bush's speech to the Iraqi people in its entirety.

September 18:
- Amidst sharp congressional questioning of Reagan and Bush administration policies toward Iraq, President Bush says at a news conference
that he "regrets" earlier overtures to establish better relations with
Iraq; White House spokesperson Marlin Fitzwater says U.S. overtures
did not give Iraq "green light" to invade Kuwait.

September 19:
- Iraq seizes all assets of nations complying with UN sanctions against
Iraq.

September 24:
- The UN passes Resolution 669 by a vote of 15–0, requesting Security
Council aid to other nations affected by trade sanctions.

September 25:
- The UN passes Resolution 670 14–1, banning all cargo flights to Iraq.

September 27:
- Diplomatic relations between Iran and Britain resumed.

October:
- Testimony before the U.S. House of Representatives Human Rights
Caucus tells of Iraqi atrocities, particularly how Iraqi soldiers had removed babies from incubators in a Kuwait hospital and taken the
incubators back to Iraq, leaving the infants to die on the hospital floor.

October 1:
- President Bush addresses the UN.

October 3:
- Amnesty International issues a public statement expressing its
concern about Iraq's widespread human rights violations in Kuwait.
Iraq's embassy in London responds with a public statement dismiss-
ing the report as "an embarrassment to the practice of reporting."

- Saddam Hussein visits Kuwait and speaks to troops.

October 8:
- The linkage issue is renewed over Temple Mount conflict in Jerusalem
when more than 20 Palestinians are killed and over 100 are wounded.

October 12:
- After the U.S. proposes a UN resolution condemning Israel for the excessive force used in the Temple Mount conflict, the UN Security Council issues a statement censuring Israel.

October 23:
- 330 French and 33 British hostages released.

October 25:
- U.S. secretary of defense Cheney announces another 100,000 troops will be sent to Saudi Arabia. U.S. reservist active duty is increased from 180 to 360 days.

October 29:
- UN Resolution 674 is passed 13–0, renewing the call for an immediate end to Iraqi hostage taking and demanding reparations for war crimes against Kuwait.

November 3:
- U.S. secretary of state James Baker embarks on a seven-nation tour to establish coalition force.

November 8:
- President Bush announces that 200,000 more troops will be sent to Saudi Arabia and also announces a shift from a "defensive position" to an "offensive military option." On ABC's *Nightline*, news anchor Ted Koppel expresses his astonishment that the U.S. had been preparing to launch a war.

November 9:
- Germany's Willi Brandt secures the release of 180 Western European hostages.

November 10:
- Formal U.S. military plans are drawn up to envelop Iraqi forces in Kuwait.

November 11:
- Nearly 500 more European, Japanese, and American hostages are released.

November 13:
- U.S. secretary of defense Cheney authorizes the call-up of 72,500 additional reserves.

November 16:
- Baker rejects "linkage" theory as a solution to the crisis.

November 18:
- The U.S. Embassy in Baghdad reports that 104 Americans are still being held at stragetic locations as human shields.

November 19:
- At a Conference of Security and Cooperation in Europe meeting, Prime Minister Thatcher announces that the use of military force will become necessary if Iraqi forces do not withdraw.

November 20:
- Iraq announces that it will release all German hostages.

November 22:
- Britian's Prime Minister Thatcher resigns.
- The United Kingdom announces that it will send an additional 14,000 troops to the Gulf region.

November 23:
- President Bush meets with Syrian president Hafez al-Assad to discuss the crisis in the Gulf.

November 26:
- Iraq frees all Swedish hostages.
- The Soviet Union demands the release of all Soviet citizens in Iraq.

November 28:
- John Major becomes the new British prime minister.
- The UN passes Resolution 677 by a vote of 13–0, condemning Iraq for attempts to alter Kuwaiti demographic records.

November 29:
- UN Resolution 678 establishes January 15, 1991, as the deadline for Iraqi withdrawal from Kuwait and authorizes "all necessary means" thereafter to effect withdrawal.

November 30:
- President Bush proposes sending Secretary of State Baker to Baghdad to meet with Saddam Hussein and invites Iraqi foreign minister Tariq Aziz to Washington, D.C., to meet with him.

December 2:
- Iraq test fires two Scud missiles within the Iraqi border.

December 4:
- Turkey announces its consideration of sending troops to the Gulf region.

December 6:
- Iraq announces it will soon release all remaining hostages.

December 8:
- The estimated 750 Americans remaining in Kuwait leave the country, along with 2,000 other Western hostages.

December 11:
- Soviet foreign minister Shevardnadze announces that Soviet troops will not be sent to the Gulf region.

December 13:
- The U.S. District Court rejects the injunction being sought by 45

House Democrats to prevent the initiation of hostilities by the president without congressional approval.

December 15:
- The UN passes Resolution 681 by a unanimous vote of 15–0, denouncing the Israeli deportation of Palestinians and calling for a monitoring of the West Bank.
- Soviet foreign minister Shevardnadze resigns.

December 24:
- Saddam Hussein announces that Israel will be the first target if war breaks out.

1991

January 3:
- The United Kingdom expells seven Iraqi diplomats for "unacceptable conduct."

January 7:
- A U.S. opinion poll indicated that almost two-thirds of Americans favored the use of force if that is what it took to solve the crisis in the Gulf.

January 8:
- President Bush formally asks Congress to authorize the use of force to get Iraq to withdraw from Kuwait.

January 9:
- In Geneva, U.S. secretary of state James Baker meets with Iraqi foreign minister Tariq Aziz. Aziz refuses to deliver a letter from President Bush to Saddam Hussein.

January 12:
- UN secretary general Perez de Cuellar arrives in Baghdad in an effort to convince Iraq to adopt the UN Resolutions.
- After debates in both the House and the Senate, U.S. Congress formally announces support of President Bush's use of military force. Vote: 52–47 Senate; 250–183 House.
- The U.S. closes its embassy in Baghdad and expells all but four Iraqi diplomats in the United States.

January 13:
- Secretary General Perez de Cuellar announces that he had no luck in his talks with Saddam Hussein.

January 14:
- The Pentagon issues official guidelines to the media.

- France outlines a peace proposal.

- The president of the European Community announces to President Bush that the EC has given up on peace efforts.

- Iraq recalls its ambassador to the U.S.

January 15:
- Both the European Community and French peace initiatives collapse.

- Bush gives written authority for military action.

January 16:
- UN deadline expires at midnight EST.

January 17:
- The air war starts at 0230 local time. First cruise missiles strike Iraq. Over 1,000 sorties flown by coalition planes in the first 14 hours.

- The first reports from journalists come in by telephone. CNN broadcasts live for 17 hours before being cut off.

January 18:
- First Iraqi Scud missiles strike Israel. A U.S. Patriot missile is launched to intercept a Scud missile fired at Saudi Arabia.

- First Iraqi prisoners of war are taken.

- President Bush warns the media against overoptimism.

- A U.S. opinion poll shows that more than four-fifths of Americans support the Desert Storm effort and that more than two-thirds of Americans disapprove of antiwar protests.

January 19:
- Three Scud missiles land in Israel; in response, the U.S. sends two Patriot missile batteries to Israel.

- Most foreign journalists are expelled from Iraq; CNN's Peter Arnett remains in Baghdad.

- An antiwar demonstration in San Francisco draws at least 35,000. Some 20,000 protesters converge in front of the White House.

January 20:
- Iraq displays seven captured coalition pilots on Iraqi television.

- The U.S. bombing of an Iraqi plant sparks controversy: was it a munitions factory or a baby milk plant?

January 21:
- CBS's Bob Simon and his three-person crew disappear on Kuwait-Saudi border.

- First Kuwaiti oil fields reported set on fire.

- Iraq announces that it will use coalition prisoners of war as human shields, in violation of the Geneva Convention.

January 22:
- Iraqi television broadcasts interviews of two more captured coalition airmen.

January 23:
- Iraq continues Scud attacks on Israel and Saudi Arabia.
- Iraq suspends sale of gasoline to civilians.
- In televised Pentagon briefings, General Powell announces that coalition forces will "kill" the Iraqi army, and General Norman Schwarzkopf provides information about U.S. military progress in the Persian Gulf.
- Island of Quarah taken by coalition forces.
- Iraq begins publishing footage of civilian damage.

January 24:
- The French air force begins bombing missions against Iraqi targets.
- Reports circulate that Saddam Hussein has his air force commanders executed.
- Iraqi-Jordanian border opened; refugees begin to enter Jordan.
- Oil begins to leak into the Persian Gulf from damaged Iraqi tankers.

January 26:
- Antiwar demonstration in Washington. Estimates in turnout range from 75,000 to 250,000. Opinion polls show that more than three-fourths of Americans approve of the military action the U.S. is taking.

January 27:
- The 25th Anniversary Super Bowl dedicated to the men and women in the Persian Gulf is telecast.

January 28:
- Iraq issues warnings of worldwide terrorist action.
- Saddam Hussein announces that Iran has offered sanctuary for Iraqi planes.

January 29:
- French defense minister Jean-Pierre Chevènement resigns, protesting that the war is counterproductive to UN objectives.
- Bush delivers State of the Union address.
- Iraqis take Khafji, a Saudi Arabian city near the border of Kuwait.
- The U.S. and the Soviet Union issue a joint statement seemingly offering terms of a cease-fire.

January 30:
- The Bush administration distances itself from the joint statement, saying that the U.S. is not backing down from its former stance.

- Eleven U.S. Marines killed, the first casualties in the ground war.
- "Total air superiority" of coalition declared.
- CNN begins live broadcasts of pictures from Iraq.

January 31:
- Coalition retakes Khafji.

February 1:
- The U.S. denounces Jordan for buying Iraqi oil, accusing Jordan of violating the UN embargoes.

February 2:
- The U.S. Defense Department acknowledges that the January 30 marine deaths were caused by "friendly fire."
- U.S. Department of Defense issues a statement that there would be no reestablishment of a draft.
- Western journalists still remaining in Iraq are taken to civilian damage sites.

February 3:
- New media-coalition guidelines are arranged.

February 4:
- Iran's offer to hold direct talks with the U.S. and Iraq is dismissed by both sides.

February 6:
- Iraq severs diplomatic relations with the U.S., Britain, France, Egypt, Italy, and Saudi Arabia.

February 7:
- Physicians for Human Rights issue report on Iraqi atrocities in Kuwait.
- Senator Alan Simpson (R-Wyo.) calls Peter Arnett a "sympathizer" with Iraq.

February 8:
- The UN authorizes investigation of the baby milk plant bombing.

February 9:
- Gorbachev expresses concerns that the coalition is going beyond UN objectives as Soviet presidential aid Yevgeny M. Primakov arrives in Baghdad.

February 11:
- Iraq issues reports of death tolls in the thousands and declares it will never accept a cease-fire.
- Two major broadcast network executives accuse CNN of making concessions to Iraqis in exchange for special access.

February 12:
- Saddam Hussein tells Soviet aide Primakov that he will consider withdrawal from Kuwait under certain conditions.
- The largest combined air-, sea-, and land-based shelling of the war is initiated by the coalition.

February 13:
- Stealth bombers hit civilian shelters, killing 400.
- Primakov leaves Baghdad.

February 14:
- Peter Arnett is interviewed on CNN to declare that he is "not under the thumb of Iraqi censors."

February 15:
- Iraq says it is willing to withdraw from Kuwait if questions of linkage are met. Coalition leaders dismiss proposal.

February 17:
- Beginning of heaviest air raids yet on Baghdad.

February 18:
- Gorbachev offers Soviet peace proposal to Iraqi foreign minister Tariq Aziz.

February 20:
- February 23 is declared the deadline for Iraqi withdrawal or the beginning of a ground war.
- Chief Pentagon spokesperson Pete Williams tells Senate Governmental Affairs Committee that press restrictions were justified but the military may have unnecessarily impeded some efforts to gather and report information.

February 22:
- Moscow announces that Iraq has accepted the U.S.S.R.'s eight-point peace plan. Bush says it does not go far enough in complying with all UN resolutions and reaffirms the February 23 deadline.

February 23:
- Deadline for withdrawal expires.

February 24:
- Ground war begins at 0400 local time. News blackout.

February 25:
- Scud missile hits Dhahran in Saudi Arabia, killing 27 Americans and injuring 98.
- Over 600 oil fields are left burning as Iraqis begin evacuation.

February 26:
- Iraq announces withdrawal from Kuwait.
- Coalition forces enter Kuwait City.

February 27:
- Iraqi foreign minister Aziz sends a letter to the UN declaring intent to comply with all UN resolutions.
- President Bush declares victory and issues a cease-fire directive to begin at midnight EST, 0800 local time.

March 1:
- First pictures of devastation on road to Basra televised.

March 2:
- Bob Simon and three others from CBS crew are freed; they report that they were beaten and accused of spying during captivity.

March 4:
- Crown prince of Kuwait returns.
- Shiite uprising against Saddam Hussein gains momentum.

March 5:
- Iraqi Republican Guards move in to battle Shiites.

March 6:
- Iraq expels all remaining Western journalists. Thirty-six reporters and photographers reported "unaccounted for."
- Forces loyal to Saddam Hussein begin suppression of Kurdish insurrection.

March 9:
- U.S. State Department warns Baghdad against use of chemical weapons to quell domestic unrest.

March 14:
- Emir of Kuwait returns.

March 19:
- Senator Simpson extends a qualified apology to Peter Arnett.

March 22:
- The UN Security Council ends embargo on food shipments to Iraq and eases other sanctions.

March 26:
- President Bush declines to intervene in Iraqi civil war.

April 3:
- The UN Security Council approves Resolution 687, establishing a permanent cease-fire in the Gulf War and outlining a gradual reduction in sanctions against Iraq.

April 5:
- Bush orders U.S. Air Force to airlift humanitarian aid to Kurdish refugees.
- UN Security Council condemns Iraqi repression.

April 6:
- Iraq accepts UN cease-fire agreements.

April 9:
- The UN Security Council authorizes deployment of a peacekeeping force along the Kuwait-Iraq border.

April 18:
- A U.S. federal judge dismisses the lawsuit filed in January by a group of news organizations against the Defense Department challenging the constitutionality of press restrictions.

May 15:
- UN inspectors from the International Atomic Energy Association begin inspection of Iraq's nuclear installations and chemical-warfare facilities.

June 7:
- U.S. and coalition soldiers begin withdrawal from northern Iraq.

June 22:
- Iraqi soldiers prevent access of UN inspectors to Iraq's nuclear facilities, firing warning shots.

June 23:
- The UN demands that Iraq allow UN inspectors free access to all Iraqi nuclear facilities and documents.

July 18:
- Syria, Jordan, and Lebanon accept U.S. proposal for Arab-Israeli peace conference.

August 2:
- The U.S. Senate votes 97–2 to support the use of "all necessary means" to rid Iraq of weapons.

August 16:
- The UN Security Council votes to allow Iraq $1.6 billion to raise money for food and medicine.

September 8:
- Iraq bars UN arms experts from flying helicopters in Iraqi airspace.

September 18:
- Bush announces authorization of U.S. warplanes to escort UN weapons inspectors in Iraq.

September 24:
- Iraqi troops detain UN weapons inspectors at a nuclear-weapons manufacturing site.

September 28:
- Iraq frees UN inspectors in Baghdad.

October 11:
- The UN Security Council announces a permanent ban in Iraq on nuclear, biological, and chemical weapons.

October 30:
- The Middle East peace conference begins in Madrid.

November 6:
- The last Kuwaiti oil well fire is extinguished and capped.

1992

January 6:
- John MacArthur's op-ed piece in the *New York Times* reveals that the congressional witness who testified in October 1990 that Iraqi soldiers had left Kuwaiti infants to die on the hospital floor was the daughter of the Kuwaiti ambassador to the United States.

January 7:
- An ABC *20/20* story airs on the deliberate U.S. public relations campaign regarding the false reports on Iraqi soldiers and incubator babies.

Bibliography

The Persian Gulf War

Abidi, A.H.H., and K. R. Singh, eds. *The Gulf Crisis.* New Delhi, India: Lancers Books, 1991.

Aksoy, Asu, and Kevin Robins. "Exterminating Angels: Morality, Violence, and Technology in the Gulf War." *Science as Culture,* no. 12, 322–336.

Arkin, William M. *On Impact: Modern Warfare and the Environment: A Case Study of the Gulf War.* Washington, D.C.: Greenpeace, 1991.

Barnaby, Frank. "The Environmental Impact of the Gulf War." *Ecologist* 21, no. 4 (1991): 166–172.

Bennis, Phyllis, and Michael Moushabeck, eds. *Beyond the Storm: A Gulf Crisis Reader.* New York: Oliver Branch Press, 1991.

Bisp, Sandy, and Kenneth Buffery. *The Gulf War: The Home Front.* London: Sutton, 1991.

Blackwell, James. *Thunder in the Desert: The Strategy and Tactics of the Persian Gulf War.* New York: Bantam Books, 1991.

Bresheeth, Haim, and Nira Yuval-Davis, eds. *The Gulf War and the New World Order.* London: Zed Books, 1991.

Brittain, Victoria, ed. *The Gulf between Us: The Gulf War and Beyond.* London: Virago, 1991.

Browne, Malcolm E., Michio Kaku, James M. Fallows, and Eric Fischer. "War and the Environment." *Audubon,* Sept./Oct. 1991, 88–89.

Bulloch, John, and Harvey Morris. *Saddam's War: The Origins of the Kuwait Conflict and the International Response.* London: Faber and Faber, 1991.

Chanchreek, K. L., ed. *The Gulf War: A Global Crisis: Causes and Future Effects.* Delhi, India: H. K. Publishers, 1991.

Clark, Ramsey. *The Fire This Time: U.S. War Crimes in the Gulf.* New York: Thunder's Mouth Press, 1992.

Clark, Ramsey, et al. *War Crimes: A Report on United States War Crimes against Iraq.* Washington, D.C.: Maisonneuve Press, 1992.

Cleaver, Harry. *The Political Economy of the Persian Gulf Crisis.* Austin, Tex.: Pamphlet Press, 1991.

Creighton, Jane. "War at Home." *Mother Jones,* May/June 1991, 22–23.

Darwish, Adel, and Gregory Alexander. *Unholy Babylon: The Secret History of Saddam's War.* New York: St. Martin's Press, 1991.

De Cosse, David E., ed. *But Was It Just?: Reflections on the Morality of the Persian Gulf War.* New York: Doubleday, 1992.

Dewar, Michael. *The Gulf War: A Photographic History.* London: Robert Hale, 1992.

Dunnigan, James F. *From Shield to Storm: High-Tech Weapons, Military Strategy, and Coalition Warfare in the Persian Gulf.* New York: W. Morrow, 1992.

Earle, Sylvia A. "Persian Gulf Pollution: Assessing the Damage One Year Later." *National Geographic,* Feb. 1992, 122–135.

Ehrenreich, Barbara. "The Long March." *Nation,* Feb. 25, 1991, 220–224.

Elshtain, Jean Bethke, ed. *Just War Theory.* New York: New York University Press, 1992.

Fox, Thomas C. *Iraq: Military Victory, Moral Defeat.* Kansas City, Mo.: Sheed & Ward, 1991.

Freedman, Lawrence, and Efraim Karsh. *The Gulf Conflict, 1990–1991: Diplomacy and War in the New World Order.* Princeton, N.J.: Princeton University Press, 1993.

Friedman, Norman. *Desert Victory: The War for Kuwait.* Annapolis: Naval Institute Press, 1991.

Friedrich, Otto, ed. *Desert Storm: The War in the Persian Gulf.* Boston: Little, Brown, 1991.

Garrett, Laurie. "The Dead." *Columbia Journalism Review* 30 (May/June 1991): 32.

Geyer, Alan F., and Barbara G. Green. *Lines in Sand: Justice and the Gulf War.* Louisville: Westminster/John Knox Press, 1992.

Gittings, John, ed. *Beyond the Gulf War: The Middle East and the New World Order.* London: Catholic Institute for International Relations, 1991.

Graubard, Stephen R. *Mr. Bush's War: Adventures in the Politics of Illusion.* New York: Hill and Wang, 1992.

Hawley, T. M. *Against the Fires of Hell: The Environmental Disaster of the Gulf War.* New York: Harcourt Brace Jovanovich, 1992.

Haykal, Muhammad Hasanayn. *Illusions of Triumph: An Arab View of the Gulf War.* London: Harper-Collins, 1992.

Helms, Robert F., II, and Robert H. Dorff, eds. *The Persian Gulf Crisis: Power in the Post–Cold War World.* Westport, Conn.: Praeger, 1993.

Hiro, Dilip. *Desert Shield to Desert Storm: The Second Gulf War.* New York: Rutledge, 1992.

Hybel, Alex Roberto. *Power over Rationality: The Bush Administration and the Gulf Crisis.* Albany: State University of New York Press, 1993.

Jarecke, Ken, and Harold Evans. "The Image of War." *American Photo* 2 (July 1991): 40ff.

Jin, Khoo Khay, ed. *Whose War? What Peace? Reflections of the Gulf Conflict.* Penang: Aliran Kesedaran Malaysia, 1991.

Johnson, James Turner, and George Weigel. *Just War and the Gulf War.* Lanham, Md.: University Press of America, 1991.

Karsh, Efraim, and Inari Rautski. *Saddam Hussein: A Political Biography.* New York: Free Press, 1991.

Kashmeri, Zuhair. *The Gulf Within: Canadian Arabs, Racism, and the Gulf War.* Toronto: James Lorimer & Co., 1991.

Klare, Michael T. "The Peace Movement's Next Steps." *Nation,* Mar. 25, 1991, 361–364.

Kopkind, Andrew. "The Wider War." *Nation,* Feb. 4, 1991, 109–114.

Kownacki, Mary Lou. "First Hearts, Then Minds: Tactics for Peacemakers." *Commonweal*, Feb. 22, 1991, 119–121.

Mariscal, George. "In the Wake of the Gulf War: Untying the Yellow Ribbon." *Cultural Critique* 19 (Fall 1991): 97–117.

Mazarr, Michael J., Don M. Snider, and James A. Blackwell, Jr. *Desert Storm: The Gulf War and What We Learned*. Boulder: Westview Press, 1993.

Miller, Judith, and Laurie Mylroie. *Saddam Hussein and the Crisis in the Gulf*. New York: Times Books, 1990.

Miller, Mark Crispin. *Spectacle: Operation Desert Storm and the Triumph of Illusion*. New York: Poseidon/Simon and Schuster, forthcoming.

Nairn, Allan. "When Casualties Don't Count." *Progressive*, May 1991, 16–19.

Nardo, Don. *The Persian Gulf War*. San Diego: Lucent, 1991.

Norris, Christopher. "Consensus 'Reality' and Manufactured Truth: Baudrillard and the War That Never Happened." *Southern Humanities Review* 26 (Winter 1992): 43–66.

Norris, Christopher. *Uncritical Theory: Postmodernism, Intellectuals, and the Gulf War*. Amherst: University of Massachusetts Press, 1992.

Robbins, Bruce, Gayatri Chakravorty Spivak, Lila Abu-Lughod et al. "Collective Conversations." *Public Culture* 3, no. 2 (1991): 119–154.

Rochlin, Gene I., and Chris C. Demchak. *Lessons of the Gulf War: Ascendant Technology and Declining Capability*. Berkeley: International and Area Studies, Institute of International Affairs, University of California, 1992.

Rourke, John T. *Presidential Wars and American Democracy: Rally 'Round the Chief*. New York: Paragon House, 1993.

Rowe, John Carlos. "The 'Vietnam Effect' in the Persian Gulf War." *Cultural Critique* 19 (Fall 1991): 121–139.

Said, Edward. "Thoughts on a War: Ignorant Armies Clash by Night." *Nation*, Feb. 11, 1991, 14–17.

Salinger, Pierre, and Eric Laurent. *Secret Dossier: The Hidden Agenda behind the Gulf War*. New York: Penguin, 1991.

Schulte-Sasse, Jochen, and Linda Schulte-Sasse. "War, Otherness, and Illusionary Identification with the State." *Cultural Critique* 19 (Fall 1991): 67–95.

Sekula, Allan. "War without Bodies." *Artforum* 30 (Nov. 1991): 107–110.

Sharkey, Jacqueline E. *Under Fire: U.S. Military Restrictions on the Media from Grenada to the Persian Gulf*. Washington, D.C.: Center for Public Integrity. 1991.

Sifry, Micah L., and Christopher Cerf, eds. *The Gulf War Reader: History, Documents, Opinions*. New York: Times Books/Random House, 1991.

Simon, Bob. *Forty Days*. New York: Putnam, 1992.

Simpson, John. *From the House of War: John Simpson in the Gulf*. London: Hutchinson, 1991.

Smith, Jean Edward. *George Bush's War*. New York: H. Holt, 1992.

Subraman, Belinda, ed. *The Gulf War: Many Perspectives*. El Paso, Vergin Press, 1992.

U.S. News & World Report. *Triumph without Victory: The Unreported History of the Persian Gulf Conflict*. New York: Times Books, 1992.

Weisberg, Jacob. "Means of Dissent: The Anti-War Movement's Dead End." *The New Republic*, Feb. 25, 1991, 18–20.

Werman, Robert. *Notes from a Sealed Room: An Israeli View of the Gulf War*. Carbondale: Southern Illinois University Press, 1993.

Woodward, Bob. *The Commanders*. New York: Simon and Schuster, 1991.
Yant, Martin. *Desert Mirage: The True Story of the Gulf War*. Buffalo: Prometheus Books, 1991.

Television, Visual Spectacle, and the Persian Gulf War

Banks, Anna. "Frontstage/Backstage: Loss of Control in Real-Time Coverage of the War in the Gulf." *Communication* 13, no. 2 (1992): 111–119.
Easterbrook, Greg. "Robowar." *The New Republic*, Feb. 11, 1991, 17–19.
Ewen, Stuart. "The Public Eye: The Gulf War: A Report from the Couch." *Artforum* 29 (Mar. 1991): 12.
Gerbner, George. "Instant History—Image History: Lessons of the Persian Gulf War." *Velvet Light Trap* 31 (Spring 1993): 3–13.
Gitlin, Todd, and Daniel Hallin. "Prowess and Community: The Gulf War as Popular Culture and as Television Drama." Paper delivered at the 42d annual conference of the International Communication Association, Miami, Fla., 1992.
Hammer, Rhonda, and Peter McLaren. "The Spectacularization of Subjectivity: Media Knowledges, Global Citizenry, and the New World Order." *Polygraph* 5 (1992): 46–66.
Hanke, Robert. "The First Casualty?" *Public 6: Violence* (1992): 135–140.
Kellner, Douglas. *The Persian Gulf TV War*. Boulder: Westview Press, 1992.
Kleinhans, Chuck, and Julia Lesage. "The Gulf War Superbowl, January 1991." *Jump Cut*, Spring 1991, 8.
Larsen, Ernest. "Gulf War TV." *Jump Cut*, Spring 1991, 3–10.
McConnell, Frank. "Nintendo from Hell: The Gulf War on the Tube." *Commonweal*, Feb. 22, 1991, 134–136.
Marvin, Carolyn. "Trooping the Colors on TV." *Public Culture* 3, no. 2 (1991): 155–158.
Morrison, David E. *Television and the Gulf War*. London: John Libbey & Company, 1992.
Smith, Perry, M. *How CNN Fought the War: A View from the Inside*. New York: Birch Lane Press, 1991.
Squiers, Carol. "Special Effects: Carol Squiers on War in the Gulf." *Artforum* 29 (May 1991): 25–27.
Stam, Robert. "Mobilizing Fictions: The Gulf War, the Media, and the Recruitment of the Spectator." *Public Culture* 4, no. 2 (Spring 1992): 101–125.
Tomas, David. "Polytechnical Observation: An Artistic and Popular Response to Political Events in the 'Age of the Smart Bomb." *Public 6: Violence* (1992): 141–154.
Wilson, Rob. "Sublime Patriot." *Polygraph* 5 (1992): 67–77.

The Press, News Information, and the Persian Gulf War

Anderson, Robin. "The Press, the Public, and the New World Order." *Media Development*, Oct. 1991, 20–26.
Boot, William. "The Press Stands Alone." *Columbia Journalism Review* 29 (Mar./Apr. 1991): 23–24.
Browne, Malcolm W. "The Military vs. the Press." *New York Times Magazine*, Mar. 3, 1991, 27–45.

Cockburn, Alexander. "The Press and the 'Just' War." *Nation*, Feb. 18, 1991, 181–186.

Dennis, Everette E., Craig LaMay, Martha FitzSimon, Jeanne Sahad, and David Stebenne, eds. *The Media at War: The Press and the Persian Gulf Conflict, A Report of the Gannett Foundation*. New York: Gannett Foundation Media Center, 1991.

Denton, Robert E., Jr. *The Media and the Persian Gulf War*. Westport, Conn.: Praeger, 1993.

Dickey, Christopher. "Not Their Finest Hour: Did the Press Fail during Desert Storm?" *Newsweek*, June 8, 1992, 66.

Fialka, John J. *Hotel Warriors: Covering the Gulf War*. Baltimore: John Hopkins University Press, 1992.

Greenberg, Bradley S., and Walter Gantz, eds. *Desert Storm and the Mass Media*. Cresskill, N.J.: Hampton Press, forthcoming.

Jensen, Robert. "Fighting Objectivity: The Illusion of Journalistic Neutrality in Coverage of the Persian Gulf War." *Journal of Communication Inquiry* 16 (1992): 20–32.

Katz, Elihu. "The End of Journalism? Notes on Watching the War." *Journal of Communication* 42 (Summer 1992): 5–12.

Lewis, Justin, Sut Jhally, and Michael Morgan. *The Gulf War: A Study of the Media, Public Opinion, and Public Knowledge*. Amherst, Mass.: Center for the Study of Communication, 1991.

MacArthur, Brian, ed. *Despatches from the Gulf War*. London: Bloomsbury, 1991.

MacArthur, John R. *Second Front: Censorship and Propaganda in the Gulf War*. New York: Hill and Wang, 1992.

Massing, Michael. "Another Front." *Columbia Journalism Review* 30 (May/June 1991): 23–24.

Mowlana, Hamid, George Gerbner, and Herbert I. Schiller, eds. *Triumph of the Image: The Media's War in the Persian Gulf: A Global Perspective*. Boulder: Westview Press, 1992.

Norris, Margot. "Military Censorship and the Body Count in the Persian Gulf War." *Cultural Critique* 19 (Fall 1991): 223–245.

Rosen, Jay. "From Slogan to Spectacle: How the Media and the Left Lost the War." *Tikkun* 6 (May/June 1991): 22–26.

Shulman, Holly Cowan. "One-Way Radio." *Nation*, May 13, 1991, 624.

Small, William, J. "The Gulf War and TV News: Past, Future, and Present." *Mass Communications Review* 19, nos. 1 & 2 (1991): 3–13.

Smith, Hedrick, ed. *The Media and the Gulf War*. Washington, D.C.: Seven Locks Press, 1992.

Taylor, Philip M. *War and the Media: Propaganda and Persuasion in the Persian Gulf*. Manchester: Manchester University Press, 1992.

Thomson, Alex. *Smokescreen: The Media, the Censors, the Gulf*. Tunbridge Wells, Kent: Spellmount, 1992.

U.S. Senate. Committee on Governmental Affairs. *Pentagon Rules on Media Access to the Persian Gulf War*. Hearing before the Committee on Governmental Affairs, United States Senate. 102d Cong., 1st sess., Feb. 20, 1991. U.S. Docs. No.: Y4.G74/9S.hrg.102–178.

Wakeman, Carolyn, ed. *The Media and the Gulf: A Closer Look*. Berkeley: Graduate School of Journalism, University of California, 1991.

Wiener, Robert. *Live from Baghdad: Gathering News at Ground Zero.* New York: Doubleday, 1992.

Zelizer, Barbie. "CNN, the Gulf War, and Journalistic Practice." *Journal of Communication* 42 (Winter 1992): 66–81.

Zoglin, Richard. "Live from the Middle East!" *Time,* Jan. 28, 1991, 69–71.

The Vietnam War

Arlen, Michael. *Living-Room War.* New York: Penguin, 1982.

Dittmar, Linda, and Gene Michaud, eds. *From Hanoi to Hollywood: The Vietnam War in American Film.* New Brunswick, N.J.: Rutgers University Press, 1990.

Edelman, Bernard, ed. *Dear America: Letters Home from Vietnam.* New York: Norton, 1985.

Epstein, Edward Jay. *News from Nowhere: Television and the News.* New York: Random House, 1973.

Faulkner, Francis. "Bao Chi: The American News Media in Vietnam, 1960–1975." Ph.D. diss., University of Massachusetts, 1981.

Hallin, Daniel C. *The "Uncensored War": The Media and Vietnam.* New York: Oxford University Press, 1986; Berkeley and Los Angeles: University of California Press, 1989.

Jeffords, Susan. *The Remasculinization of America: Gender and the Vietnam War.* Bloomington: Indiana University Press, 1989.

Karnow, Stanley. *Vietnam: A History.* New York: Viking, 1983.

Kinnard, Douglas. *The War Managers: American Generals Reflect on Vietnam.* New York: Da Capo Press, 1977.

Levy, David W. *The Debate over Vietnam.* Baltimore: John Hopkins University Press, 1991.

Lewy, Guenter. *America in Vietnam.* New York: Oxford University Press, 1978.

Meyers, Kate Beaird. "Fragments and Mosaics: Vietnam War 'Histories' and Postmodern Epistemology," *Genre* 21 (Winter 1988): 535–552.

Myers, Thomas. *Walking Point: American Narratives of Vietnam.* New York: Oxford University Press, 1988.

Rowe, John Carlos, and Richard Berg, eds. *The Vietnam War and American Culture.* New York: Columbia University Press, 1991.

Smith, Julian. *Looking Away: Hollywood and Vietnam.* New York: Scribner's, 1975.

Zaroulis, Nancy, and Gerald Sullivan. *Who Spoke Up? American Protest against the War in Vietnam, 1963–1975.* New York: Holt, Rinehart and Winston, 1984.

Women, Gender Issues, Feminism

Ahmed, Leila. *Women and Gender in Islam: Historical Roots of a Modern Debate.* New Haven: Yale University Press, 1992.

Allen, Robert. *Speaking of Soap Opera.* Chapel Hill: University of North Carolina Press, 1985.

Binkin, Martin, and Shirley J. Bach. *Women and the Military.* Washington, D.C.: Brookings Institution, 1977.

Campbell, D'Ann. *Women at War with America.* Cambridge: Harvard University Press, 1984.

Chapkis, Wendy, ed. *Loaded Questions: Women in the Military.* Amsterdam and Washington, D.C.: Transnational Institute, 1981.

Cohn, Carol. "Sex and Death in the Rational World of Defense Intellectuals." *Signs: A Journal of Women in Culture and Society* 12, no. 4 (1987): 687–718.

Enloe, Cynthia. "Tie a Yellow Ribbon 'Round the New World Order." *Village Voice,* Feb. 19, 1991, 37.

Farmanfarmaian, Abouali. "Sexuality in the Gulf War: Did You Measure Up?" *Genders* 13 (Spring 1992): 2.

Goldman, Nancy Loring, ed. *Female Soldiers—Combatants or Noncombatants?: Historical and Contemporary Perspectives.* Westport, Conn.: Greenwood Press, 1982.

Jeffords, Susan. *Hard Bodies: Hollywood Masculinity in the Reagan Era.* New Brunswick, N.J.: Rutgers University Press, 1993.

Jeffords, Susan. "Women, Gender, and the War." *Critical Studies in Mass Communication* 6 (Mar. 1989): 86–87.

Joyrich, Lynne. "All That Television Allows: TV Melodrama, Postmodernism, and Consumer Culture." *Camera Obscura* 16 (Jan. 1988): 129–153.

Mernissi, Fatima. *Beyond the Veil: Male-Female Dynamics in Modern Muslim Society.* Bloomington: Indiana University Press, 1987.

Modleski, Tania. *Feminism without Women.* New York: Routledge, 1991.

Modleski, Tania. *Loving with a Vengeance: Mass-produced Fantasies for Women.* New York: Methuen, 1982.

Moore, Molly. *A Woman at War: Storming Kuwait with the U.S. Marines.* New York: Scribner's, 1993.

Norton, Ann. "Sexuality and the Gulf War." *Middle East Report: Gender and Politics,* Nov./Dec. 1991, 27.

Radway, Janice. *Reading the Romance: Women, Patriarchy, and Popular Literature.* Chapel Hill: University of North Carolina Press, 1984.

Stone, Bonnie Domrose, and Betty Alt. *Uncle Sam's Brides: The World of Military Wives.* New York: Walker, 1990.

Williamson, Judith. "Woman Is an Island: Femininity and Colonization." In *Studies in Entertainment: Critical Approaches to Mass Culture,* edited by Tania Modleski. Bloomington: Indiana University Press, 1986.

Miscellaneous

Adams, William C., ed. *Television Coverage of International Affairs.* Norwood, N.J.: Ablex, 1982.

Anderson, Benedict R. *Imagined Communities: Reflections on the Origin and Spread of Nationalism.* London: Verso, 1983.

Baudrillard, Jean. *Selected Writings.* Edited by Mark Poster. Stanford: Stanford University Press, 1988.

Baudrillard, Jean. *Simulations.* Trans. Paul Foss, Paul Patten, and Philip Beitchman. New York: Semiotext(e), 1983.

Bird, Elizabeth, S. *For Enquiring Minds: A Cultural Study of Supermarket Tabloids.* Knoxville: University of Tennessee Press, 1992.

Boyd-Barrett, Oliver. "The Collection of Foreign News in the National Press." In *Studies on the Press,* edited by Oliver Boyd-Barrett, Colin Seymour-Ure, and Jeremy Tunstall. London: Her Majesty's Stationery Office, 1977.

Cumings, Bruce. *War and Television.* New York: Verso, 1992.

Dahlgren, Peter. "The Third World on TV News: Western Ways of Seeing the 'Other.'" In *Television Coverage of International Affairs*, edited by William C. Adams. Norwood, N.J.: Ablex, 1982.

Dates, Jannette L., and William Barlow, eds. *Split Image: African Americans in the Mass Media*. Washington, D.C.: Howard University Press, 1990.

Debord, Guy. *The Society of the Spectacle*. Detroit: Red and Black, 1983.

Donner, Frank J. *The Age of Surveillance: The Aims and Methods of America's Political Intelligence System*. New York: Knopf, 1980.

Dower, John W. *War without Mercy: Race and Power in the Pacific War*. New York: Pantheon 1986.

Fabian, Johannes. *Time and Other: How Anthropology Makes Its Object*. New York: Columbia University Press, 1983.

Fiske, John. *Television Culture*. New York: Methuen, 1987.

Franklin, H. Bruce. *War Stars: The Superweapon and the American Imagination*. New York: Oxford University Press, 1988.

Fussell, Paul. *Wartime: Understanding and Behavior in the Second World War*. New York: Oxford University Press, 1989.

Gerbner, George, ed. *Mass Media Policies in Changing Cultures*. New York: Wiley, 1977.

Gitlin, Todd. *The Whole World Is Watching: Mass Media in the Making and Unmaking of the New Left*. Berkeley and Los Angeles: University of California Press, 1980.

Gitlin, Todd, ed. *Watching Television: A Pantheon Guide to Popular Culture*. New York: Pantheon, 1986.

Hallin, Daniel. "Sound Bite News: Television Coverage of Elections, 1968–1988." *Journal of Communication* 42 (Spring 1992): 5–24.

Hammond, William M. *Public Affairs: The Military and the Media, 1962–1968*. Washington, D.C.: Center of Military History, United States Army, 1988.

Knightley, Philip. *The First Casualty: From the Crimea to Vietnam: The War Correspondent as Hero, Propagandist, and Mythmaker*. New York: Harcourt Brace Jovanovich, 1975.

Landy, Marcia, ed. *Imitations of Life: A Reader on Film and Television Melodrama*. Detroit: Wayne State University Press, 1991.

Larson, James F. *Television's Window on the World: International Affairs Coverage on the U.S. Networks*. Norwood, N.J.: Ablex, 1984.

McLuhan, Marshall. *Understanding Media: The Extensions of Man*. New York: Mentor, 1964.

Mellencamp, Patricia. *High Anxiety: Catastrophe, Scandal, Age, and Comedy*. Bloomington: Indiana University Press, 1992.

Mellencamp, Patricia, ed. *Logics of Television: Essays in Cultural Criticism*. Bloomington: Indiana University Press, 1990.

Nelson, Cary, and Lawrence Grossberg, eds. *Marxism and the Interpretation of Culture*. Urbana: University of Illinois Press, 1988.

Nelson, Joyce. *The Perfect Machine: TV in the Nuclear Age*. Toronto: Between the Lines, 1987.

Noelle-Neumann, Elisabeth. *The Spiral of Silence: Public Opinion, Our Social Skin*. Chicago: University of Chicago Press, 1984.

Ong, Walter. *Orality and Literacy: The Technologizing of the Word*. New York: Methuen, 1982.

Poster, Mark. "War in the Mode of Information." *Cultural Critique* 19 (Fall 1991): 217–222.

Riegel, Oscar W. *Mobilizing for Chaos: The Story of the New Propaganda.* New Haven: Yale University Press, 1934.

Rogin, Michael. *Ronald Reagan, the Movie, and Other Episodes in Political Demonology.* Berkeley and Los Angeles: University of California Press, 1987.

Rosen, Jay, and Paul Taylor. *The New News vs. the Old News: Press and Politics in the 1990s.* New York: Twentieth Century Fund, 1992.

Rucinski, Dianne. "Personalized Bias in the News: The Potency of the Particular?" *Communication Research* 19, no. 1 (1992): 91–108.

Said, Edward W. *Covering Islam: How the Media and the Experts Determine How We See the Rest of the World.* New York: Random House, 1981.

Said, Edward. *Orientalism.* New York: Pantheon, 1978.

Scarry, Elaine. *The Body in Pain: The Making and Unmaking of the World.* New York: Oxford University Press, 1985.

Schramm, Wilbur, and Erwin Atwood. *Circulation of News in the Third World: A Study of Asia.* Hong Kong: Chinese University Press, 1981.

Schulman, Holly Cowan. *The Voice of America: Propaganda and Democracy, 1942–1945.* Madison: University of Wisconsin Press, 1990.

Schwoch, James, Mimi White, and Susan Reilly. *Media Knowledge: Readings in Popular Culture, Pedagogy, and Critical Citizenship.* Albany: State University of New York Press, 1992.

Stafford, Barbara Maria. *Body Criticism: Imaging the Unseen in Enlightenment Art and Medicine.* Boston: MIT Press, 1991.

Stevenson, Robert L., and Donald L. Shaw, eds. *Foreign News and the New World Information Order.* Ames: Iowa State University Press, 1984.

Wyshogrod, Edith. *Spirit in Ashes: Hegel, Heidegger, and Man-Made Mass Death.* New Haven: Yale University Press, 1985.

Young, Robert. *White Mythologies: Writing History and the West.* New York: Routledge, 1990.

Zelizer, Barbie. "From Home to Public Forum: Media Events and the Public Sphere." *Journal of Film and Video* 43, nos. 1 & 2 (1992): 69–79.

Notes on Contributors

Venise T. Berry is an assistant professor at the University of Iowa, School of Journalism and Mass Communication. She is the author of a variety of articles on African-American images in the media, particularly music, television, and film. Berry is currently working on two books: an edited volume, *Mediated Messages: Issues in African-American Culture*, and *Race and Politics in the Early Film Industry: The Life of Joel Fluellen, 1909–1990*.

Victor J. Caldarola is an independent researcher in Washington, D.C. He is working on a book on mass media and Muslim Orthodoxy in the Republic of Indonesia, and is guest editor of "Culture/Media," a *Visual Anthropology Review* special issue (Spring 1994).

Dana L. Cloud is assistant professor of speech communication at the University of Texas, Austin. She has published articles on topics including racial stereotypes on television, feminist criticism, and Marxist and neo-Marxist criticism and theory. Her contribution to this book is part of a larger work examining therapeutic discourse and the decline of public engagement in popular and political culture. Dana Cloud was active in the political movement against the Persian Gulf War. She lives in Austin with her husband Keith Hutchinson and their daughter Samantha.

Tom Engelhardt, a writer and editor living in New York City, has written on the media, popular culture, and children's culture for *Harper's*, the *Nation*, *Mother Jones*, and other magazines and newspapers in the United States and Europe. He is a former senior editor at Pantheon Books and a Guggenheim Fellow. His newest book is on the collapse of victory culture in the United States (1945–1992).

Cynthia Enloe is professor and chair of government at Clark University (Worcester, Massachusetts). She received her Ph.D. in political science from the University of California at Berkeley in 1967. Among her recent books are *Does Khaki Become You? The Militarization of Women's Lives* (Pandora/HarperCollins, 1988) and *Bananas, Beaches, and Bases: Making Feminist Sense of International Politics* (University of California Press, 1990). Her newest book is *The Morning After: Sexual Politics at the End of the Cold War* (University of California Press, 1993). It uses feminist questions to understand nationalism in Yugoslavia, Kuwaiti women's postwar politics, the gay politics of the U.S., Canadian, and Australian militaries, and the role of J. Crew and other U.S. garment companies in postwar El Salvador.

H. Bruce Franklin is the author or editor of sixteen books on culture and history, including *War Stars: The Superweapon and the American Imagination* (Oxford University Press, 1988) and *M.I.A., or Mythmaking in America* (Brooklyn, N.Y.: Hill Books, 1992). He is the John Cotton Dana Professor of English and American Studies at Rutgers University in Newark.

Daniel C. Hallin is associate professor of communication at the University of California at San Diego. His writings include *The "Uncensored War": The Media and Vietnam* (Oxford University Press, 1986; University of California Press, 1989) and *We Keep America on Top of the World: Television Journalism and the Public Sphere* (forthcoming), as well as many articles on the media and public life. His essay on the shrinking sound bite in television coverage of elections won the 1990 Woodrow Wilson Center Media Studies Essay Contest.

Susan Jeffords is associate professor of English and the director of the Women Studies Program at the University of Washington. She is the author of *The Remasculinization of America: Gender and the Vietnam War* (Indiana University Press, 1989) and *Hard Bodies: Hollywood Masculinity in the Reagan Era* (Rutgers University Press, 1993) and is currently completing a book on rape and U.S. national identity.

Kim E. Karloff is a doctoral student at the School of Journalism and Mass Communication at the University of Iowa. Before returning to school, she taught at Texas Christian University in Fort Worth and worked in the news industry. She is researching several articles regarding police reporters and their coverage of crime, legal issues surrounding the rape victim identification debate, and the historical ties between media, rape, and race.

Michelle Kendrick is a graduate student at the University of Washington. Other publications and research interests include work on representations of Persian Gulf War technologies, technology and subjectivity in modern American literature, and feminist theory.

Margot Norris is professor of English and comparative literature at the University of California at Irvine, where she teaches modern literature. She is the author of two books on James Joyce and a book on modern intellectual history (*Beasts of the Modern Imagination: Darwin, Nietzsche, Kafka, Ernst, and Lawrence*, The Johns Hopkins University Press, 1985). Her current project explores the cultural representation of modern mass warfare.

Lauren Rabinovitz is an associate professor of American studies and film studies at the University of Iowa. She is the author of *Points of Resistance: Women, Power, and Politics in the New York Avant-Garde Cinema, 1943–71* (University of Illinois Press, 1991) and the forthcoming book *City in Motion: Cinema, Gender, Danger* (Rutgers University Press). She writes frequently about television.

Leonard Rifas is a Ph.D. student in the School of Communications at the University of Washington in Seattle and is also proprietor of EduComics, a small educational comic-book company. His interest in supermarket tabloid coverage of the Persian Gulf War is part of a larger interest in political discourse in low-prestige media. Rifas's master's thesis was "The Forgotten War Comics: The Korean War and American Comic Books."

Therese Saliba teaches cultural studies at Antioch University, Seattle. Her essay is from her recently completed Ph.D. dissertation, "'Saving Brown Women': Cultural Contests and Narratives of Identity" (University of Washington, 1993), which examines Western representations of Arab women in literature and media, as well as their resistant narratives and theories. She is also involved in peace and justice issues for the Middle East.

Ella Shohat is associate professor of women's studies and cultural studies at the City University of New York—Graduate Center and the director of the cinema studies program at the College of Staten Island. She is the author of *Israeli Cinema: East/West and the Politics of Representation* (University of Texas Press, 1989) and coauthor with Robert Stam of the forthcoming *Unthinking Eurocentrism* (Routledge).

Holly Cowan Shulman teaches in the Department of History at the University of Maryland, College Park. She has written *The Voice of America: Propaganda and Democracy, 1942–1945* (University of Wisconsin

Press, 1988) and a variety of articles on international broadcasting and on oral history.

Mimi White is the author of *Tele-Advising: Therapeutic Discourse in American Television* (University of North Carolina Press, 1992) and a coauthor, with James Schwoch and Susan Reilly, of *Media Knowledge* (State University of New York Press, 1992). She is an associate professor in the Department of Radio/Television/Film at Northwestern University.

Robyn Wiegman is an assistant professor of English and women studies at Indiana University. She is the author of numerous essays on race, gender, and U.S. cultural studies. Her essays have appeared in such journals as *American Literary History, Cultural Critique,* and *Journal of the History of Sexuality.* She is currently completing a book, *Economies of Visibility: Race and Gender in U.S. Culture.*

Index